# British History

## FOR

# DUMMIES®

## 3RD EDITION

# British History

## FOR

## DUMMIES®

### 3RD EDITION

by Seán Lang, PhD

A John Wiley and Sons, Ltd, Publication

**British History For Dummies®, 3rd Edition**

Published by
**John Wiley & Sons, Ltd**
The Atrium
Southern Gate
Chichester
West Sussex
PO19 8SQ
England

Email (for orders and customer service enquires): cs-books@wiley.co.uk

Visit our Home Page on www.wiley.com

For general information on our other products and services, please contact our Customer Care Department within the U.S. at 877-762-2974, outside the U.S. at 317-572-3993, or fax 317-572-4002.

For technical support, please visit www.wiley.com/techsupport.

Wiley also publishes its books in a variety of electronic formats. Some content that appears in print may not be available in electronic books.

British Library Cataloguing in Publication Data: A catalogue record for this book is available from the British Library

ISBN 978-0-470-97819-1 (paperback), ISBN 978-1-119-99180-9 (ebk), ISBN 978-0-470-97836-8 (ebk), ISBN 978-0-470-97837-5 (ebk)

Printed and bound by CPI Group (UK) Ltd, Croydon, CR0 4YY

C978047097819_250924

WILEY

# About the Author

**Seán Lang, PhD** is Senior Lecturer in History at Anglia Ruskin University. He studied history at Oxford and has been teaching it to school, college, and university students for the past twenty years. He has written textbooks and edited magazines on nineteenth and twentieth century history for school and college students and he lectures for Cambridge University's School of Continuing Education. He has acted as adviser on history teaching to two governments as well as to the Council of Europe, and he twice held the post of Honorary Secretary of the Historical Association. He broadcasts regularly on history for the BBC and for independent local radio.

# Dedication

Thanks to Richard Dargie, Fr Feidhlimidh Magennis, and Jasmine Simeone for helping me to keep it genuinely British. To Jason Dunne, Daniel Mersey, and Steve Edwards at Wiley for encouraging (okay, chivvying) me to keep the chapters flowing in. And to all my students, past and present, at Hills Road and Long Road Sixth Form Colleges in Cambridge and at Anglia Ruskin University: You shaped this book more than you know.

## Publisher's Acknowledgements

We're proud of this book; please send us your comments through our Dummies online registration form located at www.dummies.com/register/.

Some of the people who helped bring this book to market include the following:

*Commissioning, Editorial, and Media Development*

**Project Editor:** Steve Edwards

**Commissioning Editor:** Mike Baker

**Assistant Editor:** Ben Kemble

**Production Manager:** Daniel Mersey

**Cover Photos:** © Aspix/Alamy

**Colour Insert Photos:** © Alamy

**Cartoons:** Rich Tennant (www.the5thwave.com)

*Composition Services*

**Project Coordinator:** Kristie Rees

**Layout and Graphics:** Joyce Haughey, Vida Noffsinger

**Proofreader:** Laura Albert

**Indexer:** Potomac Indexing, LLC

**Publishing and Editorial for Consumer Dummies**

**Diane Graves Steele,** Vice President and Publisher, Consumer Dummies

**Kristin Ferguson-Wagstaffe,** Product Development Director, Consumer Dummies

**Ensley Eikenburg,** Associate Publisher, Travel

**Kelly Regan,** Editorial Director, Travel

**Publishing for Technology Dummies**

**Andy Cummings,** Vice President and Publisher, Dummies Technology/General User

**Composition Services**

**Debbie Stailey,** Director of Composition Services

# Contents at a Glance

Introduction .................................................................... 1

## Part I: The British Are Coming! .................................... 9
Chapter 1: So Much History, So Little Time ............................... 11
Chapter 2: Sticks and Stone Age Stuff .................................... 23
Chapter 3: Woad Rage and Chariots: The Iron Age in Britain ........ 35

## Part II: Everyone Else Is Coming! The Invaders ........... 49
Chapter 4: Ruled Britannia ................................................. 51
Chapter 5: Saxon, Drugs, and Rock 'n' Roll .............................. 65
Chapter 6: Have Axe, Will Travel: The Vikings .......................... 81
Chapter 7: 1066 and All That Followed ................................... 97

## Part III: Who's in Charge Around Here? The Middle Ages... 113
Chapter 8: England Gets an Empire ....................................... 115
Chapter 9: A Right Royal Time – the Medieval Realms of Britain ...... 129
Chapter 10: Plague, Pox, Poll Tax, and Ploughing – and Then You Die ..... 147

## Part IV: Rights or Royals? The Tudors and Stuarts ...... 161
Chapter 11: Uneasy Lies the Head that Wears the Crown ............... 163
Chapter 12: A Burning Issue: The Reformation .......................... 181
Chapter 13: Crown or Commons? ......................................... 199
Chapter 14: Old Problems, New Ideas ................................... 217

## Part V: On the Up: The Eighteenth and Nineteenth Centuries ..................................... 231
Chapter 15: Let's Make a Country ........................................ 233
Chapter 16: Survival of the Richest: The Industrial Revolution ....... 253
Chapter 17: Children of the Revolutions ................................ 267
Chapter 18: Putting On My Top Hat – The Victorians .................. 285
Chapter 19: The Sun Never Sets – But It Don't Shine Either .......... 299

## Part VI: Don't Look Down: The Twentieth Century ....... 315
Chapter 20: The Great War: The End of Innocence – and Everything Else? .......... 317
Chapter 21: Radio Times ................................................... 329
Chapter 22: TV Times ...................................................... 345
Chapter 23: Interesting Times ............................................ 359

**Part VII: The Part of Tens** .......................................... **377**

Chapter 24: Ten Top Turning Points ..........................................379

Chapter 25: Ten Major Documents ..........................................383

Chapter 26: Ten Things the British Have Given the World
(Whether the World Wanted Them or Not) ......................387

Chapter 27: Ten Great British Places to Visit ............................391

Chapter 28: Ten Britons Who Should Be Better Known ..............395

**Index** .......................................... **401**

# Table of Contents

*Introduction* ................................................................ *1*

About This Book ...................................................................... 1
Conventions Used in This Book ................................................ 2
Foolish Assumptions ............................................................... 3
How This Book Is Organised .................................................... 3
    Part I: The British Are Coming! ........................................... 3
    Part II: Everyone Else Is Coming! The Invaders ................... 3
    Part III: Who's in Charge Around Here? The Middle Ages ......... 4
    Part IV: Rights or Royals? The Tudors and Stuarts ............... 4
    Part V: On the Up: The Eighteenth and Nineteenth Centuries ........ 5
    Part VI: Don't Look Down: The Twentieth Century ............... 5
    Part VII: The Part of Tens .................................................. 6
Icons Used in This Book ........................................................... 6
Where to Go from Here ............................................................ 7

*Part 1: The British Are Coming!* ........................................ *9*

**Chapter 1: So Much History, So Little Time** ..................... 11

A Historical Tin of Beans – But Not Quite 57 Varieties .............. 12
    England ............................................................................. 13
    Scotland ............................................................................ 13
    Wales ................................................................................ 13
    Ireland .............................................................................. 14
    And all those little islands ................................................. 14
How the UK Was Born ............................................................. 15
    England: Head Honcho ....................................................... 15
    The conquest of Scotland ................................................... 16
    The conquest of Wales ....................................................... 17
    The conquest of Ireland ..................................................... 17
You're Not From Round 'Ere – But Then Again, Neither Am I ...... 18
    Any such thing as a native Briton? ...................................... 18
    Immigrants ........................................................................ 19
Whose History Is It Anyway? ................................................... 20
    Kings and queens .............................................................. 21
    What about the workers? .................................................... 21
    A global story ................................................................... 22

**Chapter 2: Sticks and Stone Age Stuff** ........................... 23

What a Load of Rubbish! What Archaeologists Find .................. 24
    Going through the trash ..................................................... 24
    Examining the tools ........................................................... 24
    Looking at tribal societies of today ..................................... 25

Uncovering prehistoric man .................................................. 25
It's life, Jim, but not as we know it................................. 25
Why the ruckus? ........................................................ 25
The Stone Age ................................................................. 26
Hey, hey – we're the monkeys! The Neanderthals................ 27
Meet your ancestors ................................................... 28
Plough the Fields, Don't Scatter – the Neolithic Revolution .................. 30
Rolling Stones: A National Institution ................................... 31
Giving It Some Heavy Metal: The Bronze Age ............................ 32
And the bronze goes to . . . ........................................... 33
Beakermania ............................................................ 33

**Chapter 3: Woad Rage and Chariots: The Iron Age in Britain . . . . . . .35**

The Iron Age: What It Was and How We Know What We Know ............. 35
Written accounts from others......................................... 36
Look what I found down the bog: Bodies ........................... 38
Figuring Out Who These People Were........................................ 38
Looking for patterns .................................................. 38
Celts in Britain? Maybe, maybe not................................. 39
Life in Iron Age Britain .................................................... 40
Warring tribes ........................................................ 41
Trading places ........................................................ 41
A touch of class....................................................... 43
Bring me my chariot, and fire!....................................... 43
Hit the woad, Jack.................................................... 44
This Is NOT a Hoax: The Belgians Are Coming!............................ 45
More Blood, Vicar? Religion in the Iron Age .............................. 45
Ye gods!............................................................... 46
Head cases ............................................................ 47
Sacrificing humans.................................................... 47

**Part II: Everyone Else Is Coming! The Invaders ............ 49**

**Chapter 4: Ruled Britannia . . . . . . . . . . . . . . . . . . . . . . . . . . . . . . . . . . .51**

A Far-Away Land of Which We Know Virtually Nothing.......................... 51
The Gallic Wars........................................................ 52
Welcome to Britain!................................................... 53
They're Back – with Elephants!............................................. 54
Caratacus fights the Romans.......................................... 54
One angry lady – Boudica ............................................ 55
Roman in the Gloamin' – Agricola ........................................ 56
'And What Have the Romans Ever Given Us in Return?' ...................... 57
Sorry, no aqueducts .................................................. 57
Another brick in the wall ............................................ 58
Urban sprawl.......................................................... 58
Get your kicks on Route LXVI ......................................... 60
All that foreign food................................................. 60

The Roman way of life ....................................................... 60
Saints alive! Christianity arrives! ..................................... 61
Time to Decline and Fall . . . and Go ..................................... 62
Trouble up North ............................................................. 62
Roman emperors, made in Britain ................................. 63
Gothic revival .................................................................. 63
Exit Romans, stage left .................................................. 64

**Chapter 5: Saxon, Drugs, and Rock 'n' Roll** .....................**65**
They're Coming from All Angles! ....................................... 66
Welcome to our shores! .................................................. 66
The Overlord of All Britain: Vitalinus the Vortigern ...... 66
Disunited Kingdoms ............................................................ 69
Celtic kingdoms .............................................................. 69
Saxon kingdoms ............................................................. 72
We're on a Mission from God ............................................... 73
Keeping the faith to themselves: The British Christians ......73
Sharing the faith: The Celtic Church .............................. 74
Enter the Roman Church ................................................ 76
Winds of Change ................................................................. 78
The rise of Mercia .......................................................... 78
I don't want to worry you, but I saw three ships come
sailing in: The Vikings ................................................ 79

**Chapter 6: Have Axe, Will Travel: The Vikings** ..................**81**
The Fury of the Norsemen ................................................... 82
A pillaging we will go ..................................................... 82
Setting up base on the Isle of Man ................................ 83
Some Seriously Good Kings ................................................. 84
Scotland the brave: Kenneth MacAlpin ........................... 85
We'll poke your eye out in the hillsides: The Welsh ....... 85
The English kings: Egbert, Alfred, and Athelstan ........... 86
The Vikings Are Gone – Now What? ..................................... 89
They're back – and this time it's personal ..................... 89
Showdown in Ireland ...................................................... 91
Scotland wasn't much better .......................................... 92
Cnut: Laying down the Danelaw ..................................... 93
The Messy Successions Following Cnut ............................... 94
Kings for (just over) a day .............................................. 94
Edward the Confessor .................................................... 95
The men who would be king ........................................... 96

**Chapter 7: 1066 and All That Followed** ...........................**97**
The King Is Dead, Long Live – er ........................................ 97
King Harold – One in a Million, One in the Eye .................... 98
Trouble on the not-too-distant horizon ......................... 98
The fightin' fyrd ............................................................. 99
When Harry met Harry .................................................... 99
Come on William, if you're hard enough! ....................... 100
Norman mods and Saxon rockers: Battle at Hastings ......... 101

William Duke of Normandy, King of England ........................... 102
Coronation chaos.................................................................103
Under new management ....................................................103
Mine, all mine! The feudal system ..................................105
Scotland turns English ......................................................107
And Wales follows suit ......................................................108
But Ireland has a breather ................................................108
The Church gets cross .......................................................108
William Dies and Things Go Downhill..................................... 109
Who wants to be a William heir? .....................................109
William Rufus as king ........................................................109
Henry Beauclerc (a.k.a. Henry I) as king........................110
Anarchy in the UK...............................................................110

## Part III: Who's in Charge Around Here? The Middle Ages .. 113

### Chapter 8: England Gets an Empire........................... 115

Meet the Family ......................................................................... 115
Good lords! (Sacré bleu!) ..................................................116
England was nice, but France was home .........................116
Henry II and the Angevin Empire............................................ 117
A trek to Toulouse .............................................................118
The Big Match: England vs. Wales...................................118
Bad news for Ireland..........................................................119
All (fairly) quiet on the Scottish front ............................120
Henry the lawgiver.............................................................121
Murder in the Cathedral .......................................................... 122
Henry's cunning plan . . . doesn't work..........................122
Recipe for Instant Martyr .................................................123
Royal Families and How to Survive Them ............................. 124
Richard I – the Lion King ......................................................... 125
A-crusading we will go.......................................................125
A king's ransom..................................................................126
King John .................................................................................... 127
The Pope goes one up .......................................................127
Er, I seem to have lost my empire ...................................127
Magna Carta........................................................................128

### Chapter 9: A Right Royal Time – the Medieval Realms of Britain...129

Basic Background Info ............................................................. 130
England – the French connection ....................................130
Who was ruling what? ........................................................130
Simon Says 'Make a Parliament, Henry!' ............................... 131
I'm the King of the Castles: Edward I ..................................... 132
War for Wales......................................................................132
It's hammer time: Scotland................................................133

You Say You Want a (Palace) Revolution: Edward II ............................ 136
    A woman scorned ................................................. 137
    Careful! Some day your prince may come ................................... 137
Conquering France: The Hundred Years War – Round One ................. 137
    Some battles ................................................... 138
    Conquering France again: The Hundred Years War – Round Two ...140
    Calamity Joan ................................................... 141
Lancaster vs. York: The Wars of the Roses – a User's Guide ................ 142
    House of Lancaster: Henrys IV, V, and VI ................................ 144
    House of York: Edwards IV and V and Richard III ....................... 144
    Guns 'n' Roses ................................................... 145

**Chapter 10: Plague, Pox, Poll Tax, and Ploughing – and Then You Die...147**

Benefits of the Cloth ................................................... 147
    What people believed in ................................................... 148
    The church service ................................................... 149
    Monastic orders ................................................... 150
    Medieval schools ................................................... 151
    Tending the sick: Medical care in the Middle Ages ...................... 152
    The advanced thinkers ................................................... 153
    A rebel: John Wyclif and the Lollards ................................... 153
The Black Death ................................................... 155
    Death by plague ................................................... 155
    Dire diagnoses ................................................... 155
The Prince and the Paupers: The Peasants' Revolt ........................... 157
    Laws to keep wages low ................................................... 157
    A poll tax ................................................... 157
    Showdown at Smithfield ................................................... 158

**Part IV: Rights or Royals? The Tudors and Stuarts ...... 161**

**Chapter 11: Uneasy Lies the Head that Wears the Crown .........163**

Princes and Pretenders ................................................... 165
    Tricky Dicky, a.k.a. Richard III ................................................... 165
    Enter Henry Tudor – and a succession of pretenders ................. 166
And Then Along Came Henry (the VIII, that is) ........................... 167
    Bad Ideas of the Sixteenth Century – No 1:
        Marrying Henry VIII ................................................... 167
    Edward VI, Queen Mary . . . and Jane Grey? ........................... 170
The Stewarts in a Stew ................................................... 172
    James IV attacks the English – and loses ................................ 172
    A new king and another power struggle ................................ 172
    Bad ideas of the sixteenth century – No 2:
        Marrying Mary, Queen of Scots ................................... 173
The First Elizabeth ................................................... 175
    The Virgin Queen vs. the not-so-virgin Mary ........................... 176
    English sea dogs vs. the Spanish Armada ................................ 178

The seeds of an empire ................................................................. 179

Protestants in Ulster .................................................................... 179

Don't let the sun go down on me ................................................ 180

## Chapter 12: A Burning Issue: The Reformation ................. 181

Religion in the Middle Ages ............................................................ 181

The role of the Catholic Church .................................................. 183

Enter the reformers ..................................................................... 185

Back in England with Henry VIII ................................................... 187

Breaking with Rome ..................................................................... 188

Closing the monasteries ............................................................... 188

The Pilgrimage of Grace .............................................................. 189

The Church of England: More Protestant or More Catholic? ....... 189

God's on Our Side! – the Protestants and Edward VI ..................... 191

We're on God's Side! – the Catholics and Queen Mary ................. 192

A good beginning, then a few bad decisions ............................... 192

Come on Mary, light my fire ......................................................... 193

Elizabeth Settles It . . . or Does She? ............................................. 193

The Catholics strike back and strike out .................................... 194

And the Protestants aren't happy either .................................... 195

Scotland Chooses Its Path ............................................................. 195

Protestant uprising ...................................................................... 195

Mary's return to Scotland ........................................................... 196

James VI steps in and muddies the waters even more ............... 197

## Chapter 13: Crown or Commons? ............................... 199

The Stewarts Come South ............................................................... 199

Know your Puritans ...................................................................... 200

Boom, shake the room – the Gunpowder Plot ............................ 201

James I fought the law and . . . who won? ................................... 202

Charles I ........................................................................................... 203

Buckingham's palace? ................................................................... 203

Dissolving Parliament ................................................................... 204

Ireland, under Strafford's thumb ................................................ 205

Getting tough with Puritans – again ........................................... 206

Parliament: It's back and shows who's boss ............................... 207

Civil War: Battle Hymns and a Republic ........................................ 208

War stories .................................................................................... 209

Can we join in? Enter the Irish and the Scots ............................ 209

The only good Stuart is a dead Stuart ......................................... 210

Oliver! ............................................................................................... 212

Levellers levelled and Scots scotched ........................................ 212

England becomes a republic ........................................................ 212

Ireland: The Curse of Cromwell .................................................. 214

Restoration Tragi-Comedy .............................................................. 214

Charles II comes to England ........................................................ 214

Some relief for Catholics and Puritans alike ............................. 215

So, Who Won – the Crown or Parliament? .................................... 216

**Chapter 14: Old Problems, New Ideas** . . . . . . . . . . . . . . . . . . . . . . .217
The Renaissance: Retro chic . . . . . . . . . . . . . . . . . . . . . . . . . . . . . . . . . . .217
    Sweet music and palaces in air . . . . . . . . . . . . . . . . . . . . . . . . . . .218
    Shakespeare: The good, the bard, and the ugly . . . . . . . . . . . . . .219
It's No Fun Being Poor . . . . . . . . . . . . . . . . . . . . . . . . . . . . . . . . . . . . . . .221
    The Poor Laws . . . . . . . . . . . . . . . . . . . . . . . . . . . . . . . . . . . . . . . . .222
    Crime or class war? . . . . . . . . . . . . . . . . . . . . . . . . . . . . . . . . . . . . .222
New Ideas . . . . . . . . . . . . . . . . . . . . . . . . . . . . . . . . . . . . . . . . . . . . . . . . .223
    Let's talk about religion . . . . . . . . . . . . . . . . . . . . . . . . . . . . . . . . .223
    A little bit of politics . . . . . . . . . . . . . . . . . . . . . . . . . . . . . . . . . . . .224
    Even science gets political . . . . . . . . . . . . . . . . . . . . . . . . . . . . . . .225
    The appliance of science . . . . . . . . . . . . . . . . . . . . . . . . . . . . . . . .226

## Part V: On the Up: The Eighteenth and Nineteenth Centuries . . . . . . . . . . . . . . . . . . . . . . . . . . . . 231

**Chapter 15: Let's Make a Country** . . . . . . . . . . . . . . . . . . . . . . . . . . .233
No Popery! No Wooden Shoes! . . . . . . . . . . . . . . . . . . . . . . . . . . . . . . . .233
1688: Glorious(?) Revolution(?) . . . . . . . . . . . . . . . . . . . . . . . . . . . . . . .234
    Going Dutch . . . . . . . . . . . . . . . . . . . . . . . . . . . . . . . . . . . . . . . . . . .235
    The Bill of Rights . . . . . . . . . . . . . . . . . . . . . . . . . . . . . . . . . . . . . . .236
Ireland: King Billy of the Boyne . . . . . . . . . . . . . . . . . . . . . . . . . . . . . . .237
    Bad heir day . . . . . . . . . . . . . . . . . . . . . . . . . . . . . . . . . . . . . . . . . . .238
    Marlborough country . . . . . . . . . . . . . . . . . . . . . . . . . . . . . . . . . . .239
Making Great Britain: Making Britain Great? . . . . . . . . . . . . . . . . . . . .240
    England and Scotland: one king, two kingdoms . . . . . . . . . . . . . .240
    Glencoe – death at MacDonald's . . . . . . . . . . . . . . . . . . . . . . . . . .241
    Act Two of Union: Scotland . . . . . . . . . . . . . . . . . . . . . . . . . . . . . .242
    Rebellions: The '15 and the '45 . . . . . . . . . . . . . . . . . . . . . . . . . . .243
    Ireland: Penal times . . . . . . . . . . . . . . . . . . . . . . . . . . . . . . . . . . . .245
    Act Three of Union: Ireland . . . . . . . . . . . . . . . . . . . . . . . . . . . . . .246
George, George, George, and – er – George . . . . . . . . . . . . . . . . . . . . . .247
    The one and only, the original, George I . . . . . . . . . . . . . . . . . . . .247
    Just when you thought it was safe to go
        back to the water – George II . . . . . . . . . . . . . . . . . . . . . . . . .247
    The badness of George III . . . . . . . . . . . . . . . . . . . . . . . . . . . . . . .248
    Completing your set of Georges . . . . . . . . . . . . . . . . . . . . . . . . . . .248
Whigs and Tories . . . . . . . . . . . . . . . . . . . . . . . . . . . . . . . . . . . . . . . . . . .249
Fighting the French: A National Sport . . . . . . . . . . . . . . . . . . . . . . . . . .250
    Round 1: War of the Spanish Succession 1701–14 . . . . . . . . . . . .250
    Round 2: War of Captain Jenkins's Ear 1739 . . . . . . . . . . . . . . . .251
    Round 3: War of the Austrian Succession 1740–48 . . . . . . . . . . . .251
    Round 4: The Seven Years' War 1756–63 . . . . . . . . . . . . . . . . . . .251

### Chapter 16: Survival of the Richest: The Industrial Revolution . . . . .253

Food or Famine? ........................................................................................ 253
    Problem: Fertiliser; Answer: Turnip ................................................ 254
    Baa baa black sheep, that's a lot of wool .................................... 255
    Reaching (en)closure ........................................................................ 255
Getting Things Moving: Road Work ........................................................ 256
Trouble Over: Bridged Water ................................................................... 257
Revolutionising the Cloth Trade .............................................................. 257
    The spinning jenny has landed ....................................................... 258
    Things speed up even more .............................................................. 259
It's (Not So) Fine Work, if You Can Get it: Life in the Factories ........... 259
    Trouble at t'mill ................................................................................ 259
    It were grim in them days ................................................................ 260
All Steamed Up ........................................................................................... 261
Do the Locomotion .................................................................................... 262
Any Old Iron? ............................................................................................. 262
Tea, Sympathy, and the Slave Trade ....................................................... 263
Why Britain? ............................................................................................... 265

### Chapter 17: Children of the Revolutions . . . . . . . . . . . . . . . . . . . . . .267

Revolutions: Turning Full Circle or Half? ............................................... 268
A British Civil War in America ................................................................. 268
    How the trouble began ..................................................................... 269
    Things get nasty: From Boston to Concord .................................. 270
    Declaring independence ................................................................... 270
    The fight's on .................................................................................... 271
    Calling it quits: The world turned upside down .......................... 273
The French Revolution .............................................................................. 273
    The nutshell version ......................................................................... 274
    Sounds good to us . . . we think ...................................................... 274
    This means war! Britain and France at it again ............................ 275
    Impeached for free speech: Restricting freedoms ....................... 276
    Cruising for a bruising – Nelson .................................................... 277
    Bonaparte's Spanish ulcer: The Peninsular War ......................... 278
    The Battle of Waterloo: Wellington boots out Napoleon ............ 278
A British Revolution? ................................................................................ 279
    Sowing discontent: The Corn Law ................................................. 279
    What the protestors wanted ........................................................... 281
    The Great Reform Act ...................................................................... 283
    Was THAT the British Revolution? ................................................ 284

### Chapter 18: Putting On My Top Hat – The Victorians . . . . . . . . . . . . .285

Queen Victoria ........................................................................................... 285
Prime Ministers and MPs of the Age ....................................................... 287
    Sir Robert Peel – tragedy of a statesman .................................... 287
    The Irish Famine ............................................................................... 288
    Peel forgets to check behind him ................................................... 288
    Lord Palmerston – send a gunboat! ............................................... 289
    Bill and Ben: The Gladstone and Disraeli show .......................... 290

Troubles at Home and Abroad ............................................... 291
   The People's Charter ................................................ 291
   The Crimean War – not Britain's finest hour ............... 292
   Did the upper classes really have the upper hand? ...... 294
How Victorian Were the Victorians? ................................... 294
   Were the Victorians really so cruel to children? ......... 294
   Were the Victorians really scared of sex? .................. 295
   Were Victorians really so religious? ......................... 295
   Did the Victorians oppress women? .......................... 296
Things Can Only Get Better .............................................. 297
   Crystal Palace's Great Exhibition .......................... 297
   Two giants: Brunel and Darwin ............................... 297

**Chapter 19: The Sun Never Sets – But It Don't Shine Either . . . . . . . 299**
New World Order ............................................................ 300
   Colonies in the New World .................................... 301
   Hey, sugar sugar ................................................ 301
India Taken Away ........................................................... 302
   Black Hole in Calcutta ......................................... 302
   The Battle of Warren Hastings ............................... 303
   Great game, great game! ...................................... 303
   This is mutiny, Mr Hindu! ..................................... 304
Cook's Tour: Australia and New Zealand .......................... 305
Opium? Just Say Yes: China ............................................ 306
Wider Still and Wider: Scrambling for Africa ................... 307
   Zulu! ................................................................ 307
   The wild Boers .................................................. 309
   One for you and two for me – cutting up Africa ......... 309
The Colonies Grow Up – As Long As They're White ........... 311
Lion Tamers .................................................................. 312
   What about the Irish? .......................................... 312
   The Anglo-Boer War: A hell of a lesson and a hell of a shock ...... 313

**Part VI: Don't Look Down: The Twentieth Century ....... 315**

**Chapter 20: The Great War: The End of Innocence –
and Everything Else? . . . . . . . . . . . . . . . . . . . . . . . . . . . . . . 317**
Indian Summer ............................................................... 317
   Go easy on the ice .............................................. 318
   Not so quiet on the home front .............................. 318
Alliance Building ........................................................... 320
   Loitering with entente ......................................... 320
   Going great guns – the naval race .......................... 321
   Bullets in Bosnia ............................................... 322
   General von Schlieffen's cunning plan and
      Britain's ultimatum ......................................... 323

The Great War....................................................................................323
    Your Country Needs YOU!.........................................................324
    Death in the trenches.................................................................324
    Death in the Dardanelles...........................................................326
    Death at sea................................................................................326
    Death on the Somme..................................................................327
    Death in the mud.........................................................................327
    The war ends...............................................................................328

**Chapter 21: Radio Times .................................... 329**

Big Troubles......................................................................................329
    Ireland – the Troubles...............................................................330
    India – massacre at Amritsar....................................................331
    Problems back home..................................................................332
The Years That Roared......................................................................334
    Party time!..................................................................................334
    Party's over: The slump.............................................................334
How Goes the Empire?......................................................................335
    Palestine – the double-promised land.....................................336
    Gandhi.........................................................................................336
The Road to Munich..........................................................................337
    The Munich Conference.............................................................338
    And then Hitler attacked Poland...............................................339
World War Two...................................................................................339
    Early battles and Churchill's finest hour.................................339
    Battle over Britain......................................................................340
    If it ain't flamin' desert, it's flippin' jungle.............................342
    Boats and bombers....................................................................342
    D-Day – fighting on the beaches...............................................343
    The war with Germany ends......................................................343
    The war with Japan continues..................................................344

**Chapter 22: TV Times ....................................... 345**

We Are the Masters Now...................................................................345
    The Beveridge Report: Fighting giants.....................................346
    Going into Labour......................................................................346
    Power for the people..................................................................347
    You may have won the war, but you can't have any sweets........348
    Discovery and recovery.............................................................349
End of Empire.....................................................................................349
    Sunset in the east . . . and the Middle East.............................349
    Wind of change in Africa...........................................................352
Losing an Empire, Finding a Role....................................................353
    A world power or just in de-Nile?.............................................353
    Into Europe?...............................................................................354
    Black and British – and brown, and yellow..............................355
    Yeah yeah, baby – groovy...........................................................356

What ARE those politicians up to? ................................................ 356

Labour pains ......................................................................... 357

**Chapter 23: Interesting Times** ............................... **359**

Mrs Thatcher's Handbag ............................................................ 359

Union power and power cuts ................................................. 360

Falklands fight, Hong Kong handover ..................................... 363

Very special relationships .................................................... 364

The Lady Vanishes ................................................................... 365

All alone in Europe ............................................................. 366

Belfast blows up ................................................................ 366

New Labour, New Dawn ............................................................. 369

Major problems .................................................................. 370

Blair's Britain .................................................................. 370

Scotland and Wales – sort-of nations once again ...................... 370

Lording it over the Lords ..................................................... 371

Shoulder to shoulder with America .......................................... 372

Britons bomb Britain ........................................................... 373

You said I could have a go! – Gordon Brown ............................... 375

_Part VII: The Part of Tens_ ........................... _377_

**Chapter 24: Ten Top Turning Points** ....................... **379**

End of the Ice Age, c. 7,500 BC ................................................ 379

The Romans Invade Britain, 43 AD .............................................. 379

The Synod of Whitby, 664 ........................................................ 380

The Norman Invasion of England, 1066 .......................................... 380

The English Invade Ireland, 1170 .............................................. 380

The Battle of Bannockburn, 1314 ............................................... 381

Henry VIII Breaks with Rome, 1532 ............................................. 381

Charles I Tries to Arrest Five MPs, 1642 ..................................... 381

The Great Reform Act, 1832 ..................................................... 382

The Fall of Singapore, 1942 .................................................... 382

**Chapter 25: Ten Major Documents** ........................... **383**

Bede's Ecclesiastical History of the English People (731) ................... 383

The Book of Kells (800) ........................................................ 383

Magna Carta (1215) ............................................................. 384

The Declaration of Arbroath (1320) ............................................ 384

The Authorised 'King James' Version of the Bible (1611) ..................... 384

The Petition of Right (1628) ................................................... 385

Habeas Corpus (1679) ........................................................... 385

Lord Mansfield's Judgement (1772) ............................................. 385

The People's Charter (1838) .................................................... 386

Darwin's The Origin of Species (1859) ......................................... 386

### Chapter 26: Ten Things the British Have Given the World (Whether the World Wanted Them or Not) .....................387

Parliamentary Government ...............................................387
The English Common Law ...............................................388
Organised Sport ...........................................................388
The Novel ...................................................................388
DNA ..........................................................................389
The BBC .....................................................................389
The Beatles .................................................................389
Tea with Milk ...............................................................390
Penicillin ....................................................................390
Gilbert and Sullivan .......................................................390

### Chapter 27: Ten Great British Places to Visit ...................391

Skara Brae ..................................................................391
Iona ..........................................................................391
Hadrian's Wall .............................................................392
Durham ......................................................................392
Stirling Castle ..............................................................392
Beaumaris ..................................................................393
Armagh ......................................................................393
Chatsworth House .........................................................393
Ironbridge ..................................................................394
Coventry Cathedral .......................................................394

### Chapter 28: Ten Britons Who Should Be Better Known ..........395

King Oswald of Northumbria .............................................395
Robert Grosseteste ........................................................396
Nicholas Owen .............................................................396
John Lilburne ...............................................................396
Olaudah Equiano ..........................................................397
John Snow ...................................................................398
Sophia Jex-Blake ...........................................................398
Emily Hobhouse ............................................................399
Dr Cecil Paine ..............................................................399
Chad Varah .................................................................400

## *Index* ..................................................................*401*

# Introduction

$O$ne day, I was sitting in my college rooms at Oxford when my dad arrived to visit. Dad was one of the British staff at the American Embassy in London, and he had said that a couple of American girls who were over from the States had asked if they could come too, because they had never seen Oxford. Would I mind? Sounded good: Were there any more who wanted to come? As they came through the door, one of the girls gasped and said, with a sort of breathless awe, 'Gee, I can't believe I'm in one of these old buildings!' Quite without thinking I said 'Oh, they're not that old. They're only seventeenth century.' You should have seen their faces.

But I was right. Just round the block from where I was sitting were other students sitting in rooms nearly four hundred years older than the ones I was in. (We reckoned our college food was even older than that.) And those rooms are still '*only* thirteenth century'. The Crown Jewels are in a tower that was built by William the Conqueror almost a thousand years ago. The amazing thing is not just that these buildings are old but that they're still in use. You can go to church in Britain in the same buildings where Saxons worshipped, and you can drive along motorways that follow lines laid down by the Romans. Complaining that the British somehow live in the Past is silly: The Past lives in the British.

## About This Book

If your idea of a history book is the sort of thing they gave you at school, forget it. Those books are written by people who want to get you through exams and give you tests and generally show off just how much they know and how clever they are at saying it. Believe me, I've written them. This book is different. Okay, it tells you the whole story, but I've tried to do so without making it seem like one whole slog. This is a great story: Don't miss it.

One important thing to note: This book is called *British History For Dummies*. A lot of people think 'British' means 'English'. And plenty of 'British' history textbooks only mention the Welsh and the Irish and the Scots when, in one way or other, they are giving the English grief. Or, more likely, the English are giving grief to them. In this book I've tried to redress the balance a bit. In here, you'll meet people like King Malcolm Canmore, James IV, Brian Boru, Prince Llewellyn, and a few others who deserve a bit more than a passing reference.

Can I promise that this book is objective and fair? Well, I present my view of British history. That view is never going to be the same as someone else's – therein lies the beauty of history. In fact, no such thing as an entirely 'objective' history book exists. Every time I choose to put something in and leave something out because there isn't space, I'm making a judgement. Every word I use to describe the events is a judgement. Americans speak of the American Revolution; for many years the British spoke of it as the American War of Independence. Do you call what happened at Wounded Knee in 1890 a 'battle', which it was in the history books for a long time, or a 'massacre'? Do I call what happened in the Highlands of Scotland after Culloden 'ethnic cleansing', as some people have? These judgements aren't just about literary style: They're judgements about the history, and not everyone will agree with them. If you think I've got it wrong, you are very welcome to write to me via my publisher, who will pass your letter on to an entirely fictitious address.

Not everyone in Britain feels happy being called British. Some prefer to put down 'Scottish' or 'Welsh' when they have to fill in a form, and many people in England routinely say 'England' or 'English' when they mean 'Britain' and 'British'. For me, I'm happy with 'British'. I have a name that shows that my ancestry is a mixture of English, Irish, and Scots. No Welsh, but then you can't have everything. So this book is very much the story of my people, of where we came from, and how we ended up the way we are today.

# Conventions Used in This Book

As you move through this book, you'll notice that a few words are italicised. These are key terms or important events from British history, and I give an explanation of what they mean, or what they led to.

Sidebars (text enclosed in a shaded grey box) consist of information that's interesting to know but not necessarily critical to your understanding of British history. You can skip sidebars if you like – I won't tell anyone.

Finally, when I mention dates, you'll need to know your BC and AD from your BCE and CE. In western historical tradition, the convention is to start with the birth of Jesus Christ (though actually they calculated it wrong by about four years!) so that anything that happened from then on was dated *AD – Anno Domini* ('Year of Our Lord' in Latin), and earlier dates were labelled *BC – Before Christ*. These terms are fine if you're happy using a Christian dating system, but not everyone is. Rather than come up with a different starting point (which would mean changing every date in every book) some people prefer to use *CE – Common Era –* instead of AD and *BCE – Before the Common Era –* instead of BC. In the end what term you use is a matter of taste: The actual dates aren't affected. I've stuck with BC and AD because I'm used to them and they tally with the dates you'll find in most books, but if you prefer to use CE and BCE, you go right on and do it.

# Foolish Assumptions

I may be wrong, but I've made a few assumptions in writing this book. Assumptions about you. I'm assuming that you probably:

- ✔ Did a bit of British history at school, but found it all got very confusing or else you quite liked it, but your memory's a bit hazy about who did what

- ✔ Did some English history but only touched on Wales or Scotland or Ireland when they were having trouble with the English

- ✔ Enjoy a good story and want to know more

# How This Book Is Organised

I've organised this book so that you can read if from beginning to end or by jumping from topic to topic. To help you find the information you want, I've divided the material into parts. Each part represents a particular period in Britain's history and contains chapters with information about that era. The following sections describe the type of information you can find in each of this book's parts.

## Part 1: The British Are Coming!

No, this part isn't about Paul Revere. Part I is about Britain's early days – the *really* early days. You can find information on life in Stone Age and Iron Age Britain – or as good a guess as archaeologists can come up with from the evidence these early people left behind, This part also introduces you to the mysterious Celts and takes a look at their religion (the weird and wacky ways of the Druids), their monuments, and the opinions that others (like the Romans) had of them. Basically, this part gives you a better picture of this dim and distant and rather mysterious, but also rather wonderful, world.

## Part 11: Everyone Else Is Coming! The Invaders

Suddenly *everyone* wants to conquer Britain. Romans, Saxons, Angles, (maybe Jutes), Vikings, Normans. What was the attraction? It can't have been the weather, and I don't believe it was the food. The Romans made Britain part of their great Empire, and then left them at the mercy of Picts, who invaded from the north, and the Angles and Saxons, who came from over the sea. Then came the Vikings, who plundered and raided, and eventually settled down in Ireland, in England, and in the Scottish islands. Finally, Britain began to form into the units we recognise today – Wales, Scotland, and England. And then, just when you thought it was safe, a new breed of Vikings – the Normans (these guys were of Norse descent, they weren't French) – conquer Anglo-Saxon England. And not just England reels.

## Part III: Who's in Charge Around Here? The Middle Ages

Knights in armour, fair maidens, and all that. Welcome to the Middle Ages, a time period when England finds herself in a great power game fought across Europe and in the Holy Land. We begin with one big, unhappy family who just happened to be ruling an empire that included England: The Plantagenets, who were on the English throne for some time and who took over a few other thrones. Ireland for one, and then, when Edward I stormed through Wales, the Welsh throne, too. Edward came pretty close to getting the Scottish throne as well. In fact, the Plantagenets did take the Scottish throne – they took it all the way down to London. In this part, you meet some colourful characters like Thomas à Becket, who was murdered in his own Cathedral; Wat Tyler, the leader of the Peasants' Revolt who was killed before the king's eyes; William Wallace, a freedom fighter (yes, the film *Braveheart* is set during this time); and the ordinary people who lived and prayed and died far away from the world of knights and kings, and whose lives we glimpse in Chaucer's *Canterbury Tales*.

## Part IV: Rights or Royals? The Tudors and Stuarts

In this part, you find out about the Tudors in England (and Wales and Ireland) and the Stuarts in Scotland, two families who had such power yet were let down by that oldest of problems: Getting an heir. Here you meet Henry VIII, who was to become history's most famous serial husband; Queen Elizabeth, who became history's second most famous virgin; Mary, Queen of Scots, who was driven from her kingdom by religious zealots and scandal; and others, like Oliver Cromwell, who shaped the political and religious landscape of the time. This part also examines religion, as Catholics burned Protestants, Protestants tortured Catholics, and the Reformation raged through England and Scotland. It also explains how the power struggles between Parliament and Charles I pushed the country into a violent and bloody Civil War. Yet, despite the horrors of civil war, revolution, fire, plague, and long wigs on men, this era was also the one that brought the Renaissance to Britain, and with it new ideas that changed the way people saw and understood their world.

## Part V: On the Up: The Eighteenth and Nineteenth Centuries

When the eighteenth century opened, no one would have believed that the British were on their way to creating the most powerful nation the world had ever known. No one planned this nation, no one even particularly wanted it, but its formation happened nonetheless. The British created their own country, a strange hybrid affair with a long and clumsy name – the United Kingdom of Great Britain and Ireland – by passing Acts of Parliament, crushing the life out of the Highlands of Scotland, and fighting the French all over the globe. Even seeming set-backs (like when the British-over-the-sea in America decided that enough was enough and declared their independence) only made the country stronger. Not all the momentous changes during this period took place on the world stage, however. Several remarkable people were busy solving practical problems – like how to spin thread more efficiently and where to build a canal – and, in the process, changed not just Britain but the world for ever. By the time the Victorian age began, Britain had become the world's first industrial superpower, with a global empire to match.

## Part VI: Don't Look Down: The Twentieth Century

Boy, were the British in for a shock. All that confidence in themselves, all that self-belief – it all fell apart in the trenches, literally. This part is where you can find out about Britain in the twentieth century, already troubled as it went into the First World War, deeply scarred and shell-shocked at the end of it. But the events of the Great War weren't the only ones that left Britain reeling. Back at home, Ireland rose in rebellion, the whole country succumbed to the global Depression, and another world conflict loomed on the horizon and then arrived before Britain was in a position to handle it. But fight Britain did, standing alone against the might of Hitler's Germany. Yet even as the RAF won the Battle of Britain, the sun was finally setting over Britain's mighty Empire. This part ends by bringing the story up to date, as Britain searches for a new role – in the Commonwealth? In Europe? Or shoulder to shoulder with the USA?

## Part VII: The Part of Tens

Want to impress strangers with the depth of your knowledge and insight? Read this part. If someone talks about turning points in world affairs, you can say, 'I know all about them' – and then offer one (or more) of the ten turning points that helped shape Britain (you can find them in Chapter 23). Then you can go on to ten major British contributions to world civilisation, or ten documents that helped shape Britain as much as, if not more so, than any of the battles that had been fought. In this part, you can find lists like these and more. And, for those times when you want to *experience* British history rather than merely read about it, I've listed a few (okay, ten) places you may want to see for yourself.

## Icons Used in This Book

History isn't just about telling stories: It's about thinking. How do we know these things happened? What are we to make of them? To highlight some of these points, you'll see some icons that indicate something special about the text next to them.

British history is full of good stories. Unfortunately, not all of them are true! This icon means I'll be checking.

The Present is a gift from the Past. Where you see this icon, you'll see examples of how events even long ago in history have helped shape life in Britain to this day.

History is always being rewritten, because historians often disagree about what to think about events in the past. Where you see this icon, you'll see some very different interpretations!

There are some points you need to remember in order to make sense of what's coming. This icon tells you the main ones.

Odd facts, small details. You can skip these bits if you like, or else learn them by heart and amaze your friends.

# *Where to Go from Here*

'Begin at the beginning,' says the King of Hearts in *Alice's Adventures in Wonderland*, 'and go on till you come to the end: Then stop.' You don't have to follow that advice in this book. If you want to know about the Tudors, head off (appropriate phrase – as you'll see!) to Chapter 11, or if you want to know about the Georges, read Chapter 15 and don't you worry about Chapters 13 or 14 along the way. But, of course, history connects in all sorts of ways, and you may find that information in one chapter links up with something in another chapter. If you want to read that other chapter you can, and if you don't want to, you don't have to. Did they give you this much choice at school?

If you're still not sure where to plunge in, have a read of Chapter 1. This chapter's a sort of survey of the whole scene, to give you a good sense of what you're letting yourself in for. And I bet you didn't get *that* at school.

# Part I
# The British Are Coming!

The 5th Wave · By Rich Tennant

'Wait! That's better! Now try leaning one of the stones a little to the left!'

## In this part . . .

Britain is an ancient land, with a lot of history. It was formed thousands of years ago by the continental shifts of the Ice Age; the first people to come to Britain and to Ireland came on foot, before the ice melted and the seas came. In time they learned the arts of metal, first tin and copper, then bronze, and finally iron, the 'daddy' of all metals in the ancient world. With these metals they made weapons for hunting and fighting, and they crafted tools, learning painfully but steadily how to adapt this land, with its hills, dales, mountains, and lakes, and to tame it.

These people weren't 'English' or 'Irish' or 'Scots' or 'Welsh' – that was all to come a lot later. But their descendants still live here, sometimes in the same places, and they laid the foundations of modern Britain and of Ireland. This part looks at who these people were, and at the culture they forged in the ages of stone and bronze and iron. This is the beginning.

# Chapter 1

# So Much History, So Little Time

*In This Chapter*
- Listing the kingdoms that make up the United Kingdom
- Figuring out how the UK was formed
- Identifying the people who make up the UK

*B*ritish history is a history of a variety of people inhabiting a variety of regions. In fact, all this variety is one of the reasons why the country's name is so ridiculously long: The United Kingdom of Great Britain and Northern Ireland. This name's a mouthful, for sure, but it reveals a great deal about the people – past and present – who have inhabited these islands.

When you think of history lessons at school, what comes to mind – before your eyelids droop, that is? Probably endless lists of kings or Acts of Parliament and confusing tales of people named after places ('Ah! Lancaster! Where's Worcester?') who spend their time swapping sides and cutting each other's heads off. You may think of the stories of Drake playing bowls as the Spanish Armada sails up The Channel, or Robert the Bruce watching a spider spinning his web, or Churchill hurling defiance at Hitler. Good stories, yes, but is there a connection between these events and *you*? If you tend to think of history as merely a series of disconnected events, you miss the bigger picture: That history is about people.

British history is full of wonderful people (quite a few of whom were clearly stark raving mad, but that's history for you) and exciting events – all of which helped make Britain the sort of place it is today. In examining what made Britain Britain, you'll also discover that the British helped make the world. In that sense, whoever you are, British history is also probably part of your history. Enjoy.

# A Historical Tin of Beans – But Not Quite 57 Varieties

British history is incredibly varied. That variety is partly because any country that can trace its history back to the mists of time is going to have a motley tale to tell, but it's also because of the nature of the country itself. To get a glimpse of how the union was formed, head to the section 'How the UK Was Born'. To find out *who* makes up the UK, see 'You're Not From Round 'Ere – But Then Again, Neither Am I'.

TECHNICAL STUFF

## Where the name came from

The country's full name is the United Kingdom of Great Britain and Northern Ireland. Of course, no one actually calls the country by that name. You hear 'United Kingdom' in top international gatherings like the UN or the Eurovision Song Contest, and 'the UK' has become more common in recent years. Even so, most English people say 'England' when they mean 'Britain', but they're in good company: The Victorians used to do that all the time, too – even the Victorian Welsh and Scots and, yes, Irish. You may think *Britain* would be a safe term to use, but apart from the fact that using it is a good way to get yourself lynched in Glasgow or West Belfast, Britain's not actually accurate.

You see, *Britain* was the name the Romans gave to the whole island, which contains modern-day England, Wales, and Scotland. Ireland was *Hibernia,* so even Northern Ireland was never part of 'Britain'. This old Roman distinction between Britain and Hibernia (or Ireland) is why the full name of the country is so cumbersome.

For a long time after the Romans went the term *Britain* disappeared and was only used to refer to the time before the Saxons – like in Shakespeare's *King Lear,* for example. Educated people knew *Britain* was an ancient term for the whole island, but no one actually used it, or if they did, they used it to mean Brittany! When King James VI of Scotland became King of England in 1603 (see Chapter 13) he tried to revive the term *Britain,* but no one really took him up on it.

Then, a hundred years later, England and Scotland joined together in the Act of Union, and they had to think of a name for the new joint kingdom. Someone suggested 'Great Britain', which not only sounded good but was actually accurate – when England and Scotland united, they reformed the old Roman province of Britain, and the 'Great' helped to distinguish it from Brittany. When, a hundred years after *that,* another Act of Union brought Ireland into the fold, they didn't just lump all three countries under the name Great Britain (because Ireland had *never* been part of Britain, great or small) so the name changed again to *the United Kingdom of Great Britain and Ireland.* (To find out more about the Acts of Union, head to Chapter 15.)

When the Romans left, the *Britons* were the Celtic peoples they left behind. When the Angles and Saxons came raiding and settling, they subsumed the Britons of 'England' into the new people who eventually got called the English. So the people with the best right to be called British nowadays are actually the very people in Wales and Scotland who object to the term most strongly!

Before the Romans came, the whole island was one big patchwork of different tribes: No-one had any sense that some tribes were 'Scottish' and some 'English'. In fact, since the Scots were an Irish tribe and the English, if they existed at all, lived in Germany, no one would have understood what either term meant!

# England

After the Romans left, the Angles and Saxons set up a whole network of different kingdoms: Kent, East Anglia, Northumbria, Mercia, Wessex, and some other less important ones. Not until the Vikings arrived did the English start to unite under a single king. It was this united kingdom that William the Conqueror took over when he won the Battle of Hastings in 1066. He would hardly have bothered if he was only going to become King of Wessex.

After the Norman invasion, although it was easier to speak of 'England', it was much harder to talk about 'the English'. The ordinary people were of Saxon blood, but the nobles were all French – Normans to start with and later from other parts of France. A whole sweep of famous Kings of England including Richard the Lionheart, King John, the first three Edwards, and Richard II would never have called themselves English. Not really until Henry V and the Wars of the Roses can you talk of everyone from top to bottom being part of an English people.

# Scotland

The Romans did have a sense of 'Scotland', or *Caledonia* as they called it, being a bit different, but that was just because they were never able to conquer it completely. There were Britons in Strathclyde and Picts in most of the rest of Caledonia, and then Scots came over from the north of Ireland and settled. It took a long time, but eventually these three groups all learned to get along with each other. It was a Scottish king, Kenneth MacAlpin, who finally managed to unite the groups, so the whole area came to be called after his people – 'Scot-land'.

# Wales

'For Wales', it used to say in indexes, 'see England'! Which is desperately unfair, but for many years that was how the English thought about Wales. The Welsh are descended pretty much directly from the Ancient Britons, and they have kept their separate identity and language. You still find Welsh being spoken in parts of Wales today.

## The border regions

Whole areas of southern Scotland and northern England were forever changing hands. For example:

- The English Lake District isn't included in *Domesday Book* (explained in Chapter 7) because it was part of Scotland at the time.

- For many years, southern Scotland was colonised by the Angles – the English.

- The border city of Berwick upon Tweed actually got a sort of separate status, neither English nor Scottish, so that peace treaties and things had to be made in the name of 'the United Kingdom of Great Britain and Ireland and the City of Berwick upon Tweed'!

For many years, more or less continual warfare raged all along the border. The fierce border family clans, like the Nixons or the dreaded Grahams, lived wildly, beyond anyone's control. They raided and murdered each other and stole cattle, and when wars broke out between Scotland and England, they helped whichever side they liked, regardless of which side of the 'border' they actually lived on. The border clans were known as *Reivers* – the most terrifying raiders since the Vikings: They've given us the word *bereaved* and *bereft* to mean devastated, which is pretty appropriate.

# Ireland

Most people think of Irish history in terms of Ireland being invaded by the English, but if anything, it was the other way round in the beginning. Apart from one or two trading posts, the Romans left Ireland alone (except, that is, for a certain Roman Briton called Patrick, who did make something of an impact). After the Romans left Britain, the Irish started to come over as missionaries, not conquerors. They set up the great monasteries of Iona and Lindisfarne, and Irish monks and preachers like St Columba brought Christianity to Scotland and northern England. Some Irish did cross over to settle, and one of these tribes, the *Scotti* or *Scots*, gave their name to Scotland. Once the Normans settled in England, however, things changed.

# And all those little islands

Islands play an important part in what is, after all, the story of an island people. Scottish missionaries worked from Iona and Lindisfarne, and Queen Victoria governed a worldwide empire from Osborne Palace on the Isle of Wight. The islands are a reminder of the cultural and ethnic variety that makes up the British peoples.

### The Shetland Islands and the Isle of Man

The most northerly parts of Britain are the Shetland Islands. You may think of these islands as Scottish, but you'd be badly wrong. The Shetlanders are of pure Viking stock and proud of it. You can touch the Viking heritage in the Manx people of the Isle of Man, though ethnically they are Celtic. They say you can see five kingdoms from Man – England, Ireland, Scotland, Gwynedd (Wales), and the Kingdom of Heaven! – and the Vikings used it as a base for controlling all of them. The Isle of Man boasts the world's oldest parliament, Tynwald, a descendant of the Viking 'parliament', the *Thing*.

### The Channel Islands

At least with the Shetlands and the Isle of Man, you know you are still in the United Kingdom. You can be forgiven for wondering when you drop in on the Channel Islands. The islands all look English enough, but their English road signs carry French names, the police are called the *Bureau des Etrangers*, and the money looks like British money, but isn't. The Channel Islands were part of the Duchy of Normandy, and when you look at the map, you can see that they're virtually in France. These islands have kept many of their distinctive customs and laws including, as rich people found out long ago, much more relaxed tax regulations.

The Channel Islands were the only part of British territory to fall to the Germans in the Second World War, and Hitler made full use of them for propaganda purposes. Perhaps not surprisingly, historians who have looked into the German occupation have found just as much evidence of active collaboration and collusion in the Channel Islands as anywhere else in occupied Europe. Even more tragically, Alderney became a slave labour camp for prisoners from all over the Nazi empire.

# How the UK Was Born

How did this strange hybrid country with the long-winded name that no one actually uses actually come into being? If you want a full answer, you'll have to read the whole book, but here's a quick overview. As you'll see, the creation of the United Kingdom was a mixture of conquest, immigration, and Acts of Union, all going to produce a very British sort of melting pot.

# England: Head Honcho

England was bound to play the leading role. The country's much bigger than any of the other parts of Britain, and closer to the Continent. England had been part of the Roman Empire, and the Viking invasions gave the English a strong sense of unity against a common enemy. The English didn't consciously set out to conquer their neighbours: They had been fighting the Welsh on and off since Saxon times, so when King Edward I finally conquered Wales in 1284 it seemed a natural conclusion to a very long story. With Scotland, despite all those battles, the English were never trying to overrun the country: They simply wanted a pro-English monarch on the Scottish throne for their own safety's sake.

The real problem for the English was Ireland, because they were never able to control it. England's great worry was always that the Irish or the Scots would ally with the French – and they often did. The English managed to persuade the Scottish parliament to agree to an Act of Union in 1707 (which, as it turned out, enabled the Scots to benefit to the full from England's Industrial Revolution!). The English imposed direct rule in Ireland in 1801, but mainly as a security measure: Ireland never benefited from union with England to the same degree as Scotland did.

For most of the nineteenth and twentieth centuries the English took their commanding position within the United Kingdom more or less for granted. England was what counted; the rest were the 'Celtic fringe'. But by the 1990s that confidence had gone. After years of having no governing body of their own, the 'Celtic fringe' once again had their own parliaments and assemblies; England was beginning to look like the Rump of the United Kingdom. So the English began to rediscover a national sense of their own: they began to fly the flag of St George at football matches, and there was even talk of setting up special assemblies for the English regions, though ultimately nothing came of it.

## *The conquest of Scotland*

Like England, Scotland began as a collection of different tribes, which slowly and painfully began to form themselves into a nation. Of course, hostility to the English was a great help, and it's no coincidence that Scotland's most important statement of national identity, the 1320 Declaration of Arbroath, dates from the period of the fiercest wars for independence from England. Well into the sixteenth century the Scots maintained an anti-English alliance with France – the *Auld Alliance*, as it was called – which was guaranteed to stop the English government from sleeping at night.

But although Scotland and England spent plenty of time at war with each other, by no means were all Scots anti-English. The English negotiated marriage alliances with the Scots – Henry VIII's sister became Queen of Scotland – so a pro-English faction usually existed somewhere at court. When the Protestant Reformation took hold in the sixteenth century, Scottish Protestants naturally looked to Tudor England for support against the Catholics of the Scottish Highlands, and especially against the Catholic and very accident-prone Mary, Queen of Scots. People usually know that it was the English who cut Mary's head off; they often forget that the Scots had already overthrown her and locked her up themselves.

In the end, it wasn't the English who got their own man on the throne in Edinburgh, but the Scots who got their man on the throne in London. When

Elizabeth I died childless in 1603, King James VI of Scotland inherited the English throne. It was a Union of the Crowns but not yet of the nations: That had to wait a hundred years until the Act of Union of 1707. From then on Scotland played an active role in the United Kingdom: The British Empire could hardly have carried on without the large number of Scottish missionaries, doctors, soldiers, and administrators who served it. But the Scots kept their strong sense of separate identity, and in 1999 they finally got their parliament back.

## The conquest of Wales

The Normans began the conquest of Wales, and for many years, parts of Wales were ruled by the powerful Norman 'Marcher Lords' (see Chapters 8 and 9 for a bit more on this). The Welsh princes Llewellyn the Great and Llewellyn ap Gruffyd fought back, but eventually King Edward I conquered Wales and planted massive castles all over it. Owain Glyn Dŵr had a good go at pushing the English out, but it was not to be.

Ironically, the people who finally snuffed out Welsh independence were themselves of Welsh origin: The Tudors. Henry Tudor landed at Milford Haven to challenge King Richard III and become King Henry VII, and it was his son, Henry VIII, who got Parliament to pass an Act of Union making Wales, in effect, a province of England. And Wales stayed like that until Tony Blair set up a Welsh Assembly in 1999. A long wait!

## The conquest of Ireland

Ireland's great Christian heritage was to prove her undoing. Pope Adrian IV (who also happened to be the only English pope there's ever been) gave King Henry II permission to go over to Ireland and bring the Irish church into the Roman fold whether the Irish liked it or not. So a great wave of Anglo-Norman knights crossed the Irish Sea and claimed Ireland for the English crown.

### Religious strife

When the Reformation started in the sixteenth century, the descendants of those Anglo-Norman knights went along with the new Protestant religion, but the Celtic Irish stayed Catholic. Queen Elizabeth, I, and her ministers came up with a clever solution: Plant Scottish Protestants in Ireland. Hey presto! The Catholic province of Ulster became the most fiercely Protestant and loyal area in the kingdom.

When the English threw out their Catholic King James II in 1688, the Irish rallied to help him, but the Scots-Irish of Ulster were having none of it: They defied King James, thrashed him at the Battle of the Boyne, and sent him packing. Their descendants in modern-day Ulster have never forgotten it, and they make sure their Catholic neighbours don't forget it either.

### Famine and Fenians

After the seventeenth century, the British brought in all sorts of laws to take away Catholics' civil rights, which in effect kept Ireland in poverty for generations. Pockets of affluence existed – Dublin was a very elegant eighteenth-century city – but Ireland was a bit like modern-day India in its mixture of extreme poverty and great wealth. Even the Protestant Irish were beginning to feel that the laws against Catholics were unfair and dragging the whole country down, and they began to argue for *Catholic Emancipation*, especially the right to vote.

By the time emancipation came, the British had closed Ireland's parliament down, and were governing Ireland directly from London. Then, in the 1840s, the potato crop in Ireland failed and produced one of the worst famines of modern times. Those who could, got out of Ireland and spread around the world, taking their hatred of England and the English with them. Those who stayed in Ireland campaigned all the more vigorously for self-government, or *Home Rule*, while armed groups like the *Fenians* turned to bombings and shootings.

Finally, in 1922 the British had to agree to grant Ireland its independence. The Ulster Protestants were dead against an independent Ireland, and immediately voted to stay in the United Kingdom, which is why part of the ancient province of Ulster is still within the UK. Many Irish saw this division as a stop-gap measure, and the violence that erupted in the 1960s was about trying to get – or to resist – a united Ireland. Ultimately, neither side would surrender, and the different parties had to agree a compromise peace settlement. Although the shooting has ended and Northern Ireland is now peaceful and prosperous, the story of a united or divided Ireland shows no sign of ending quite yet.

# You're Not From Round 'Ere – But Then Again, Neither Am I

Working out exactly who the native peoples of Britain are is very difficult. The Victorians talked about the 'British race', but doing so is silly: By definition there's no one British race, but a collection of different ethnic groups.

## Any such thing as a native Briton?

The closest anyone can come to being an original native must be the Celts: The Welsh, the Scottish Gaels, the Irish, and the Cornish – though there are people of Celtic origin throughout Britain. But even the Celts weren't originally native to Britain; they came from the continent, as did the Romans, the Angles and Saxons, and the Normans.

The Scots and the Irish have a better claim to be 'natives', but the situation's complicated because of all the swapping they've done over the years. The Celtic Irish are certainly native to Ireland, but on the other hand, just how long do you have to be settled in a place before you can call yourself a native? Ulster Protestants have been in Ireland for as long as whites have been in America, and a lot longer than the Europeans have been in Australia and New Zealand, yet some people still have a problem calling them Irish.

# Immigrants

As if working things out between the English, Welsh, Irish, and Scots isn't complicated enough, Britain has long been a country of immigrants, from all parts of the globe.

## Asylum seekers

During all the religious wars of the seventeenth century large numbers of Protestants took shelter in England because it was the largest and most stable of the Protestant powers. French Huguenots fleeing Louis XIV settled in London and made a very prosperous living as craftsmen and traders. The Dutch had started coming over in Elizabethan times during their long war of independence from Spain, and many others came over when William of Orange ousted James II in 1688. Some of these immigrants were nobles, like the Bentincks, who became Dukes of Portland. Others were ordinary folk brought over to help drain the fens of East Anglia, and you can still see their Dutch-style houses today. Britain did very well by welcoming these asylum seekers.

---

## Spreading Britain's wings

A famous Victorian painting by Ford Madox Brown called *The Last of England* shows a couple looking thoughtfully at the disappearing English coastline as they set off for – well, maybe America, Australia, South Africa, Argentina or any of the other places where the British emigrated in such large numbers. The Welsh populated Patagonia in the Argentinean pampas, and one of Chile's great national heroes has the distinctly Irish name of Bernardo O'Higgins. Plenty of Brits settled in the American West, including a large number who responded to Brigham Young's mission to Liverpool and went out to settle at Salt Lake City. British engineers and navvies went all over Europe designing railways and laying the tracks: The lines in northern Italy were all the work of British engineers. The British have always been a people of immigrants – and emigrants.

### A right royal bunch of foreigners

Of course, if you want a good example of a family with very little English – or even British – blood in its veins, then look at the Royal Family. The Normans and Plantagenets were French, the Tudors were Welsh, the Stuarts were Scots, the Hanoverians were German, and, until George III, they couldn't even speak the language properly. Victoria's family was the union of one German family with another, and its name was the House of Saxe-Coburg-Gotha – doesn't sound very English, does it? The Royal Family changed the name to Windsor during the First World War (and their relatives the Battenbergs anglicised theirs to Mountbatten), but the British have never entirely forgotten that their royal family is not quite as Made in Britain as it may look. The British probably liked Diana, the Princess of Wales, so much because she was indisputably *English*.

### There should be black in the Union Jack

People often assume that the first black faces appeared in Britain after the Second World War. Not a bit of it! Black people were in Britain in surprisingly large numbers from Tudor times, though, of course, most of them were slaves (many society portraits of the seventeenth and eighteenth centuries have a small black child servant in the corner). By Queen Victoria's time, whole communities of black people existed, especially in London, perhaps because, by then, Britain had abolished the slave trade.

### Other ethnic groups

Victorian Limehouse in London's docklands was a regular Chinatown and, as Britain extended her rule in India, more and more Asians came to London: Gandhi trained as a barrister in the Middle Temple in London and Nehru studied at Cambridge. Duleep Singh, the exiled Maharajah of the Punjab, was a frequent visitor to Queen Victoria's court (okay, it was because of the British that he was exiled in the first place). Victoria also took on an Indian manservant known as the *Munshi*, who wasn't at all the high caste sage he claimed to be, but what the heck.

# Whose History Is It Anyway?

Most history books tell you a lot about what the kings and queens and leaders got up to. For many years British historians thought the only point of reading history was to find out about how the British constitution developed, so they concentrated on parliaments and laws and pretty much ignored everything else. More recently, historians have pointed out that history involves a lot more than royals and politicians, and there are all sorts of people whose history has a right to be heard.

## Kings and queens

You can't entirely get away from kings and queens – they were important, and it would be an odd book of British history that left them out altogether. But beware of the 'Fairy Tale' approach to these people. Kings couldn't just give away half their kingdoms to young men who came and married their daughters, and the kings who *did* try to divide up their realms among their sons, like William the Conqueror and Henry II, found doing so didn't work. Even the most powerful rulers relied heavily on their ministers' advisers. Some advisers, like Sir William Cecil with Queen Elizabeth I, gave good advice (in fact, some historians reckon it was really Cecil who was ruling England); some advisers were disastrous, like Charles I's ministers, Strafford and Archbishop Laud.

By the time you hit the Georges, working out exactly how much is being done by the King and how much by his ministers is very difficult. 'This house believes the power of the crown has increased, is increasing, and ought to be diminished' ran one famous parliamentary motion in 1780, and three years later George III, completely on his own initiative, dismissed a ministry which had a big parliamentary majority – and got away with it. But on the whole, the power of the crown had decreased, was decreasing, and was going to go on decreasing, too, whatever Queen Victoria or Prince Albert might have thought about it.

## What about the workers?

History isn't just about the people at the top. Sure, these folks have left lots of evidence behind them – all their writings, houses, and furniture – so finding out about them is easy. But a lot of people worked hard to keep the people at the top in the style to which they were accustomed, and these working people have a history, too.

An English historian called E. P. Thompson showed how to discover the history of ordinary people when he constructed his *Making of the English Working Class*. He used all sorts of source material, including ballads, posters, and court cases (a lot of working people ended up in front of a magistrate) to trace how the working people of industrial England developed a sense of identity. Many stately homes open up the kitchens and the servants' quarters to visitors, and if you really want an idea of how the other half lived, go to Henry VIII's palace at Hampton Court and have a look at the Tudor kitchens. Think how much *work* it took to keep him so fat!

## My grandfather was . . .

Go into any archive or records office in Britain and you'll find it surprisingly busy with ordinary people researching their family history. Explaining exactly why family history has taken off in the way that it has in recent years is difficult, but genealogy is phenomenally popular. People learn how to use censuses, parish registers, and hearth tax assessments to work out who their ancestors were and where they came from. You may be surprised how far back you can go if you know what you're doing – and if the records have survived. Most people get back to Victorian times, and some trace the line to Tudor times and beyond. These family history searches are a sign of just why history is important: It helps us work out exactly who we are.

## A global story

'What should he know of England,' asked that great poet of Empire, Rudyard Kipling, 'who only England knows?' Allowing for that Victorian use of 'England' to mean 'Britain', Kipling had a point, though not perhaps in the way he expected. To know the story of Britain and the British, you ought really to look at the story of Britain's Empire and at how all these different places – Canada, Jamaica, Tonga, Malta, Punjab, Kenya, Aden (Qatar) – were brought into the British story. Their histories are part of Britain's history, and British history is part of theirs, especially for the descendants of people from these parts of the world who are at school in Britain now. Okay, there's a limit to what I can do in this book, but bear this in mind: If you know British history (and by the end of this book you'll have a pretty good idea of it) you only know half the story of *Britain's* history.

# Chapter 2

# Sticks and Stone Age Stuff

. . . . . . . . . . . . . . . . . . . . . . . . . . . . . . . . . . . . . . . . . . . . . . . .

## In This Chapter

▶ Digging into the prehistoric past

▶ Understanding the Stone Age and the people who lived then

▶ Advancing into the Neolithic period

▶ Beakers, barrows, and the Age of Bronze

. . . . . . . . . . . . . . . . . . . . . . . . . . . . . . . . . . . . . . . . . . . . . . . .

*1*magine a roll of toilet paper laid out on the ground. Pretty long, isn't it? That roll's the history of planet Earth. Walk along its length, and you find the Jurassic and the Devonian and the Cretaceous periods. You see where the dinosaurs come in and where they go out, and you see volcanoes and sabre-toothed tigers and all the rest of that really old prehistoric stuff. What you *don't* see are any cavemen in bearskins fighting off dinosaurs: They didn't come anywhere near living at the same time. In fact, you can look as hard as you like, but you won't find any human life at all, at least not until you've got to the very end of the roll. Not to the last few squares, not even to the very last square. See on the *edge* of the last square? Those perforations? That edge is human history on earth. All 800,000 years of it. All the Stone Age stuff and the Middle Ages and your Tudors and Stuarts and Abraham Lincoln and Winston Churchill and the Cold War – in the history of the world, human history takes up no more space than that last edge on the roll.

Now put the toilet roll back before someone misses it and take a sheet of paper. Mark out 100 squares – in a square, in a line, it doesn't matter. The squares represent human history on earth. Now you colour the squares in according to the different periods – blue for the Middle Ages, red for the Romans, and so on – and start with the Stone Age. How many squares do you reckon it will need for the Stone Age? Ten? Fifteen? Fifty? Take your coloured pencil and colour in ninety-nine squares. And colour a little into the hundredth square as well. The Stone Age dwarfs all other periods of human history. Nothing else in human history lasted so long, and nothing that came later came anywhere near matching this period for the changes and inventions it produced. Come on, these guys deserve some respect. They lasted a long time, and they had a lot to put up with.

# What a Load of Rubbish! What Archaeologists Find

Prehistoric people didn't leave behind any Stone Age manuscripts or tales and legends telling their own story. To piece together what life was like for prehistoric people, archaeologists have to play detective.

## Going through the trash

What we do have is what prehistoric people left behind, and you'd be surprised how much archaeologists can work out from it. Nosy journalists know how much you can learn from going through people's rubbish bins, and archaeologists work on the same principle. Stone Age people (and everyone else after them) left lots of their rubbish behind – literally – and mighty informative all those chicken drumsticks and broken bones are, too.

Archaeologists don't just look at evidence of prehistoric life. They study all periods right up to the modern day, and the sort of evidence they can provide is still very useful for periods where written history exists. When a new building or road is being constructed, you'll often see archaeologists close by, watching the newly-exposed soil for signs of our ancestors.

## Examining the tools

Once you start examining the tools, pretty soon you get to thinking about what they used these tools for. A hand-axe means they were cutting things, but what? Wood? Food? An arrow suggests hunting, and hunting suggests a whole set of rituals and roles, so immediately you can begin to build up a picture of the life of a tribe. Animal bones can give a good idea of what they hunted and ate, and sometimes what they did with the bones. Scientists have even been able to get hold of prehistoric seeds and grain, so we know what plants they sowed, and when. Impressive.

As farming took hold, new tasks abounded for everyone: Seed had to be sown, crops harvested, harvests stored, grain ground, food baked, and all sorts of tools to be thought of and created. So these are the things that archaeologists start finding, and from what they find, experts make deductions about how people were living and how quickly technology was advancing.

## Looking at tribal societies of today

In addition to poring over the detritus of these prehistoric people, sometimes archaeologists have a look at what anthropologists have found studying the social patterns in tribal societies today, so as to get an idea of how Stone Age tribes may have operated. Next are biologists and palaeobiologists and geologists and geophysicists until you can hardly move for experts – because we're not just looking at what the Stone Age people left behind; we're looking at who and what they were in the first place. And being sure of your findings isn't always easy.

# Uncovering prehistoric man

Most people didn't have any concept of prehistoric man before 1856, when in the Neander Valley in Germany some quarry workers were out doing whatever quarry workers do when they found a skull and some bones. Not knowing whether they had found animal or human bones they took the bones along to their local doctor who had a look at them and said, 'Yup!' – or more likely, 'Ja!' – they were human bones all right.

## It's life, Jim, but not as we know it

The next question was what kind of human bones were they? The skull had no real forehead – the whole thing looked low and long, which is why some people thought it was an ape. It certainly didn't look like the locals. Could the bones be Asiatic? Cossack troops had been in the area during the Napoleonic Wars; was it one of those? And because the bones were a bit bow-legged, they wondered if the Cossack had had rickets.

Then two prominent British scientists, Charles Lyall and Thomas Huxley, crossed over to Germany to have a look. They decided this chap was definitely human, but a lot older than the Germans realised: This was the skull, they said, of a primitive man.

## Why the ruckus?

The bones were discovered in 1856: Victorian times. The idea of a primitive man was dynamite. Many people weren't even sure what Lyall and Huxley meant. The Bible said that God created Adam: It didn't say anything about a prototype. But Huxley and Lyall seemed to be saying this skeleton was just such a prototype man.

---

## Darwin

Darwin's *The Origin of Species* contains fourteen long chapters. Here is the section on the origins of humankind: 'In the distant future I see open fields for far more important researches. Psychology will be based on a new foundation, that of the necessary acquirement of each mental power and capacity by gradation. Light will be thrown on the origin of man and his history.' That's it. And that's all of it. But Darwin's timing couldn't have been better – he published just as bones began to appear which did indeed throw light on the origin of man.

---

Three years later Huxley's friend Charles Darwin published his famous book *The Origin of Species*. Darwin put forward the theory of evolution based on survival of the fittest, and his ideas have created huge arguments ever since about which is right: The theory of evolution or the Book of Genesis.

 You may not realise that Darwin's book is entirely about plants and animals: Except for a brief bit at the end (which you can read in the sidebar 'Darwin'), *The Origin of Species* makes no mention of human beings at all. But that omission wasn't going to stop people making a connection between his ideas and these mysterious bones. Things were beginning to evolve.

With Darwin's book selling like hot cakes it was obvious that people would begin talking about those bones, and they did. They were horrified. The Neander Valley skull (or Neanderthal in German) had a thick ridge over the eyes and the bones were so chunky. Were we really related to *that* man?

## The Stone Age

We talk about the Stone Age because people used stones – in a surprising number of ways. A smooth, round stone? It may look at home on a beach, but had you ever thought of it as a hammer? If you look carefully at some of the stones that have turned up at Stone Age sites you can see that they still carry all the little marks and chips from hammering other stones into place.

Then consider sharp tools. If you were stuck in the wilds without a blade of any sort, would you know which sort of stone to pick up and how to break it so you got a sharp cutting edge? Even if you did, you'd probably end up with something pretty crude: Just a large pebble broken in two. Congratulations. You've reached the technological level of some of the earliest hominids!

Stone Age people were a lot more skilled than just splitting rocks. They crafted and shaped their tools, and some of those flint knives cut like a razor. They made tools out of bones, too. Through their cave paintings, we can really get a clue of what was going on inside all those skulls that keep cropping up. Here's what we can tell:

- ✔ **They knew they needed tools for some jobs**, and we can see those jobs growing in sophistication.

- ✔ **They could identify the best materials**. Picking the best materials probably started as trial-and-error, but this knowledge got passed down through the generations. That suggests skill and education.

- ✔ **They were highly skilled and imaginative**. Every tool they made had to be invented first.

## Hey, hey – we're the monkeys! The Neanderthals

Thanks to Darwin and his *The Origin of Species*, published in 1859, you could hardly walk along a cliff in the nineteenth century without tripping over a fossil hunter, with a hammer in one hand and a copy of the book in the other. Soon these people began to find more bones and skulls just like the German ones. Bits and pieces of Neanderthal turned up in Belgium, France, Spain, and Greece. Bits started emerging outside Europe, in the Middle East, and in central Asia. But it was always bits: A skull here, a thigh bone there – that was him all over. Then, in 1908, they finally unearthed a whole Neanderthal skeleton in France. At last archaeologists could work out what these strange people really looked like. It was Bad News.

This French Neanderthal had big bones, bent legs, a bent neck, stiff joints – it looked more like a lumbering ape than anything human. So people thought that's what Neanderthals were: Great big apes, with ugly faces and knuckles dragging along the floor. And dim. Stands to reason, doesn't it? Big ape-like thing living in caves going 'Ug, ug' and wearing animal skins. Yes, people told themselves, whatever else we thought about these Neanderthals, we had to be better than them. And if we *did* evolve from them, well didn't it make sense that we would be cleverer? Think again, friend.

Scientists have done a lot more work on these Neanderthals, and we've got them so badly wrong that they should get a good lawyer and sue. And if they had lived a bit longer they might have done it, too.

Here are some facts:

- ✔ **That skeleton they found in 1908 came from an elderly Neanderthal with chronic arthritis.** Other skeletons – and we've found lots of them by now – don't show any of the same deformities. Allowing for a slightly squashed face and a slightly heavier bone structure, you wouldn't look twice at these guys if you passed them in the street.

- ✔ **Neanderthals were not stupid.** In fact, their brains were bigger than ours. They were highly advanced tool makers, they were organised enough to hunt even the biggest animals around, and from the way they buried their dead they seemed to have had some sense of spirituality and religion.

- ✔ **No one alive today is descended from Neanderthals.** Not even England football supporters.

We simply don't know for certain what happened to the Neanderthals. We know they survived the Ice Age, and it may be that the shape of their skulls and faces helped. Scientists have made comparisons with the Inuit in the Arctic. Looking at some of the breaks and twists in their bones we think they must have had an incredibly high pain threshold. Their stocky bone structure was an advantage in the Ice Age, but it made them much less agile for hunting in the big open areas that opened up as the ice retreated. Neanderthals used short stabbing spears for hunting: Good for getting up close and personal in an Ice Age forest, but not so good out in the open where your dinner has plenty of space to run away.

Whatever the reason, the Neanderthals died out. And they didn't give birth to us lot, either. Because one of the biggest mysteries about the Neanderthals is that we've found definite human bones from the same time. That is, at one time there were *two* human races walking the earth (since the Neanderthals died out, you could say it makes them our first cousins once removed).

## Meet your ancestors

Modern humans, what scientists call *Homo sapiens sapiens*, first appeared in the Middle East, possibly at about the same time that the Neanderthals first appeared in Europe. It took a long time, but eventually this new type of people began appearing in Europe, too.

### The Swanscombe woman

The oldest identifiably human remains in Europe come from England – a female skull, which turned up at Swanscombe in Kent. But what was she? She looks a bit like a really early type of human called *Homo erectus*. *Homo* because we are definitely talking humans, not apes here; *erectus* because these people walked upright – no stooping. But she's not entirely like other *Homo erectus* finds: Her big, round brain section is more Neanderthal. Maybe Swanscombe woman was *Homo erectus*'s swan song.

# Ice Age

The Ice Age was long, about 990,000 years, long enough to go from Swanscombe woman, part *Homo erectus* and part *Homo sapiens*, through the Neanderthal story, and on to *Homo sapiens sapiens*. That's us.

Don't get the wrong idea about the Ice Age. It didn't mean the whole world was covered in ice the whole time. It didn't even mean it was cold the whole time. We reckon they probably had some quite hot summers in the Ice Age. But the winters were very long and very cold, and the earth's temperature was definitely falling. It was certainly cold enough for people to make their homes in caves and to wrap themselves up in animal skins. They had to hunt, and in those days plenty of woolly mammoths were walking around well wrapped up against the cold. Lots of meat covers a woolly mammoth, but how would you feel about facing it armed only with a few spears tipped with flint? Hunting it took guts.

### *Paint your Cro-Magnon*

Some of the people worrying woolly mammoths were our friends the Neanderthals, but by the time of the last Ice Age some new kids were on the block. Rounder heads but sharper brains. We call them *Cro-Magnon*, after the place in France where we found something very special they left behind. These guys could paint. Cro-Magnon created those amazing paintings in the caves at Lascaux in France. Painting doesn't just take skill or brains: You need imagination and artistic sensitivity. Perhaps we're looking at the first artistic tantrums in history. Tools and arrows and hunting parties are all very practical: What exactly was the point of cave painting? We don't know exactly, and we probably never will.

The paintings may have had some ritual or religious purpose, or they may have been the Cro-Magnon equivalent of holiday snaps – 'Here's one of me with a bison' and 'That's Sheila and the kids when we walked over to France for the summer'. But with Cro-Magnon, we can be pretty sure that we are looking in the mirror and seeing ourselves. Literally. A DNA test carried out on some Middle Stone Age bones in the South West of England found an exact match with a local history teacher. His pupils probably weren't surprised, but think this one through: Despite all those waves of Celts and Romans and Saxons and Normans (which you can read about in Chapters 3–7), some people never moved from where their ancestors lived. Our gene pool goes back all the way to the Stone Age. Perhaps the teacher even lived in the same house.

Cro-Magnon Man had culture. Archaeologists have found needles and pins, which suggests they had worked out how to make proper clothes out of all those animal skins. The discovery of fish hooks and harpoons means they went fishing (which could account for all that imagination). They even had jewellery. But the Cro-Magnon were a nomadic people, regularly upping sticks and following the deer. Hunter-gatherers. But all that was about to change. The Cro-Magnon didn't know it, but their world was about to get turned upside down.

## Who says No Man is an Island?

Although we've been talking about 'Britain', the term doesn't really make much sense for the prehistoric period for the simple reason that 'Britain' and 'Ireland', as separate islands off the European mainland, didn't actually exist. They were simply outlying parts of the whole European continent, and they stayed that way until the end of the Ice Age. When the great thaw came, round about 7,500 BC, the water levels rose dramatically, creating what we call the English Channel and the Irish Sea. This development must have taken the Neolithics by surprise: They were islanders now and they were going to have to get used to it.

# Plough the Fields, Don't Scatter – the Neolithic Revolution

As far as we know, the first people to work out that you could get food by sowing seeds and waiting for them to grow came from the 'fertile crescent' in the Middle East. The idea really caught on, and when farming spread to Europe, it created what historians call the *neolithic revolution*. (*Neo* = new, *lith* = stone; so *neolithic* = New Stone Age.) Okay, so the revolution didn't happen overnight. And it didn't necessarily make life easier: Farming is a lot more work than hunting.

People may have taken up farming because they probably needed extra food to feed an increasing population. Whatever the reason, farming changed everything. Hunters blend into the landscape, but farmers change it. People stopped following wherever the deer went; instead, they settled down and learned to plough. You can date big human impact on the environment to the New Stone Age.

As farming became more common everyone found new jobs to do: From sowing seeds, to harvesting, to storing and using the crops. And making tools to make these jobs easier. All this activity left signs and artefacts for archaeologists to find.

The innovation didn't stop with farming. Neolithic people learned how to tame pigs, horses, cattle, and how to use them for work or for food. They already knew about skinning animals, but somewhere along the line, they met sheep and figured out how to get textiles without killing the beast who provided it. Exactly how these people worked out that you can shear a sheep, play about with the wool, and tease it into a long thread to be used in making cloth no one really knows (it's not, you must admit, the most *obvious* use of a sheep).

Maybe Neolithic people got the idea of shearing or learned the technique from trading contacts. During the Neolithic period, fully-fledged cities existed with walls and streets and a crime problem at Jericho and Çatal Hüyük in Turkey.

And then consider religion. If you're hunting, you invoke the spirit of the deer or wild boar. When you take up farming, however, you're putting your life entirely in the hands of the sun, the rain, the earth, and the British weather. No wonder these things began to get worshipped as gods. The British weather still is.

What survives from the Neolithic period is amazing:

- ✔ **In southern England, a wooden track leading over marshland was found; it may have been one of many.** That's a prehistoric road network!

- ✔ **At Star Carr in Yorkshire, antlers, bones, and tools, including a wooden paddle (which seems to indicate that these people worked out some kind of boats), were found.** Star Carr goes back to 7,500 BC, which is almost twice as old as the little commune settlement of seven huts, which has survived at Skara Brae on Orkney.

- ✔ **At Skara Brae, beautifully crafted jewellery and pottery have been found.** These were highly resourceful and sophisticated people.

- ✔ **Burial chambers under long grassy mounds called long barrows have been discovered,** and let's not forget Stonehenge, the Neolithic equivalent of a massive public works project.

# Rolling Stones: A National Institution

Stonehenge. Neolithic people built it, and the Beakers (explained in the section 'Beakermania', later in this chapter) helped complete it. Stonehenge was huge. If it looks impressive now, think how it must have looked when it was new. Stonehenge is a massive circle of upright stones supporting lintels, with another horseshoe-shape set of stones inside it, and an altar stone inside that. The circle is aligned with the sunrise at the summer solstice and the sunset at the winter solstice, so it seems a pretty safe bet that Stonehenge was a religious or ritual centre of some sort. If size and scale are anything to go by, we are looking at a place of national importance.

The stones aren't local; they were probably brought all the way from Wales. For a long time archaeologists assumed the stones were transported by hauling them on log rollers. Now they think they were brought most of the way by boat, even though Salisbury Plain, where Stonehenge is located, is a long way from the sea. The effort, the organisation, and the sheer number of people required to pull off such a massive undertaking were enormous. We're not just talking a few druids cutting mistletoe: Stonehenge meant meticulous planning, technical know-how, communication, logistics, and some very good rope-making. Not to mention how you persuade all those people to do the dragging.

## Puzzles and mysteries no one's answered – yet

We simply don't know why the Neolithics and Beakers built Stonehenge, and short of finding the makers' instructions one day, we're not likely to know either. But Stonehenge is just one of many things we don't know about these people. We know they had a language, but we don't know what it was; we know they made music, but we don't know what it sounded like; we don't know who their leaders were or whether they enjoyed the sun or if they ever got tired of eating deer.

People who don't like unsolved mysteries come up with their own ideas, no matter how wacky. Some people suggest, for example, that Stonehenge was a clock or a computer or the launch pad for a space ship. And modern-day druids carry out not-very-ancient ceremonies at Stonehenge every summer solstice, and hikers follow imaginary *ley lines* between ancient sites of completely different periods. Well, it's a free country. But if you really want to know what ancient Britain looked like, stick to the evidence with a little leeway for imagination. Leave the spaceships to the loonies.

And Stonehenge isn't the only circular formation of importance. Others include Woodhenge, not far from Stonehenge (but made of, er, wood) and even a wooden henge on the coast known as Seahenge. The stone circle of Tara is in Ireland, where the kings would be crowned in due course. Still in existence are simple circles, like Castlerigg in Cumbria, and big, complex circles, like Avebury, which has two sets of concentric circles inside the bigger one and a ditch around the whole thing. These stones tell us a lot about the Beakers and the Neolithics, but of course they don't tell us the one thing we're dying to know: What did they build them *for?*

# Giving It Some Heavy Metal: The Bronze Age

Someone, probably in the Middle East, found out one day that if you leave some types of shiny rock in the fire, the shiny stuff melts and then sets hard again when it cools. And then some bright spark realised that with a bit of ingenuity, you could set the material in particular shapes. Like ploughs or swords or spearheads. Welcome to the age of metal.

# And the bronze goes to . . .

We used to think that metal first came to Britain through invasion. The British are so used to the idea of waves of invaders, that it seemed only natural to assume that the first bronze age people came leaping out of landing craft, kicking neolithic ass. Well no, no evidence supports that theory, and anyway, why should anyone want to go to all that trouble? Much better to do what probably happened: Take this new technique to the big island over the sea and make your fortune – especially as Britain had some very useful deposits of copper and tin. And that process seems to be what happened. New people began to drift in from the continent bringing this interesting technique with them, starting in Cornwall, where the metals were, and spreading out from there.

What should we call these newcomers? You may think they'd be called the Metalworkers or something suitable like that, but no. You see, when they weren't busy making metal they enjoyed a drink, and we know this was pretty important for them because they put their very distinctive beaker-like beer cups in their graves. So archaeologists called them the *Beaker people*. A bit like classifying us as the Tupperware folk.

# Beakermania

The Neolithic people may have started making things in metal even before the Beaker People began to arrive – we're pretty sure they had in Ireland – but the Beakers were able to take the process an important step further. At this stage, everyone who worked with metal was using copper, which looks nice but isn't very strong. But the Beakers knew how to mix copper with tin – Britain had lots of both – to make bronze. Now, okay, Britain and the Beaker people were not at the, er, cutting edge of metal technology. That was the Minoan civilization, which was under way in Greece (for more about the Minoans, see *European History For Dummies* (Wiley)). But it was the Beakers who brought Neolithic Britain gently into the early Bronze Age and Britain never looked back.

We're pretty sure that the Beakers and the Neolithic people got on. All the signs are that the Beakers shared their technology and even helped to do up Stonehenge in the latest fashion. Like the Neolithics, the Beakers were hunters to start with, but settled down to farming in time. Archaeologists have found what look like the foundations of cattle enclosures, though they might have been the Beakers' huts. Caves were, like, so last era. Now they were building proper round huts, with wooden fences around them for protection, sometimes grouped together in little hill-top forts.

## Wheels and barrows

We don't know who exactly invented the wheel, but it was someone in Ancient Sumer (modern-day Iraq). The wheel was without question the greatest invention in the history of the world. (Heaven help us if it ever turns out the Sumerians took out a patent.) We're pretty certain the Neolithics didn't have wheels, but they certainly came in during the Bronze Age. Wheels made all the difference. They made travel easier, they made transporting heavy goods easier, and they even made ploughing easier.

The Beakers seem to have had a thing about circles. The circle is a mystical shape, of course: No corners, just a line forming a perfect O. The Neolithics had buried their chiefs under great long mounds known as barrows. The Beakers went for round barrows. Different types existed. You could have a simple bowl barrow, very popular and seen everywhere, or else a bell barrow, which had an extra mound for protection. Also available were the flatter, more complex disc barrow, the low-lying saucer barrow, and the communal chuck-in-your-dead pond barrow, which was just a large dip where you could dump your aunt.

With bronze pins and needles you could make finer clothes, and with bronze shears you could cut them to a better fit. A bronze plough cuts better and straighter than a bone one, and a bronze sickle harvests more easily. You could have really fancy brooches and highly decorated daggers and belt buckles. We know they did, because these artefacts have been found in burial sites in the West Country. And then consider the famous beakers themselves: Ornate drinking cups made on a potter's wheel.

You did get that, didn't you? A potter's wheel. Because at some point in the Bronze Age, someone invented the wheel. It was a revolution.

# Chapter 3

# Woad Rage and Chariots: The Iron Age in Britain

. . . . . . . . . . . . . . . . . . . . . . . . . . . . . . . . . . . . . . . . . . . . . . . . . . . . . . . .

### In This Chapter

▶ Finding out when the Iron Age began and how it differed from earlier ages

▶ Debating whether the early Britons were actually Celts

▶ Glimpsing life in the Iron Age

▶ Seeing is believing: The Belgians invade Britain

▶ Finding out about the Druids and the religion of the period

. . . . . . . . . . . . . . . . . . . . . . . . . . . . . . . . . . . . . . . . . . . . . . . . . . . . . . . .

*T*owards the end of the Bronze Age a new technology began to make its way into Britain from the continent – iron. And a new people – the Ancient Britons. We have tended to get our picture of the Britons from Roman accounts, and the Romans didn't like them. But now we have a much better idea of what the Britons were really like. They mastered iron, that most powerful but difficult of metals, and changed Britain into a land of tribes and nations, of traders, and of huge hill-top cities. The Ancient Britons had craftsmen who created artifacts of stunning beauty, which still take your breath away, and Druids who took more away than just your breath.

## The Iron Age: What It Was and How We Know What We Know

The Iron Age in Britain goes from about 750 BC up to the Roman invasion in AD 43 (though obviously the Iron Age people were still around after that). Iron smelting originally came from the Middle East, and it came into Britain through contacts with continental Europe.

## Any old iron?

Making bronze is easy. You dig up some copper ore, heat it, and then pour out the copper. While you're doing that, put some tin on a low heat and pour when molten. Mix together and leave to simmer. Heat up some zinc and add into the mixture. Stir well, and when brought to the boil, pour into moulds. The liquid hardens as it cools and produces a shiny, dark reddish-gold colour. That's bronze.

Iron is different. You don't have to mix it with anything, but iron is very difficult to extract from its ore. Doing so requires really high temperatures, and when you do get the iron out, you have to go at it like fury with a hammer while it's still red hot. It comes in such small quantities that initially the early iron workers could only make little things like brooches and buckles. Smelting iron ore took so much wood that, when these folk started making iron on the island of Elba, they used up all the trees and had to move to the mainland. (And you thought deforestation was a modern problem.)

We've got a lot more evidence about the Iron Age in Britain than we have about the Bronze Age. The usual sites and artefacts exist: Burial chambers, traces of buildings, and bits and pieces of cooking pots or farming tools. The Druids, discussed in the section 'More Blood, Vicar?' later in this chapter, had a thing about water and were always throwing things into rivers as a sacrifice to the gods, which is good news for us because that way a lot of objects got preserved in the mud.

The first people to work out how to equip an army with proper iron weapons were the Assyrians, but the Greeks weren't far behind, and thanks to them it spread. Those early ironmasters really knew what they were doing: Some of their swords are still springy when you bend them back today.

## Written accounts from others

During this period, people started visiting Britain and Ireland to see what they looked like. Britain had been cut off from the continent since the ice melted at the start of the Bronze Age (Ireland got cut off even earlier) and ever since an air of mystery had surrounded the islands. How big were they? What sort of people lived there? Were they of any use to anyone? These travellers and others wrote of their impressions of the people and things on the British Isles.

### Greek accounts

The Greek historian Herodotus mentioned that British tin was worth having; Strabo (another Greek) wrote a geography book that included Britain and Ireland, or Albion and Ierne as the people who lived there were beginning to call them; and Pytheas of Massilia (yet another Greek) actually sailed all round Britain and showed that it definitely was an island. But the most detailed accounts we have of Iron Age Britain come from a rather more suspect source: The Romans.

## What the Romans wrote

Although Chapter 4 is devoted to the Romans we can't entirely ignore them in this chapter because so much of our evidence for the Iron Age comes from them. That wouldn't matter too much if they were detached and objective, but they weren't.

### From Julius Caesar

Caesar wrote about how he beat the Britons in battle. His account was designed to show how great he was and how brave he was to face up to the Big Bad British Barbarians. Take this excerpt from Book V of Caesar's *Gallic Wars*:

> *Most of the inland inhabitants do not sow corn, but live on milk and flesh, and are clad with skins. All the Britons, indeed, dye themselves with woad, which occasions a bluish colour, and thereby have a more terrible appearance in fight. They wear their hair long, and have every part of their body shaved except their head and upper lip.*

Biased? Just a tad. First, early Britons did sow corn. They had been farming since the Neolithic period. Second, they weren't clad in skins. The Bronze Age introduced sewing implements that made it possible to tailor clothing. Third, not every Briton was dripping with woad. Some people covered themselves in it; some didn't, but the use of woad was more complicated than Caesar's account makes it seem. (See the section 'Hit the woad, Jack', later in this chapter, for details.) And, okay, so early Britons went in for moustaches. But so did everyone else in Western Europe at the time – including the men.

### From Tacitus

Roman senator and historian Tacitus wrote a book all about his father-in-law Agricola, who served as Governor of Britain. Agricola got recalled in disgrace by the Emperor Domitian, so Tacitus sticks up for him by pointing out how Agricola rescued the Britons from savagery and made them into model Roman citizens.

### From Suetonius

Roman historian Suetonius wrote a strange book called *The Twelve Caesars*, which is half-serious, half scandal-sheet history about the first batch of emperors. The one who actually conquered Britain was Claudius, but Suetonius didn't think much of him, so he said 'Claudius's sole campaign [that's Britain, folks] was of no great importance.' Gee, thanks, Suetonius.

## Look what I found down the bog: Bodies

Believe it or not, the best evidence for Iron Age life didn't come from archae-ologists; it came from peat cutters, of all people. You get peat in marshes and bogs, and peat cutters keep finding dead bodies buried in it. These bodies started turning up in Denmark, one at Tollund and another at Grauballe. At first, people suspected foul play and called in the police. And very foul play it looked too, because these poor dead people hadn't fallen in; they'd been tied up, strangled, and pushed.

The amazing thing about the bodies was how well preserved they were: These bog bodies aren't skeletons, they are whole human beings, complete with faces, hands, and clothes – a bit distorted by two and a half thousand years of being stuck down a Danish peat bog, but then who wouldn't be?

Archaeologists had a look in the stomach of one bog body (Lindow Man's; head to the section 'Sacrificing humans' later in this chapter for info on him) and found that he had eaten toast and mistletoe. Mistletoe was sacred, so it really does look as if these bog bodies were human sacrifices. Creepy.

# Figuring Out Who These People Were

One thing we can be pretty sure of: No great 'wave' of Iron Age invaders occurred. The people living in Britain were still descended from the old Neolithics and Beaker folk, but new people were always coming and going, and some of them clearly knew how to smelt iron. Plenty of iron ore existed in Britain, so anyone who knew the secret could settle and make a fortune. But where did these newcomers come from?

## Looking for patterns

Since the early iron workers in Britain tended not to leave forwarding addresses archaeologists have had to trace where they came from by looking at the things they left behind. If you look carefully at the decoration on Iron Age shields and brooches and so on, two main styles can be discerned:

- **Hallstatt style:** Named after a village in Austria where a lot of it has been found, including very long and powerful swords. Some evidence of Hallstatt culture can be found in Britain, but not much.

- **La Tène style:** Named after a village in Switzerland where archaeologists have found pottery and ironwork decorated with circles and swirling patterns. Lots of La Tène culture has turned up in Britain.

## Celts

Poor old Celts. They've had a raw deal from history. Julius Caesar thought they were a bunch of savages and for a long time historians tended to follow his lead: They talked dismissively of the 'Celtic fringe'. Only recently have people learned to respect the Celts for their craftsmanship or for their technology. Apart from a few heroic figures like Boudica and Caratacus (and even they lost in the end), the Celts are everyone's favourite losers: Invaded by the Romans, overrun by the Angles and Saxons, conquered by the Normans and then hammered by Edward I and the English. They're on the losing side in every civil war and just about every football match. They can't even go out in the sun thanks to all that red hair.

Two main types of Celt exist: Q-Celts, who are the modern Irish, Scots, and Manx (people from the Isle of Man), and P-Celts, the modern Welsh, Cornish, and Bretons of northern France. Yes, folks, the Celts had to mind their Ps and Qs! However, what they certainly did was to develop bronze and then iron, and they could create some stunning craftsmanship. A big Celtic revival is happening nowadays thanks to the New Age movement, and you can relax to CDs such as *Celtic Sounds* or *Celtic Moods*, unless you're at a football match, in which case you're more likely to hear the sound of moody Celts.

Some historians say you can trace the movement of people by tracing patterns and styles, in which case, there seems to be a link between La Tène and Britain. But other historians say that people of different ethnic groups often adopt the same styles independently of each other. In which case, the link between Britain and the people at La Tène isn't proven.

You may think clarifying this point sounds a bit finicky, but it matters, because one thing we do know about the people of La Tène and others who used their patterns and designs is that they were Celts. If these folk really were the people who brought iron to Britain, then they also made Britain a Celtic land.

## Celts in Britain? Maybe, maybe not

The Celts first appear on the European scene in about 500 BC. We don't know exactly where they came from except that it was probably a long way to the east, possibly well into modern Russia, but they scared the life out of the Classical world. The Romans didn't know what had hit them when the Gauls – Celts who had settled (in so far as the Celts ever settled anywhere) in modern-day France – invaded Italy and sacked Rome in 390 BC, killing everyone they could find. The Romans treated them very warily after that.

### What we used to think: The Invasion Hypothesis

People used to assume that any new group of settlers must have attacked and forced the indigenous people out. This theory is known as the *Invasion*

*Hypothesis.* If this process is what happened when the Celts arrived in Britain, the west coast of Britain would've resembled a massive refugee camp.

According to this theory, two sorts of Celts possibly arrived in two different phases between 200 and 100 BC. One lot, called the Gaels, headed for Ireland and the northern parts of Scotland, where they are the ancestors of today's inhabitants, and their language survives as Scots and Irish Gaelic. The others, who settled in modern-day England, Wales, and the lowlands of Scotland, were known as Brythoni (Brythoni = Britons, geddit?), and their language survives in modern Welsh and Breton, though Cornish would have counted, too, if it had survived.

All these people had wild red hair and long moustaches, spent all their time fighting each other, and had to build massive great hill-top strongholds for protection. They were brave and very handy with a chariot, but they didn't have the discipline to stand up to the Romans when it came to the crunch. Head to Chapter 4 for details about the Romans in Britain.

### Now we don't know what to think

Other historians say the arrival of the Celts wasn't like that at all. France and Belgium – Gaul – were Celtic, and Celtic language and culture certainly crossed into Britain, but, they say, that doesn't mean the Britons (to use the term the Romans gave them) were Celtic. Think of the situation this way: You can find American culture all over the world, but that doesn't mean everyone who wears jeans and watches *The Simpsons* is American.

The Romans called these people Britons, not Celts; in fact, the Romans only grouped these folk together under one name at all because they all happened to inhabit the same island. No one called them Celts until the eighteenth century when people got very interested in the whole idea of building up a composite 'British' identity (to find out more about this, see Chapter 12).

Confused? No wonder. Some historians say pretending the Britons weren't Celts is silly; others say that calling them Celts is positively misleading. No one's ever going to prove the Britons–Celts connection one way or the other. What we do know is that, whoever they were and wherever they came from, the Iron Age tribes of Britain and Ireland kept up close links with the Iron Age tribes of the continent, which, in the end, was to bring down on them the full wrath of Rome. And for the Romans, invasion was never just a hypothesis.

# Life in Iron Age Britain

The Romans took a dim view of the Iron Age people of Britain. But what were the Britons really like?

# Warring tribes

In the Iron Age, the people of Britain seem to have developed a very strong tribal structure. Talking about 'tribes' in a loose way for the Beaker folk and the Neolithics before them is probably okay (see Chapter 2 for info on these people), but there was nothing loose about Iron Age tribes. In fact, 'tribe' is a bit misleading: Iron Age tribes were something closer to nations, rather like the Iroquois or the Sioux in North America. Following are some tribes of note (take a look at Figure 3-1 for a fuller picture of who lived where):

- ✔ **The Ulaid:** In Ulster, this tribe built an impressive fortified capital at Emain Macha, still one of the most important Iron Age sites in Ireland.

- ✔ **The Durotriges:** In Dorset, this tribe had the biggest capital in the isles, at *Mai Dun* (the 'Great Fort') now known as Maiden Castle. (The Durotriges managed this feat, and they weren't even in the premier league, with big nations like the Brigantes, the Catuvellauni, the Iceni, the Trinovantes, and others.)

- ✔ **The Brigantes:** Named from the Celtic *briga*, meaning a hill, these people dominated the North Country.

- ✔ **The Picti:** Living in what would later be Scotland were the mysterious Picti, also known as the Painted People, who could be very violent.

# Trading places

The people along the coast, like the Dumnonii or the Cantiaci, traded regularly with the continent, not just with the Gauls, but through them with the Romans and Greeks. Some trade was carried on directly: Phoenicians, for example, regularly stopped off in Cornwall to buy tin.

Archaeologists can trace this sort of contact by seeing what remains turn up. Hundreds of Roman wine jars, dating from before the Roman conquest, for example, have turned up in the land of the Trinovantes, in East Anglia. Interestingly, no such jars have been found in Iceni territory, which is just next door. Based on this evidence, it looks as if the Trinovantes were very open to a Roman tipple, but the Iceni – for whatever reason – didn't want anything to do with it. The Iceni may have been teetotalers, or they may have distrusted the Romans (maybe the Romans selling liquor was a bit like the Victorians plying the Chinese with opium or the Americans selling 'fire water' on the Frontier).

In addition, pottery and jewellery from all over the continent have been found at sites in Britain, and we know something about how the Britons paid for these items because we've found a lot of their coins. Sometimes coins turn up with lots of other artefacts; other times, a lucky archaeologist digs up a real treasure trove: A hoard of coins buried for safe-keeping. Either the original owner got killed, or the skies of Iron Age Britain were filled with angry wives shouting 'What do you mean you can't remember where you hid it? Think!'

**Figure 3-1:**
The Iron
Age tribes
of Britain.

All these bits of pottery and jewellery show that the tribes in the South East kept in close touch with their cross-Channel neighbours, especially after those neighbours fell to the Romans. In fact, the Romans seem to have regarded some of the Britons, like the Cantiaci of Kent, as virtually Romanised even before they landed. Which isn't surprising, because, although the Britons couldn't match the Romans for buildings or roads, their social structure wasn't all that different.

# A touch of class

An Iron Age tribe wasn't just a bunch of people in a village with a chief, oh no. These people had class – four classes, to be precise:

- ✔ **The nobles:** This group included the King (or Queen – a number of British tribes were led by women) and other highly respected people like warriors, Druids, poets, and historians, and quite right too.

    Among the Gaels of Ireland a tribal chief was called a *toisech*, which is where we get the word *taoiseach* for the Irish prime minister.

- ✔ **The middle class:** This group was made up of farmers, craftsmen, and merchants. These people paid rent to the nobles.

- ✔ **The working class:** These people did all the chores. Iron Age tribes may not have had a permanent working class: They may have used children for things like shepherding or washing up and older people for heavier jobs like harvesting or mining (though it sounds a bit dicey to rely for your supply of iron on the most clapped-out people of the tribe).

- ✔ **The slave class:** Slaves, who were usually criminals or prisoners of war, were known as *mug*, which sounds about right.

# Bring me my chariot, and fire!

The Britons knew how to fight. Even Julius Caesar allowed them that. He also said they spent a lot of time fighting each other, which is why the Romans were able to defeat them. With all those hill forts and weapons around, this probably looks about right, though archaeologists now think a lot of those weapons were more for show and not all of the hill forts were built for fighting. (Just when you thought everything looked clear, trust an archaeologist to come along and spoil it!)

The Celts had a special group of elite fighters who guarded the tribal king. In Ireland they were called the *Fianna* or *Fenians* – much later on the Irish would use the name again when they were fighting against the British. The most famous of the Fenians was the legendary Finn MacCool, who stars in all the Celtic literature that got handed down in the oral tradition from generation to generation. Much later, someone started writing these stories down, and they may be the basis for the stories of King Arthur and the Knights of the Round Table.

## Hill-top des res

You have to visit these Iron Age hill forts to get a real idea of just how vast they were. You can read about the early Britons building ramparts, but until you stand at the bottom of, say, Maiden Castle and look up at the sheer slope that towers above you, you can't truly understand just what these people achieved. And that description's just the view from the bottom level: Two more levels are above that.

Knowing exactly how many of these hill forts were in Britain is difficult, because some of them almost certainly had Norman castles built on top of them later, but if Ireland is any guide, there must have been a lot. Over 30,000 Celtic ring forts and sites exist in Ireland: That's a lot of ramparts.

Archaeologists say that, because some of these forts were so vast, they'd have been difficult to defend, so they must have been built for something else; but no one knows what alternative purpose these huge ramparts could have served.

But it is true that these hill forts weren't really forts any more than a walled town in the Middle Ages was a castle. Hill forts were towns, cities even, with hundreds of families living inside them and large warehouses for trade. But the archaeologists do have a point: When it came to the crunch, these mighty hill forts fell to the Romans fairly easily.

But the Britons' real secret weapon – and it seems to have been something peculiar to Britain – was the swift, light chariot, pulled by a couple of sturdy British ponies. Each chariot carried two men, one to drive, and the other to throw spears. The spear thrower could either throw the spear from the chariot or he could leap down and fight on foot, and then call up a chariot when he needed to get out in a hurry. Caesar was impressed. He wrote this in Book IV of *Gallic Wars*:

> *By daily practice and exercise they reach such expertness that, even on a steep slope, they can check their horses at full speed, rein them in and turn them in an instant, and run along the pole and stand on the yoke, and then with the utmost speed get back in the chariot again.*

## Hit the woad, Jack

Everyone knows about woad, the blue dye made from the woad plant. Julius Caesar says the Britons were covered in great buckets of the stuff when he landed with his men, and the sight of these woad-covered men quite unnerved them. A bit later, Roman historian Pliny says that British women wore woad and nothing else when they went to be sacrificed – which, had the women been on the beach, would have unnerved Caesar's men even more. This business about did they or didn't they wear woad and, if they did, how much, is the sort of thing that we just have to rely on Roman eye-witnesses for. Unless, of course, an archaeologist unearths an ancient British woad-compact.

Finding tribes using war paint isn't unusual, but the use of woad may not just have been for ritual purposes. Woad is a type of mustard plant that is supposed to help stop bleeding and heal wounds: Very useful in battle. Also, if the Britons did wear woad, they probably didn't just splash it all over like blue emulsion: Much more likely is that they put it on in those rather nice swirling patterns they may or may not have got from La Tène (see the section 'Looking for patterns' earlier for info on the Le Tène connection).

# This Is NOT a Hoax: The Belgians Are Coming!

Some time between 200 and 100 BC Britain really did get some invaders: But they weren't Romans, they were Gauls. Some of the Parisi tribe had already left the banks of the Seine to settle in Humberside (not a very common exchange nowadays!) but these latest Gauls who started landing along the south coast were from the Belgae and the Atrebates, two of the most powerful nations of northern Gaul. Yes, folks, these were Belgians – and they weren't sightseeing. They were after slaves, which they used to buy wine from the Romans (maybe the Iceni were right to steer clear of it; see the section 'Trading places' earlier in this chapter for details).

After a few pillaging raids both invading tribes set up in the south, more or less in modern Hampshire. They stayed in close touch with their 'parent' tribes back in Gaul, so they knew all about Caesar launching his invasion of Gaul, and they seem to have sent some of their men over to help in the fight against him. That the Belgae and the Atrebates in Britain were sending reinforcements back home was one of the main reasons Caesar thought about crossing over to Britain and teaching the inhabitants a lesson. But after Caesar had conquered Gaul, these British Belgae and Atrebates became a sort of Roman fifth column within Britain. Caesar even put his own man, Commius, in charge of the Atrebates before he crossed over himself, and very useful to the Romans Commius proved to be. Head to Chapter 4 to see how this alliance turned out.

# More Blood, Vicar? Religion in the Iron Age

Welcome to the weird and wonderful world of the Druids. Real Druids, not those characters who dress in sheets and blow rams' horns at Stonehenge every summer solstice. The religion of the Britons was based on reverence for nature and their surroundings, and the Druids were its priesthood. These Druids were surprisingly learned: They probably knew how to read and write, and they certainly had a good grasp of mathematics. They knew something of medicine and law, and could trace the stars and the planets. Druids even had a sort of holy headquarters on the Isle of Anglesey.

Druids also had immense power. They could tell everyone what to do, even kings and chiefs. They shut themselves away in sacred groves, offered up sacred mistletoe, and led all the sacred rituals the tribe needed to get through another year. They could read the future in the flight of birds, and could weave dark and terrible magic. Above all, they knew when to offer the gods blood and (Druid opens envelope, whole tribe holds its breath) whose blood it should be.

## *Ye gods!*

Rather a lot of gods existed in Iron Age Britain: Over 400 in fact. Most of them were local, and historians still dispute over which ones are genuine and which ones were made up later. Some of these gods went on to become Christian figures – the Irish goddess Birgit, for example, may have become St Brigid, one of the patron saints of Ireland.

As if all those gods (and many others) weren't enough, the Britons also treated various animals as gods, including horses, bulls, deer, wild boar, and bears. Rivers and lakes were sacred, too, which is why the Druids kept making sacrifices to them.

Little echoes of that belief in the sacredness of rivers and lakes are evidenced later on: All those statues of Father Thames, for example, and the legend of King Arthur getting Excalibur from the Lady of the Lake.

---

## Trust me, I'm a bishop

Geoffrey of Monmouth was a Welsh writer and chronicler who lived in the twelfth century and ended his days as Bishop of St Asaph in Wales (though by then he was living a very comfortable existence in Oxford and had no intention of leaving it to go and see St Asaph just because he'd been made bishop of it). Geoffrey decided the English and Welsh needed an epic history of their origins, like the Greeks and Romans with the story of Troy. Hardly anything was known about the history of the Celtic kings, but Geoff didn't let that stop him. He wrote a *History of the Kings of Britain*, borrowing a bit from Bede, a bit from Gildas, and a smattering from other writers; the rest he just made up. He invented an entirely fictional Trojan called Brute who sailed north and became the father of the Britons. He included a King Lud, which rather confuses matters because some historians claim Lud was a genuine British god, who may have given his name to Ludgate in London and even to London itself. Read Geoffrey's account and you'll meet Shakespeare's British kings, Cymbeline and Lear, as well as – inevitably – King Arthur.

Yes, all in all, Iron Age religion was enough to make anyone's head swim, but if you have a headache, don't, whatever you do, go and tell your local Druid. Druids are very, *very* interested in heads.

# Head cases

The Druids believed in an afterlife and that, when a person died, the soul went from one world to another. They also believed that capturing someone's soul gave you really powerful magic and that the soul was stored in the head. So Druids collected people's heads, some of which they kept to use in rituals, and others that they offered up to the gods.

The prize head in any collection was an enemy's and horrified Romans came across Druid caves with heads strung up like French onions. They found huge collections of heads at Bredon in Shropshire and in Wookey Hole in Somerset. British warriors even rode around with severed heads tied to their saddles, hoping to get the benefit of the victim's spirit: I suppose they thought it would give them a head start.

# Sacrificing humans

One thing about the Britons that the Romans found really revolting was all that human sacrifice. The Druids triple-killed their human sacrifices, not just to make sure the sacrifice was dead but as three different ways into the afterlife. Archaeologists know this because of the bog bodies, all of which had been thrice killed (head to the section 'Look what I found down the bog: Bodies', earlier in this chapter, for more information). If you had any sense, you chose someone you could make do without: A lot of those bog bodies had little distortions of one sort or another. (Woad-covered virgins were very acceptable, too, if you could find one.)

Take Lindow Man, for example, who turned up in 1984 in a peat marsh at Lindow in Cheshire. The archaeologists worked out how he died – head smashed in, strangled (he still had the leather garrotte tied tightly round his neck), and finally drowned. This description tallies with what Caesar says happened at ritual killings.

The notion of sacrifice was done on the basis of exchange. If you wanted something from the gods, you offered them a sacrifice to appease and please them and maybe they would give you what you wanted. Then again, maybe they wouldn't. Neither Lud nor Lug nor Teutatis nor St Brigid herself was able to predict, let alone prevent, the storm that was fast heading Britain's way from Roman Gaul.

.

# Part II
# Everyone Else Is Coming! The Invaders

The 5th Wave                    By Rich Tennant

'Who knows what day it is?'

## In this part . . .

When the Romans arrived, they changed the course of British history. The Romans brought order and law and the Britons learned to live peacefully in the Roman world. But Roman rule stopped at Hadrian's Wall, and the Roman legions never crossed the sea to Ireland. While the people of southern Britain lived the Roman way, with roads and cities, the people of the north rejected Rome and all she stood for.

The Romans left and the people of Britain and Ireland had to face the Angles and the Saxons who came over the sea, first to raid and then to settle. These people were followed by the Vikings, who also raided and settled. Britain became a land of many kingdoms, but William of Normandy had his heart set on the English crown. In 1066 William arrived off the south coast with an army and brought the Anglo-Saxon world to a bloody end.

# Chapter 4

# Ruled Britannia

*In This Chapter*

▶ Figuring out what led to the Roman invasion of Britain

▶ Fighting the good fight: Britons who resisted

▶ Understanding what the Romans did, and didn't do, for us

▶ Heading back home: Why the Romans eventually left Britain

For a nation that prides itself on having resisted invasion attempts so successfully, the British are surprisingly warm towards the Romans who conquered them two thousand years ago. The Romans were the first to call the main island Britain, or *Britannia*, and the British never forgot it: They dug the term out again when they were feeling pretty strong themselves and ready to take on the world eighteen centuries later (see Chapter 15 for details on that).

The Romans hadn't been intending to conquer Britain at all, and it was by no means all plain sailing when they did, but once they got settled, things went very well. Britain became totally integrated into the Roman world; it even produced some emperors. But a Roman Britain couldn't last. Soon Saxon raiding ships appeared off the east coast, and the Romans pulled out and left the Britons to cope as best they could. Which wasn't very well.

# A Far-Away Land of Which We Know Virtually Nothing

Before Julius Caesar appeared on the scene, most Romans knew only two things about Britain: One was metals, especially Cornish tin, which sold very well all over the Roman world and even beyond; the other was Druids. Britain was the centre of the strange religion of the Celts, just as Rome herself would one day be the centre of the Catholic Church. Basically, most Romans thought, Britain was a long way away and not doing Rome any harm. The best thing to do was to leave it alone? Right? Wrong.

Julius Caesar landed in Britain in 55 BC, but he left the job unfinished, and it was left to the Emperor Claudius, who conquered most of Britain in AD 43. So what made the Romans change their minds?

# The Gallic Wars

Ancient Rome was meant to be a republic: The Romans got rid of their kings years before, and they didn't want them back. But an ambitious and ruthless general called Gaius Julius Caesar had other ideas (for more on the Roman republic and empire, check out *The Romans For Dummies*, by Guy de la Bedoyere). To seize the power he wanted, he needed political support, and the best way to get that was to win a nice little military victory followed by a great triumphal procession. All he needed was a war.

### Taking on one Gallic tribe at a time

Caesar got a really plum posting in charge of the Roman army on the French Riviera, and right on cue, an entire tribe called the Helvetii, who lived up in the Alps, decided to go on a massive migration through Roman territory to find somewhere else in Gaul to live. Caesar seized his chance. 'Migration my foot!' he said (or, more likely, *migratio meus pedus!*); 'This is an invasion. Sound the trumpets!' And so began Caesar's famous Gallic Wars.

Caesar got his men together, took on the Helvetii, and beat them. Along the way, however, he alarmed some of the other Gallic tribes and before he knew it, Caesar found himself fighting just about every tribe in Gaul. Luckily for him, they didn't all band together at once, or that would have been the end of Caesar and his grand ambition. Instead they came at him tribe by tribe. First he beat one tribe, then another, and another, until, almost without realising it, he was conquering Gaul. Very handy.

### Gallant little Belgae

But not all of Caesar's campaigns went smoothly. He ran into stiff resistance when he turned north and took on the Belgae. In those days, the Belgae were tough customers: They hadn't yet descended to putting mayonnaise on chips.

Gradually, Caesar figured out that the Belgae resistance was so successful because the Belgae had been getting help. Some of the prisoners Caesar's army captured spoke in strange accents and, when interrogated, finished each sentence with 'Don't you know?' They wore socks with sandals and apologised when people trod on their feet – leaving no doubt that they were British.

British warriors were bad enough, but British Druids seemed to be coming over as well, and that meant bad trouble (for information on the Druids, refer to Chapter 3). The Gauls would fight a lot harder with Druids egging them on. Caesar decided the time had come to teach the Britons a lesson they wouldn't forget.

## Gallic Wars

Like all media-savvy, power-hungry generals, Julius Caesar didn't just conquer Gaul, he also churned out a best-seller of his exploits (telling his version of events, of course), *The Gallic Wars*. Later on, when everyone learned Latin at school, *The Gallic Wars* got into British classrooms, and generations of weary schoolchildren learned to hate its famous opening line 'All Gaul can be divided into three parts'. (Which is a bit unfair on Caesar, because he wasn't writing for British schoolchildren having to translate Latin into English.) To the Romans of Caesar's day, however, his book was a rattling good story with plenty of good battle scenes, especially as the Romans kept winning them. And, there was the added benefit of making him seem a very dangerous man, and it gave him the confidence he needed to cross the River Rubicon into Italy and seize power in Rome. *Alea iacta est*, as he put it: The die is cast.

# *Welcome to Britain!*

When Caesar turned up off the south coast of Britain in 55 BC, the shore was full of Britons, armed to the teeth and painted with woad, shouting and screaming at the Romans to come and fight if they thought they were hard enough.

According to Caesar, quite a sharp battle followed on the beach, but once enough Romans were able to get ashore and into formation, they forced the Britons back and got a foothold. They then moved inland, had a look round, crushed a few tribes, and went back home to Gaul.

The next year (54 BC), Caesar came back with a much bigger force. Was he intending to stay? Probably not, but the Britons couldn't be certain. The British tribes did manage to get together under one high king, Cassivelaunus (well, that's what the Romans called him), but Cassivelaunus couldn't beat Caesar's men, and in any case, not all the Britons were on his side: Some signed alliances with the Romans.

### *I came, I saw, I decided it wasn't worth conquering*

People often think Julius Caesar conquered Britain. He didn't. He invaded Britain twice, in 55 BC and then again, in greater strength, in 54 BC, but he returned home to Gaul each time. Of course, he did more than enough to show that he could have conquered Britain if he'd wanted to, but really there was no need – the British kings agreed to pay tribute to Rome (*tribute* is a posh word for protection money) and to leave pro-Roman tribes, like the Trinovantes in East Anglia, alone (to find out about the Trinovantes, refer to Chapter 3). Then Caesar sailed away, back to Gaul and to Rome, where in the end they knifed him before he could make himself emperor. 'Infamy! Infamy!' as he says in *Carry on Cleo*, 'They've all got it in for me!'

### We'll invade them, we'll invade them not: Roman dithering

But what about Britain? The Romans dithered between a 'who's going to be the one to finish off what Julius started?' attitude and one of 'Caesar went there and didn't think it was worth bothering about, so why should we?'

In any case, Britain was no threat: Quite the reverse. Most of the southern part, which was the bit that mattered to the Romans, was ruled by a king called Cunobelinus (Shakespeare's 'Cymbeline'). Cunobelinus got control of the Trinovantes tribe, who were Roman allies, and he made southern Britain a Roman-friendly zone. So no need for a full-blown Roman invasion of Britain existed. Yet.

# They're Back – with Elephants!

Claudius is the Roman emperor who stammered and limped and who everyone thought was a fool. Ah, but we know better, don't we? Because we've seen Derek Jacobi in *I, Claudius*. Great TV series, rotten history. Claudius wasn't the wise old sage *I, Claudius* makes him out to be; Roman historians like Tacitus and Suetonius reckoned he was just as bloodthirsty as any of the Julio-Claudian emperors. But one thing Claudius didn't have was any military street cred, and that bothered him. So when a British chieftain turned up in Rome complaining that he'd lost his kingdom, Claudius was very interested. Very interested indeed.

In Britain, Rome-friendly King Cunobelinus had died, and his two sons, Caratacus and Togodumnus, began taking over neighbouring tribes. One of these neighbouring tribes was the Atrebates, and it was their king (or rather, ex-king), Verica, who was now in Rome bending Claudius's ear. The Atrebates were also Roman allies: Did this mean that Caratacus and Togodumnus weren't going to continue their dad's pro-Roman policy? Claudius decided that it was time to remind the Britons of what happened to people who got on the wrong side of the Romans.

## Caratacus fights the Romans

Claudius had learnt a few lessons from Julius Caesar's time in Britain. He made sure he had enough men to conquer the place and to stay. On this excursion, the Romans didn't hang around at the beach: They swept ashore and moved inland. Togodumnus, Caratacus's brother, was killed early on, so it was down to Caratacus to try to put up some resistance. He did, but the Romans were just too strong for him.

When the Romans moved in on Caratacus's capital, Camulodunum (Colchester), Claudius decided to come and see Caratacus's defeat for himself, and he brought some elephants with him, which scared the life out of the Britons. Camulodunum fell, but Caratacus escaped and led the Romans a merry dance, hiding out in the Welsh hills and up in the north, launching guerrilla attacks just when the Romans were least expecting it. The Romans took ages to catch Caratacus, and even then, they only managed it by treachery.

The Romans finally defeated Caratacus's men in open battle, but Caratacus and his family got away and took shelter with the Brigantes of Yorkshire. But Queen Cartimandua of the Brigantes, a Roman stooge if ever there was one, had him put in chains and handed him over to the Romans, who led him through the streets of Rome. But everyone was so impressed by how dignified Caratacus was and how he hurled defiance at the emperor and the crowds, that Claudius let him go on the condition that he stay in Rome. As for Cartimandua, she got lots of money and favours from the Romans, as you would expect. But if the Romans thought that with Caratacus safely out of the way everything was safe in Britain, they were in for a very nasty shock.

## One angry lady – Boudica

In AD 58, the Emperor Nero appointed a new governor in Britain, Suetonius Paulinus. Suetonius decided to head west and deal with the Druids once and for all, so he led a big army into Wales and on to the Isle of Anglesey. The Druids gathered on the hills, screaming curses down on Suetonius and his men. The curses didn't save the Druids, but one of them may have hit home, because while Suetonius Paulinus was away in Wales disaster struck back.

### That ain't no way to treat a lady

The trouble began with the Iceni, who lived in modern-day Norfolk. Although the Iceni had fought against the Romans during the invasion, they seemed to have settled down since then. The Romans didn't actually control them directly: The Iceni king, Prasutagus, was what the Romans called a *client-king* (if you were going to be unkind you could call him a puppet-king). But when Prasutagus died in AD 60, everything suddenly began to go wrong.

As a good Roman client-king, Prasutagus left half of his estate to his wife, Queen Boudica, and half to the Roman emperor. An incredibly stupid Roman tax-collector called Catus Decianus then made his way to the Iceni capital at Norwich to claim Rome's share and to tell the Iceni that all the money the late Emperor Claudius had given them was not a gift but a loan and was to be paid back now. With interest.

Demanding money was never going to make for an easy meeting, but something obviously went horribly wrong when Catus Decianus and his men got to Norwich. According to Roman accounts (yes, *Roman* accounts), Roman soldiers flogged Boudica, and then raped her two daughters. How on earth a tax-collecting expedition ended up like that – and whether these actions were done on Catus Decianus's orders – no one really knows. Catus Decianus and his men were lucky to get out alive. A lot of other Romans weren't going to be so lucky.

### Hell hath no fury . . .

All hell broke loose after the attack on Boudica. The Iceni went on the rampage, attacking anything Roman they could find. Even more worrying for the Romans, their old allies the Trinovantes joined the Iceni. The Roman legions went to pieces. The Ninth Legion got pushed back, the commander of the Second Legion refused to move. Everyone else was with Suetonius Paulinus in Wales killing Druids. Boudica led her tribe to Camulodunum (modern-day Colchester), the great town the Romans had built up as their capital with an enormous temple dedicated to the Emperor Claudius (they'd made him a god for conquering Britain). All the Romans fled to the temple because it had a big walled compound, but it wasn't enough to keep Boudica's people out. They broke in, burned the temple to the ground, and killed everyone they could find. Then they headed for London.

London wasn't the capital, but it was an up-and-coming port, and a lot of Romans and Romanised Britons lived there. Suetonius Paulinus couldn't get troops to London in time, so he gave the order for everyone to get out. Boudica burned London to the ground. Then she headed to Verulamium, modern St Albans, and destroyed that.

In a matter of months Boudica had run rings round the Roman army and totally destroyed all three of the major Roman towns in Britain. The destruction was so devastating that you can still see the blackened layer of burnt and charred remains in the ground today.

No Roman emperor could allow a whole province to fall out of control like that. Suetonius Paulinus raced back from Wales and lured Boudica into open battle near Mancetter, in the West Midlands. The Romans won – well, they were bound to – but they didn't catch Boudica. According to legend, which may well be true, she and her daughters poisoned themselves. And according to the popular version, Boudica is buried underneath one of the platforms at King's Cross Station.

# *Roman in the Gloamin' – Agricola*

The Romans in Scotland? You're probably thinking the Romans didn't conquer Scotland. Think again. The Roman governor Agricola led an army through the Lowlands and on into the Highlands. Agricola conquered the Lowlands without too much trouble. Some tribes made peace quickly, and he soon dealt with the ones that didn't. The whole area became a Roman province, with a big Roman camp called Trimontium at modern-day Newstead. Agricola carried on building forts as he moved north to take on the Caledonians of the Highlands. An almighty battle occurred between the Romans and the Caledonians at Mons Graupius in AD 84, and the Caledonians lost. Heavily. But to Agricola's surprise, the Caledonians didn't come and surrender. They burned everything and took to the hills. Agricola knew he couldn't follow them, so he and his men turned back.

Still, most of Caledonia was in Roman hands, which meant the Romans had conquered modern-day England, Wales, and most of Scotland. A few years ago, archaeologists even found the remains of what looked at first like a Roman fort in Ireland, but we now think the spot's more likely to have been a trading post. At any rate, Agricola could feel pretty pleased with himself: Britannia was firmly in Roman hands. Then he got recalled to Rome.

Agricola's recall was politics, of course: The Emperor Domitian was intensely jealous of him. And thanks to Agricola, fewer troops seemed to be needed in Britain, so the legions began to be pulled out and sent elsewhere. With the departure of Agricola and many Roman legions, the Caledonians saw their chance. They began to attack the forts Agricola had built, and without enough men to defend them, the remaining Romans had to pull out of Scotland. Soon, not much was left of the Roman occupation of Scotland.

# 'And What Have the Romans Ever Given Us in Return?'

The Romans weren't great ones for original thinking: They built on other people's ideas and inventions, especially the Greeks'. In Britain, they even 'borrowed' the local gods: They built Roman temples to British gods, and named *Aquae Sulis* (Bath) after Sul, a local British river god.

Iron Age people were more sophisticated and advanced than we tend to give them credit for, but the Romans were in another class altogether. The Britons' first introduction to Roman technology was in battle, when they probably didn't have much time to admire the Romans' craftmanship or their grasp of mathematics and angles of projection. Roman siege artillery could hurl huge rocks through the air, smashing the Britons' wooden palisades into pieces, and a Roman *ballista* catapult could fire metal darts so rapidly, with such deadly accuracy, that it was almost like having a machine gun. The following sections, however, examine how Roman technology affected the Britons once the fighting was over.

## Sorry, no aqueducts

Despite Monty Python, apart from a bit of raised piping and a pump system in Lincoln, we haven't actually found any Roman aqueducts in Britain. Shame. We know that they set up a proper waterworks system: A beautifully preserved network of baths exists in Bath to prove it, not to mention smaller bath houses up and down the country. But instead of sending the water over long distances by aqueduct, the Romans seem to have made more use of local pipes and lead pipes underground.

The Latin for lead is *plumbum* – hence 'plumb line' and Pb, the chemical term for lead – which is why someone who deals with your water pipes is called a *plumber*. But if the Romans didn't actually bring the aqueduct to Britain, they brought plenty of other goodies.

## Another brick in the wall

Probably the most famous thing the Romans built in Britain was Hadrian's great wall, which extends from the River Tyne over to the Solway Firth (which is roughly Newcastle to Carlisle). The wall doesn't, and never did, mark the boundary between England and Scotland.

No one knows exactly why Hadrian built the wall. It may have been for defence, or to stop the troublesome Brigantes (from the North Country) from ganging up with the Caledonians (from Scotland), or the wall may just have been to get his name into the *Guinness Book of Records*. What we do know is that he took the project seriously, because he came over in person to help plan the thing. The job was massive: All along the wall's length were forts and milecastles, and a huge military ditch and rampart ran parallel to it. Hadrian's Wall still looks impressive today, as it snakes its way across countryside, but it was a lot higher in Roman times. Its construction was a tremendous feat of engineering.

A few years later, however, the Romans moved north again. This time, the emperor was Antoninus Pius, and he ordered a second wall to be built much further north. Called the Antonine Wall, after Antoninus Pius, this wall went across Scotland, more or less from Edinburgh to Glasgow. The Antonine wall made a lot more sense than Hadrian's Wall because it protected the peaceful tribes of the south from the wild Caledonians of the north. And the southern tribes needed protecting, too, because the Caledonian attacks were so fierce that the Romans had to abandon the Antonine Wall and head back to Hadrian's Wall. And after all that *work*!

## Urban sprawl

Look at a map of Roman Britain (shown in Figure 4-1), and the first thing that hits you is the sheer number of towns. The place was covered with them, all linked by those famous straight roads. Some of these towns started off as big tribal centres before the Romans arrived, like Camulodunum (Colchester), which had been Cunobelinus's capital, or Verulamium (later St Albans), which had been the capital of the Catuvellauni. When the Romans arrived, they took these large centres and built them up in the Roman style, which was sensible in two ways:

✔ **Taking advantage of a good thing:** Usually, if a town already exists somewhere it's there for a good reason – good water supply or easy access to the river, or whatever.

✔ **Romanising the population:** Making the Britons' towns Roman helped to give the Britons a sense that they were now part of the Roman Empire whether they liked it or not.

The Romans also set up *coloniae*: Settlements for soldiers who had left the army and were looking to settle down. The first big colonia was at Colchester, but others followed at places like Gloucester, Lincoln, Wroxeter, and York.

**Figure 4-1:**
Roman
Britain.

## Get your kicks on Route LXVI

What the Romans lacked in aqueducts they made up for in roads (take a look at Figure 4-1 to see where the main ones were built). At some point, two of the three big roads got rather homely English names: Watling Street (London to Wroxeter in Wales) and Ermine Street (London to Hadrian's Wall). Only the Fosse Way, which goes from Exeter in Devon across country to Lincoln, has a Roman ring to it. And yes, these roads are straight.

You can drive along stretches of Roman roads today because later road builders followed the same routes. You can virtually go onto autopilot, except that they're so straight that they're full of hidden dips.

You can see why they're so straight – consider that 'The shortest way between two points is a straight line' stuff you did at school – but the Romans might have been a bit more sensible. A straight line may be the shortest way up a hill, but it sure ain't the easiest. Still, you've got to hand it to the Romans: They knew their business. They used the old three-sticks-in-a-line technique to keep the roads straight: Simple, but very effective. They knew about drainage. They knew all about laying good foundations and having a layer of small stones to keep the big top stones in place. And they knew all about cutting the trees back so they couldn't be taken by surprise in an ambush.

## All that foreign food

The Romans probably started the international custom of moaning about British cuisine. Not that the British ate badly; just that their range was very limited: Lots of meat and bread, followed by bread with meat, with meat (or bread) as a bedtime snack. The Romans brought some better agricultural techniques over with them, along with the latest in ploughs (cutting edge technology!) and showed the Britons how to grow things like cabbages and carrots. A few copies of Roman recipes still exist and they're surprisingly good. Lots of fruit – the Romans introduced that as well – and things like fish paste and honey.

## The Roman way of life

How Roman were the Britons? We know that the leading Britons took to the Roman way of life. They stopped talking about 'chiefs' and called themselves 'kings' – much more posh. One king, Cogidubnus, who was a good friend of the Emperor Vespasian, probably had the big Roman-style villa at Fishbourne in West Sussex built for him. Anyone who lived in a town – and a lot of people did – was in effect living the Roman way. The Emperor Caracalla even made all Britons citizens of Rome, but he was doing the same throughout the Roman Empire, so perhaps we shouldn't read too much into that.

Nevertheless, most Britons still lived in their villages, doing things pretty much as they'd always done them. Despite some changes – new crops, new tools, new roads, no woad – if their Iron Age ancestors had been able to visit, they wouldn't have found things all that different.

## Saints alive! Christianity arrives!

We don't know exactly who first brought Christianity into Britain (except that we can be pretty sure it wasn't Joseph of Arimathea, which is what they liked to claim in the Middle Ages). But Christianity only became widespread when the Romans started to worship as Christians.

The town of Verulamium got called St Albans after Britain's first ever Christian martyr, a Roman soldier called Alban, who was put to death in Verulamium for sheltering a Christian priest. This event may have happened in AD 304 or AD 209 (no one said ancient history is an exact science), and it shows that Christianity did indeed reach Roman Britain.

Early British Christians had to keep their heads down, or they'd end up like poor old Alban. After the Emperor Constantine gave Christianity the thumbs up in AD 312 (and he became emperor at York – a local lad, by Jove!) and the Emperor Theodosius made it the official religion in AD 380, the Christians could come out of hiding and worship in the open.

To judge by the number of Roman churches and chapels that cropped up, that's just what they did. These early Christians must have started appointing bishops, too, because three of them set off from Britain for a big church conference at Arles in Gaul in AD 314.

### You mean you thought St Patrick was *Irish*?

Prepare yourself for a shock. St Patrick was British. He came from the west of Britain, and he wasn't christened Patrick but Succatus. Okay, Patrick sounds better. He probably wasn't even the first person to bring Christianity to Ireland: That was probably a monk called Caranoc who took over from St Ninian at Candida Casa.

In fact, St Patrick can't have liked his first taste of Ireland because, as a boy, a boatload of Irish raiders came and carried him off there as a slave. It would be nice to say that he instantly converted his captors then, but that's not quite how it happened. St Patrick managed to escape back to Britain, where he went into the Church. We know he spent many years studying and training as a monk in Gaul, until he eventually went, or more likely got sent, back to Ireland. His mission seems to have gone well, and he may well have used the shamrock to explain the idea of the Trinity. But he didn't drive the snakes out of Ireland: There weren't any there to begin with.

In addition, a monk called Ninian – later St Ninian – took the religion north of Hadrian's Wall to the warlike Picts (find out more about the Picts in Chapter 3). Quite a scary thing to do, but Ninian seems to have got away with it, and he founded a big monastery up there called *Candida Casa*, which means the White House. (No, archaeologists haven't uncovered anything the right shape to be the oval office, but they're looking.)

# Time to Decline and Fall . . . and Go

By the fourth century AD the Roman Empire was no longer the mighty edifice it had been in Caesar's day. It was divided into two halves, and continual power struggles occurred, which often ended up with Roman armies fighting each other, or commanders in one part of the Empire declaring war on other parts. As if that in-fighting wasn't enough, Rome's neighbours started moving in for the kill. The tribes of Germany and Hungary, as well as migrating tribes from Asia, started attacking the Empire, penetrating far beyond the frontier. Try as they might, the Romans couldn't recover the discipline and organisation that had once made them seem invincible. They were well into decline, and about to fall. Roman Britain was no exception. If you want to find out more about how the Romans declined and fell, and about the tribes that helped them do so, take a look at *European History For Dummies* (Wiley).

## Trouble up North

Cue the Brigantes: The northern tribe who handed Caratacus over to the Romans (explained in the section 'Caratacus fights the Romans'). Well, maybe they wanted to make up for their past treachery, because just when you thought Britain was nicely Romanised and everything was settled, the Brigantes started raising merry hell.

The Brigantes had caused Hadrian to come to Britain for a look – and he probably built his wall specifically to keep the Brigantes apart from the Caledonians, who were always causing trouble as well. But it took more than a wall to keep the Brigantes down, and they spent most of the second century (the 100s AD) in revolt against the Romans, until in the end the Romans divided Britain into two: *Britannia Prima*, which was the South, where it was peaceful and prosperous, and *Britannia Secunda*, which was the north, where all the trouble was. This ancient division was a bit like the north–south divide still evident in Britain today.

## Roman emperors, made in Britain

Britain was also caught up in an endless and deadly struggle for power between the Roman emperors and their military commanders. Here are a few British highlights in this long, drawn-out death march:

- ✔ **AD 186:** Huge mutiny in the Roman army in Britain, put down by Governor Pertinax. Pertinax then heads off to Rome and becomes emperor but only lasts a few months before being bumped off.

- ✔ **AD 208:** Emperor Septimius Severus (the only black African Roman emperor) arrives in Britain to sort out the Caledonians. He does, for a while, but then dies at York – the first Roman emperor to do so, but not the last.

- ✔ **AD 259:** Would-be Emperor Postumus declares a break-away Roman Empire of Gaul, Spain, and Britain. It gets put down in the end.

- ✔ **AD 286:** Carausius, Admiral of the Roman fleet in Britain, declares a Roman British Empire all on his own. His self-declared empire lasts about ten years until Caesar Constantius comes over and wins Britain back for the proper Roman Empire. Constantius goes on to become emperor and has another go at the Caledonians.

- ✔ **AD 306 and onwards:** In 306, Emperor Constantius dies. At York. After that, Roman emperors steer clear of York.

Constantius's death at York explains how his son Constantine came to be declared emperor (also at York). Constantine is the one who built the great city of Constantinople as a 'New Rome' in the east. While Constantine was busy building cities on the Bosphorus, things were going badly wrong back in Britain.

## Gothic revival

The Picts, now joined by their pals the Scots, were launching more and more raids over Hadrian's Wall. They ran rampage and stole anything they could carry or, in the case of cattle, drive. The problem just wouldn't go away: No matter how many times the Romans beat them, those Picts and Scots kept coming back. These troublesome events combined with an even more worrying development. Boatloads of raiders had started landing all along the east coast of Britain. These raiders weren't Picts or Scots: They were Saxons, and they came from Germany.

Germany was the big area along the frontier of the Roman Empire that the Romans were never able to conquer. Not only had the Romans not been able to conquer the Saxons, but the Saxons kept leading incursions into Roman territory. By the time of the Saxon landing parties in Britain, various German tribes – Vandals, Ostrogoths, Visigoths, all with black eye liner and white faces of course! – were attacking Rome, charging into the Roman Empire and heading down towards Italy. The Romans were in deep trouble, so when Saxons started landing in Britain, they took special precautions.

## Exit Romans, stage left

The Romans appointed a special officer to keep the Saxons at bay. The whole of the east coast of Britain became known as the Saxon Shore, so the officer was called the Count of the Saxon Shore. The Romans built a string of forts along the shore, with lookout posts and early warning signals. These forts worked well until AD 367 when everything went wrong.

The Picts, the Scots, and another lot called the Attacotti, got together and planned a simultaneous attack. Simultaneously, the Saxons stepped up their raids. The Romans were caught completely on the hop and the Count of the Saxon Shore was killed. It looked like the end for Roman Britain. But no! A new Count, Theodosius, zoomed in, beat the Picts, scotched the Scots, sent the Saxons packing, and rebuilt Hadrian's Wall. Then he stopped for lunch. He even found time to put the Roman governor to death for treason (well, the governor had tried to pull out of the Empire, and who can blame him?).

Frankly, Theodosius needn't have bothered with saving Roman Britain from the wild tribes and the Saxons. In AD 407, Emperor Constantine III started withdrawing troops from Britain to deal with a crisis along the Rhine. He may not have meant this action to be a permanent withdrawal, but it became one. By AD 409 the Romans had all gone.

# Chapter 5

# Saxon, Drugs, and Rock 'n' Roll

*In This Chapter*
▶ Finding out how the Angles and Saxons arrived in Britain
▶ Dividing Britain into Saxon and Celtic kingdoms
▶ Converting Celtic and British Christians to the Roman Church
▶ Developing political and religious centres of power and influence

*W*hen you start talking about the Anglo-Saxons, things get a bit tricky. Up until the middle of the fifth century the two groups who lived in Britain were Celtic Britons – different tribes, sure, but basically all the same type of people – and Romans (head to Chapters 3 and 4 for information about these groups). Once the Anglo-Saxons arrive, in about AD 450, however, things change. The English are descended (in theory) from the Anglo-Saxons; the word *England* comes from *Angle-land*, and some historians even talk about this period as 'The Coming of the English'. The Scots still call the English *Sassenachs*, which means 'Saxons', and the Welsh sing about 'Saxon hosts' invading their hills in 'Men of Harlech'. Clearly we're deep into National Identity territory (not to say National Identity Crisis territory). If you're a Celt, or like to pretend you are, then the story looks like a straightforward one of invasion and oppression with the Saxons as the Bad Guys. Some people even accuse the Saxons of trying to wipe the Celts out completely. But if you're of Saxon descent, then the story looks like a fairly standard one of conquest and settlement, the sort of thing people – including Celtic people – have done throughout history.

Not all the moving and settling was violent. This was also the time when Christian missionaries travelled through Britain and Ireland spreading a gospel of peace to some very war-like people. But here, too, an identity crisis was evident: Were the English going to keep to their Celtic heritage, or throw in their lot with Europe? This period may be a long time ago, but it was crucial in shaping the Britain we know today.

# They're Coming from All Angles!

When the Romans left Britain, you could hardly move in Europe without bumping into a wave of people who'd upped sticks and gone off to find somewhere nice and overrun it. Ostrogoths, Visigoths, Huns, Avars, Bulgars, Slavs, Franks, Lombards, and Burgundians were all running rampage and generally helping the Roman Empire to get a move on with its Decline and Fall (you can get all the gory details in *European History For Dummies* (Wiley)). Across the North Sea, the Angles and Saxons, who came from what is nowadays north Germany and Denmark, were on the move. They came to Britain for all sorts of reasons – a taste for adventure, overpopulation at home, even plague coming in from Asia.

## Welcome to our shores!

Although the Romans had built a string of forts along Britain's Saxon shore precisely to stop such invaders, the Romans had gone now. Protecting Britain was down to the two groups of people remaining:

- ✔ **Romano-Britons**, or *Cives* (that's *kee-ways*, which means 'Roman citizens'), who had been thoroughly Romanised for generations and probably spoke Latin rather than any British language.
- ✔ **Celts**, who spoke their own Celtic language and had lived alongside the Romans, usually fairly peacefully, for a long time, too.

You'd think that with boatloads of Angles and Saxons landing all along the east coast, pinching anything they could carry, and burning anything they couldn't, this would be the Time for All Good Men to Come to the Aid of the Party, but it wasn't. The Cives and the Celts just couldn't get on, and soon they were engaged in a full-scale civil war. Which was very good news for the Angles and Saxons: With the Cives and Celts fighting each other, the invaders could carry on with their raids and no one was likely to stop them.

## The Overlord of All Britain: Vitalinus the Vortigern

Ascertaining for certain exactly how and why the Angles and Saxons settled in Britain is difficult. Very few written sources exist and they're very patchy. What follows is the story that the British monk Gildas told in his history, but how much is truth and how much is legend (possibly all of it) we just cannot know for certain.

According to Gildas, the Celtic king, Vitalinus, managed to get the upper hand for a while in the war with the Cives and declared himself *Vortigern*, or Overlord of All Britain. However, what the Vortigern was now up against was a classic problem: how to fight a war on two – or rather, three – fronts. Firstly, he was still fighting the Cives. These guys were Roman citizens, and no way were they going to take orders from a mere Briton. Secondly, the Angles and Saxons were raiding the coast. And then a third problem landed in his lap: The Picts. The Picts, who lived up in the north, were so fierce that Hadrian had built his wall to keep them back (head to Chapter 4 to find out more about the Picts, Hadrian, and Hadrian's Wall). They had given up attacking the wall – it was too well defended, and were now raiding the coast instead.

Naturally, the people along the coast appealed to the Vortigern for help, but he didn't have any men to spare. So he decided to do exactly what the Romans had often done in the past: Buy in some help. The Vortigern wasn't to know that he was making one of the biggest mistakes in history.

## Shedding light on the Dark Ages

For many years historians talked about the period after the Romans left as the Dark Ages because we have so little evidence from it. Actually, plenty of archaeological evidence does exist, but it is true that only a handful of writers chronicled the events of these years. First up is a British monk called Gildas. Gildas wrote about a hundred years after the time that Hengist is supposed to have arrived, and he wasn't a happy bunny. He called his book Concerning the Ruin of Britain, and he doesn't have a good word to say about the Saxons or about the Vortigern who let them in. 'A race hateful to God and men,' he calls them: 'Nothing was ever so pernicious to our country, nothing was ever so unlucky.' Still, at least you know where he stands on the topic.

Next up is Bede, who was a Northumbrian monk living about a hundred years after Gildas. Bede's greatest work is his Ecclesiastical History of the English People, which is often called the first history of the English. This book is a great work,

no question, but in his way Bede is just as difficult a source as Gildas because Bede was a great Northumbrian patriot. All the heroes in his history tend to be Northumbrian kings or saints, and all the villains tend to be people who went to war with them, like the Welsh or the Mercians. In addition, Bede wrote a history of the English people; he had no time for the native British, who always come across in his history as hot-headed, insular, and, well, stupid.

Finally, comes the Anglo-Saxon Chronicle, which is essentially an enormous timeline, going right the way back to the Romans. The Chronicle has dates, a lot of which, unfortunately, we now reckon are wrong. But the real problem with the Chronicle is that it isn't quite what it seems. It looks like an impartial record of events; in fact, King Alfred the Great of Wessex commissioned the work specifically to make him and his kingdom look good. Which it does. In other words, the Chronicle is propaganda. Handle with care.

### My kingdom for a Hengist (and possibly a Horsa)

The man the Vortigern got in touch with was probably a Germanic chieftain called Hengist. According to Gildas, Hengist (and possibly his little bruv Horsa) arrived in three ships off the coast of Kent at Thanet. Don't read too much into those three ships: Writers at the time always described invaders as arriving in three ships. But Hengist must have had some ships, because apparently he sailed up north, sank the Picts, and then went and raided their homeland, giving the Picts a taste of their own medicine. Some of Hengist's men may even have settled in Pictland. As you can imagine, the Vortigern was very pleased and paid Hengist his fee. But then Hengist did something very odd. He sent home for reinforcements from the Angles. And when they came, they were in a lot more than three ships.

You can probably guess what followed. The more the Vortigern dropped hints about how it was time for Hengist and his pals to go home, the more shiploads of Angles and Saxons arrived. Eventually Hengist suggested a big meeting of all Vortigern's Council to discuss matters. And when the Council gathered for the meeting, Hengist's men sprang out from behind pillars and killed them all. All except the Vortigern, which was probably quite cruel. He had nothing left to be Vortigern of: Hengist was in charge now.

## But what about King Arthur?

A story exists that a British chief called Arthur led a sort of resistance movement against the Saxons. Arthur is supposed to have beaten the Saxons in a great battle at a place whose Latin name is Mons Badonicus, or Mount Badon, until eventually he was killed by treachery. If you really go for myths and legends, then he's still supposed to be sleeping somewhere with his men, ready to come charging out whenever England is in deadly danger (though if that's true he should have been playing in nearly every World Cup for the past forty years).

As with most myths, a smidgen of truth may be at the heart of this story. There was a Roman-Briton called Ambrosius Aurelianus (doesn't sound very like 'Arthur' does it?), and the battle of Mount Badon probably took place in AD 500.

The Celts took up the legends of Arthur, especially in Cornwall, where Arthur is supposed to have lived at Tintagel Castle. A round table hangs on the wall in Winchester, which is supposed to be the Round Table, though in fact it's medieval and the names of the knights painted on it date from the reign of Henry VIII.

Later, the story was adopted by the English – the very people Arthur is supposed to have been fighting in the first place! Since then, different people have used the Arthur story to put across their own messages. In the Middle Ages, the Arthur legends were all about chivalry, thanks to the stories of Thomas Malory, who wrote them down in prison. The Victorians were in love with the Middle Ages, because they reckoned it was a time of innocence and ideals, so they lapped up Tennyson's version of the legend. Over in Germany, Richard Wagner used the stories to give the Germans a sense of their national heritage (which is a cheek, considering that Arthur is supposed to have been fighting Germans). They even dug up the imagery of Camelot to describe the Kennedy White House, though I can't quite see Sir Galahad approving of Marilyn Monroe.

### Being a Briton in Saxon England

Some of the Britons left the areas that the Saxons took over. We know, for example, that some Britons moved west to get away from the Saxons and ended up in Wales and Cornwall, or Kernow, as they called it. Those further north may have gone to a British kingdom up in Strathclyde. Some got in boats and headed over to Gaul (though with the Franks overrunning it, people were beginning to call it Frank-land, or France). These folk ended up in what became known as Brittany. Most of the Britons, however, stayed put and learned to live alongside the Angles and Saxons, just as you would expect.

Of course, in the beginning, these two groups didn't have much in common. The Romanised Britons were used to living in towns; the Saxons went in for farming. By this time, the Britons were mainly Christian; the Saxons had their own religion, with Odin the King of the Gods, Thor the Thunderer, Freya, Tiw, and all that crowd. At first, the Britons and Saxons lived pretty separate lives. But in time, they started inter-marrying and making the part-German-part-Celtic people we call the English.

# Disunited Kingdoms

If Hengist arrived at all, it was probably in or around AD 450. The last Celtic king to lose to the Saxons was Cadwallader of Gwynned in AD 682 – two hundred and thirty years later. So, the Saxon invasion of Britain wasn't some fifth-century blitzkrieg (lightning war), all over in a matter of weeks. The Angles and Saxons spent at least as much time fighting each other as they spent fighting the Celts. But they did push the independent Celtic kingdoms back so that the only places outside Pictland and Ireland where the Celts still ruled themselves were in Wales, Cumbria, Cornwall, and a British tribe who lived in Strathclyde (take a look at Figure 5-1 for more details of the kingdoms during this period). The Saxons called these Celts *Strangers*, which in their language came out as *Welsch*. The Welsch had other names that they called the Saxons, but my editor won't let me print them.

# Celtic kingdoms

Meanwhile, what was happening in the largest of the Celtic kingdoms – Ireland?

### The luck of the Irish

The Irish had five Gaelic kingdoms – Ulster, Leinster, Munster, Connaught, and a smaller one in County Meath – with a High King who was crowned at the royal hill of Tara. For the most part, the High King probably didn't have much real power, but exceptions existed, like High King Neill of the Nine Hostages, so called because, at one point, he had hostages from every one of the other nine royal houses of Ireland. Ireland had a detailed legal code called *Brehan Law*, which treated everyone the same, and a rich oral tradition telling their history, which later got written down in four great epic Cycles. Above all, the Irish had taken to Christianity in a big way, a fact that plays a crucial role in their history, as explained in the section 'Sharing the faith: The Celtic Church', a bit later in this chapter.

**RHEGED** — Celtic Kingdoms
*ELMET* — Germanic Kingdoms

PICTLAND

Iona

DALRIADA

GODODDIN
BERNICIA

STRATHCLYDE

NORTHUMBRIA

DALRIADA

ULSTER

RHEGED

DEIRA

CONNAUGHT

ELMET

MEATH

GWYNEDD

Offa's Dyke

LEINSTER

EAST
ANGLIA

POWYS

MERCIA

MUNSTER

DYFED
GLYWYSING

WESSEX

KENT
SUSSEX

DUMNONIA

**Figure 5-1:**
Saxon
and Celtic
kingdoms in
Britain.

With the Angles and Saxons putting on the pressure over in Britain, the Irish began to expand their kingdom. They took over the Isle of Man and started crossing over to Wales. The main Welsh kingdoms were Gwynedd in the north and Dyfed in the south, and the Irish virtually made parts of Dyfed an Irish colony. The people of Dalriada in modern County Antrim crossed over to Pictish territory and carved out a kingdom for themselves in modern-day Argyll which they also called Dalriada, probably to remind them of home.

### Picturing Pictland

Four main groups lived north of Hadrian's Wall:

- **Picts:** Also known as the Painted People, these were the largest of the tribes and fearsome fighters.

- **Irish Dalriadans:** Recently arrived from Dalriada in Ireland (as explained above) and settled in Argyll, or 'New Dalriada' as you might call it.

- **Britons:** Moved north, possibly to get away from the Saxons, and settled in the Kingdom of Strathclyde.

- **Angles:** Possibly – *possibly* – descended from some of Hengist's men who settled on Pictish territory. At any rate, a large Angle kingdom existed in what is now the Scottish lowlands.

---

# Place that name! Name that place!

One way we can trace Saxon settlement is through place names. The Saxons believed in telling it like it was, so if they had a settlement (tun) by a winding river (cridi) they called it 'Settlement by a Winding River', or Cridiantun, now Crediton in Devon. You also get Cyninges (King's)-tun: Kingston, which was a royal tun and is still a Royal Borough today. And talking of boroughs, that word comes from burh, a fortified town, as in Gæignesburh (Gainsborough) and Mældubesburg (Malmesbury). Consider -feld for field and -ing for people, which gives Haslingfeld: The field of the Hasle people (now Haslingfield) or Hæstingacaester, the camp of the people called Hæstingas, modern Hastings.

You can even trace the chronology to an extent because, when the Saxons first arrived, they tended to name places after the people who settled there: Malling, for example, just means 'the Malling folk live here'. As the Saxons got more settled and started building things, their place names began to reflect that: Grantanbrycg means 'Bridge on the River Granta (or Cam)' – Cambridge, and all those felds had to be cleared and all those burhs had to be constructed. Of course, not everyone likes to be reminded of their ancient Saxon history. Modern Nottingham was Snotingaham in those days, which means 'The place of Snot's people'.

### So how did they all become Scots?

A lot of fighting occurred between these groups. The Angles pushed deep into Pictish territory: They took Dun Eidyn (now Edinburgh) and might have conquered the highlands if they hadn't been sent packing by the Pictish king, Brudei. Meanwhile, the Picts – in between conquering the Britons of Strathclyde – were finding the Irish of 'New' Dalriada a wretched nuisance – thieves, they called them, or in Pictish, *Scotti*.

The Picts attacked the Scotti relentlessly – at one point the Picts very nearly destroyed Dalriada – but in the end the Picts and the Scotti (okay, we can call them Scots now) gradually merged together. Scots married into the Pictish royal family, and because King Kenneth I MacAlpin, who finally united the Picts and Scots and led them against the Vikings, was one of the Scottish kings of Dalriada, they all took the name of his people – Scots.

## Saxon kingdoms

In 'Angle-land' the Angles and Saxons were setting up some kingdoms of their own:

- **Northumbria:** Angles (made up of two smaller kingdoms, Bernicia and Deira)
- **Mercia:** Angles
- **East Anglia:** Angles
- **Sussex:** Saxons
- **Essex:** Saxons
- **Wessex:** Saxons
- **Kent:** Possibly Jutes from Jutland, but more likely Saxons

These seven kingdoms were known as the *Heptarchy*. Some evidence exists that one of the kings would be recognised by the others as Overlord (many books will tell you the term was *Bretwalda* – 'Lord of Britain' or possibly 'Wide (meaning broad) Ruler' – though the evidence for this is very shaky) but quite what this meant in practice is not entirely clear. This Overlord idea may be a bit of spin applied by later 'English' historians.

Don't forget: Celtic British kings still ruled in Wales and up in Pictland, and they could be just as powerful as their Angle and Saxon neighbours. At one time Mercia even forged an alliance with the Celtic king, Gwynedd, (in Wales) against Anglo-Saxon Northumbria, and a lot of trouble this alliance gave the Northumbrians, too.

# We're on a Mission from God

Here's a story. One day, as Pope Gregory I walked through the streets in Rome, he passed a slave market and his eye fell on some handsome young lads with rather fair skins. 'Hello,' says he, 'where are you from?' 'We are Angles,' replied one of the lads. 'Ho ho,' says Gregory, 'you're not Angles but Angels' – or to put it another way, a cute Angle! So Gregory chatted with the boys, and when he gathered that they still worshipped all the wrong gods, he summoned one of his monks, a chap called Augustine, and sent him off to Angle-land to preach the gospel. Augustine landed in Kent, converted King Ethelbert (the Saxon Bretwalda, also known as Lord of Britain, from Kent), and became the first Archbishop of Canterbury. Nice tale.

But wait a minute. Hadn't the Romans made Britain Christian? Yes. And weren't there all sorts of Celtic saints? Yes, again. So how can the story start with Augustine? Well, it doesn't.

Britain already had two church traditions long before Pope Gregory met those boys in the slave market. First was the British Church, still going strong but not really doing anything about preaching to the Saxons. Then there was the Celtic Church, with Irish missionaries on Iona and Lindisfarne.

This is a story of strong faith, high hopes, and precious little charity. Welcome to the Conversion of England.

## Keeping the faith to themselves: The British Christians

Towards the end of the Romans' time in Britain, they'd turned Christian, and all the Roman-Britons followed suit. By the time the Romans left, plenty of British Christian priests and bishops were at work. Britain even had its own home-grown heresy movement led by a priest called Pelagius, who reckoned sending so many people to Hell because of Original Sin was a bit harsh (Pelagius got condemned by the Pope for his trouble). British missionaries existed like St Ninian, who took his life in his hands and went to convert the Picts, and St Patrick, of course, who went to Ireland.

The Angles and Saxons didn't want anything to do with this strange religion, and the Britons don't seem to have done anything to tell them about it. They were probably sulking: 'They've taken over our land; they can jolly well keep their own gods, and I hope they all burn.' So Christianity didn't exactly die out in Britain: The British just kept it to themselves.

# Sharing the faith: The Celtic Church

With the British Church just treading water, as explained in the preceding section, it was down to the Irish to go out and spread the word. Irish missionaries went all over Europe preaching, and of course they also crossed the Irish Sea. Irish colonies were evident in Wales and in Scottish Dalriada, remember, so starting there made sense. The man this section is interested in got in a boat and sailed over to Scotland. His name was Columba.

## Columba sails the ocean blue to Iona

Columba was a tough cookie. He was no obscure peasant: He came from the royal clan of O'Neill, who went on to be High Kings of Ireland. Columba needed to be tough because the Picts weren't going to drop their old gods just like that. The Picts were used to Druids working magic and raising people from the dead, and when a Christian missionary came along they expected him to match the Druids' performance.

We don't know exactly how Columba did it, but he obviously impressed the Picts because one of their kings gave him the island of Iona as a base.

Columba made Iona the nerve centre of a big mission to Britain. Just in case you're ever faced with the task of converting a tribal kingdom to a new religion, take these tips on how to do it from the Irish missionaries of Iona:

- ✔ **Go straight to the top:** Convert the king and the rest will surely follow.

- ✔ **Give them a few simple stories:** Finding the Trinity tricky? Try a shamrock – three leaves: One leaf. Simple! Our brief span of life on earth? Tell about the sparrow who flies through a mead hall, full of light and laughter, and then out the other end into the night. Works every time.

- ✔ **Perform miracles:** Sorry: I'm afraid miracles are expected. Note: Posthumous miracles are very acceptable.

- ✔ **You've got to win a battle or two:** Nothing succeeds like success. The Romans turned Christian because the Emperor Constantine reckoned it would win him more battles, and the Saxon kings were much the same.

## A very Holy Island – Lindisfarne

Getting on God's good side was more or less what King Oswald of Northumbria was thinking when he sent a message to Iona to ask if they could send him a missionary. The Mercians had got together with the Welsh to crush Northumbria, and they pretty nearly succeeded. Oswald decided his best chance was to get God on his side.

# Saxon saints – a User's Guide

Half the towns and railway stations in England seem to be named after obscure Celtic saints. Consider St Pancras, St Neots, St Austell – does anyone know who these people actually were? (St Pancras was a Roman martyr; St Neot was a hermit so short he had to stand on a stool to say mass; and St Austell was a monk who founded a church in Cornwall, and may have done lots of other things but we don't know what.) Some saints are of, frankly, very dubious authenticity. St Ia, after whom St Ives in Cornwall is named, is supposed to have crossed the Irish Sea on a leaf, and some scholars are pretty sure that St Brigid, Ireland's other patron saint, was simply a Christianised version of a pagan goddess of the same name, though the Catholic Church gets very defensive of her. The following are some saints who definitely did exist.

**St Cedd:** An Irish monk, one of St Aidan's crew. Cedd spoke Anglo-Saxon and acted as inter- preter in the crucial Synod of Whitby before becoming bishop of the East Saxons, and you can still see his seventh-century (yes, seventh-century) church at Bradwell-on-Sea.

**St Chad:** English monk trained at Lindisfarne, who became Bishop to the Mercians. Chad said bad weather was a reminder of the Day of Judgement; if so, it looks like the English still need a lot of reminding.

**St Cuthbert:** The big Daddy of all these saints and missionaries. Cuthbert was a much-loved Saxon Abbot of Lindisfarne, a holy man (he was another one who liked to set off to the Farne Islands to be alone), and also a pretty shrewd politician. When he died the monks of Lindisfarne built a shrine to his memory and produced the beautiful Lindisfarne Gospels to go in it. They moved his bones to Durham to keep them safe from Viking raids, where they still are today behind the altar in the Cathedral.

**St Hild:** Formidable abbess of the mixed monas- tery of Whitby (the Saxons rather approved of mixed monasteries. Hild made sure there was no hanky-panky). Hild, or Hilda, was a good friend of St Cuthbert, and she hosted the famous Synod of Whitby in Whitby Abbey. (If you're wondering what this Synod of Whitby is that keeps cropping up, head to the section 'Showdown at Whitby Abbey' later in this chapter).

**St Wilfrid:** Not everyone likes Wilfrid. He was another Lindisfarne product, but he went over to the Continent and picked up the Roman way of doing things. He came back to Northumbria determined to bring the Celtic Church to heel, and at the Synod of Whitby, where he led the Roman side, he did just that. You can still see Wilfrid's throne in Hexham Abbey.

**St David:** Or Dewi, to give him his proper name. David is the patron saint of Wales, and he went out from Wales to preach to the people of the English West Country. David's monasteries followed the Rule of St Columba, which said, among other things, that you shouldn't speak unless you really needed to. You won't be sur- prised to hear that Celtic monks were absolute masters of sign language.

**St Boniface:** A Saxon monk from Devon. He went over to Germany to preach to the Germans in their own homeland and even chopped down one of their sacred trees without getting struck down from on high. He converted thousands of Germans. They murdered him.

The abbot of Iona sent Oswald a monk called Aidan, and since Oswald reckoned anyone from Iona would operate best from an island, he gave Aidan the island of Lindisfarne (also known these days as Holy Island), within sight of his royal burh. Aidan seems to have been at court quite a lot, probably because Oswald and King Oswin who came after him wanted to make absolutely sure they had his blessing for the way they ruled. But Aidan didn't feel happy with the swanky life: He disapproved of riding horses, and when King Oswin gave him one, he passed it on to a beggar (donkeys were okay for long journeys – good biblical precedents – but otherwise Aidan went on foot and told his followers to do the same).

Lindisfarne may have been an island, but it was still within easy reach of the royal court, so Aidan often used to go off on his own to the much more lonely Farne islands for a bit of peace. Even so, Aidan made Lindisfarne the real religious centre of England, much more important than Canterbury. Which meant, of course, that Northumbria was much more important than anywhere else. Which situation suited the Northumbrian kings just fine.

# Enter the Roman Church

If Britain already had two church traditions going (as explained in the preceding sections), why did Pope Gregory decide to send someone else to convert England? Good evidence exists that he was genuinely interested in Britain, but another reason was that the church in Rome was very wary about the Celtic Church. The Irish Celtic Church was a long way away, and it had its own way of doing things. The Roman Church believed in powerful bishops; the Celtic Church was more interested in monasteries and abbots. Irish monks wore their hair in a different style from Roman monks: Instead of that shaved bit on top, the Irish shaved it across the top, from ear to ear. And above all was the difference in the date at which the two churches celebrated the most important Christian feast day of all, Easter. So the Pope probably thought it time to remind everyone in Britain who was in charge. And Augustine was just the man for the job.

### Now hear this! Augustine has landed!

In AD 597 Augustine set off for Britain with a group of 40 monks. Augustine was lucky: The king he intended speaking to, Ethelbert of Kent, had overlordship of the other southern kingdoms at the time, so winning him to his cause would have a big impact. He also had a head start because Ethelbert's queen was a Christian, and it may have been thanks to her that Ethelbert agreed to be baptised and told all his leading nobles to do the same.

Just one problem existed: The British bishops. They didn't see why they should accept Augustine's authority over them, and they set off to meet him and tell him so. When the bishops arrived, instead of rising to greet them politely, Augustine stayed firmly seated and told them he had orders from Rome that they were to clean up their act about Easter and accept him as their chief. No ifs or buts. The meeting ended up as a shouting match, with Augustine threatening the bishops with divine vengeance and the British bishops going back to Wales in a huff.

Augustine was right to target the top. King Ethelbert married his daughter Ethelburga off to King Edwin of Northumbria and when she went, she took a Roman monk called Paulinus with her. Paulinus converted King Edwin and brought the Roman version of Christianity up to Northumbria, right in Celtic Church territory. Unfortunately, after Edwin's death, the Welsh and the Mercians tore Northumbria apart, and Paulinus fled back to Kent. As a result, King Oswald sent to Iona for his bishop and Christian Northumbria stayed firmly in the Celtic camp. (See the section 'A very Holy Island – Lindisfarne' earlier in this chapter for the story of Oswald, St Aidan, and Northumbria.)

### Showdown at Whitby Abbey

The Celtic Church and the Roman Church could have carried on happily at opposite ends of the island for years, but once again the royal house of Northumbria took a hand. By AD 651 Northumbria had a new king, called Oswy. Oswy decided to get married, and he too looked to Kent for a bride. The girl he chose was Eanfled, the daughter of old King Edwin and Queen Ethelburga.

Eanfled had fled back to Kent with Paulinus when she was little; now she was grown up and Christian just like her mother. The trouble was Eanfled had grown up learning the Roman way of doing things, which proved a problem when Easter came round. The Celtic way of calculating the date of Easter was a week ahead of the Roman church (you don't want to know the details about how they calculated all this, believe me), so while the king and his pals were making merry at one end of the palace, at the other end the queen and her Roman monks were still fasting and marking Palm Sunday.

The Roman monks saw their opportunity to get this issue settled once and for all. They persuaded King Oswy to summon both sides to a big summit meeting or *synod* at Whitby Abbey.

AD 664. Mark it down well: This date is as significant in British history as 1066 or 1940. It was the year the English turned their backs on their Celtic heritage and came down on the side of Europe.

The Celts brought out all their big guns for Whitby. Abbess Hild was there, so was Cedd and the new Bishop – Abbot of Lindisfarne, a fiery Irishman called Colman (keen as mustard!). The Romans struggled to find anyone eminent enough to match the Celtic team, but they did have Wilfrid, who had trained at Lindisfarne but had gone over to the Roman side. King Oswy chaired the debate, which wasn't much of a debate at all:

**Colman:** The Celtic Church has been working out the date of Easter in the same way ever since St Columba's day. What was good enough for him should be good enough for the rest of us.

**Wilfrid:** Who do you Celts think you are, you and your obstinate pals the Britons and the Picts? You live out here in the sticks, yet you think you're right and the whole of the rest of Europe is wrong. You may have St Columba on your side, but we've got St Peter. So there.

**King Oswy:** St Peter's in charge of the gates of Heaven, isn't he? I reckon we ought to go with him; otherwise, when I die, he might not let me in. I find in favour of the Romans.

And that was that.

# Winds of Change

All sorts of trouble could have occurred after Whitby, but luckily a new and very wise Archbishop of Canterbury, called Theodore, took things nice and smoothly, and didn't ruffle too many feathers. But things were changing. Northumbria's days were numbered. Down south, King Cedwalla of Wessex was expanding his kingdom as far as Kent, but it was Mercia that was really making people sit up and take notice.

## The rise of Mercia

Mercia was Northumbria's great heathen rival: King Penda of Mercia had beaten and killed King Oswald, and then King Oswy did the same to Penda. It didn't stop Mercia: By AD 754 it was the most powerful kingdom in Britain under its most famous and powerful ruler, King Offa.

### An Offa you can't refuse

Offa had a very simple way of doing things. He showed the King of East Anglia he meant business by capturing him and cutting his head off (it worked), and he kept the Welsh out by building a huge earthwork, known as Offa's Dyke, in much the same way that Hadrian had built his wall. Offa's Dyke was one of the main reasons the Welsh developed in such a different way from their Saxon neighbours. Offa drew up a full law code and a remarkable survey of who owned what in his kingdom, called the *Tribal Hideage*, though it was probably just a way of making sure he knew exactly how much money to demand with menaces. Offa even stood up to the great Frankish emperor, Charlemagne, who recognised him as his 'brother' king. Offa had turned

England into a Mercian empire: Only Wessex was left outside it, and even Wessex had to do more or less what Offa wanted. Pope Adrian I called Offa 'King of the English', and it's hard to disagree with him.

### Offa and out

Offa was clearly hoping that his family would continue to rule England, but it was not to be. He died in AD 796 and, five months later, so did his son and heir. More warrior kings of Mercia came and went – they particularly enjoyed taking on the Welsh – but Mercia's glory days had gone. In any case, some new kids had arrived on the block.

# I don't want to worry you, but I saw three ships come sailing in: The Vikings

In AD 787, according to the not-always-accurate *Anglo-Saxon Chronicle*, someone spotted three ships off Portland on the Wessex coast. 'Better tell the reeve,' the ship-sighter said, and off he went to fetch him. The reeve, the royal official who was supposed to check out anyone coming into the country, rode down to the coast to see who these people were and what they wanted.

''Ello, 'ello, 'ello,' says the reeve, 'what 'ave we heah, then?' What he had was three boatloads of Vikings. And Vikings dealt very expediently with royal reeves who came to see what they were up to. They killed him. They would be doing a lot more killing in the years to come.

# Chapter 6

# Have Axe, Will Travel: The Vikings

*In This Chapter*

▶ Figuring out what drew the Vikings to Britain and what they did once they arrived

▶ Getting familiar with England's first kings

▶ Introducing famous rulers from Scotland, Ireland, and Wales

▶ Understanding how a Dane – Cnut – became an English king

▶ Describing events leading up to the Norman Invasion

For two hundred years, from the 800s to the millennium, and beyond, Britain was part of the Viking world. Everyone knows – or thinks they know – about the Vikings. Horned helmets, great longboats, and plenty of rape and pillaging. This portrayal, while not entirely wrong, isn't entirely right. Sure, everyone – kings, commoners, and clergy alike – suffered at the Vikings' hands. Lindisfarne, the religious centre in Northumbria, got trashed, and so did the monasteries of Ireland: You can still see the tall towers with the doors half-way up them that the Irish monks built to protect themselves. In one sense, the Viking raids helped to bring the different peoples of Britain closer together, because they all suffered together. In another sense, England, Wales, Scotland, and Ireland really began to go their different ways, slowly evolving from regions peopled by Celts and Saxons to regions with their own national identities.

In the years from the first Viking raiding ship off the coast of Britain to 1066, when the Normans invaded England (see Chapter 7 for that bit of history), a lot was going on in Britain. It was a time of national heroes – Brian Boru in Ireland and Kenneth MacAlpin in Scotland who united their countries, and England's Alfred the Great, who was able to push the Vikings out of England entirely – and royal embarrassments like King Ethelred the Unredy, who was reduced to paying protection money to get the Vikings to leave him alone.

No matter how many times the Vikings were beaten, they always came back, and in the end their tenacity paid off. The Norse of Normandy finally conquered England in 1066 and changed British history forever.

# The Fury of the Norsemen

'From the fury of the Norsemen,' went one Saxon prayer, 'Oh Lord, deliver us.' Or at least, so the story goes, although no one's ever found a source for the prayer. But who were these people, and why did they want to set off in longboats to go and ruin other people's lives?

'Norsemen' simply means 'people from the North', which the Vikings were. 'Viking' isn't really a noun, but a verb (or if you're really into this sort of thing, the word's a gerund) meaning 'going off as a pirate': You might say you were going off a-viking for the day. Even 'Dane' doesn't actually mean someone from Denmark: The term's simply a variation on the Saxon word *thegn* (or, as the Scots spell it, *thane*), which meant 'a warrior'. So the Saxons and the Irish tended to use the words Norsemen, Vikings, and Danes pretty much interchangeably.

## A pillaging we will go

Like the Angles and Saxons before them, the Vikings came to Britain for many reasons. They came from the fjords, so going by boat came naturally to them. Britain was really only a hop, skip, and jump away. And even if they didn't want to settle (and sooner or later they would), raiding was very lucrative and quite safe really. If they got beaten, they could always come back the next year.

---

## Equal opportunity raiders

The Norsemen didn't just go to Britain and Ireland. They sailed west, to Iceland and Greenland (which is anything but green – they called it that to try to persuade more Vikings to go there). They even went to the land they called Vinland, which was North America, where they were driven off by the Skraelings, who were presumably either the Algonquins of Canada or the Inuit. They also sailed up the Seine to raid Paris, and they settled the area of northern France that was named Normandy after them (from the French *normand*, meaning Norsemen and Normans). They raided deep into Germany, and they headed east, sailing along the rivers deep into Russia. The locals called them *Rus*, which comes from the Norse word for 'route', and in turn the Rus gave their name to Russia. They founded Kiev and Novgorod and Smolensk, and traded with the Chinese. They pressed south and attacked Miklagard, that is, Byzantium or Constantinople (modern Istanbul), the capital of the Roman Empire. They didn't take Byzantium but many of them did join the Roman emperor's elite Varangian Guard.

The Vikings who killed the reeve at Portland (refer to Chapter 5 for that tale) were probably just on a recce, but they would've given a very favourable report. England and Ireland (we can more or less use the modern terms from now on) were both very wealthy, especially all those defenceless monasteries. If the Vikings had believed in Christmas, they'd have believed it had come early.

So, very sensibly, the Vikings started off by attacking monasteries. After all, the Saxons were ever so thoughtful to put their really important religious centres, Iona and Lindisfarne, on undefended islands just off the coast. The location was just right for seagoing raiders coming from the north. The Vikings must have thought it would be a sin not to raid them and probably wondered why the Saxons hadn't done it years ago.

## Setting up base on the Isle of Man

The great thing about coming from Scandinavia was that all sorts of areas that the Saxons and the Picts thought of as remote, like the Orkneys or the Hebrides, were actually very easy to get to. Take the Isle of Man, for instance. Most people in Britain and Ireland probably hardly gave the Isle of Man a thought, but the Vikings did. If you look at a map from their angle (shown in Figure 6-1), you can see why.

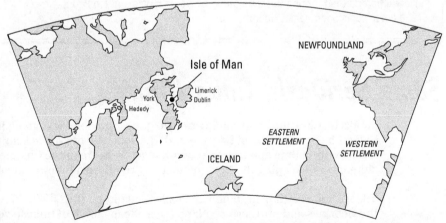

**Figure 6-1:** The Viking view of Britain and Europe.

To the Vikings, Britain and Ireland were simply two parts of a group of islands with a big sound (the Irish Sea) running down the middle, and in the middle of the sound is a very handy island, the Isle of Man. So they seized it, and found Man gave them control of the whole area. The Viking parliament, Tynwald, still survives on Man – the oldest parliament in the world.

## Long ships and tall tales

The Vikings took their raiding very seriously. Their ships were long, but they weren't packed with men because they needed room for a lot of luggage: Food, weapons of course, and sometimes even the chief's tent or his bed. Planning a raid took a lot of thought and care. Those who were planning a trip would listen carefully to people who had got back from raiding and judge whether going back to the same place was worth it or whether striking out somewhere new would be better.

Without doubt the Vikings knew just how to scare the wits out of people. Although most of the written evidence about the Norsemen comes from people like the Lindisfarne monks, who were on the receiving end of a Viking raid, so much evidence exists of people being absolutely terrified of these guys that we can't just put it all down to biased reports and scare stories. The Norse raiders seem to have had a neat trick of sliding a live snake down a hollow tube and then forcing the tube and the snake down some poor monk's gullet. But even

without these little refinements, the Vikings were so fierce and apparently invincible that no wonder people were scared of them.

Nevertheless, we do need to put the Viking image in proportion. For example, many Viking helmets have been found, but not one of them has horns. The traditional image of the Vikings' horned helmets probably comes from people thinking the Vikings must have looked scary and a horned helmet seems scarier than a helmet without horns. More importantly, when they weren't raiding, the Vikings could be much the same as other folk, ploughing, harvesting, hunting – they even played chess, as you can see from those rather beautiful Island of Lewis chessmen in the British Museum. But the best fun for a Viking was drinking in the mead halls and listening to a bard retelling one of the long Viking sagas, like Sigurd the dragon-slayer, or the sayings of Odin. Then after dinner, there was just time to torture a hostage or two, and then it was early to bed.

# Some Seriously Good Kings

Monks just moaning and wailing was no good: Someone was going to have to fight back. King Offa of England and Charlemagne of France sank their differences for a time and agreed to work together to keep the Channel safe for shipping, but keeping the Norsemen at bay required a bit more than that.

Vikings were settling in Dublin and sailing inland up the Liffey. They seized the Hebrides and northern Scotland (Hebrideans think of themselves as Nordics rather than Scots to this day). And they settled at Thanet in Kent. Under their terrifying leader Ivar the Boneless (because he was so slippery, you just couldn't catch him), the Norsemen also took the Northumbrian capital, York, and killed the Northumbrian king. The story goes that they opened up his ribcage and pulled his insides out through his back in what they called the 'Blood Eagle', but, like so many grisly Viking tales, this is almost certainly not true.

Several Saxon and Celtic kings answered the Viking challenge – some with spectacular success, some not. But in almost every case, battling the Norsemen was not only an objective in itself (they had to get rid of these guys), but also a means to an end: Consolidating power and creating nations.

## Scotland the brave: Kenneth MacAlpin

Scotland was vulnerable to Norse attacks because the Scots and the Picts were still fighting each other (head to Chapter 5 for details on how the brou-haha started). The Picts were still trying to crush their neighbours, the Irish Scotti, who had come over from northern Ireland and set up a kingdom called Dalriada, and the Britons who lived in the Kingdom of Strathclyde. But all these people were going to have to unite if they were to stand a chance against the Vikings. The question became how to unite these warring factions.

The man who worked out a solution was the Scottish king of Dalriada, Kenneth I MacAlpin, and his plan was very effective. First, he tricked his own men into believing that he had God on his side by sending a man dressed as an angel to tell them so (I couldn't entirely guarantee that you'd get away with this trick nowadays). Then he invited all the Scottish and Pictish leaders to a peace banquet. The purpose of the banquet? To bury the hatchet. And bury it they did – in the Pictish leaders' skulls.

MacAlpin's intention wasn't to join in some big anti-Viking alliance with the Angles and Saxons: What he wanted was a strong Scottish kingdom, which he called by the Gaelic name of *Alba*, and the Angles out of the Lowlands. He certainly did fight the Vikings, but he was also quite happy to join up with the Vikings against the Angles, thus starting a long Scottish tradition of support-ing absolutely anyone who picks a quarrel with the English.

Forcing the Angles out of Scotland took a long time: Not until the Battle of Carham in 1018 did the Scots finally manage it, and they lost a lot of battles along the way. Nevertheless, it was the Alban kings founded by Kenneth MacAlpin who moved the capital out of remote Dalriada to a more central loca-tion in Perthshire and were crowned sitting on the Stone of Destiny at Scone.

## We'll poke your eye out in the hillsides: The Welsh

The Welsh also developed much more of a separate identity during the Viking period. The days when Welsh kings like Cadwallader could charge around Northumbria spreading terror among the English were long gone: Gwynedd in the north and Dyfed in the south had been cut off from the rest of Britain by King Offa and his famous dyke (refer to Chapter 5 for info on that), and the Welsh had been developing stronger ties with Ireland.

The King of Gwynedd, Rhodri the Great, managed to get the Welsh to unite against the Vikings, but unfortunately, he ran into English trouble. In 878, the Mercians went to war with the Welsh, and Rhodri was killed. His son Anarawd swore vengeance. Anarawd didn't care which Saxon kingdom had actually killed his father, he wanted to teach all the English a lesson. So he made an alliance with the Vikings against Wessex (not Mercia, mind you) and even against the southern Welsh in Dyfed (who thought he'd gone mad). Alfred the Great, the King of Wessex, had to take time out from fighting the Vikings to deal with Anarawd and force him to come to terms.

Eventually, it was King Hywel the Good who finally moulded the Welsh into a single nation, and he did it by working very closely with the English. Nations don't always have to be formed by fighting the neighbours.

## The English kings: Egbert, Alfred, and Athelstan

Important things were happening in southern England. In 829 King Egbert of Wessex was briefly recognised as Overlord of England, and although his own power was shaky – he was up against the Mercians, the Welsh, and the Cornish, not to mention the Vikings – it was a sign of the growing importance of Wessex. By the 860s the Vikings had started to settle a large area of northern and eastern England, which became known as the *Danelaw* (because the law of the Danes applied there). Hitherto the Vikings had been raiders, and they had left the government of the English kingdoms alone, but if they were going to start settling and introducing their laws, then they posed a real threat to the stability and security of all the English kingdoms. By 870 the Vikings had crushed East Anglia, murdered its king, and taken over most of Mercia. Only Wessex was left. But was Wessex strong enough to challenge the power of the Danes? The signs didn't look good.

Egbert had finally won his war with the Vikings, and his son Ethelwulf had managed to join forces with the Mercians against the Welsh. But then the situation all seemed to go to pot. Ethelwulf's sons came to the throne, but they didn't last very long – Ethelbald 858–9; Ethelbert 859–65; Ethelred 865–71 – and they could only sit by and watch as the Vikings crushed the neighbouring kingdoms. Then in 871 the Vikings launched their long-awaited attack on Wessex. King Ethelred and his younger brother led the forces of Wessex out to meet the invaders at Ashdown. To everyone's amazement, they won a great victory. King Ethelred died soon after, and that younger brother of his became King. His name was Alfred.

### Alfred the Great – 'King of the English'

Although the English tend to date all their history from 1066, the only monarch to be called 'the Great' is Alfred, who lived in the 800s – and rightly so. Alfred was a remarkable man, a scholar as well as a soldier, and an amazingly clear-sighted, even visionary, soldier at that. He was wise enough to know when to buy time, and he began his reign by doing just that: The Vikings soon recovered from their defeat at the Battle of Ashdown, so Alfred paid them to leave Wessex alone. This strategy gave Wessex time to prepare for the big showdown they knew was coming.

In 878 the Vikings under their king, Guthrum, tore into Wessex. The Saxons could hardly have known what hit them. Alfred had to go into hiding in the marshes at Athelney in Somerset and conduct a guerrilla war against the Vikings. As long as the Vikings couldn't catch him, Alfred was a powerful symbol of resistance, living proof that the Vikings weren't going to have it all their own way.

When Alfred came out of hiding, he gathered a huge army and fell on King Guthrum's Vikings at Edington like a ton of bricks. In the peace settlement that followed, King Guthrum was lucky to get away with keeping East Anglia, and he even had to agree to be baptised. Alfred was his godfather.

Alfred called it the turn of the tide, and he was right. He completely over-hauled Wessex's defences and he organised the first proper English navy with a new design of ship so that he could take the Vikings on at sea. Which he did – and won. Then he marched east and forced the Vikings out of London. Alfred was definitely on a winning streak. When the Vikings came back at him; he beat them (with some very useful help from the Welsh). When King Anarawd of Gwynedd came at him; Alfred beat him, too. By the time Alfred died in 899 his coins were calling him King of the English, the first time anyone had been called that since Offa's day (refer to Chapter 5), and Wessex was poised to take the fight to the enemy and invade the Danelaw.

## Let them eat (burnt) cake

The most famous story about Alfred dates from Saxon times. While Alfred was hiding out in Athelney marshes, he took shelter with an old woman who told him to watch her cakes while she popped out. Alfred, thinking furiously about how to beat the Danes, forgot to watch the cakes. When the old woman came back, the cakes were burnt. The woman was furious and started to beat Alfred until some of his thegns arrived, and she realised who he really was.

So what's the point of the story? Well, it shows Alfred in an appealingly human light – it would've been stretching things a bit if he'd been able to plan a campaign *and* keep an eye on the cakes at the same time. The story also shows that he was fair: The woman was quite right to be cross, and he didn't pull rank or have her punished. Did it happen? Does it matter? The story's important because of what it tells us about how the English saw Alfred: Hero but human.

In addition to beating the Vikings, Alfred is credited (not always accurately) with the following:

- ✔ **Expanding education and translating great works into Anglo-Saxon:** Ireland was still the great centre of learning – Alfred's contemporary, King Cormac of Munster, was a great scholar in his own right – and Alfred very sensibly brought a group of Irish monks over to set up a school at Glastonbury. He even set up a school for the sons of noblemen within his own household, nurturing the future leaders of Wessex. Since so many people no longer spoke Latin, Alfred had important works translated into Anglo-Saxon. So well known was Alfred's patronage of scholars that many years later, in Richard II's reign (1377–99), University College, Oxford successfully (though entirely falsely) claimed special royal privileges on the grounds that it had supposedly been founded by King Alfred the Great.

- ✔ **Drawing up legal codes:** Alfred drew up a proper code of laws saying exactly what rights people had, how much tax and rent they had to pay, and who they had to pay it to.

- ✔ **Commissioning the *Anglo-Saxon Chronicle*, one of the first histories of Britain:** Not surprisingly for such a learned king, Alfred had an eye on how history would judge him, and he decided to get his retaliation in first. He commissioned the *Anglo-Saxon Chronicle*, a huge year-by-year story of English history from Roman times, and a biography of himself, from Bishop Asser. Which, it may not surprise you to learn, was very complimentary.

### Athelstan – King of Britain

You know how it is: You get a really great leader, but then he dies, and the next ones don't live up to him. Well, prepare yourself for a shock: Alfred's successors were just as tough and well organised as he was. His son Edward the Elder invaded the Danelaw to start the reconquest of England. He had help from his sister Athelfled who deserves to be better known – picture a Saxon Joan of Arc, and you've got the idea. You can imagine their dad looking down very approvingly. But there were more excellent relatives to come.

Next up was Athelstan, Edward's son (illegitimate but don't tell anyone), and Alfred's grandson, and they would both have been proud of him. Athelstan began by expelling the Vikings from York, and then he reconquered Northumbria. The Scots and the Vikings teamed up to try to put a stop to him, but Athelstan took them on at Bromborough on Merseyside and slaughtered them. Literally – according to the *Anglo-Saxon Chronicle* – the ground was slippery with blood. Bromborough was Athelstan's greatest triumph. He was an ally with the Welsh and the Mercians, and he'd beaten the Scots and the Vikings: Athelstan called himself King of All Britain, and he deserved the title.

# *The Vikings Are Gone – Now What?*

Let's take stock of the situation. By the 940s or so, the people of Britain were doing fairly well. The Welsh had been united by King Hywel the Good (read about him in the section 'We'll poke your eye out in the hillsides: The Welsh' earlier in this chapter) and had found that lining up with Wessex (see the section 'Athelstan – King of Britain') was a very smart move. The Scots had come off worst in an attack on Wessex and had had to give Strathclyde to Athelstan and recognise Athelstan as Lord of Britain. The Scottish king, Constantine II, had decided to retire to a monastery.

But most importantly, Wessex is riding high. The Kings of Wessex had more or less conquered England, and kept on good terms with the Welsh. They'd beaten the Scots and taken Strathclyde, and they weren't expecting any more trouble from the Vikings. Why not? Because Wessex had beaten the Vikings.

Those Norsemen weren't invincible: Alfred and Edward the Elder and Athelstan had all shown that. Of course plenty of Norsemen were still living up in Northumbria, but they were Athelstan's subjects now, and they would have to learn to like it.

Of course, the Vikings tried to come back – they always did. The Viking king of Dublin teamed up with Eric Bloodaxe (best Viking name in the book) to take York back, but Athelstan's half-brother Edred kicked them out again. Still, give or take the odd raid, from the 930s to the 990s – a span of 60 years – Britain was largely free of Viking attacks. You can see this period of peace in the stunning artwork that dates from this time – beautiful carvings and metal-work and gorgeous illustrated books and manuscripts. All thanks to the Kings of Wessex. You can see why the English call Alfred 'the Great'. If there were any justice, Athelstan would be called the Great, too.

And then, ever so slowly, the situation went pear-shaped.

## *They're back – and this time it's personal*

Just when you thought that period of history was all over, the Vikings came back. In 991 a huge Viking invasion force landed on the English coast. Who was there to meet them? Ethelred II, one in a long line of Wessex kings. Unfortunately, he wasn't one of the successful ones.

### Ethelred to the rescue – not!

King Ethelred the Unredy rushed to meet the invading Vikings at Maldon in Essex. Disaster! The Battle of Maldon became one of the biggest Viking victories ever. The Norsemen even wrote an epic poem about it, just to rub it in. Ethelred was faced with a choice. He could:

- ✔ Carry on fighting the Vikings and hope for better luck next time.

- ✔ Give the Vikings Essex and hope they would be satisfied.

- ✔ Pay them to go away.

Ethelred chose the last option: He paid the Vikings to go away. The Saxons called this arrangement *Danegeld* – we'd call it a protection racket. To be fair, even Alfred the Great, at the start of his reign, had paid the Danes to go away. But he did it to gain a bit of time so he could be ready for the Norsemen when they came back (see the section 'Alfred the Great – King of the English' earlier in this section for details). Biding time doesn't seem to have been Ethelred's strategy, though. Every year, the Vikings came back, beat up some of Ethelred's men, and then negotiated that year's Danegeld rates. You'd have thought Ethelred would have got a clue from all those Norse cries of 'Bye bye, Ethelred. Same time next year, ja?'

### You really shouldn't have done that

In 1002 Ethelred did a very silly thing. He gave orders for a terrible massacre of thousands of Danes – men, women, and children – at Oxford. He wanted all the Danes and Norse and Vikings to take note. They took note all right, but if Ethelred thought the senseless bloodbath was going to scare them off, he was badly wrong.

The Danish king, Svein Forkbeard (don't you just wish you had the courage to call yourself that), launched massive reprisal raids on England. Ethelred offered Danegeld; Svein told him the rates had shot up. Svein's men even raided Canterbury and murdered the Archbishop. (They pelted him with bones after dinner, and if you're wondering how anyone could die from that – what can they have been eating? – they finished him off with an axe. Which probably renders the bones irrelevant to the cause of death, but they make a good story). And Svein, to coin a phrase, had not yet begun to fight.

In 1013 Svein launched a full-scale invasion. He wasn't after Danegeld this time: He wanted the throne. The Danes of Danelaw flocked to him, and he marched down to London. You couldn't see Ethelred for dust. Ethelred's son Edmund Ironside (incidentally, the first decent name the Saxons have come up with) carried on the fight and managed to force the Danes to agree to divide the kingdom, but Cnut, Svein Forkbeard's son, murdered Edmund before it could happen. With Edmund dead, Svein Forkbeard became King of England. He ruled for a short time before he died and handed the kingdom over to Cnut. Or, as he is better known, King Canute.

After everything all those Kings of Wessex had achieved, England was now ruled by the Danes. Well, thank you, Ethelred the Unredy.

## Showdown in Ireland

While the Danes were taking over England, those Danes who'd settled in Dublin were having a fine old time, not just because of the night life, but also because the Irish were always fighting each other and the Vikings (or Dublin Norse, as they get called) started up a very lucrative business hiring themselves out as mercenaries to whichever side wanted them. The Irish got quite attached to the Dublin Norse and were very sorry when in 902 the King of Leinster (one of the kingdoms in Ireland) pushed them out. But as Vikings were wont to do, they soon came back, and they didn't need to wait long before the mercenary business picked up again.

The Ui Neill clan were the High Kings of Ireland. They had been for years and the other clans resented it deeply, especially the Kings of Leinster. But although the Ui Neills were able to dominate the Irish clans, they weren't able to defeat the Dublin Norse; in fact, in 914 more Vikings arrived and settled in Waterford, to the south of Dublin, and the Ui Neills didn't seem able to do anything about it.

The man who emerged to challenge both the Ui Neills and the Vikings was Brian Boru, the King of Munster. Boru loathed the Vikings, who'd decimated his tribe and killed his mother when he was a child. Boru had fought his way to the kingship of Munster and built up such a power base in the south of Ireland that in 998 High King Malachy Ui Neill agreed to divide his kingdom with Boru, and in 1002 Boru took over the High Kingship himself.

Like Alfred, Brian Boru was a patron of scholars, but he was also a formidable fighter, which was just as well, because he had plenty of enemies, among them the Dublin Norse and the King of Leinster.

The Dublin Norse also got in touch with the Vikings of Orkney, Iceland, and Norway. By 1013, they were all ready. They rose up in a mighty rebellion against High King Brian Boru, and the following year he faced them in battle at Clontarf. And crushed them. But Brian did not live to savour his victory: One of the Vikings fleeing the field killed him.

Clontarf broke the power of the Dublin Norse, but Brian Boru's death led to further civil war in Ireland. Which, as the Danes said, was very good for business. If you want to learn more about Brian Boru and the Dublin Norse, have a look in *Irish History For Dummies* (Wiley).

# Scotland wasn't much better

The Scots were having a difficult time keeping the English at bay, beating off Viking attacks, and stopping people from taking Strathclyde, which is what everyone seemed to end up doing. The fact that the Scots couldn't agree who should be king didn't help any. When the Scottish king, Malcolm I, lost to the English, his own people murdered him, and soon everyone was fighting for the crown.

### It's (not so) good to be king – at least not in Scotland

Here's a handy guide to the murder and mayhem of the Scottish court:

| | |
|---|---|
| **954** | Men of Moray murder King Malcolm I. New king is Malcolm's cousin, Indulf. |
| **962** | Danes kill Indulf. New king is Malcolm's son, Dubh. |
| **966** | Indulf's son, Culen, has Dubh kidnapped and murdered and his body dumped in a ditch. Culen then becomes king. |
| **971** | The King of Strathclyde kills Culen in revenge for Culen raping the king's daughter. New king of Scots is Kenneth II. |
| **995** | Kenneth II is murdered, possibly by a booby-trapped statue (!), and Constantine III becomes king. |
| **997** | Constantine III killed in battle – against Scottish rebels led by his cousin, Kenneth, and Constantine's own illegitimate son. Kenneth becomes King Kenneth III. |
| **1005** | Kenneth III is killed by his cousin, who becomes King Malcolm II. |

And then things get *really* interesting.

### 'Is this a dagger I see before me?'

Malcolm II linked up with the King of Strathclyde and beat the English at the Battle of Carham in 1018 – one of the most important dates in Scottish history. The battle more or less settled the border along the River Tweed, where it is today.

But when Malcolm died (killed in battle against the men of Moray, in case you're wondering), there was trouble. His grandson, Duncan, seized the throne. This is the same Duncan who appears in Shakespeare's play *Macbeth*, where he's portrayed as a nice old man; in reality, he was young and a really nasty piece of work. Not a particularly good leader either: He tried to attack Durham, but only had cavalry – not much use against high stone walls. The English cut his men to pieces and stuck their heads along those same walls as souvenirs. Then Duncan lost against the Vikings – twice. No wonder Macbeth reckoned he could do better.

Macbeth was an important Scottish nobleman (he may well have been helping the Vikings, not fighting them the way Shakespeare shows it), and Duncan didn't go to his castle in 1040 to stay the night: He went to attack it. And, true to form, he lost. Duncan was probably killed in the fighting; some like to say that Macbeth killed him in open combat. When (or how) Duncan died doesn't matter: That he was dead is the important point. Everyone gave a sigh of relief, and Macbeth was elected High King of Scots. He remained king for 18 years, which is a bit longer than Shakespeare allows him and a major feat for the Scotland of those days.

Macbeth was actually quite a good king and very devout: He went on pilgrimage to Rome and gave a lot of his money away to the poor. In the end, it was Duncan's son Malcolm who had it in for Macbeth. Malcolm ran off to complain to the English, who joined up with the Danes (the Danes were ruling England by now) to invade Scotland on Malcolm's behalf. An almighty battle occurred at Dunsinane in 1054 (Shakespeare gets that bit right), but it took another three years of conspiring and plotting before Malcolm was finally able to kill Macbeth in battle. With a dagger? No, more likely with an axe.

## Cnut: Laying down the Danelaw

Everyone – the Irish, English, Welsh, and Scottish – had to submit to Cnut, the Dane who became king on Ethelred's watch (see the earlier section 'You really shouldn't have done that' for details). Cnut was one of those really powerful kings like Offa (see Chapter 5) or Athelstan (see the earlier section 'Athelstan – King of Britain' in this chapter) who controlled the whole of England so that even continental monarchs sat up and took notice.

Of course, the little problem existed that Cnut had seized the throne, and some of Ethelred's family might not like that, but Cnut had a very simple way of dealing with possible challengers: He killed them. As soon as the crown was on his head, Cnut rounded up every relative of Ethelred's and every leading Saxon he could lay his hands on and had them all put to death. He even reached over the North Sea and took Denmark off his brother Harald. No one who knew Cnut thought there was anything remotely funny about him (even though, much later on, the English took to calling him Canute in an attempt to make this formidable king a figure of fun). But Cnut was a very good king in many ways. He reformed the law and gave England twenty years of peace. Perhaps Danelaw wasn't such a bad thing after all.

# The Messy Successions Following Cnut

After Cnut, the Dane who ruled all of Britain – despite what the Welsh, Scottish, and Irish kings may have thought (see the earlier section) – the question became who would be king when he died? And finding the solution got a bit complicated, because everyone started having two wives (in Cnut's case, both at the same time) and several people had more or less legitimate claims to the throne. Here are the various claimants – hold tight:

- **Ethelred the Unredy had two wives.** With Wife 1, he had a son, Edmund Ironside, who got killed by Cnut. End of that line. With his second wife, Emma of Normandy, he had two sons, Alfred and Edward (also known as Edward the Confessor). Note: Ethelred and Emma were so worried about the Viking threat that Emma took the boys over to Normandy for their own safety, so they grew up more Norman than English. Remember this fact – it will be important.

- **When Ethelred died, Cnut married his widow, Emma.** They had a son, Harthacnut. But Cnut had already married a 'temporary wife' called Ælfgifu of Northampton. He and Ælfgifu had two sons, Swein, who became King of Norway, and Harold 'Harefoot'.

As you can see, lots of half-brothers were knocking around, and they were all determined to have their day as king.

## Kings for (just over) a day

When Cnut died in 1035, Harold 'Harefoot' (Cnut's son by Ælfgifu) and Harthacnut (Cnut's son by Emma) had a big row about who should succeed. Harold was the elder, but Harthacnut said that his mum was Cnut's real wife, so there. Harold said, 'Insult my mother, would you?' and seized the throne.

Meanwhile, over in Normandy, Ethelred and Emma's young son Alfred thought 'Hang on, shouldn't I be King?' and crossed over to England to have words with his step-brother Harold Harefoot. But Alfred was murdered by an ambitious English nobleman with an eye to the main chance, called Godwin. (Godwin was a man to watch: Think of him as the Thegn Most Likely to Succeed in the Class of 1035. Alfred's little brother, Edward the Confessor, certainly didn't forget what Godwin had done).

Harold Harefoot ruled for a time and then died, and then Harthacnut came over and ruled, and fell dead in the middle of a wedding banquet (it was probably the fish). The obvious person to put on the throne was Ethelred and Emma's rather pious and fiercely pro-Norman son, Prince Edward, 'the Confessor'. No one could quarrel with that: Through his dad, Edward was descended from Alfred the Great, and his mum had been married both to Ethelred and to Cnut. So Edward it was.

# Edward the Confessor

Although Edward was of the Royal House of Wessex, he never really liked England. His mum was from Normandy, and he'd grown up there. When he took up his throne in England, he brought a lot of Normans over with him, which didn't go down well with the English. Edward liked to surround himself with scholars and builders: He was having Westminster Abbey built, and he wanted to look over all the details. But one problem existed, which really preyed on his mind: How to get back at the Godwins.

Edward's nickname, 'The Confessor,' means pious or God-fearing, though it may just mean 'chaste', which in turn may just be a tactful way of pointing out that Edward and his queen, Edith, didn't have any children. Which was a shame, really, because an heir would have saved an awful lot of trouble.

King Edward hated Godwin: He never forgot that Godwin had killed his brother Alfred. But Godwin had too many powerful friends for Edward to do anything about avenging his brother's death. In fact, Edward even had to marry Godwin's daughter, Edith, though he was a rotten husband and got rid of her as soon as he could.

Edward did not want a Godwin on the throne; he wanted the throne to go to William, the new Duke of Normandy. When trouble occurred at Dover between Godwin's men and some Normans, Edward seized the opportunity to drive Godwin and his family into exile and to lock up poor Queen Edith. If Edward really did promise the throne to William, as William always claimed he did, this was probably when he did it.

Then the Godwins came back. With an army. Edward gritted his teeth, welcomed them home, pretended their banishment had all been a misunderstanding, and gave them some smart new titles. Godwin's son Harold Godwinsson became Earl of Wessex, and his other son Tostig became Earl of Northumbria.

The two Godwin brothers went to Wales to deal with King Gruffudd ap Llewellyn, who'd united the Welsh and launched a fierce war against the English. Harold Godwinsson soon had the Welsh king on the run, and then Gruffudd's men murdered their own king. Harold won a lot of friends through his Welsh campaign (though probably not among the immediate family and friends of King Gruffudd ap Llewellyn). A number of Saxon nobles thought Harold Godwinsson was just right to become king. Even King Edward seemed impressed with Harold. But was he impressed enough to promise Harold the throne?

## The men who would be king

All the following people had some sort of claim to Edward's throne after his death:

- **Edgar the Ætheling:** Ethelred the Unredy's grandson by his first wife. That gave Edgar (*Ætheling* means 'crown-worthy') a better claim to the throne than anyone – even Edward the Confessor himself, who was Ethelred's son by his second wife.

- **Harold Godwinsson:** He won the popular vote with the Anglo-Saxon council, the *witenagemot* – or *witan* for short. Harold even said Edward had promised him the throne, but then he would say that, wouldn't he?

- **William of Normandy:** William was very ambitious but had no support in England. Except – crucially – from King Edward.

- **Harald Hardrada:** The Viking king of Norway. Harald Hardrada had a rather complex – not to say specious – claim to the English throne: Harthacnut promised Harald Hardrada Denmark, but Harald Hardrada claimed it was a package deal: Denmark and England. Not very likely, is it?

All these people were just waiting for Edward the Confessor to die, which he did on 5 January 1066. And then the fun really began.

# Chapter 7

# 1066 and All That Followed

*In This Chapter*

▶ Providing a who's who of the claimants to the throne after Edward the Confessor's death

▶ Battling it out at Hastings: King Harold and William, Duke of Normandy

▶ Considering how the Norman Conquest changed England, Scotland, and Wales, and how Ireland escaped – for now

▶ Understanding how the fighting between King Stephen and Empress Matilda threw England into anarchy

The year? 1066. The event? The Battle of Hastings. The most famous date and the most famous battle in English history. The year that William, Duke of Normandy crossed the Channel and King Harold got an arrow in his eye. The English sometimes need to be reminded that William conquered only England: The Battle of Hastings didn't put him on the throne of Scotland or Ireland or Wales. But if the people of Scotland or Ireland or Wales thought that what happened at Hastings was just an English affair, they were in for a very nasty shock. The Norman Conquest changed everything, for everyone. For ever.

## The King Is Dead, Long Live – er

Saxon England didn't have any firm rules about who should be king. Basically, when the old king died, the crown passed to whoever could (a) show that they had some sort of blood claim, and (b) grab the crown before anyone else got it.

By the time Edward the Confessor died on 5 January 1066, the king's council – the *Witan* (or *Witenagemot*, if you like showing off), a sort of Saxon Supreme Court – had the job of finally saying who was to be the next king. They had four candidates to choose from:

- ✔ **Harold Godwinsson:** Everyone's favourite, he was popular, a gifted soldier, and had a good head for politics. Ideal.

- ✔ **William Duke of Normandy:** No blood link, but William claimed that Edward promised him the throne.

- ✔ **Edgar the Ætheling:** Although he was only 14 years old, he had the best bloodline claim to the throne. In 1066, he was too young to rule on his own, but give him time.

- ✔ **Harald Hardrada, King of Norway:** He had a tenuous claim, and no support in England. But he also had a strong nuisance value. He needed watching.

# King Harold – One in a Million, One in the Eye

The Witan chose Harold Godwinsson to succeed Edward the Confessor, and it had no doubts about its selection. Harold was the man on the spot, and he also said that Edward's dying wish had been that he, Harold, should have the crown. (No, there were no actual witnesses to this event, but the claim was good enough for the Witan.) So Harold went to Westminster Abbey, where the Archbishop of York (not Canterbury, a point that becomes important when William arrives on the scene) put the crown on his head.

## Trouble on the not-too-distant horizon

Harold's coronation went fine, but two little problems were already on their way back to haunt him.

### Tostig, Harold's brother and soon-to-be ex-Earl of Northumbria

Harold's brother, Tostig, had been a very harsh Earl of Northumbria, and in 1065, his thegns got together to get rid of him. Harold took the thegns' side against his brother, forced Tostig to go into exile, and gave the earldom of Northumbria to a useful potential ally called Morcar. Tostig got sore (wouldn't you?) and headed straight off to Norway to have a quiet word with King Harald Hardrada.

### Harold's earlier trip to Normandy and the oath he swore there

In 1064, two years before he was crowned king, Harold had gone to Normandy. We still don't really know why. Some historians think Harold went over to talk with William about the succession; Harold's story was that he was shipwrecked, though what he was doing so close to the Norman shore he doesn't say.

However he ended up in Normandy, William made Harold an honoured guest for a while, but then William turned nasty. When Harold wanted to head home, William forced him to put his hand on a box and swear an oath to help William become King of England when Edward died. After Harold had sworn the oath, William told Harold to open the box. And guess what was in it? Holy relics.

Harold had a serious problem on his hands. Swearing an oath on holy relics, even if you didn't know you'd done it, was the most solemn type of oath there was. As soon as Harold got home, every churchman he asked, from his local vicar to the Archbishop of Canterbury, said that an oath taken under false pretences or duress doesn't count (it still doesn't), but you could bet your bottom dollar William wouldn't see it like that.

## The fightin' fyrd

It didn't take a genius to work out that William was probably going to cross the Channel and fight, so Harold called up the fyrd and stood guard along the south coast of England.

The *fyrd* was Anglo-Saxon England's secret weapon: An instant army. Every free man trained in how to fight, and when the local lord or the king needed men quickly, he only had to summon the fyrd and – presto! – he had an army behind him. Of course, when the fyrd marched off, no one was left to do any of the work around the farm, but hey, that's progress.

But when the invasion came, it didn't come along the south coast. It came up in Yorkshire.

## When Harry met Harry

William wasn't the invader; it was Harald Hardrada. And guess who was with him? Tostig. Tostig and Harald Hardrada landed with a massive army, took York (a good Viking city, see Chapter 6), and declared Harald Hardrada King of England.

Then King Harold (the Saxon one) did an amazing thing. He and the fyrd raced up north. Napoleon always said that speed was his greatest weapon, and Napoleon would've been impressed with Harold. Just when Harald Hardrada and Tostig were sitting back, thinking it would be weeks before Harold even knew they were there, Harold arrived with the Anglo-Saxon fyrd at his back. And boy, was he in a fighting mood. 'So this Norwegian wants England, does he?' said Harold. 'I'll give him a bit of England. Six feet of it.' The two armies met at Stamford Bridge, just outside York. The Saxons crushed the invaders.

The Battle of Stamford Bridge was one of the most impressive victories any Saxon king ever won. The Vikings – the *Vikings* – didn't know what hit them. Harold's men killed Harald Hardrada and Tostig. This battle puts Harold right up there with Alfred, Athelstan, and all the other Kings of Wessex who'd made their names by standing up to the Vikings (refer to Chapter 6 for a rundown of the impressive Kings of Wessex). And Harold hadn't finished yet.

## Come on William, if you're hard enough!

While Harold was defeating Harald Hardrada and Tostig, William had been sitting around at the mouth of the Seine waiting for the wind to change. He'd gathered a huge army and, according to the Bayeux Tapestry, his men had been chopping down trees and building boats big enough to take William's men and their horses across the Channel and into England. By the time the wind changed and the Normans set sail, no one was left along the English coast to stop them. Everyone had gone north to fight the Battle of Stamford Bridge.

William was lucky. Or you could say, he knew how to make his own luck.

- ✔ **A heavenly sign:** Just before the Normans set sail, a shooting star flew overhead. The Normans were really scared that the star was a sign of bad luck. William told them, yes, it was a sign of bad luck – for Harold.

- ✔ **Blessing from the Pope:** The Pope said William was the rightful king of England, based on the fact that Harold had supposedly sworn an oath – on holy relics, no less – swearing William was the rightful king. In addition, Harold had been crowned by the Archbishop of York, not Canterbury (if you want to know why this even mattered, see the sidebar 'Who crowned whom and why it was important'). The Pope gave William a special papal banner to fly so he could show everyone God was on his side. Useful.

- ✔ **Slip sliding away:** As the Normans were coming ashore, William slipped and fell. When they saw their Duke come a purler the moment he set foot on English soil, the Normans were bound to think, 'Uh-oh, is that a bad sign?' But one of William's quicker-thinking barons saved the day. He called out, 'Looks like you've already grabbed England with your bare hands, sir!' and William quickly grabbed a handful of sand and held it up triumphantly. Everyone cheered.

## Who crowned whom and why it was important

Harold was crowned by the Archbishop of York, not the Archbishop of Canterbury, and here's why. Years earlier, back in King Edward's time, Harold's dad, Earl Godwin, had led a sort of anti-Norman purge. He got rid of a lot of Norman bishops – including the Archbishop of Canterbury – and lots of Saxon bishops, all loyal to the Godwin family, took over. One of these bishops was Stigand, who became the new Archbishop of Canterbury.

The Pope wasn't happy at all about all these changes. In particular, he said that Stigand had no right to be archbishop while the previous Norman archbishop (whose name was Robert, if you're interested) was still around. The English told the Pope to go and boil his head.

When it came time for Harold to be crowned, he didn't want to take any chances. Because there was no dispute about the Archbishop of York, Harold made sure that he was the one who did the coronation.

So when William got in touch with the Pope about going to England to overthrow Harold, he promised the Pope that if he won, he would get rid of Archbishop Stigand. The Pope was delighted, and said that God was clearly on William's side. Official.

## *Norman mods and Saxon rockers: Battle at Hastings*

As soon as Harold had dealt with the Vikings up north (see the earlier section 'When Harry met Harry' for info about the Battle of Stamford Bridge), he and the fyrd had to about turn and head back down south to deal with William. In double-quick time. Harold and his men must have been shattered, but you would never know it from the battle that followed. When the Normans woke up, they found the entire Saxon fyrd occupying Senlac Hill.

Basically, in an eleventh-century battle, if you were on top of a hill, you had all the aces. The other side had to run up at you, while you could hurl whatever you wanted down at them. All the Saxons had to do was keep their shield wall firm and hack at anything that managed to struggle to the top. The Normans charged again and again, but they couldn't break through the Saxon shield wall and had to ride back down.

Then the Saxons made their fatal mistake. Some of them broke out of the shield wall and ran after the Normans. Which was very silly because, once they got to the bottom, the Normans simply turned round and cut them to pieces.

## The Bayeux Tapestry – embroidering the truth?

Strictly speaking, of course, the Bayeux Tapestry isn't really a tapestry: It's a very long (70-metre) piece of embroidered linen. The tapestry is also a very long piece of propaganda; it tells the story of the Battle of Hastings from the Norman perspective. William's brother, Odo, bishop of Bayeux, was probably the one who had the tapestry made, and it probably hung on the wall in his palace (maybe it covered a particularly nasty 70-metre stain).

The tapestry tells the story of William's invasion of England and the Battle of Hastings in great detail. Harold comes out very much as the bad guy: The tapestry portrays him as an oathbreaker, shows that both Edward and Harold had promised William that he should be king, and makes it look as if Harold was crowned by Stigand, the 'wrong' archbishop – which he wasn't. (See the sidebar 'Who crowned whom and why it was important' for the truth about Harold's coronation and why the Normans would have deliberately portrayed it wrongly.)

The Bayeux Tapestry is such an extraordinary piece of art and such wonderful source material that historians sometimes have to remind themselves that it's not exactly objective. Kings in those days were no strangers to spin and propaganda – look at King Alfred and his carefully crafted Anglo-Saxon Chronicle (see Chapter 6) – but it took the Normans to turn it into an art form.

Then William brought in his archers, and Harold's luck ran out. The arrows didn't break the Saxon line, but if the Bayeux Tapestry (head to the sidebar 'The Bayeux Tapestry – embroidering the truth?' for an explanation of that) is to be believed, one of them hit Harold in the eye. Then, if the tapestry has got the events right, the Normans charged with their cavalry, and Harold got cut down.

Of course, how the battle ended doesn't really matter; what mattered was that Harold was dead. And in a battle about who was to be king, that fact was all that mattered.

# William Duke of Normandy, King of England

When King Harold died at the Battle of Hastings, William became King of England. The fact that Harold was killed was really handy for William. That Harold's brothers (his heirs) were killed too made things even better. The Saxons might not like having William on the throne, but for the moment, there wasn't anyone else around that they could put up instead. So William made his way cautiously to London and announced he would be crowned on Christmas Day in Westminster Abbey.

# Coronation chaos

We like to call William *the Conqueror*, but that wasn't the message he wanted to send. In William's view, Harold was the conqueror, the one who had seized the crown illegally; he himself was the rightful monarch being restored to his throne. So William chose Westminster Abbey (which was new, don't forget) quite deliberately.

Westminster Abbey was Edward's abbey. By having his coronation take place there, William was showing that he was Edward's heir, not Harold's. William also made sure that, like Harold, he was crowned by the Archbishop of York and not by Stigand the 'illegal' Archbishop of Canterbury.

No one knew how the people of London might react to William's coronation, so William posted guards on the abbey doors. When the people inside the abbey let out a shout, probably something like 'God save the King!' or 'Yessss!', the guards thought William was in trouble. Instead of running in to rescue him, however, they set fire to all the nearby houses. The abbey filled with smoke, everyone ran out to see what on earth was happening, and William, according to the one detailed account we have, was left shaking with fear as the archbishop finally put the crown on his head. Not a good start.

# Under new management

As the English (and the Welsh and the Scots) were about to learn, William was a tough customer. No sooner was he crowned than his men set to work building the Tower of London, a massive fortress meant to warn the Londoners against trying anything on: The Normans, the Tower said, were here to stay. Soon the whole country was getting used to the sight of these Norman castles. Because if you thought Hastings was the end of the war, think again: The fighting had only just started.

### Trouble in Kent and Exeter

First there was trouble in Kent. Then there was trouble in Exeter, down in Devon. Because Exeter was always causing trouble, William marched down in person with a big army and dealt with it. Then Harold's sons landed with an Irish army. Sure, William was able to deal with all these threats, but it meant that already other people were claiming the throne. And a much more dangerous claimant than Harold's family had just thrown his hat in the ring: Edgar the Ætheling.

### It's grim up north

Edgar the Ætheling was of the Royal House of Wessex and a direct descendant of Alfred the Great. A lot of important people were very interested in Edgar the Ætheling:

- ✔ **Edwin and Morcar (or Morkere, if you prefer):** Edwin of Mercia and Morcar of Northumbria were the two most important English thegns still left alive after Hastings. They defied William and backed anyone who opposed him.

- ✔ **Malcolm Canmore III, King of Scots:** The English had sheltered Malcolm and helped him get his throne back (see Chapter 6 for details) so naturally Malcolm felt very kindly towards them. When the Normans conquered England, Malcolm decided to help the English fight back.

- ✔ **King Svein of Denmark:** It wasn't that long since the Danes had ruled England, and they were still very interested in it. If there was a chance of helping put Edgar the Ætheling on the throne, then you could count Svein in.

So William had to spend two years, 1068 and 1069, fighting Edgar the Ætheling and his allies. A lot of blood was spilt, especially in York where the Saxons massacred 3,000 Normans. But William won. Edwin and Morcar had to give in, the Danes had to go home, and Edgar the Ætheling had to flee to Scotland. That was when William decided he was going to teach the North a lesson it would never forget.

It was called 'Harrying the North'. William led his army through the north of England destroying everything – a total scorched earth policy. As if that wasn't enough, King Malcolm invaded the north the next year and virtually destroyed the city of Durham. Thousands of English were shipped off to Scotland as slaves. But William wasn't having that either, so he headed back up north again, invaded Scotland and forced Malcolm to acknowledge him not just as King of England, but as overlord of Scotland, too.

### In Hereward's wake

One little bit of England still held out against the Norman invader – the Isle of Ely. Nowadays, the isle isn't an island any more and it's got a magnificent cathedral on it, but in those days, it was marshland, ideal for a hideout. The man hiding out was Hereward, later known (wrongly – a local family called Wake tried to claim him as their ancestor) as 'the Wake'. Hereward (that's Herra-ward) was a Saxon thegn who had always been a bit of a troublemaker, and now he made himself even more of one. He joined up with King Svein's men to attack the city of Peterborough, and then he teamed up with Earl Morcar in a sort of guerrilla campaign from the Ely marshes.

Hereward became such a folk hero, ambushing Norman patrols and going into their camp in disguise, that the Normans just had to deal with him. And that meant bringing in ships and engineers and virtually draining the marshes. The Normans managed to capture Morcar and take over Ely Abbey, which had been supplying Hereward and his merry men with food and shelter, and they caught some of Hereward's men, but they didn't catch Hereward.

## An Englishman's home is his castles

The Normans knew just how to leave their mark on the land: They built castles. Not nice, romantic, fairy tale castles: These things were big and ugly and built to strike fear into everyone. First, the Normans forced all the locals to dig a huge great earthwork like a vast upside-down pudding bowl and called a *motte*. Then they built the main fort on the top. We're talking a 1 in 1 gradient here, so you wouldn't be able just to run up the side of it. Then, down at the bottom, they built a smaller mound for all the horses and cattle and people who weren't going to be based in the fortress itself. They put a strong wooden fence round that and called it a *bailey*. Motte and bailey castles sprang up all over England and along the frontier with Wales. When you remember that most people had never seen a building higher than a barn, you can see why these castles really made their point: The Normans were in charge now, and don't you forget it.

# Mine, all mine! The feudal system

William had promised his barons land in England, but he had to be sure that a baron wouldn't use his land and wealth to get above himself and try and take the throne. William hit on a very simple solution: He created the feudal system in England.

## How the system worked

First, William declared that all the land in England belonged to him. Then he appointed several of his trusted barons as tenants-in-chief (William tactfully used the old Saxon title *Earl* instead of the Norman French *Count*), but they had to pay William rent, just like any other tenant. That obligation could be in money; it could also be in loyalty. Tenants-in-chief were supposed to provide the king with a lot of men in time of war.

Down at the bottom of the feudal system were the peasants, or villeins, who had to work the land and pay rent – and who were always Saxons. The word villein gives us villain, which gives you a pretty good idea of what the Normans thought of them. If the feudal system sounds a bit confusing, take a look at Figure 7-1 to help you along.

## The Domesday Book

The Normans quickly worked out that Knowledge is Power. William wanted to get taxes in from his kingdom, and he didn't want anyone to escape paying. So he sent his men out to conduct the first doorstep survey in history. They went to every single village in England and wrote down exactly who owned what and how much.

## Extremely interesting linguistic point

Modern English has got bits of Norman French and bits of Anglo-Saxon, and you can use it to see the relationship between the two groups. Animals had Saxon names, like cow or sheep or swine, while they were alive and Saxon peasants had to look after them, but as soon as they got served up on a plate to a Norman lord and his lady, they got French names like beef or mutton or pork. The peasants who had to carry the heavy plates knew some other Anglo-Saxon words, too, and used to mutter them under their breath.

Ever get that feeling that Big Brother is watching you? The Normans started it. They wrote their findings up in a vast book known as the *Domesday Book*, so-called, according to Richard FitzGerald, Treasurer of England, 'because it is not permissible to contradict its decisions, any more than it will be those of the Last Judgement'. And they weren't far wrong: the *Domesday Book* was last used in settling a legal dispute in 1982!

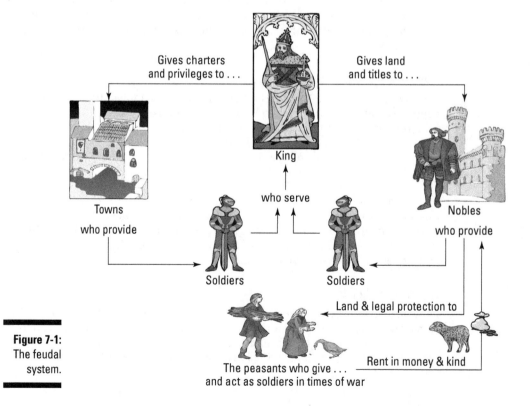

**Figure 7-1:** The feudal system.

# Scotland turns English

Scotland's king, Malcolm III (who got rid of Macbeth; see Chapter 6), was a remarkable man. Although he had a Gaelic title, *Canmore*, which means 'Chieftain', Malcolm was a moderniser at heart. He had spent a long time in England and on the continent, and he could see that Scotland had no future if she kept to her old tribal customs.

Malcolm gave his children English names, and he moved his capital away from the Highlands into the Lowlands, where there were still plenty of people descended from the Angles. He even built a proper Norman-style castle at Edinburgh. So the fact that pro-English Malcolm was killed in an English ambush, fighting to keep hold of his English lands, is ironic.

## Queen Margaret: A saint for Scotland – made in England

King Malcolm III's wife was Edgar the Ætheling's sister, Margaret. Margaret was highly intelligent and a very devout Christian. She stopped the Celtic habit of holding markets and festivals on Sundays, and she invited English monks of St Benedict to come over and set up their first monastery in Scotland, at Dunfermline. Her chapel in Edinburgh Castle is still there today. She set up the Queen's Ferry on the River Forth so that pilgrims could cross over to visit the shrine of St Andrew. She even held big dinners for the poor in the royal hall. No-one can doubt that Margaret was a much-loved figure, and after her death they made her into a saint: She is a patron saint of Scotland to this day. After all, she did actually live in Scotland, which is more than you can say for St Andrew, Scotland's other patron saint.

## Old McDonald came to harm . . .

A lot of Scots didn't like what Malcolm III had been doing, including his brother, Donald Bane. After Malcolm's death, Donald Bane wanted to take Scotland back to the old ways so he got all the Celtic Scots behind him, seized Edinburgh Castle, and declared himself king.

Malcolm's sons were having none of this succession, and a right old battle broke out between King Donald and his nephews, with the crown going back and forth between them. Donald even had one of his nephews, Duncan II, put to death, or 'mrrrdrrrd' as they say in Glasgow. But in the end, King Donald was no match for our old friend Edgar the Ætheling. Edgar (who was having much more success in Scotland than he had had in England) led an Anglo-Norman army into Scotland, sent Donald Bane packing, and put his nephew – and Malcolm's son – Edgar on the throne. In fact four of Malcolm's sons ruled Scotland, and they all helped to make Scotland a more modern country, more like England.

## And Wales follows suit

To the Normans, the Welsh border was Injun country. William stationed some of his best barons along it and built some of his strongest castles there – nearly five hundred of them, some in stone. The Normans weren't content to sit around on the border, however, so they crossed the frontier and started to take over. The fact that the Welsh were fighting each other helped the Norman incursion, so much so that, by the time William died, the Normans had taken over North Wales and were moving into the south. Then they took over the south and went right through to Pembroke on the west coast. This action was the Norman Conquest of Wales.

## But Ireland has a breather

The Normans didn't try to invade Ireland. Well, not in this chapter. While England, Scotland, and Wales were slogging it out with the Normans, the Irish were having something of a golden age. Brian Boru's dynasty was on the throne, and the Danes had given up fighting and settled down into respectable careers in the import–export business. The Irish Church was beginning to do things the Roman way, building beautiful Romanesque chapels like Cormac's Chapel at Cashel, while Irish monks produced illustrated books of the great Irish sagas. The situation looked as though Ireland might turn into a strong feudal state, like England. It didn't, because disaster struck, but you'll have to have a look in Chapter 8 to find out what befell them.

## The Church gets cross

William kept his promise to the Pope, who had backed his invasion of England: He started sacking Saxon bishops and replacing them with Normans. His choice of Archbishop of Canterbury was inspired: An Italian called Lanfranc. Lanfranc firmly reminded the Archbishop of York who was in charge, told the Irish Church to clean up its act, and told priests in England they had to remain celibate – not a popular message when most priests had live-in partners. Lanfranc enjoyed full backing from William, but trouble was brewing between Church and Crown: the Investiture Contest.

The trouble was about who should appoint bishops. The Pope said only he could do it, but William – like just about every other king in Europe – said it was a matter for the Crown. Things got worse when William's son, William Rufus, and then Henry I, came to the throne (see the next section). The new archbishop, Anselm, was staunchly pro-Pope, and he had to be sent into exile until eventually a compromise was reached: The Pope would appoint bishops, but the bishops would pay homage to the king. The arrangement was never likely to last, and it didn't.

# William Dies and Things Go Downhill

William died in 1087. If I tell you he was away fighting his own son, you'll have an idea of how things had deteriorated in the William household. They were about to get a whole lot worse.

## Who wants to be a William heir?

William had three sons, and they all wanted to be king:

- **Robert Curthose:** The name *Curthose* means shorty. Robert was the eldest son, always arguing with his father. He got Normandy when William died, but wasn't quick enough off the mark to get England.

- **William Rufus:** *Rufus* meant red-faced. The artist of the family, he liked music and poetry. His enemies said he was gay, which may be true. He was certainly a tough and cruel soldier. As soon as his father died, William Rufus crossed over to England, took possession, and blew a raspberry at Robert.

- **Henry Beauclerc:** The clever one, which is more or less what *Beauclerc* means. Henry was the third son. As such, he didn't stand to get anything when his father died. But don't count him out. This was a man who once threw one of William Rufus's supporters from the top of a tower. Utterly ruthless.

Robert, as you may expect, felt pretty sore at not getting England, but he felt even sorer when his brother William Rufus invaded Normandy and made Robert mortgage it to him. (Robert wanted to go off on crusade and needed the money.)

## William Rufus as king

William Rufus (1087–1100) was a pretty bad king – one historian called him the worst king England ever had – and he had a minister called Ranulph Flambard who was even worse. But, not to worry: William Rufus wasn't king for long because one day, while he was out hunting in the New Forest, a French knight called Walter Tyrrel shot him with an arrow.

Accident or contract killing? Tyrrel didn't hang around to say. Robert had a motive, but he also had an alibi because he was on crusade in Jerusalem. Prince Henry, however, was close by, and he immediately seized the treasury and got himself crowned king before Robert could claim the throne himself. Poor old Robert. Henry beat him at the Battle of Tinchebrai, took Normandy from him, and then locked him up. (Henry also captured our old friend Edgar the Ætheling (see earlier in this chapter), but you'll be pleased to hear that Henry let him go.)

## Henry Beauclerc (a.k.a. Henry 1) as king

Henry I did a lot of good work with the legal system, laying down that every-one was entitled to be protected by the law. He also sorted out the Investiture Contest with Archbishop Anselm (see the earlier section, 'The Church gets cross'). But his real concern was the succession. Too many kingdoms had fallen apart because the succession wasn't clear – England, for one – so Henry gave the issue a lot of thought. Ironically, his legacy was one of the worst succession crises in English history.

Henry married Edgar the Ætheling's niece, Edith (which is why, inciden-tally, the present royal family can claim, by a very, very windy route, to be descended from the Royal House of Wessex). Edith (also called Matilda, but don't ask me why, this story has enough Matildas in it as it is) had three chil-dren: Two boys, William and Richard, and a girl called, er, Matilda.

The two princes grew into handsome young pin-ups, and the future looked promising, until one terrible day in 1120 when Henry and his sons set out from Normandy to England in a couple of ships. Henry's ship crossed safely, but the *White Ship*, with both princes on board, hit a rock and sank – with no survivors. So Henry had to turn to his daughter, Matilda, to be the heir to his throne.

## Anarchy in the UK

Matilda was a widow: She'd been married to the Holy Roman Emperor, which is why she was known as the Empress Matilda. She remarried, to Count Geoffrey of Anjou, and had two sons.

Henry got all his barons together to swear loyalty to Matilda. But he knew that they didn't like the idea of having a queen, and they knew that he knew. And the situation wasn't helped by Henry quarrelling with Matilda's husband, Geoffrey, and specifically saying he was not to inherit the throne.

So when Henry finally died in 1135, lots of those barons who had sworn loy-ally to support Empress Matilda through thick and thin suddenly decided they preferred her cousin, Stephen. So Stephen, along with his wife, who was called – really sorry about this – Matilda, crossed over to London and got himself crowned.

But no daughter of Henry I and granddaughter of William the Conqueror was going to take that lying down. Had William given up just because Harold got himself crowned? Well, quite. And so (deep breath):

*Empress Matilda's husband Geoffrey of Anjou invades Normandy and Queen Matilda (Stephen's wife) attacks Empress Matilda's supporter Robert of Gloucester at Dover while King David of Scotland, who supports Empress Matilda, invades England to get some of his father Malcolm III's lands back, but David gets beaten at the Battle of the Standard; then Stephen attacks Empress Matilda and Geoffrey of Anjou at Arundel, but they escape, and the Earl of Chester takes Lincoln, and Stephen has to go and besiege it, but he gets captured, and the barons have to accept Geoffrey of Anjou as king until Geoffrey swaps Stephen for Robert of Gloucester, after which Geoffrey goes off to get Normandy and won't come back to help Empress Matilda, so their son Henry comes to lend her a hand, which is just as well since she's been thrown out of London and has had to take refuge in Oxford, but Stephen comes and besieges Oxford, and Empress Matilda has to escape down the walls over the river which – luckily for her – was frozen over, during which time the Welsh take the opportunity to chuck the Normans out, and King David of Scotland takes over a huge area of northern England – from Cumbria to Northumbria – and people say God and his angels slept, and Stephen is exhausted, and Matilda is exhausted, too, so exhausted, in fact, that she gives up her claim and goes to live in France, but her son Henry vows to jolly well make sure he is next in line when Stephen dies and WHAT DO YOU MEAN YOU STOPPED READING THIS AGES AGO?!*

Well, you can see why they called this period the Anarchy. Things didn't really calm down until Stephen died in 1154 and handed over to Empress Matilda's boy, Henry Plantagenet. But that's another story . . .

# Part III

# Who's in Charge Around Here? The Middle Ages

Oh for gosh sake, Richard! It's a couple of mice in the basement stealing grain. Quit making a crusade out of everything!

## In this part . . .

The medieval world revolved around its kings. This was the age of the Plantagenet dynasty, but others claimed the throne, too. The Plantagenets sought to conquer their neighbours in Ireland, Wales, and Scotland – and in France, which led to a prolonged era of warfare.

The Church also played a vital role in the medieval world, setting up monasteries and sending out friars to pray with the people and bring help to the poor, and continually vying for power with the king. And all the while the ordinary people were ploughing the land and grinding the corn and making the very wealth that gave these nobles their power. The ordinary people were at the bottom of the feudal system: They fought in the battles and they died of the plague.

# Chapter 8

# England Gets an Empire

### In This Chapter

▶ Discovering how England goes Angevin

▶ Describing Henry II's battles, with Becket, Strongbow, Wales, Ireland, Eleanor, Young Henry, Geoffrey, Richard, John – you get the idea

▶ Following the reigns of Henry's sons: King Richard the Lionheart and King John

▶ Messing things up with King John, angry lords, and the Magna Carta

*M*esdames et Messieurs, bienvenue à l'Angleterre au moyen âge! Or, to put it another way, welcome to merrie medieval England, a land of maypoles and castles and knights in armour, and a country and a time that are probably not quite what you thought – if you think of it as British history. Sure, this chapter tells you about people like Archbishop Thomas à Becket, who was murdered in his own cathedral; Richard the Lionheart, who fought it out with Saladin on the Third Crusade; and King John, who unwillingly agreed to the great charter of liberties known as Magna Carta. You can even find a glimpse here of Robin Hood and his Merry (sorry, Merrie) Men, and a discussion of how the kings of England first began acting on their claims to Ireland. But this isn't British history. For this chapter, my friends, we are well and truly in French history. These 'English' kings spoke French, they acted French, they had French names and French titles, they ate baguettes and smelt of garlic, and opened a new pharmacy every week. They *were* French. Now, don't get the wrong idea: England wasn't ruled by France, or even by the king of France – he should be so lucky. But Merrie England was neither quite so Merrie nor quite so English as it looked.

## Meet the Family

If you've seen the film *The Lion in Winter*, you'll have a good idea of the dysfunctional family that ruled England in the late twelfth century (some things don't change much, do they?) First, is the king, Henry II, who's tough, but easily hurt if you know how to do it. Next, is his wife, Eleanor of Aquitaine, who's more than a match for Henry, except that Henry's got her locked up and only lets her out for Christmas and birthdays. And finally, are the boys: Young Henry, who resents his dad and can't wait to be king; Geoffrey, who hates his parents for calling him that (well, did you ever hear of a King Geoffrey?); Richard, who is arrogant and impatient and thinks he's better than his elder brothers; and John, the daddy's boy who's nasty and horribly spoilt. These people are the Plantagenets.

If the name Plantagenets seems a bit of a mouthful, it's because the word is French. The name came from Henry's personal badge, which he wore in his hat and which happened to be a sprig of broom – *plante à genêt* in French.

The obvious question to ask is: How did England's royal family suddenly turn French? It's tempting to say it all started with the Normans (read Chapter 7 to find out about them), and in a way it did. But the real explanation lies in the Middle Age concept of lordship.

## Good lords! (Sacré bleu!)

Nowadays, if you own a bit of land, that plot's yours and you can do what you like with it, but in the Middle Ages, you held land from someone. Different names existed for the land that you held: A castle, and the farms around it, was known as a *manor* or an *honor*; any land you held in return for helping in war was known as a *Knight's Fee* or a *feof* – and some feofs could be pretty large.

If you traced all the lines of lordship back as far as they would go, everyone held their land from the king and had to pay him *homage*. Paying homage was a ceremony where you knelt before your lord, placed your hands between his, and promised to be his loyal subject while he promised to be your good lord and protect you from your enemies. Which system is fine when it involves, say, a French lord paying homage to the French king for a bit of French land, but when nobles started getting kingdoms for themselves, things got a bit complicated.

William the Conqueror was a king in England, but he still had to pay homage to the King of France for Normandy because it was a French duchy. In fact, the Normans regarded Normandy, not England, as the main bit of William's legacy, which is why Normandy went to his eldest boy, Robert, and his second son, William Rufus, got England. If the situation had stayed like that, England and Normandy would have gone their separate ways, but as Chapter 7 reveals, William Rufus got greedy and grabbed Normandy for himself, so from then on, if you became King of England, you got Normandy for free.

## England was nice, but France was home

When Henry I died, there was a lot of trouble (see Chapter 7 for the details). Henry wanted his daughter Matilda to succeed him, but a lot of the Norman barons didn't like the idea and supported her cousin, Stephen of Blois, instead. The main reason the Normans supported Stephen was the Normans weren't happy with the idea of having a queen. There was another reason as well: Everyone assumed that if you had a queen her husband would run the show, and they didn't like Matilda's husband one bit. Not so much because his name was Geoffrey, which it was, but because (are you ready for this?) he came from Anjou.

Now if you or I met someone from Anjou, we'd probably smile politely and say 'Really? How interesting,' and all the time we'd be thinking 'Where the heck is Anjou?' but the Normans really hated people from Anjou, or Angevins, as they were called.

Have a look at the map, and you'll see that Anjou is a fairly small French duchy, much smaller than its neighbours. Maybe that was the problem. The Normans couldn't stand the idea of being ruled by the duke of such a tiny little place. And while you're looking at the map, cast an eye over the other places nearby: Poitou and Maine and Touraine and Limousin, and all the other ones. Get to know them, because those were the places, unlike England, that really meant something to the Angevin Kings of England. England wasn't somehow less important, but these kings just felt completely at home in France. Because, well, they were French.

King Stephen won the great civil war with the Empress Matilda, but he didn't have any children to succeed him. That lack of an heir meant that Matilda's son Henry had the best claim to be next in line (in fact, if you really follow the family tree, Henry had the best claim to the throne whether Stephen had any children or not). Henry was young and ambitious, and no one but no one wanted any more fighting. So Stephen and Henry did a deal. Stephen could stay on the throne until he died (which, Henry rightly reckoned, wouldn't be long) and then Henry could become Henry II, King of England (and still Duke of Anjou, naturally).

# Henry II and the Angevin Empire

Being King of France in the twelfth century really can't have been much fun. That all the Dukes of Normandy had gone and become Kings of England was bad enough; now Henry, the Duke of Anjou, was doing the same thing. And of course Henry wouldn't just get England, he'd get Normandy, too. And he'd gone and married Eleanor of Aquitaine, one of the most powerful women in France. (And why was Henry able to marry Eleanor of Aquitaine in the first place? Because King Louis VII of France had gone and divorced her, that's why. Ouch!). Eleanor just happened to own both Aquitaine and Gascony, which meant, to put it bluntly, the whole of the south west of France right down to the Spanish border, and Aquitaine even stretched across to the border with Italy. So Henry, through marriage, got the whole of western France except Brittany. And he even got Brittany because his kid brother, as Duke of Brittany, owed him allegiance. In fact, when he became King, Henry would end up with almost as much of France as the King of France had.

## Eleanor of Aquitaine

Eleanor of Aquitaine was quite a lady. Like all her family, her first loyalty was to her lands and her rights and titles, and woe betide anyone who got in the way, even her husbands. Eleanor's first husband was Prince Louis, who soon became King Louis VII of France. Not a happy marriage. Louis was all very good and pious and really rather boring, whereas Eleanor was fiery and full of zip. Louis decided to go off on the Second Crusade – a silly idea because sequels are never as good as the original – and he was a hopeless soldier: He soon had the Second Crusade going nowhere fast. Eleanor started flirting with her uncle, the Count of Antioch, and when Louis refused to march and help him against the Saracens, she stormed out of the royal tent and demanded a divorce. While the Saracens cut her uncle's head off, Eleanor and Louis returned home in separate ships. Poor old Louis got shipwrecked on the way home (it just wasn't his day), and even the Pope couldn't patch things up with him and Eleanor. So Eleanor got her divorce and immediately made a beeline for young Henry of Anjou, who was going to be the next King of England – after all, not many women get to be Queen of France *and* Queen of England. Henry and Eleanor had plenty of children, but their marriage wasn't a happy one. They were both unfaithful, and soon Eleanor started scheming with her sons against Henry until he had her locked up. She didn't get out till he died. If you're into girl power, then you'll like Eleanor of Aquitaine. Just be thankful she wasn't your mother.

Then in 1154, King Stephen died. Henry simply dropped what he was doing (which just happened to be fighting Normans – you can see why they didn't like him) and went to London for his coronation. And what a list of titles he had: King of England, Duke of Normandy, Anjou, Maine, Touraine, Poitou, Aquitaine – shall I go on? Poor old Louis VII. All he was left with was Paris and all the boring bits up near Belgium.

## A trek to Toulouse

One of Henry's first moves as king was to try to get even more land in France. He fancied adding Toulouse to his collection, because it would look so much neater on the map and that way he would have all of the south and the west of France. With this additional land, he would be as powerful as King Louis. But Louis got to Toulouse first and dared Henry to do his worst. Henry tried, but Louis and the Count of Toulouse threw him out. Okay, thought Henry, Plan B. If I can't expand in France, I'll expand in England. Or rather, to be more precise, in Wales.

## The Big Match: England vs. Wales

The Normans had had a pretty good go at conquering Wales. They knew only too well that the Welsh had been very good at breaking into England in Anglo-Saxon times, and William the Conqueror didn't want that sort of thing happening again. So he had built a huge line of castles along the border with Wales and gave whole swathes of land to a set of tough Norman barons who became known as the *Marcher Lords*. ('Marcher' comes from 'march' or 'marches', meaning 'border'.) These Marcher Lords had pushed further into Wales until they controlled all of the south and east, and the Welsh princes were stuck up in the north, in what they called *Wallia Pura* or 'pure Wales'. During all the fighting in England between Stephen and Matilda (see the earlier section, 'England was nice, but France was home'), the Welsh had managed to get some of their lands back off the Marcher Lords, but now the Norman Marchers were hoping that Henry II would give them the green light to hit back. He did.

Henry was no fool. He didn't want any of these Marcher Lords doing to him what he had done to Louis VII, so he came to Wales to sort things out himself: He would decide who got what, which meant, in effect, that everything went to him. The Welsh princes had to give the Marcher Lords their lands back and recognise that Henry ruled in north Wales. All in all, things were going very satisfactorily for Henry, when he blew it. Absolutely blew it.

Henry decided to do for Wales what William the Conqueror had done for England: Declare himself overlord and require everyone to come and pay him homage. Well! The Welsh may have lost some battles, but they were not about to accept that Henry had the right to the whole country. So just when Henry was drawing up plans for a statue of himself trampling on a set of Welsh princes and eating a leek, his messengers brought news that he had a full-scale war on his hands – and he was losing. Henry set off again, but this time, the campaign was much harder. It rained like there was no tomorrow, and Henry just seems to have decided that conquering Wales himself wasn't worth the trouble. He was a top-rank European monarch, don't forget: He had better things to do. So he left the Welsh and the Marchers to it, and they carried on hammer and tongs for a good few years, though a number of the Marchers were rather wishing they'd tried taking over somewhere a bit easier. And then someone suggested, Have you thought of Ireland?

## Bad news for Ireland

The Pope was losing patience with the Irish because they were still doing things their way, celebrating Easter at the wrong time and generally not going along with the rest of the Church (this problem went back a long way. See Chapter 6 to find out how it had all started). Pope Adrian IV, formerly Nicholas Breakspear, an Englishman, decided to settle the matter once and for all, so he wrote a special papal order known as a *bull* saying that if Henry II wanted to go over to Ireland to sort things out, he would have the full backing of the Pope. Hint, hint. But Henry didn't take the hint. He wasn't interested in taking on a whole new war. And then one day, an Irish king turned up at Henry's court in France, and everything changed.

### Even worse news for Ireland: a king with a grudge

Dermot (or Diarmait Mac Murchada to give him his full Gaelic name) was the King of Leinster; or rather the ex-King of Leinster, because he'd run off with another king's wife, and Rory, High King of Ireland, had thrown him out. Now Dermot wanted Henry II to help him get his own back. (Dermot was no fool: The Normans and Angevins fought as great knights in armour, whereas the Irish were still playing around with slings and stones.) Henry was interested – he hadn't forgotten the Pope's letter – but he didn't have the time to invade Ireland himself. On the other hand, some of those Norman Marcher Lords from Wales might be interested (see the earlier section 'The Big Match: England vs. Wales'). They were. A great army of them set off for Ireland, headed by the Earl of Pembroke, Richard FitzGilbert de Clare, known to his friends, enemies, and to history as Strongbow.

Everything about the invasion went according to plan. The Irish hadn't faced such an invasion since the Vikings (see Chapter 6 for more about that little problem). The Normans conquered Leinster, Waterford, Wexford, and Dublin. Strongbow married Dermot's daughter, and when Dermot died Strongbow became King of Leinster in his place. And that little detail rang alarm bells in Henry II's mind back at base.

### Look out! Here comes Henry

A nobleman who owes you homage suddenly becoming a king in his own right? Remind you of anyone? The scenario certainly reminded Henry II – of himself! – and he wasn't going to stand by while Strongbow declared independence, or even war. So Henry got a huge army together, raced over to Dublin, and demanded to see Strongbow. But if Henry was expecting trouble, for once he got a pleasant surprise. Strongbow knew there was no point in fighting Henry: The two men reached a deal. Strongbow would hand most of the important parts of Ireland over to Henry and stay on as Henry's Keeper or Guardian of Ireland, a Governor-General, if you like. And Strongbow did like. He died a very powerful man. He's buried in Christchurch Cathedral in Dublin.

## All (fairly) quiet on the Scottish front

Now you may be expecting that, along with campaigns in Wales and Ireland, the Anglo-Normans would've launched some sort of campaign in Scotland, but just for once you'd be wrong. Scottish King Malcolm Canmore and his sons had been redrafting Scotland more along English lines (see Chapter 7 to find out why), and the next Scottish kings weren't looking to change tack. Malcolm's youngest son, David I, had grown up in England at Henry I's court, and he even held an English title, as Earl of Huntingdon (for which, of course, he had to pay homage to the King of England). David was very loyal to Henry I. He supported Matilda in the civil war, and it was he who first knighted her son, Henry of Anjou. In fact, David did pretty well out of the anarchy in England. He got Cumbria and Northumberland to add to his Huntingdon title, and he was on very good terms with the Angevins when they finally came to the throne. He even started getting Anglo-Normans, like the de Bruces, the Comyns, and the Stewards (yes, they'll be the Stuarts in years to come), to move up to Scotland and serve him.

If you're feeling let down because there wasn't more mutual bashing between the Scots and the English, look at the situation from David I's point of view. Peace with England meant that he could get a proper grip on Scotland. His new Anglo-Norman barons built strong castles, and David invited some of the most important religious orders to build monasteries in Scotland. Thanks to David, Scotland got a proper money system for the first time, which helped trade to flourish. If Scotland developed as an independent kingdom, a lot of it was down to the wise rule of King David I.

The situation couldn't last, of course. The next King of Scotland was a wee lad called Malcolm – Malcolm IV to be precise, but he's known in the books as Malcolm the Maiden because he never married, and he had no children. Henry II reckoned the time had come to take Northumberland and Cumbria back, so he did and poor little Malcolm had to agree to it. When Malcolm died, his brother William 'the Lion' became king. William decided it was time to remind Henry II that Kings of Scotland couldn't be pushed around, but unfortunately for him, Henry showed that they could. Here's what happened. When Henry's sons rose in revolt against him (see the later section 'Royal Families and How to Survive Them' for details), William thought joining in would be a good idea. Bad mistake. Henry won, William got taken prisoner, and Henry only let him go when William agreed to recognise Henry as his overlord and to do him homage, not just for Huntingdon, but for Scotland itself. Scotland had become an English feof.

## Henry the lawgiver

You'll be pleased to hear that Henry didn't spend all his time as king fighting. Henry completely revamped the English legal system. Royal justices went travelling round, and instead of having to wait for the victim or the victim's family to bring a case, a special Jury of Presentment drawn from local people could accuse someone. The Jury of Presentment is the origin of the Grand Jury system in the USA.

Henry also brought in new methods of dealing with cases quickly, with the whole idea being to strengthen his authority over his subjects. One more area of law that Henry didn't control was that in the Church. But Henry had plans for the Church, and he knew just the right man to carry them out.

# Murder in the Cathedral

Every ruler in Christendom had a problem with the Church, not just Kings of England, and certainly not just Henry II. The Holy Roman Emperor once even had to kneel in the mud and the snow for two days before the Pope would agree to see him.

In England, the big problem was the law. As things stood, if anyone within the Church got arrested (even the lowest ranking scribe) that person could claim the right to go before a Church court instead of a royal court. A Church court would be more likely to let the offender off with a caution, and because Church courts couldn't impose the death penalty, a criminous clerk, as these people were called, could quite literally get away with murder. When Henry tried to get the Church to change the rules on criminous clerks, the Church threw up its hands in horror and said he was trying to take away its holy and ancient privileges. So when the Archbishop of Canterbury died, Henry decided it was time to put someone more biddable in charge. He chose Thomas à Becket.

Becket was one of those people who really stood on ceremony. He'd been Henry's legal adviser and had served as Henry's Chancellor, the most important post under the king. Becket was good, but boy, did he insist on everything he was entitled to. When Becket went over to France on a mission, the French had never seen anything like it: Becket had so many servants and horses and fine rich clothes, you'd think he was a pharoah. But, of course, the message was this: If you think *this* is impressive, wait till you see my master. So Henry must have thought using Becket to bring the Church to heel was a stroke of genius.

## Henry's cunning plan . . . doesn't work

Perhaps Henry should have guessed what would happen, but he wasn't the only one who got caught out. Once Becket became Archbishop, he changed completely. If he was going to be a churchman, he was going to *be* a churchman. He stopped giving lavish parties and started praying regularly. Underneath his archbishop's robes, he wore a rough hair shirt that scratched his flesh raw. And he insisted on his rights. This insistence was a big problem because Henry was seriously expecting Thomas à Becket to give up the Church's ancient rights of hearing its own legal cases.

Henry tried to reduce the Church's power. He got the Church leaders together for a big meeting at Clarendon, and they drew up a new set of rules called the *Constitutions of Clarendon*. The most important bit said the following:

- ✔ Any clerks charged or accused of anything are to be summoned by the King's justice (the *King's* justice, note, not the Church's).

- ✔ The King's (not the Church's) court shall decide which cases it would hear and which cases should go to the Church courts.

- ✔ The King's justice shall keep an eye on what the Church courts are doing.

- ✔ If the clerk confesses or is convicted, the Church ought not to protect him further (bad luck, criminous clerks, your happy days are over).

At first, the bishops didn't think they should sign this document, but, rather surprisingly, Becket said they should, so they did. Then Becket seemed to change his mind: He declared that signing up to the Constitutions of Clarendon had been a great sin, and that meant the Pope decided not to sign them either. Henry was no further forward than he had been at the beginning, but now he was very angry. No one, repeat no one, undermined Henry II and got away with it. Henry came up with a whole set of charges against Becket, most of which were pretty obviously made up. Becket got up in his full canonical robes, complete with his archbishop's processional cross, declared the king had no right to try an archbishop – and promptly slipped away to France. Becket was a brave man, but he was no fool!

## *Recipe for Instant Martyr*

Henry had a problem. You simply couldn't carry on in the twelfth century in open dispute with the Church. True, Becket could be impossible, and many of his fellow bishops couldn't stand him, but he was the Archbishop of Canterbury, and Henry had selected him. When all was said and done, Becket was defending the Church. So Henry had to find a compromise. Eventually Henry and Becket met up in France. The meeting was surprisingly congenial. The two men just forgot all their quarrels and arguments and let their friendship flow. Tears poured, and Henry said he was sorry, and Becket said he was sorry, and Henry said Becket could come home, and Becket said he would come home, and no doubt violins played in the background. And then Becket got back to England – and immediately excommunicated the Archbishop of York and everyone else who had supported the king while he'd been away.

Henry had had enough. 'Will no one rid me of this turbulent priest!' he roared. Of course, he didn't really mean it, but a group of four knights decided to take Henry at his word. They slipped over to England, went fully armed into Canterbury Cathedral, and tried to drag Becket away. When he resisted, they hacked him to pieces.

## St Thomas à Becket

Who won, Henry or Becket? Henry, you may think, since the man who had plagued him was now gone. But if you're after hearts and minds, then Becket won hands down. Priests do get murdered, but killing an archbishop in his own cathedral was going way too far, even for the twelfth century. Henry had to pay a harsh penance: He was stripped naked while the monks of Canterbury whipped him mercilessly. Becket became St Thomas of Canterbury, and his shrine in Canterbury Cathedral became one of the most popular places of pilgrimage in England. Chaucer's pilgrims in Canterbury Tales were all heading there, nearly two hundred years later.

English kings weren't very fond of St Thomas, however. He had defied the king, and they didn't want other people getting ideas. Henry VIII had Becket's shrine destroyed and told everyone to scratch out St Thomas's face from any picture of him they may have in their local churches. You can still see these defaced Beckets today. And to add real insult to injury, the French playwright Jean Anouilh wrote a play about Becket, which has him as a Saxon. That misnomer would really have had him spinning inside his shrine!

# *Royal Families and How to Survive Them*

As if fighting the Welsh and the Irish, trying to work out a legal system, run the biggest empire in western Europe, and deal with the most difficult Archbishop of Canterbury in history wasn't enough, Henry II ended up fighting his own family. Eleanor was angry because of all Henry's affairs, especially the really serious one with 'fair Rosamund', the real love of his life. (Henry was considering divorcing Eleanor so he could marry Rosamund, which would have meant that Eleanor had been married to the Kings of France and England and lost both of them.) Another problem was Henry's will. In it, Henry said Young Henry was to get England, Normandy, and Anjou; Aquitaine was to go to Richard (not a bad second prize); Geoffrey was getting Brittany (very acceptable); and John 'Lackland' was getting Ireland. John wasn't overjoyed, and neither were the Irish. Henry even had Young Henry crowned king while he was still alive, just in case anyone was thinking of trying to seize the throne ('Seize the throne? Moi?' said Richard, Geoffrey, and John all together). Young Henry's coronation caused more trouble with Becket, because the Archbishop of York did the crowning and Becket thought he should have done it. But the crowning also created even more trouble with Young Henry, because he was getting impatient for his old man to hurry up and die. So the battles began:

✔ **Henry vs. Young Henry, Round One:** Young Henry staged a rebellion against his father. Practically the whole family, except John, joined in, including Eleanor. Even King William the Lion of Scotland joined in. This involvement didn't do any of them any good. Henry won the war, captured Eleanor and William (Eleanor was trying to escape dressed as a man), made William submit (see the earlier section 'All (fairly) quiet on the Scottish front' for details), and locked Eleanor up. Then he met the boys. Following lots of tears and manly hugs, Henry agreed to give the boys a bit more pocket money. So that was all right then.

✔ **Henry vs. Young Henry, Round Two:** Young Henry was getting into debt, and his dad refused to bail him out. So Young Henry started plotting another rebellion. This time Richard stuck by his dad, but Geoffrey joined in and so did the new King of France, Philip Augustus. Henry won again (You win again, as the Bee Gees would say!), and Young Henry had to run away. And he died. Dysentery. Very sad (and messy).

Henry now had to do some re-jigging of his will. Geoffrey could keep Brittany, but Henry wanted Richard to give up Aquitaine to John (because, duh, Richard was going to be getting England and Normandy and Anjou – everything Young Henry had been down for, in fact). But Richard had become very attached to Aquitaine (he was very close to his mum), and he decided he didn't trust his father. So that led to the battle between Henry and Richard (see the next bullet item).

✔ **Henry vs. Richard:** Richard got together with the French king, Philip Augustus, and ambushed Henry after a peace conference to try to sort everything out. Henry escaped to Anjou (his home), but then came the bad news. John had joined in the rebellion. John! Henry's favourite, the one he had always felt closest to. And the whole quarrel had started because he was trying to get John some land. It broke Henry's heart. And killed him.

# Richard 1 – the Lion King

A rather splendid statue of Richard I stands outside the Houses of Parliament, though the reason for it isn't very clear. Richard was a very good example of an Angevin who was French first, second, and last. The land he loved was Aquitaine, and as far as he was concerned, England existed only to help finance the Third Crusade.

## A-crusading we will go

Richard had promised his father to go on crusade, and this was one filial promise he kept. He set off with his old friend-rival King Philip Augustus and the rather alarming German Emperor, Frederick Barbarossa. The three kings soon fell out (literally in Barbarossa's case – he fell into a river and drowned), and Philip Augustus ended up turning round and going home. Richard proved a very effective Crusader and a fearsome fighter – he wasn't called *Coeur de Lion* ('Lionheart') for nothing. He took on Saladin, the formidable Kurdish Sultan who was leading the Muslims in Syria and the Holy Land, and beat him at the Battle of Arsuf. Saladin recognised Richard as a very worthy enemy.

## Christians and Muslims

The Crusades were *not* about trying to kill as many Muslims as possible (though the Crusaders did try that with Jews). Nor were they a sort of early version of European imperialism, even though the Crusaders did set up kingdoms in the Holy Land. People didn't get rich by crusading; in fact, it often ruined them. Crusading was about one thing and one thing only: Jerusalem. Nothing else mattered. Christian Europe believed that it was a scandal that Jerusalem should be in Muslim hands. They were also badly scared by the speed with which the Turks were advancing into Europe. Both sides believed they were fighting in God's cosmic battle of Good and Evil, and that they'd get their reward in heaven. The First Crusade did retake Jerusalem and set up Christian kingdoms, but the Turks recovered and took back one of the kingdoms, which is why a Second Crusade was necessary. The Second Crusade was a complete shambles, and then Saladin moved in for the kill: He destroyed the Latin Kingdom of Jerusalem and took back the Holy City. Hence, the Third Crusade was needed. Richard won back a lot of the land Saladin had taken, including the port of Acre, but he didn't get Jerusalem. (And neither did the Fourth Crusade.)

But Richard didn't manage to take Jerusalem, and in the end doing that was all that counted. And then he heard about what John was up to back in England, so he decided the time had come to head home. (For more about the Crusades, see *European History For Dummies* (Wiley)).

## A king's ransom

Richard had made a lot of enemies in the Holy Land. He'd quarrelled with Philip Augustus, been very short with the Duke of Austria, and even threw his banner off the walls of Acre in his temper. But you know what they say: Don't kick people on the way up; you may meet them on the way down.

When Philip Augustus got home, he quickly got in touch with Prince John to see if the two of them couldn't get rid of Richard and put John on the throne. Philip Augustus also started taking some of Richard's lands in France. 'What?!' said Richard when he heard all this, and he set off home at once. But he got shipwrecked in Italy and decided to take a short cut home through, er, Austria. Bad idea.

The Duke of Austria's men (yes, the one Richard had had a quarrel with) caught him and locked him up. The Duke handed Richard over to his boss, the Holy Roman Emperor. And the Emperor started cutting letters out of illustrated manuscripts for a ransom note to send to London: 'WE HAVE GOT HIM. PAY 100,000 MARKS IN USED NOTES.'

If John had been making the decisions, Richard would probably have rotted in jail, but Richard was Eleanor's favourite, and she wasn't allowing that to happen. She jacked up everyone's taxes to pay the ransom. John was going to have to act fast if he wanted to take power before Richard got home, and he wasn't quite fast enough. Richard came home. John said he was very sorry and that he would never try to usurp the throne again, and Richard said, 'That's Okay, kid. I know Philip Augustus was really to blame,' and he set off back over the Channel to deal with him. And deal with Philip he did.

Richard knocked Philip's army into the middle of next week, crushed the rebels Philip had been encouraging down in Aquitaine, linked up with the Holy Roman Emperor (amazing how quickly these guys forgave and forgot!), and launched Operation Take Over The Rest Of France And Do Something Very Nasty To King Philip Augustus. This operation was going very well when disaster struck in the form of a crossbow bolt. It hit Richard in the shoulder and the wound turned septic. No penicillin in those days. If a cut turned septic, you died. Lionhearts were no exception.

# King John

John shouldn't actually have been king at all. When Richard died, the next in line was Geoffrey's little boy, Arthur of Brittany, but when did that sort of thing ever count? John seized the throne, had Arthur locked up, and, after a little while, had him murdered as well, just to be on the safe side. And then John's troubles really began.

## The Pope goes one up

John got into an even greater mess with the Church than his father had with Becket (refer to the section 'Murder in the Cathedral', earlier in this chapter). The lesson John learned from the Becket business was to make very sure you got the right archbishop, and as far as he was concerned, that meant not having one foisted on him by the Pope. So when the Pope tried to choose a new archbishop, John refused to accept him, even though the man the Pope had chosen was actually very good. 'All right,' said the Pope, 'In that case I'm putting England under Interdict.' An Interdict is an order barring people from the sacraments of the Church – think of it as a complete strike by the English Church. No masses, no confessions, no burials, no baptisms, no sins forgiven, no people going to heaven, nothing. For a deeply God-fearing age, this prospect was terrifying. John had to give way and accept the archbishop.

## Er, I seem to have lost my empire

Next, John made a mess in France. Philip Augustus was scared of Richard, but he wasn't scared of John. The French started attacking John's Angevin and Norman lands, and even the Holy Roman Emperor couldn't help him.

Philip beat the Emperor in a huge battle at a place called Bouvines, and the upshot was that John lost Anjou, Poitou, and Normandy – and he was lucky not to lose his mum's lands in Aquitaine. For once, John's Anglo-Norman barons and the Angevin barons all agreed on one thing: King John was a disaster. Something had to be done.

## Magna Carta

The Anglo-Normans and Angevin lords made John agree to Magna Carta, the Great Charter of English liberties that got the British and Americans so excited many years later. No, the Magna Carta didn't make the world safe for democracy, but don't get too cynical. This charter wasn't just about rights for the rich either. The barons thought John had been treading on their rights and privileges too much. He needed reining in, and certain things, like the rights of the Church, needed to be clarified on paper. The Magna Carta was about good lordship. It lays down certain rights that a good lord would recognise, like the right only to be taxed by consent and the right to proper justice.

John agreed to the Magna Carta because he had to, but he wasn't going to keep to it if he could avoid doing so. He had no trouble persuading the Pope to declare Magna Carta null and void (because it went against the rights of kings). So the barons had to decide what to do with him. John had to go, and the barons invited the French over to help get rid of him. Suddenly everything was chaos. French soldiers and barons' soldiers and John's soldiers were involved. When John tried to take a short cut across a tricky bit of seaway called the Wash, all his baggage was washed away, and in the end he had just had enough. He ate too many peaches in cider and died. And the moral of this story is: Go easy on peaches in cider.

## Robin Hood

Between the time that Richard was captured in Austria and returned to England, Robin Hood usually puts in an appearance. First you get all those jolly scenes with Little John and Will Scarlet tricking the Sheriff's men, and Friar Tuck stuffing his face; then it's Robin entering archery contests in disguise and taking First Prize ('Who are you, sirrah, that hath shot so well?') before rescuing whichever poor girl the Sheriff or Sir Guy of Gisborne is due to marry; until at the end you get the Sheriff of Nottingham in cahoots with Prince John, and King Richard coming back in disguise and finding his most loyal subjects all living in the middle of Sherwood Forest and wearing bad tights. Great stories, and people did tell them in the Middle Ages, but sadly not until a lot later.

People did exist with names that may be the basis for 'Robin Hood', but none of them seems to have lived as an outlaw robbing innocent travellers in Sherwood Forest, Barnsdale Forest, or any of the other forests that claim to have had Robin Hood in them. Sorry, but you didn't really expect anything else, did you?

# Chapter 9

# A Right Royal Time – the Medieval Realms of Britain

*In This Chapter*

▶ Getting a parliament: England

▶ Fighting for, gaining, and losing independence: Wales and Scotland

▶ Edward II gets sacked – by his queen and her lover

▶ Cutting the apron strings and cutting loose: Edward III launches the Hundred Years War

▶ Following the War of the Roses: The uncivil civil war

This chapter marks the beginning of the High Middle Ages in Britain, a time when knights were bold, all those magnificent gothic cathedrals went up, and people built castles that began to look the way they do in fairy tales. During this period, the Kings of England conquered Wales and very nearly conquered Scotland. The High Middle Ages also saw battles in France and in England: The Hundred Years War, which didn't really last 100 years, and the Wars of the Roses, which had absolutely nothing to do with gardening.

Now, you can easily look at this period and try to spot 'your' nation – be it England, Scotland, Ireland, or Wales – asserting itself. Years later, Shakespeare saw this period as the time when England gradually sorted itself out so that, by the time Henry Tudor killed Richard III at Bosworth, it was ready to be a great nation under the Tudors – which, of course, just happens to be when Shakespeare was living. Nowadays, the Welsh take pride in how Llewellyn and Owain Glyn Dŵr (he's Owen Glendower to everyone else) resisted the wicked English, and the Scots learn about Bannockburn (the battle that routed the English and sent them packing), and watch endless repeats of *Braveheart*.

Although simplistic, these interpretations aren't entirely wrong. By the end of this period you can talk about England being more 'English' than it had ever been, and that includes the king. And the Scots, Welsh, and Irish all issued documents declaring that they were (or ought to be) nations free from foreign (that is, English) rule.

# Basic Background Info

Let's get a grip on the line-up before play begins.

## England – the French connection

French kings had ruled England since William the Conqueror won at Hastings in 1066 (see Chapter 7 to find out what that was all about). Henry II had made England part of a huge French-based empire (for more on this, you need Chapter 8) but his son King John had lost most of it. John's son, Henry III, was only a baby when he came to the throne, and wasn't a very promising youth.

The Kings of England had to pay homage to the Kings of France for the French lands they still held in Aquitaine and also still had to promise to be their loyal subjects. And these not-very-English kings often brought other French nobles over to England, usually Gascons from Aquitaine, to act as advisers and enforcers – a move that didn't go down well with the 'English' nobles who were already here.

## Who was ruling what?

In the meantime, things had progressed in Scotland, Wales, and Ireland:

- **Scotland:** Scotland was separate from England and had even ruled part of northern England for a time. Unfortunately, the Scots king, William 'the Lion', took the wrong side in a family rebellion against the English king, Henry II (more details in Chapter 8), so the Scots had to give up their lands in the north of England and accept the Kings of England as their overlords.

- **Wales:** Although Henry II had declared himself overlord of Wales (see Chapter 8), the Welsh made it so hot for Henry II's men that Henry's men went and invaded Ireland to give themselves a break. The Anglo-Norman Marcher Lords (lords from the Welsh borders) ruled the south and west, but the Welsh ruled the north, and they wanted the Marchers out. So Prince Llewellyn the Great's grandson, Llewellyn (it saved on name tags) began to gear up for war. Watch this space.

- **Ireland:** Richard de Clare ('Strongbow') and his Anglo-Norman chums invaded Ireland back in 1170 (see Chapter 8) and had stuck around. They stayed mostly around Dublin and along the west coast. The rest of Ireland was too wet and boggy for them, and you couldn't get a decent cup of tea for love nor money, so the Anglo-Normans built a big protective wall called the Pale round their bits of Ireland and they sat tight behind that. (They controlled Ireland from behind the Pale for the next six hundred years.)

# Simon Says 'Make a Parliament, Henry!'

Meet Simon de Montfort. He's French, he's the Earl of Leicester, and he's important. He came over to England to claim his earldom, and King Henry III took an instant liking to him. The English barons were less impressed. They thought, 'Here's another of Henry III's poncy French favourites,' before forcing Henry to send Simon de Montfort into exile. Henry allowed Simon to come back, but when he returned, Simon didn't want to be the king's favourite any more. This time, he started making friends among the barons. He listened to all their grumbles about Henry's favourites and his alarming habit of losing battles. About this time, Henry began to demand a lot of money so that he could make his younger son King of Sicily. The barons reckoned that, if Henry wanted money, he was going to have to give something in return. Simon became their spokesman.

What the barons wanted – demanded, even – was a parliament. They laid their demands out in a document called the *Provisions of Oxford* (not a marmalade shop, though it sounds like one). The Provisions stated that Henry would have to agree to summon a parliament consisting of the following:

- **The Church:** Everyone needed the Church behind them.
- **The Nobles:** Well, naturally.
- **The Commons:** That's people who weren't royal or lords or churchmen but were just plain folks. You and me.

That last bit was Simon's idea. He suggested that each town and each shire or county should send two people to represent the ordinary, or common, folk.

Henry had to go along with the Provisions of Oxford, but he didn't like it. He got the Pope to declare the Provisions invalid (the Pope had done that with the Magna Carta, too, as you can see in Chapter 8), and as soon as he could, Henry III tore up the Provisions of Oxford. That action meant war! At the Battle of Lewes, Simon de Montfort captured Henry and his son Prince Edward. Sounds good for Simon, but unless you're planning to take the throne yourself, which Simon wasn't, capturing your king is tricky. You can't keep him locked up, but if you let him go, what will he do? Simon was saved from making a decision, however, because Prince Edward escaped, gathered an army, and counter-attacked. Seconds out, Round Two: The Battle of Evesham. Simon de Montfort was beaten. And killed.

## Order, order!

Don't get too excited about these medieval parliaments. To start with, they're not actually the oldest parliaments in the world – that honour goes to the Isle of Man parliament, Tynwald, which dates back to Viking times (head to Chapter 6 for that era in British history). In the early parliaments, barons mostly just met to discuss important decisions, usually legal disputes – parliament can still act as a court to this day.

You didn't have to call the Commons to a parliament, and they often didn't. But Simon de Montfort recognised that having the Commons on your side could be a very good idea, especially if you were going to war with the king. Edward I found the same idea true when he needed money for his wars. But the Commons tended to want to talk about other things as well as money, so gradually parliament began to become more important.

# *I'm the King of the Castles: Edward 1*

After all the excitement of dealing with Simon de Montfort, Henry III was a nervous wreck and went into retirement. Henry's son Prince Edward took over as king. When Henry finally died (he had one of the longest reigns in British history, and no one's ever heard of him), Edward became King Edward I. (He used the number to distinguish himself from all those Saxon King Edwards). Edward I didn't close parliament down, but he stopped it from trying to run the whole kingdom. Edward had other enemies in his sights: The Welsh.

## *War for Wales*

While Henry III was battling the creation of a parliament out with Simon de Montfort (refer to the earlier section 'Simon Says "Make a Parliament, Henry!"'), Prince Llewellyn of Wales was playing his favourite game, 'Let's Kick the King of England':

- ✔ **When Henry III invaded Wales he was so useless that Llewellyn ran rings round him,** and even the Marcher Lords thought they'd be better off on their own.

- ✔ **Then Llewellyn went off and joined in with Simon de Montfort's rebellion,** just so he could see the look on Henry III's face.

- ✔ **Then Llewellyn went home and attacked the Marchers,** so that, by the time Edward I came to the throne, the only bits of Wales Llewellyn didn't control weren't worth controlling.

Llewellyn's relationship with Edward I wasn't any less fractious than his relationship with Edward's father had been. When Edward I told Llewellyn to come to Westminster for his coronation and to pay him homage, Llewellyn told Edward to go boil his head. Five times! You didn't do that to Edward I. Edward got together a vast army and headed for Wales. The Welsh fought back. Edward built huge castles to keep them down; The Welsh captured the castles. Edward sent more troops; Llewellyn beat them. Then the troops beat Llewellyn. The Welsh started raiding and ambushing, Llewellyn was killed by an English soldier who probably didn't know who he was, and that was the end. The revolt petered out, and the *Statute of Rhuddlan* was drawn up. This statute said that English law now applied in Wales. Edward gave the Welsh a 'Prince of Wales' who, he promised, could speak no English. Ho ho. This prince was Edward's infant son who couldn't speak anything except gurgle. No one was fooled: Edward I was in charge now, and he had all those castles to prove it.

## It's hammer time: Scotland

Saying that next it was Scotland's turn to fall under English rule would be nice and neat, but the truth is, Edward wasn't actually planning to invade Scotland. The Scots simply ran out of monarchs. King Alexander III's children had all died, and Alexander's horse fell over a cliff (with King Alexander on it). The only person left was Alexander's little granddaughter who lived in Norway. Poor thing: She died on the ship en route to England to marry Edward I's son. The Scots call her 'The Maid of Norway', which is nice, but it didn't hide the fact that they now had a major problem. Who was to rule them?

Job vacant: King of Scotland. Edward said he would settle Scotland's monarch problem. He sifted through 13 applicants and boiled the possibles down to two: Robert the Bruce, one of those Anglo-Norman lords whose families had been settling down in Scotland, and John de Balliol, an English nobleman. And the winner was…John de Balliol. Edward was hoping that Balliol would be under his thumb so that Edward would end up controlling Scotland on the cheap. Unfortunately for Edward, Balliol wouldn't play ball. When Edward planned a war with France and told Balliol to help, Balliol not only refused, he signed a treaty with the French. Then Scots started raiding northern England.

'Right,' said Edward fiercely, 'so that's how you want to play it, is it?' Edward got his army together and marched north. He took every Scottish castle he came to, and in the end he took Balliol, too. Balliol had to take off his crown and his entire royal bits and bobs and hand them over to Edward. It was the Tower of London for Balliol; it looked like another kingdom for Edward I.

---

# What's in a name?

The Scots call him Robert the Bruce but he would have called himself by the French form of his name, Robert le Bruce. Bruce was of pure-blooded French stock. He was descended from Robert de Bréaux, one of the Norman barons who came over to England with William the Conqueror in 1066 (read more about that in Chapter 7). We'll call him Robert the Bruce, since that's the name by which he's known to history, but don't forget he was every inch a French nobleman by upbringing – he certainly never forgot it.

---

### William Wallace's grand day out

But just when Edward seemed to have won in Scotland, a low-ranking Scottish nobleman called William Wallace (who looked nothing like Mel Gibson and certainly wouldn't have painted his face blue) gathered the Scots together, murdered some English officials, and ambushed the English at Stirling Bridge. The ambush was a famous victory but it spelled disaster for the victors. Edward stormed back, defeated Wallace in open battle the next year, captured him, had him hanged, drawn, and quartered, and took over Scotland himself. He also removed the sacred coronation Stone of Destiny and sent it down to London to sit under his own coronation throne in Westminster Abbey. No wonder they called Edward I the 'Hammer of the Scots'.

### Robert the Bruce declares himself Robert 1 of Scotland

Edward went home and left two guardians to govern Scotland while he was away. One was a Scottish nobleman called John Comyn; the other was Robert the Bruce, the runner-up to John de Balliol in the Who's Going to be King of Scotland stakes. As soon as Edward's back was turned, Bruce struck. Literally. He stabbed Comyn and declared himself King Robert I of Scotland. And he dared King Edward I of England to do his worst. Edward took the challenge, marched north (again!) – and died. That death changed everything.

### The Battle of Bannockburn . . .

Edward I's son, Edward II (nice and easy to remember) could not have been more different from his father. Edward II couldn't lead an army for toffee. When he finally got round to invading Scotland in 1314, he walked straight into the trap Robert the Bruce had laid for him at Bannockburn. It was total victory for the Scots. Edward II only just escaped being captured himself. Robert the Bruce was king and Scotland was free.

### . . . Is not quite the end of the story

It's easy to think of Bannockburn as a sort of Scottish Yorktown (see Chapter 17 to find out what happened at Yorktown). The English go home, the credits roll, 'The End'. Only Bannockburn wasn't the end. Now that the Scots were clearly a strong, independent nation, they started acting like one – they invaded Ireland. Robert the Bruce's brother Edward declared himself King of Ireland. The Scots tried to claim the invasion was all in the cause of Celtic solidarity, but the Irish weren't fooled – and neither were the Anglo-Norman barons who actually ruled Ireland (see Chapter 8 for more about them). The Scots destroyed the Irish people's already sparse crops, which plunged them into famine, and marched on Dublin. The people of Dublin set the town ablaze rather than hand it over to the Scots and in 1318 the Anglo-Normans defeated Edward the Bruce in battle, cut off his head, and sent it to Edward II of England.

Then things started collapsing in Scotland itself. The new king, Robert the Bruce's son David II, was no fighter. The English invaded Scotland and David II fled to France. Then the English invaded France and David got himself captured. He made a deal with the English: They let him go and in return he agreed to hand Scotland over to them when he died. The result was as if Bannockburn had never been fought.

### An initial glimpse of the Stewarts

While David II was away in France, one of the leading Scottish noble families acted as *stewards* of the kingdom, which is why they came to be called *Stewarts* (and later *Stuarts*). Sadly, these early Stewart kings were a fairly sorry lot:

- **Robert III (1390–1406):** Took over after David II was captured but never really controlled the country.
- **James I (1406–37):** Murdered by his own nobles.
- **James II (1437–60):** Invaded England but was killed by an exploding (Scottish) cannon.
- **James III (1460–88):** Killed in battle against his own nobles.

## Declarations of Independence

In 1320, six years after Bannockburn, King Robert I decided to try to strengthen his newly independent kingdom. He got some Scottish churchmen at Arbroath Abbey to draw up the Declaration of Arbroath addressed to the Pope, asking him to recognise Scotland as an independent nation. It was quite a document. 'As long as but a hundred of us remain alive,' it said, 'never will we on any conditions be brought under English rule.' Then it added that the Scots were fighting for freedom, 'which no honest man gives up but with life itself'. The Irish and the Welsh came up with similar documents. These documents weren't just an expression of anti-English feeling. These people were beginning to think of themselves as nations. Mind you, that didn't stop the English controlling them.

# *You Say You Want a (Palace) Revolution: Edward II*

Piers Gaveston was a favourite of Edward II of England (probably he and Edward II were lovers). Gaveston was another of those cocky characters stepping off the boat from Aquitaine and looking down their noses at the locals; the nobles couldn't stand him. So began a series of palace revolutions, with everyone tussling for power:

- ✔ **1308:** Nobles force Gaveston into exile, and Edward brings Gaveston back.

- ✔ **1311:** Nobles force Gaveston into exile again, and Edward brings him back again.

- ✔ **1312:** Nobles seize hold of Gaveston, try him for treason, and cut his head off. (As a nobleman Gaveston was supposed to have immunity. From then on, any nobleman who got captured could be killed, and most of them were.)

- ✔ **1315:** After the English lose to the Scots at Bannockburn, Thomas of Lancaster decides enough is enough and takes over the government.

- ✔ **1318:** Edward II's new favourites arrive – Hugh Despenser and his father, Hugh Despenser Senior.

- ✔ **1321:** Thomas of Lancaster forces Edward to send the Despensers into exile.

- ✔ **By 1321:** Edward would like to know just who is king around here?

Edward was angry. He gathered up everyone who was loyal to the Crown (even if they didn't think much of who was wearing it) and challenged Thomas of Lancaster to a battle at Boroughbridge in Yorkshire. And for once

Edward won. He cut Thomas's head off. End of the problems? Not on your life. Edward's wife Queen Isabella then got involved.

## A woman scorned

One person Edward hadn't considered in all of this palace intrigue was his queen, Isabella. In fact, he never did consider her much – that was the problem. Isabella was young and pretty and French, and trapped in a nightmare marriage. She felt humiliated by Edward spending so much time with his favourites, and when Edward sent her to Paris on business she saw a chance to do something about it. In Paris, Isabella met an ambitious young English noble called Roger Mortimer, started an affair with him, and hatched a plot. Isabella and Mortimer crossed back to England at the head of a French army. They got rid of Edward II (according to legend, they murdered him by putting a red hot poker up his...but no evidence exists one way or the other, so you can use your imagination) and replaced him with young Edward, the Prince of Wales. But since the young Edward – King Edward III as he now was – was only a boy, Isabella and her lover, Roger Mortimer, had the real power.

## Careful! Some day your prince may come

With Isabella and Mortimer running everything, the barons soon began to feel that they'd just exchanged Edward II for a His 'n' Hers version of Gaveston or the Despensers. The young king, who was growing up fast, wasn't too happy with the arrangement either. After a year, he decided he had had enough of taking orders from his mother and her lover. He gathered some men together, and they made their way through a secret passageway into Mortimer and Isabella's chamber in Nottingham Castle and arrested them. Mortimer was hanged (English politics was beginning to look decidedly dangerous) and Isabella retired from politics. And Edward III had only just started.

# Conquering France: The Hundred Years War – Round One

Edward III decided conquering France would be fun. He had a perfectly good claim to be King of France. His mother, Queen Isabella, was the next in line, but because the rules said a woman couldn't inherit the throne, Edward came next. Instead, the throne had gone to Edward's first-cousin-once-removed, King Philip VI. So Edward III told the Bishop of Lincoln to go over to France and tell King Philip most politely to kindly get off the French throne and hand it over to Edward. Whose face would have made the better picture, we wonder – the bishop's, when Edward told him what he had to do, or King Philip's, when he heard the message!

Everyone thought Edward was crazy. France was the biggest country in Western Europe. It had more people, more knights, and more wealth than any of its neighbours – certainly more than the English. French ships controlled the Channel, and the English couldn't do much about it. All in all, the best thing for Edward to do about being cheated of the French throne seemed to be attending anger management classes and forgetting all about being passed over. But, as Edward would have put it, where's the fun in doing that?

People came to call what ensued the Hundred Years' War. They weren't keeping count; they just meant that the fighting seemed to go on for ever.

## Some battles

By all the laws of averages and physics, the English ought to have lost every battle – the French had many more men, and they were fighting on home ground. But the English had a special weapon – the longbow – that the French never seemed to take into account properly however many times they encountered it.

The longbow is a very simple weapon, but absolutely deadly. In the hands of a skilled bowman – and English bowmen were very skilled – it was highly accurate and could pierce armour almost as easily as a bullet. Edward III knew just how much he owed to the longbow, and when people started skipping Sunday archery practice to play football he issued a law banning the game. ('Football' in those days consisted of a sort of all-out war between rival villages, with everything allowed except weapons. Maybe Edward was worried about losing half his supply of archers before he even went to war.)

Here's what the longbow could do:

- ✔ **Battle of Sluys 1340:** English archers destroy the French fleet. So many French are killed, people say the fish could learn French. (In speech bubbles?)

- ✔ **Battle of Crecy 1346:** Crushing English victory – 10,000 French slaughtered by English archers.

- ✔ **Siege of Calais 1347:** Edward captures the main French port close to England. According to tradition, six burghers (leading citizens) of Calais tried to save the town from being sacked by offering Edward their lives instead. Edward was inclined to take them up on their offer until his queen, Philippa of Hainault, persuaded him to spare them. This event is the subject of Rodin's famous sculpture *The Burghers of Calais*.

✔ **Battle of Poitiers 1356:** Edward's son, the Black Prince, doesn't just decimate the cream of the French army (those archers again) – he captures the French king, Jean II. England had won – or so it looked.

The French just didn't give in: Edward found he couldn't get into Rheims, where all French kings are crowned, because the city wouldn't surrender, and the French kept up an exhausting guerrilla war against Edward's men (they were too canny to risk another open battle). In the end, Edward and the French signed a peace treaty, which said:

✔ Edward would give up his claim to the French throne and to Henry II's old lands of Anjou and Normandy.

✔ In return, Edward got to keep Calais and a much bigger Aquitaine.

If Edward seems to have given in rather easily, bear in mind that while all this was going on, the Black Death was ravaging Europe. Any sort of peace looked very attractive. All that was left of Edward's French adventure were some French fleurs-de-lis on his coat of arms to show that he ought to be King of France really.

## The Black Prince

Edward III's son, the Black Prince, is one of those heroes of history who don't bear too close an inspection. His nickname may come from his black armour, though no one seems to have called him the Black Prince in his lifetime. The Black Prince was unquestionably a fearsome fighter. When the prince was in a tight spot in one battle and people were urging King Edward to go and help him, the king is supposed to have shaken his head and said, 'No, let him win his spurs.' The Black Prince became England's first duke, fought a war in Spain, and won it, too. He even married for love. But then the details get less glamorous.

Edward III left his son in charge of his lands in Aquitaine, but before long the people of Aquitaine were appealing to the King of France against the high taxes the prince was making them pay. The French king tried to confiscate the prince's lands, which triggered the war off again. The prince was sick with dysentery by this time, but he was so angry with the French that he got off his sick bed to supervise the destruction of the city of Limoges and the massacre of some 3,000 of its people. Not such a nice guy.

## Conquering France again: The Hundred Years War – Round Two

Just when the French thought they were safe, a new English king came to the throne: Henry V. Henry became king at a very dangerous time in England. His father Henry IV had seized the throne quite illegally, and a major rebellion occurred against him (I deal with all this in the following section: 'Lancaster vs. York: The Wars of the Roses – a User's Guide'). Now some nobles had hatched a plot to kill Henry V. A war in France seemed just the thing to take people's minds off thoughts of rebellion.

### Heading back to France

Henry looked at all the old documents about Edward III's claim (have a look at the earlier section 'Conquering France: The Hundred Years War – Round One'), liked what he saw, and in 1415 he set off for France. Things started badly for Henry:

- ✔ **Henry took the city of Harfleur** (this is the 'Once more unto the breach' battle), but it took up precious time, and his men were dying like flies from dysentery.

- ✔ **Henry had to give up any thoughts of marching on Paris.** The best he could do was march through northern France to Calais, thumbing his nose at the French king with a sort of 'Yah! You can't stop me!' as he went. Only, the French could stop him. Or so they thought.

- ✔ **A massive French army was shadowing Henry's men** and on 25 October 1415, it barred Henry's way near the village of Azincourt. Or, as the English called it, Agincourt.

### Battle at Agincourt

Forget the films, the plays, and all the fine words – Agincourt was slaughter from start to finish. The French charged across a muddy field, and the English archers just mowed them down. The chroniclers talk of mounds of dead, and for once, we don't think they were exaggerating. Then Henry gave his most ruthless order of the day: 'Kill the prisoners!' His army was so small, he couldn't hope to control large numbers of prisoners. Only a few of the very top people were spared (you could get a hefty ransom for them). Then Henry came home in triumph.

Winning at Agincourt really was a triumph. This time the peace treaty said that Henry's little son, also called Henry, was to be the heir to both the English and the French thrones. Then Henry V died – of dysentery, like so many of his men.

## Joan of Arc

No one comes out very well from the story of Joan of Arc except Joan herself. As far as we know, she was simply a peasant girl who had an incredible capacity to inspire people. The French Dauphin became King Charles VII thanks to her, but he never showed her much gratitude. The French nobles were jealous of her and resented being shown up by a peasant. They also didn't like it that she told them off for swearing. The English, of course, were convinced Joan was a witch – only evil powers could explain how she was able to beat them.

Nowadays, the French like to accuse the English of having burnt Joan of Arc, but in fact French soldiers captured her, and a French court, with a French bishop on the bench, condemned her to death. The French were fighting each other as well as the English, and the French Duke of Burgundy had made an alliance with the English. The Duke of Burgundy's men caught Joan and handed her over to the Church, which didn't like Joan breaking its monopoly on hearing sacred voices. In the end, Joan was a victim of grubby politics, and as French politicians like to latch onto her for their own causes – even the pro-Nazi wartime government at Vichy – she has more or less remained in that position.

## *Calamity Joan*

But Henry V hadn't quite won. The King of France's son, known as the *Dauphin* (because his personal badge was a dolphin, which is *dauphin* in French) was pretty sore about the peace treaty because it meant he would never be king. So a sort of resistance movement grew against the English. This movement didn't seem to be getting anywhere until a young girl called Joan turned up one day and said she was hearing voices in her head telling her that God wanted her to drive the English out of France. No one quite believed her, but things were so desperate, the Dauphin felt ready to try anything. So he kitted Joan out in armour, and to everyone's surprise, she went down to the city of Orleans, where there was a big siege going on, and drove the English away. The French victory at Orleans put heart into the French, and they began to fight back much more fiercely. Joan was captured and tried as a witch and burnt, but these events didn't save the English. The Dauphin was crowned King of France in Rheims Cathedral, and when the last English towns in Normandy fell, the English had to give in. After all that fighting and all that blood, all the English had left was Calais.

# Lancaster vs. York: The Wars of the Roses – a User's Guide

Richard II was the little son of the Black Prince (see the earlier section 'Some battles', as well as Figure 9-1 for the family tree), and he became king when he was still only a baby, so his uncle, John of Gaunt, ran the kingdom. When John of Gaunt went off to do some campaigning in Spain, everything fell to pieces. (For more on the adventures of John of Gaunt – like the Poll Tax that sparked off the Peasants' Revolt – head to Chapter 10.)

Richard II is one of the last kings we ought to think of as more French than English, and his nobles, who by now were much more English than French, didn't like some of Richard's French ideas, especially his notion that he ought to be able to rule as he liked, answering to nobody. Soon serious trouble was brewing between Richard and his nobles. The nobles forced Richard to execute his chancellor, and Richard started to arrest and execute the nobles. John of Gaunt came back from Spain and managed to calm things down a bit, but he was a sick man and died soon afterwards. The situation was not looking good.

Basically, each side thought the other was trying to get rid of all it held most dear. Richard thought the nobles were trying to take away his very power as king; the nobles thought Richard was trying to destroy the nobles of England as a class. Then Richard banished two leading nobles, the Duke of Norfolk and John of Gaunt's son, Henry Bolingbroke, Duke of Lancaster, and confiscated all Bolingbroke's estates. Now the nobles were really alarmed. Bolingbroke was the most powerful noble in England; if Richard could do this to Bolingbroke, he could do it to any of them. So when Richard went off to deal with a rebellion in Ireland, Henry Bolingbroke slipped back across the Channel. He said he only wanted his lands back. But what he actually seized was the throne.

Richard came racing back, but he was too late. Henry Bolingbroke, now King Henry IV, was firmly in place, and he had Richard put in chains. Within months, Richard was dead – almost certainly murdered. This death was a tragedy in many ways. But for the English, the tragedy was just beginning.

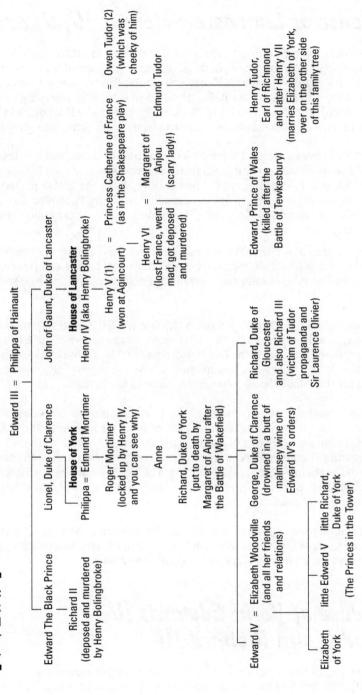

**Figure 9-1:**
The York
and
Lancaster
family tree.

## House of Lancaster: Henrys IV, V, and VI

Did Henry Bolingbroke actually have any right to the throne? He was Edward III's grandson, but so were plenty of others, and many of them had a better claim. But frankly, so what? Henry was on the throne now and everyone else would have to learn to like it. But Henry had set a very worrying precedent: If he could seize the throne just because he didn't like the current king, what was to stop anyone else from doing the same? And, sure enough, they tried:

- ✔ **The Percys:** Henry Percy, Earl of Northumberland, and his dashing son Harry 'Hotspur' were fresh from crushing the Scots, so they were formidable foes to Henry IV. They got help from the Welsh prince, Owain Glyn Dŵr, and even from the French, but Henry IV moved too quickly for them: He and his son Prince Henry defeated the Percys and killed them both in battle.

- ✔ **Owain Glyn Dŵr:** Owain came very close to turning the English out of Wales. A full-scale military campaign, as well as lots of bribery, were necessary for Henry to re-establish English control. No one knows what happened to Owain.

Henry IV had to spend all his reign fighting battles just to stay on the throne, and Henry V spent his short reign, as explained in the earlier section 'Conquering France again: The Hundred Years' War Round Two', fighting to get the throne of France. Which should have meant that all was secure and well for the infant Henry VI when he came to the throne.

Unfortunately, Henry VI couldn't have been less like his warlike predecessors: He was deeply religious and rather timid. He married a formidable Frenchwoman, Margaret of Anjou, which made him even more timid. The in-fighting at court got even worse, with everyone blaming each other for the disasters in France and accusations of treason and even witchcraft going backwards and forwards; and then something quite unexpected happened. The king went mad.

Not running-through-the-fields-like-George III-mad, but Henry VI certainly seems to have lost his reason. He had no idea who he was or who anyone else was, or what he'd come in here for or anything.

## House of York: Edwards IV and V and Richard III

When Henry VI's mind went, a Regency seemed the obvious solution, but another little point had to be considered. If you could get rid of Edward II and Richard II because you didn't think they ruled very well, what should you do with a king who couldn't rule at all? That was when the heir to the throne, the

Duke of York, began to take an interest. His was thinking: (a) Why shouldn't someone else take over from Henry VI? and (b) Why shouldn't that someone else be me?

The Duke of York started looking carefully at his family tree (and so can you, in Figure 9-1). If he'd read the tree correctly, didn't he actually have a better claim to be king than Henry VI had? Edward III had claimed the French throne when a perfectly good French king was on it; why shouldn't the Duke of York claim the English throne when a patently incapable English king was on it?

# Guns 'n' Roses

The wars were a tragedy for England. The fighting was bitter and very bloody. One of the battles, at Towton in 1461, was one of the bloodiest ever fought on British soil. No one at the time called what transpired the Wars of the Roses – that detail's a much later piece of romance based on the badges each side wore (red rose for the Lancastrians, and white rose for the Yorkists). There was nothing romantic – or rosy – about them at all. These were brutal wars, fought with all the latest weaponry, including cannon. As with all civil wars, there was a lot of changing sides, which makes it hard to get a clear picture of what was going on. Here's an outline.

### Round 1: 1455–60 War!

The Duke of York won the Battle of St Albans against King Henry VI. In theory he fought the battle to show how loyal he was to Henry and to liberate him from his 'evil advisers' but Henry didn't believe it and neither should you. Five years later, in 1460, the duke finally came clean and claimed the throne for himself. Seizing the throne didn't do him much good. Henry VI's wife, Queen Margaret, got an army together and cut the duke off at Wakefield. Then she cut his head off, too. **Advantage: Lancaster**.

### Round 2: 1461 Revenge!

The new Duke of York (son of the old one) beat Queen Margaret's men at Towton and forced Henry VI and his family to flee to Scotland. The Duke was crowned King Edward IV. **Advantage: York**.

### Round 3: 1462–70 Yorkists split and people change sides!

Yorkist Earl of Warwick arranged for Edward IV to marry a French princess, but Edward married an Englishwoman called Elizabeth Woodville behind Warwick's back. Elizabeth brought lots of friends and relations to court. Warwick, knowing when he's not wanted, slipped away to have a quiet word with Queen Margaret and join the Lancastrians. Then Edward IV's brother, George, Duke of Clarence, changed sides, too. The Lancastrians landed in England, seized London, and declared Henry VI the true king. Edward IV had to run for his life. Warwick became known as 'the Kingmaker'. **Advantage: Lancaster**.

### Round 4: 1471 Edward's revenge!

Edward IV got the Duke of Burgundy on his side and came back to England in force. He defeated (and killed) Warwick at Barnet, and then he beat Queen Margaret and the Prince of Wales (and killed him) at Tewkesbury. Edward retook London and sent Henry VI to the Tower, where he, er, died. (Just in time, George Duke of Clarence changed sides again and re-joined Edward.) **Game, set, and match to York.**

Edward IV reigned for twelve years, from 1471–83, and he was able to bring a bit of stability to the country. He carried on giving land and titles to his wife's family, the Woodvilles. He had Clarence arrested for plotting against him (very wise), but his other brother, Richard, Duke of Gloucester, did him very good service fighting the Scots. When Edward IV fell seriously ill and had to hand over to his young son, Edward V, Richard made sure he, and not the Woodville family, was the boy's protector.

When Edward IV finally died, Richard put the young king and his younger brother in the Tower of London for safe-keeping – and they were never heard of again. Then Richard staged a coup (boy kings had caused England nothing but trouble) and declared himself King Richard III. (You can find out more about these events in Chapter 11.)

### Round 5: 1485 The Lancastrians come back!

Distant-relative-by-marriage-to-the-House-of-Lancaster Henry Tudor, Earl of Richmond, landed at Milford Haven (he was Welsh) and claimed the throne. Richard III dashed off to fight Henry, but Henry beat him (and killed him) at the Battle of Bosworth. Henry Tudor became King Henry VII. **Game, set, and championship to Lancaster.**

# Chapter 10

# Plague, Pox, Poll Tax, and Ploughing – and Then You Die

*In This Chapter*

▶ Understanding religion, religious institutions, and rules for getting to Heaven

▶ Falling to the Black Death – how to tell if you've got it and what not to do about it

▶ Revolting peasants – and the king strikes back

Kings and nobles weren't the only people who lived during the Middle Ages, and battles weren't the only significant events (though Chapter 9 makes it seem that way). Ordinary people lived during this time too, and this chapter examines what their lives were like. Of course, finding out about the ordinary people is tricky, because they didn't leave behind the sort of things that make learning about them easy. They couldn't read or write, so no letters or chronicles of them exist; they didn't live in castles, and for the most part, the places they did live in are long gone.

Still, we get occasional little glimpses of the lives of ordinary folk in pictures or woodcuts from the Middle Ages, in church records and scrolls, or in literature of the time like Chaucer's *Canterbury Tales*. Some of the most interesting evidence comes when they burst onto centre stage, as they did in the famous Peasants' Revolt, and start speaking for themselves – though even then we only hear about it through the people who opposed them. From all these pieces of evidence, we can draw a surprisingly detailed picture of what life for ordinary people was like, and for most it was hard and short.

## Benefits of the Cloth

To understand medieval people, you have to start with what they believed. Religion went through all aspects of medieval life – everything. You avoided meat on a Friday because that was the day Jesus died. When people wanted to fix a date, they didn't use the ordinary calendar – 22 July, 8 November, or whatever – they used church festivals: St Bartholomew's, Corpus Christi,

Whitsun, and so on. The most important building in any community was the church, and cathedrals were the biggest buildings people had ever seen. Rich and poor alike put money into the church, and not just to restore the roof. They paid for new chancels or transepts, for golden candlesticks or stained glass windows, and for masses to be said for the souls of the dead – and sometimes people who had enough money kept whole chapels going just for that purpose. People put money into almshouses and schools and hospitals – all run by the holy and not-so-holy men and women of the church.

# What people believed in

People in Middle Ages saw death regularly. Their average lifespan was a lot shorter than ours – you counted as a senior citizen if you reached your late forties – and they were very aware of their own mortality. What might happen after death wasn't just for late-night discussions sitting up with friends, it was urgent, everyday business. The essential thing was not to end up going to Hell, because Hell was terrifying. Pictures and plays showed poor souls being dragged down into everlasting torment by hideous fiends armed with long forks. The trouble was, ending up in Hell seemed very easy unless you had some special help. That point was where the Church came in. These people were faithful members of a Catholic Church that spread over all of Europe. For spiritual leadership, they looked firmly to the Pope.

### Oh, you'll never get to heaven . . .

The problem with getting into Heaven began with Adam and Eve in the Bible. Here's the theory: After Adam and Eve got thrown out of the Garden of Eden (this was known as the Fall of Man or just the Fall), everyone who came after them was born with Original Sin. Unless you got rid of it, the Original Sin would stop you getting into Heaven. Getting rid of Original Sin was quite easy. The Church laid out the rules:

1. **First you had to be baptised.** And with infant mortality so high, you had to be baptised quickly. If you died still with the Original Sin on your soul, you got sent to a dreadful place floating in the middle of nowhere known as Limbo (think Ipswich on a bad day. Actually, think Ipswich on a good day).

2. **After being baptised, you needed to take care not to add new sins of your own to your soul.** If you did (and the new sin may mean no more than having lustful thoughts on a Friday), you needed to get along to confession. Here, you told a priest all the sins you'd committed; he'd give you some sort of penance to do (usually saying a prayer or two) and then give you absolution, wiping your soul clean until you started dirtying it again.

You could also do all sorts of other things to build up your credit with the Recording Angel: Helping people, going on pilgrimage or crusade, and above all receiving Holy Communion at least on big feast days like Easter and Christmas. Since the Church taught that Communion meant receiving the actual body and blood of Jesus Christ, you can see that it was pretty important.

If you did all these things – and remembered to confess and take Communion on your death bed (most important) – then you stood a chance when you went to Purgatory.

### Heaven's Gate: Purgatory

Purgatory sounds at first a bit like Hell: It was a massive fire that was supposed to purge your soul of the sin still ingrained in it by the time you died – hence the name. The living could help souls in Purgatory by praying for them, especially by asking a favourite saint to put in a good word on their behalf. Saints were your friends in high places (literally) and they could be very useful, which is why places get named after them and they get adopted as patrons of this and that. Assuming you weren't a mass murderer or addicted to lustful thoughts on Fridays, the hope was that, when Judgement Day came, you'd have enough good things in your ledger to outweigh all the really bad sins Purgatory couldn't get rid of. Then trumpets would blast, the Pearly Gates would open wide, and in you'd go. Phew.

But you couldn't reach Heaven without the Church.

# The church service

Putting across just how big and important the Church was to people in the Middle Ages is difficult. It was everywhere, like a parallel universe. Even the smallest village had a church, and the towns had hundreds of them. The church was specially designed to give a sense of awe and wonder – unsurprisingly, the modern theatre grew out of the medieval church.

- ✔ Unless your family was rich and could afford a special pew (within a lockable box, to keep the common people out), you had no benches to sit on – you either brought your own stool or you stood.

- ✔ The church was usually highly decorated with lots of vivid pictures on the walls or in the windows to show some of the stories in the Bible. In addition were statues of saints or of the Virgin Mary in areas where you could light a candle and say a prayer.

- ✔ At the end of the church was a special area, separated by a wooden wall called a *rood screen* (*rood* is an old word for the cross) and often on top of many rood screens were crucifixion scenes. Behind the rood screen, all the important ceremonies happened.

> ✔ There would be sweet-smelling incense, and bells ringing at special moments, and music from the choir, and the priest in his brightly coloured robes, who would lift up the bread and the cup and speak the words that made them into Christ's body and blood.

People often assume that because the service was in Latin the ordinary folk couldn't understand any of it, but all the evidence is the other way. People were used to the Latin words – they heard them every week – and the priests explained what all the different parts of the Mass meant. When the Tudors started introducing services in English – see Chapter 12 – big protests occurred.

The whole layout of the church and the form of the services emphasised that the priest had special, almost magical powers, and that the people needed him to get into Heaven.

## *Monastic orders*

Monks and nuns were people who had decided to devote their lives to God in a special way, by joining a monastic order. Monks had been around since the earliest days of the Church, and the Celtic Church had set up great monasteries on Iona and Lindisfarne (have a look in Chapters 5 and 6 for more info on the Celtic Church). But the idea of monasteries and convents as we know them came from St Benedict, who drew up a famous *Rule* for living as a monk, laying down a regular regime of prayer and work, and the idea caught on. St Augustine was a Benedictine, and so was the Pope who sent him to England (see Chapter 5). Soon different groups of monks began to put down roots in Britain:

> ✔ **Benedictines:** First of the 'Roman-style' monks on the scene in England. Some of their churches became great cathedrals, including Canterbury, Durham, Norwich, Winchester, and Ely.

> ✔ **Carthusians:** Very strict but popular order. Each 'Charterhouse' had a set of two-storey little houses known as cells, and each monk lived and worked in his cell. You can still see cells beautifully preserved at Mount Grace Priory in Yorkshire. The monks of the London Charterhouse opposed Henry VIII when he broke away from the Church, so he had them all put to death (see Chapter 11 for information about Henry VIII's reign and Chapter 12 for the details of the religious turmoil during the Reformation).

> ✔ **Cistercians:** Fairly strict and austere Benedictine group. The Cistercians liked to set up in remote valleys and anywhere that was hard to get to. Some of the most spectacular monastic ruins (ruins thanks to Henry VIII) are Cistercian, such as Fountains Abbey, Rievaulx, and Tintern Abbey in Wales.

✔ **Dominicans:** The intellectual hot-shots – top-notch preachers, specialising in taking on heretics in unarmed debate and wiping the floor with them. Dominicans ran schools and were important in getting the universities going at Oxford and Cambridge.

✔ **Franciscans:** Friars founded by St Francis of Assisi. They worked out in the community with the poor and sick. Their big moment came in the Black Death, though they rather fell apart into different groups and factions after that. Head to the section 'The Black Death' for details on the plague in Britain.

✔ **Augustinians:** Named after St Augustine of Hippo (an African bishop, not the missionary who came to England in Chapter 5 – and not a hippo, either), also known as the *Austin canons* or *black canons* – because they wore black. A popular order, the Augustinians ran schools and hospitals, and worked with the poor. Their rules were a bit less strict than the others', so they tended to be rather more independently minded. You won't be surprised to hear that Martin Luther was an Augustinian. Head to Chapter 12 to find out more about Martin Luther and the Reformation.

## *Medieval schools*

Most children didn't go to school. Doing so was expensive, for one thing, unless a local charity would pay for you. Those who did go to school were usually boys planning to go into the Church, so the main thing taught was Latin (which is why the schools were called *Grammar Schools*). Paper and books were expensive, so the children used little plates of horn with a stylus. Any trouble and the schoolmaster used the birch. If you did well at school, you might get accepted by one of the colleges at Oxford or Cambridge.

The universities at Oxford and Cambridge started off as small groups gathered around a particular teacher, and grew into colleges. The idea was to study philosophy, but that didn't just mean reading Aristotle. Philosophy meant the study of the world, and it could take in things as varied as mathematics, theology, logic, astronomy, and music. All subjects were, of course, studied, discussed, and even debated in public, in Latin.

*College* means a religious group or gathering – the Catholic Church still talks about the College of Cardinals. These colleges were monastic foundations. Like all churchmen, the students wore gowns, and the big elaborate gowns and hoods that graduates wear nowadays developed out of the monks' habits and hoods of the Middle Ages.

## Tending the sick: Medical care in the Middle Ages

Some monks and nuns made a speciality of looking after the sick – good biblical precedents existed for this, after all. Often a monk or nun looked after the monastery's *physic garden*, growing the herbs needed to make medicines and poultices. Many monasteries had a small hospital or hospice attached to them, usually for pilgrims who fell ill en route to one of the big shrines like Canterbury or Walsingham, but some more isolated hospitals existed for lepers (very common in the Middle Ages). Later on some of these hospitals grew larger, with a resident physician to look after the sick. By the fourteenth century these physicians and apothecaries were organising themselves into proper guilds and companies.

There's a famous story about how Rahere, jester at the court of King Henry I, fell ill on a pilgrimage to Rome and dreamed that if he recovered and returned home, he should found a hospital. He did recover, and his hospital was named St Bartholomew's, after the character he saw in his dream. St Bart's Hospital in London is still there today.

Medieval doctors got their ideas from the Greeks and Romans. They believed that the body was made up of four fluids, which they called the four humours. These were yellow bile, black bile, phlegm, and blood. Each humour was associated with one of the elements that made up the world, had particular characteristics, and tended to predominate at different times of the year. One of the humours, for example, was phlegm (sorry, were you eating?), which tends to make its presence felt in winter when the weather's cold and wet, but less so in the summer when it's hot and dry. Table 10-1 lists the four humours.

| Table 10-1 | The Four Humours: No Laughing Matter | | |
|---|---|---|---|
| *Humour* | *Type* | *Characteristics* | *Element* |
| Yellow bile | Choleric | Dry and hot | Fire |
| Black bile | Melancholy | Dry and cold | Earth |
| Phlegm | Phlegmatic | Cold and moist | Water |
| Blood | Sanguine | Hot and moist | Blood |

These four humours existed in each individual, too. When they were in balance, you were well. If you fell ill, it was because one of the humours had become too big for its boots, and your physician would give you something to counteract it. If, for example, you were too hot and choleric, your doctor would give you something cooling to counteract all that yellow bile, maybe some cucumber or cress. If you felt hot and wet – a fever, for example – you had too much blood racing around, so your doctor would bleed you to let some of the excess blood out and put the humours back in balance. Simple!

## The advanced thinkers

Some very clever people came out of the English and Scottish churches in the Middle Ages. Here's a taste:

- **Robert Grosseteste (ca. 1170–1253):** Pioneering Bishop of Lincoln. He had a big anti-corruption drive and got into trouble with the Pope and with the king along the way. The Pope even threatened to excommunicate him. He didn't let it put him off.

- **Roger Bacon (1214–94):** Franciscan friar and experimental scientist. Bacon worked out how to use glass to magnify things and how to mix gunpowder. The Pope reckoned Bacon one of the greatest minds in Christendom, but that didn't stop the Franciscans taking fright and having Bacon locked up for his dangerously novel ideas.

- **Duns Scotus (ca. 1265–1308):** Scottish theologian and leading opponent of the teachings of Thomas Aquinas. Aquinas had used Aristotle to support the Bible. Duns Scotus said Aristotle was all theory, and that faith should be much more practical. The Dominicans didn't like Scotus's ideas; Thomas Aquinas was one of their boys.

- **Julian of Norwich (1342–ca.1416):** Dame Julian (yes, she's a girl) was a normal Benedictine nun until she received a complex and intense vision. She spent the next 20 years working out what her vision might mean and then wrote it all out in *Sixteen Revelations of Divine Love*, in which she states that love is the basis of faith and that knowing God and knowing yourself are part of the same thing. Interesting note: Julian had no difficulty in talking of God as 'She'.

## A rebel: John Wyclif and the Lollards

One problem with the medieval Church was that it kept preaching poverty while still being fabulously wealthy. Not everyone was prepared to take that inconsistency lying down. John Wyclif was an Oxford theologian who concluded that the Church's wealth was a symptom of a church that had got things wrong from the start.

## An English holocaust

If you go to York, you'll see a rather beautiful castle on a steep mound, or motte. This castle is called Clifford's Tower, and you'll probably want to take a photo of it. But make sure you read the information about it before you move on. Clifford's Tower is the scene of one of the most appalling examples of anti-Semitism in English history. Jews had been in England since the Normans came in 1066 (see Chapter 7). They offered banking and credit services to William the Conqueror and his court. But people in England fell for all those stories about Jews murdering babies, and the anti-Jewish feeling got worse when crusade was in the air. Jews were then 'the people who killed Christ'. When the First Crusade was proclaimed in Germany, people slaughtered so many Jews that the Church had to remind them who the real enemy was.

In London, serious anti-Jewish riots broke out when Richard I was crowned, and in 1190, the people of York went on the rampage. The Jewish people who lived in York took refuge in Clifford's Tower, which was a royal castle, perhaps hoping that would give them some protection. They were wrong. With a mob outside baying for blood unless the Jews agreed to convert to Christianity, most of the Jews decided to kill themselves rather than give in. The ones who gave in to the crowd got killed anyway. This horrible tale is worth bearing in mind when you visit York. In the end, Edward I threw the Jews out of England in 1290, and they weren't allowed back in until Cromwell's time, in 1655.

During this time, as if to prove Wyclif's point, all the arguing and in-fighting in Rome produced not one Pope but two, each claiming to be the real one and saying the other was an antipope. Wyclif decided to show them what a real antipope was like. He said the Church didn't pay enough attention to what was written in the Bible and that all the bishops and cardinals and popes (and antipopes) ought to go. He even said that the Church was wrong about the bread and wine at communion becoming the body and blood of Christ.

Wyclif's ideas were radical stuff, and the Church wasn't pleased. The Church called Wyclif and his followers *Lollards* (which meant 'mumblers') – which was a lot ruder then than it sounds now. But Wyclif had some powerful friends at court, including the Black Prince (Edward III's son) and John of Gaunt (Richard II's uncle who ran the country until Richard was old enough), who were glad of anything that annoyed the Pope. Richard II didn't agree, though, and he started rounding up the Lollards, who were mainly poor priests, and their followers. Wyclif himself wasn't arrested, but Oxford threw him out, and 30 years after his death, on orders from Rome, his bones were dug up and scattered just to teach him a lesson. Some Lollards got involved in plots against Henry V, which did their reputation a lot of harm. But in effect Wyclif was only saying the sort of things that would be the ordinary doctrine of the Church of England by Queen Elizabeth's reign. (Head to Chapter 11 for information about England during Elizabeth's time.)

# The Black Death

One day in 1348, a ship put in to the southern English port of Weymouth. We don't know exactly what its cargo was but we do know one thing it was carrying: Plague. The Black Death had arrived in Britain.

The plague epidemic probably started in China and had been spreading westward relentlessly. The Black Death (so called because of the black spots it left on its victim's skin) was a form of bubonic plague that was spread by the fleas you got on rats – and rats were always in ships. In fact, in 1348 the plague came in two forms – bubonic (the basic strain of plague) and pneumonic, a more deadly variety (linked to pneumonia) that spreads from person to person through coughing, sneezing, and speaking. The bubonic strain hit in the summer, when most fleas are evident, and then the pneumonic strain took over through the winter.

## Death by plague

Bristol was the first major English town to be hit, but the epidemic soon spread. And one of the most terrifying things about the plague was that it spread so easily. Before long, it reached London, and Parliament had to clear out fast.

So what happens if you get bubonic plague? First, you get chest pains and have trouble breathing. Then you start coughing and vomiting blood, and you develop a fever. Next you start bleeding internally, which causes unsightly blotches on your skin, and buboes begin to appear – large white swellings in the armpits, the groin, and behind your ears. You become restless and delirious and then you sink into a coma. Finally, you die.

And you die, moreover, within a day or so of first feeling unwell. The numbers of dead were staggering. In London, the plague killed between a third and a half of the entire population. Some smaller places were literally wiped out. The epidemic couldn't have come at a worse time. Not only had Edward III started his wars in France (explained in Chapter 9), but only a few years before, England had gone through a terrible famine, so the people were in a pretty poor state to start with.

## Dire diagnoses

No one knew what really caused the plague or allowed it to spread so easily. But various people thought they knew and came up with treatments and preventatives. The treatment, of course, all depended on what you thought had caused the plague in the first place:

- **Too much blood:** Because people were coughing up blood, the doctors with their tables of humours (refer to the earlier section 'Tending the sick: Medical care in the Middle Ages') decided that the problem was too much blood, so they bled their patients. Imagine their surprise when that treatment didn't work.

- **God's punishment:** Those who believed the disease was a punishment from God (and lots of people thought it was) thought the answer clearly lay in prayer and fasting. Even better was to say an extra big 'Sorry!' by going round in a big procession whipping yourself. Lots of these *flagellants* were around until the Pope decided they were just spreading panic and told them to stop.

- **Something in the air:** If the plague was caused by something in the air, the answer was clearly to get in some pomade and air freshener. Well, it won't have done any harm.

- **Infected bodies:** More sensible were new burial regulations to bury people outside the city walls. Over in Dubrovnik, an Italian colony, they introduced a system of keeping visitors in isolation for 40 days. The Italian for 40 is *quaranta* – hence quarantine. Isn't that interesting to know?

- **An enemy among the people:** The usual suspects were – surprise, surprise – the poor old Jews (though the Irish said it was the English). People said the Jews had poisoned the wells, so they got their ropes out and went lynching. The attacks in England weren't as bad as they were in Germany, where thousands of Jews were massacred in revenge for the plague. And guess what? These murders didn't stop the plague either.

Eventually, people just had to let the epidemic run its course. And even then the plague kept coming back. More big outbreaks occurred, and you could usually count on the plague hitting somewhere or another just about every year until the seventeenth century.

You can see the shock effect of the plague in pictures and writings from the time. Illustrated books and manuscripts from the fourteenth century often have images of death or skeletons, reaping people in the hundreds. Nowadays, we reckon that the Black Death was the worst disaster of its kind ever. The plague hit the very people you would least expect – the young and fit. It was particularly deadly to children. Old people, on the other hand, seemed to get off relatively lightly. And this pattern of death had a most surprising effect on the labour market.

# The Prince and the Paupers: The Peasants' Revolt

In the Middle Ages, if you were a peasant, you were right at the bottom of the heap. You had no rights, you had to work on the local lord's manor, and all in all, life was one long round of ploughing. There wasn't much in the way of entertainment, and if you engaged in what entertainment was available, you ran the risk of getting gonorrhoea (not syphilis though, that was a souvenir Columbus brought back from America). Then the Black Death arrived. Which sort of people fell victim to the Black Death? Poor? Check. Adult? Check. Strong and healthy? Check.

If you managed to survive the Black Death, you found yourself in a very serious peasant shortage. This shortage had some potential to make your life a bit easier. Well, all those lords with their estates depended on the peasants working their lands. But with so few peasants around, what was to stop the peasants from offering their services to the highest bidder? A little gleam comes into thousands of peasants' eyes, and you see just the beginnings of a smile.

## Laws to keep wages low

The king and Parliament acted fast. They weren't going to have peasants getting ideas above their station. They drew up a special proclamation called the *Ordinance of Labourers* saying that no wages would be raised, and if the peasants were thinking of taking advantage of the labour shortage, they could think again. And when the *Ordinance of Labourers* didn't work, they backed it up with a new law called the *Statute of Labourers* saying the same thing. So there.

## A poll tax

The man who'd come up with the idea for the *Statute of Labourers* was John of Gaunt, Richard II's uncle. He was worried because it looked as if the kingdom might run out of money: The war in France was still going on (see Chapter 9 to find out what that war was about), and thanks to the great French captain Bernard du Guesclin, it wasn't going well. The war effort was going to need even more money, and John of Gaunt had an idea for how to get it. A poll tax.

## Did you ever hear the like?!

The *Statute of Labourers* gives a pretty good idea of what the ordinary people had been doing. It talks about 'the malice of servants which were idle, and not willing to serve after the pestilence without taking excessive wages.' This law was clearly for the rich against the poor. At one point it complains that the peasants were taking no notice of the *Ordinance of Labourers*: 'they do withdraw themselves (which means "refuse"!) to serve great men and other, unless they have livery and wages to the double or treble of that they were wont (used) to take.' People were even demanding to be paid daily rates! Shocking, isn't it? The Statute said you could go to prison for asking too much in wages. But the Statute still didn't change anything. The peasants had created what we would call a labour market, and the days of the old feudal system were numbered.

The poll tax didn't come out of the blue. John of Gaunt had been imposing taxes to pay for the war over the previous four years. But the poll tax was the worst because it simply said everyone over the age of 14 had to pay a shilling. Whether you were rich or poor didn't matter – it was a flat rate for everyone. The peasants were pretty fed up with the whole feudal system as a whole by now: It wasn't doing them any good, and if they complained or tried to charge a fair rate for their labour, they got locked up. So this poll tax was the last straw. But what could they do about it? One man seemed to know.

His name was John Ball. Ball was a priest, and like some of his fellow priests and monks, he was angry about how the poor were being kept down by the rich. He went around the country preaching, and he came up with the tag 'When Adam delved and Eve span, who was then the gentleman?' I know it may sound a bit obvious ('Er, Adam,' I hear you cry), but what he meant was not 'Who was the man?' but 'Who was the *gentle*man?' In other words, did God create people as lords and peasants? Answer: No. He created people as equals. So what, went Ball's message, were some people doing lording it over others? You can see where Ball was heading – and the poll tax was only the start. John Ball was saying that the whole feudal system was wrong.

## Showdown at Smithfield

We don't know exactly where the trouble started. Outbreaks occurred all over England. But the situation was most serious in Kent and Essex because you can easily march to London from there, and the angry peasants did. One of the Kentish rebels, called Wat Tyler, became a sort of ringleader as the peasants burst into London and went wild. They burnt down the prisons and then made straight for John of Gaunt's palace at the Savoy and burned it to the ground. John of Gaunt could thank his lucky stars that he wasn't in, because he'd never have survived. Consider what happened to the Archbishop of Canterbury. They broke into the Tower of London, grabbed the archbishop, hacked him to pieces, and stuck his head on a pole (using pole tacks, no doubt!).

Richard II, who was fourteen at the time, had to do something. So he agreed to meet the rebels outside the city at Smithfield. The meeting was very tense. Wat Tyler was there on a horse, and the king rode out with the Mayor of London beside him. Richard asked what the peasants wanted, and Wat told him:

- ✔ **No more villeins:** Peasants wanted to be agricultural workers, free to sell their services as and where they liked.

- ✔ **Everyone should be equal under the law:** No more special privileges for nobles. A little bit of Marxist analysis here.

- ✔ **No more wealthy churchmen:** Church lands and wealth should be distributed among the people. Wow! This was revolutionary stuff. The Lollards had been saying this, of course (refer to the earlier section 'A rebel: John Wyclif and the Lollards'), but Richard II was a devout Catholic. He wasn't going to like that idea one bit.

- ✔ **One bishop and one bishop only:** The peasants reckoned that the elaborate hierarchy of bishops and cardinals in the Church wasn't necessary. Have one chap in charge and leave the rest to the ordinary priests in the parishes who knew what the people wanted.

- ✔ **Oh, and a free pardon** for having risen in revolt, burnt down the Marshalsea Prison, murdered the Archbishop of Canterbury, rioted the wrong way down a one-way street, and walked on the grass while burning down the Savoy Palace.

Richard listened carefully and then said that all the demands sounded fair enough, while the mayor nearly had apoplexy sitting beside him. And then things turned nasty. According to the chronicle we have of the revolt, Wat Tyler, who was obviously enjoying putting terms to the king, called for a drink 'and when it was brought he rinsed his mouth in a very rude and disgusting fashion before the King's face'. Maybe he gargled the *Internationale*, too. At any rate, someone in the crowd then called out that Wat Tyler was a thief, and Wat Tyler took out his dagger to go and kill him. 'Just one moment!' shouts the mayor, but before he could do anything, Wat Tyler had turned his dagger on the mayor who, luckily for him (but unluckily for Tyler) was wearing full armour. So the mayor took out his sword and brought it down on Wat Tyler's head.

Utter confusion reigns – everyone started shouting, and some of the peasants started firing arrows. English bowmen could skewer a French knight at four hundred paces (head to Chapter 9 to read about the skill of the English archers), so the mayor had every reason to be very scared. He and the rest of the king's retinue turned round to leg it for the city.

And then King Richard, all of 14 years old, rides forward – forward, mind – towards the peasants. Pause. Everyone calms down. This isn't the mayor or the Archbishop of Canterbury. He's the king. Richard tells them he'll be their leader, and they all should come to meet him at Clerkenwell fields a little later.

And what happened at Clerkenwell? Well, they dragged Wat Tyler out of St Bartholomew's Hospital and finished him off. Then Richard told the peasants he was letting them go free and even giving them an escort to see they got home safely. Wasn't that nice of him? But they didn't quite all live happily ever after. As the chronicler puts it:

> *Afterwards the King sent out his messengers into diverse parts, to capture the malefactors and put them to death.*

Did they really expect anything else?

# Part IV
# Rights or Royals? The Tudors and Stuarts

# In this part . . .

Tudor England had two of the strongest monarchs ever
to sit on the English throne: Henry VIII and his daughter, Elizabeth I. Their portraits spell power and control, and
so did their governments, yet neither could crack the most
basic problem of all: Who was to succeed them? Henry
VIII's desperate search for a male heir led him into his
famous six marriages, while Elizabeth sought refuge in her
image as the Virgin Queen. But as long as the succession
was unclear, even these great monarchs could not lie easy.

Things were even worse in Stuart Scotland where monarch after monarch died, leaving a child to inherit the
throne. This situation led to murderous in-fighting among
the powerful Scottish lords.

Underlying the whole era was the terrible destructive
power of religious conflict. As new religious learning
found its way into Britain, the British people were divided
between those who embraced change, and those who
upheld their old faith. Meanwhile, the English Parliament
was speaking with increasing confidence: Arguments
broke out about religion and about the Crown, but
Parliament became a central part of the political scene.
This conflict between Parliament and Crown led to civil
war, which heralded a short-lived republic.

# Chapter 11

# Uneasy Lies the Head that Wears the Crown

*In This Chapter*

▶ Finding out how the Tudors seized the throne and tried to keep it

▶ Getting to know Elizabeth I, Queen of England and Mary, Queen of Scots

▶ Gaining security through succession: What the Tudors did to produce heirs to the throne

▶ Out-manoeuvring the Spanish Armada

▶ Seeing the first signs of an English Empire

*T*he Tudors were a family to be reckoned with. Everything about these people spoke Power. You can see it in their portraits. But don't be fooled. Power doesn't mean security, and this was a deeply worried family.

Henry Tudor (later Henry VII) seized the throne by force, and others were only too ready to do the same. The Scots and the French had an 'auld alliance', which meant that they would help each other fight the English. Henry VIII's quarrel with the Pope meant that every Catholic was a potential rebel – or assassin – especially when the Catholic King of Spain turned his eyes on England and prepared to invade. Producing a few heirs would've helped. But producing heirs was one thing the Tudors were exceedingly bad at. (Figure 11-1 gives you an idea just how bad.)

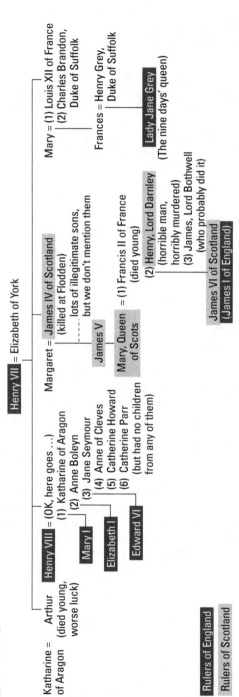

**Figure 11-1:**
The Tudor
family tree.

# Princes and Pretenders

England in 1483 was still getting over the great civil war between the Houses of York and Lancaster that nowadays we call the Wars of the Roses (see Chapter 9 for the full story). The Yorkists seemed to have won pretty comprehensively. They had more or less wiped out the Lancastrian royal family, and the Yorkist King Edward IV had been ruling peacefully for the past twelve years. (You may like to sneak a look at Figure 9-1 here.) Edward had two young sons: Edward (aged 12) and Richard, Duke of York (aged 10), but he caught a bad chill and died in 1483. His elder son now became King Edward V. Child kings always brought trouble, and Edward V was to prove no exception.

## Tricky Dicky, a.k.a. Richard III

Everyone's heard of Richard III, though usually through the Shakespeare play, which is great drama but rotten history. Who was Richard, and why is there still so much fuss about him?

Richard, Duke of Gloucester, was the younger brother of King Edward IV. Before he died Edward IV had asked Richard to look after his two young sons, and after Edward died Richard sent them to the Tower of London 'for safe-keeping'. Richard also took the opportunity to make a bid for power. He arrested every one of Edward IV's relatives-by-marriage – the Woodville family – that he could find. He had Lord Hastings, an important member of England's ruling Council who was utterly loyal to Edward IV and his family, arrested on a trumped-up charge of conspiracy to murder, and executed. Then he publicly announced that his late brother, King Edward IV, had not in fact been properly married. His two children – safely tucked away in the Tower of London, remember – were therefore illegitimate and couldn't inherit the crown. So who should be king? Parliament met and considered the matter, and offered the crown to Richard. 'Well,' said Richard, 'if you insist. . . .' And so he was crowned King Richard III.

Little Edward V and his brother – the Princes in the Tower as they are known – were never seen alive again, but two small skeletons turned up in Charles II's day (that's the seventeenth century) which we reckon belonged to them.

Richard III is one of the most controversial figures in history. Shakespeare shows him as an evil hunchbacked murderer, but that was just Tudor propaganda. Next to no evidence exists for the hump, for example, but in Shakespeare's day people regarded a hunched back as an evil sign. Most historians see Richard III in a much more positive way. He was an able king, a good soldier – he made very short shrift of a rebellion by the Duke of Buckingham and a Scottish invasion – he worked well with Parliament, encouraged overseas trade, and was quite popular really, especially in his home base in the north. But what everyone wants to know about Richard is this: Did he murder the princes? We don't actually know – and probably never will – and his fans (yes, folks, there's even a Richard III Society!) deny it vehemently, but the evidence to suggest that he did is very compelling. In any case, in the circumstances he would have been crazy not to. Young princes grow up and seek revenge – especially on wicked uncles.

But if the princes were in no position to get revenge, someone else was around who could. In 1485 Henry Tudor, Earl of Richmond, landed with an army at Milford Haven in Wales and challenged Richard for the crown.

## Enter Henry Tudor – and a succession of pretenders

Henry Tudor was a fairly distant relation of Richard's, and he certainly didn't have a good claim to the throne (see Figure 9-1 to work out just how distant a relation Henry Tudor was). But he was Welsh, and the Welsh supported him. Richard raced to head him off and the two sides met at Market Bosworth, near Leicester. And at that point Richard's luck ran out. The Stanley family, some of his most important supporters, decided to change sides and join Henry, and Richard was killed in the fighting. Someone found his crown and Lord Stanley placed it on Henry Tudor's head. Henry was now King Henry VII.

### Claiming the throne

Even with the princes dead (see the earlier section 'Tricky Dicky, a.k.a Richard III'), plenty of people had a better claim to the throne than Henry Tudor. The person with the best claim was Edward IV's daughter, Elizabeth of York. So Henry married her. Good move. Their marriage united Lancaster (Henry) and York (Elizabeth) so that even Yorkists could accept Henry as their king – in theory. The Yorkists, however, didn't see the situation that way.

The next best claim to the throne lay with the Earl of Warwick, the son of Edward IV's brother George, Duke of Clarence (see Figure 9-1 to work out who everyone is in this section), and in 1487 the Yorkists crowned him king over in Ireland. Which was odd, because Henry VII said that the Earl of Warwick was in the Tower of London, and he paraded him through the streets of London to prove it.

### Pretender No 1: Lambert Simnel

In fact, the 'Earl of Warwick' in Ireland was a pretender – a (fake) claimant. His real name was Lambert Simnel, and he was a baker's son from Oxford – a fact that didn't stop the Yorkists putting him at the head of an army and landing in England to claim the throne. So Henry had to fight another battle, this time at Stoke. Henry won, and poor Lambert ended up a prisoner. Henry was surprisingly merciful. He didn't cut his head off. He sent him down to work in the royal kitchens.

### Pretender No 2: Perkin Warbeck

Henry still couldn't relax. In 1491 another pretender, Perkin Warbeck, claimed he was the little Duke of York, the younger of the princes in the Tower. This claim was a serious threat to Henry's reign, because Warbeck had support from Henry's enemies in France and Burgundy. When Warbeck finally invaded, however, Henry quickly captured him and put him in the Tower. Then the silly lad escaped, so Henry had him dragged back and executed. And, just for good measure, he had the poor little Earl of Warwick (the real one, not Lambert, the pretender-turned-kitchen-lad) executed too. The Earl of Warwick hadn't done anything wrong, but Henry had had enough of people saying they had a better claim to the throne than he had. And Warwick really did.

# And Then Along Came Henry (the VIII, that is)

Henry VII didn't just spend his time fighting off pretenders. He married his children into the leading ruling houses in Europe, and he negotiated good trading agreements with the Netherlands. So there was a lot of money in the treasury that he handed over to his handsome and gifted son, who in 1509 became King Henry VIII.

## Bad Ideas of the Sixteenth Century – No 1: Marrying Henry VIII

Henry VIII was a good example of the ideal Renaissance prince (see Chapter 14 for a bit more on what the Renaissance was all about) – he was handsome, strong, good at jousting and wrestling but also highly educated, good at music, interested in theology, and a good mover on the dance floor. He seemed to have everything he could possibly want – except a son.

To avoid lots of squabbling over the succession in the sixteenth century you needed a good supply of sons. (Daughters could succeed, but the last time a daughter assumed the throne, England had fallen into a civil war, explained in Chapter 7. As a result, people weren't too keen on trying that again.) All those paintings of large Tudor families through the generations are saying 'there's nothin' wrong with our virility' – and Tudor men wore those enormous cod-pieces to show off their manhood for the same reason. Henry VII had managed two boys, Henry VIII and his older brother Prince Arthur, who died young, and two girls, Margaret and Mary (see Figure 11-1 for details here). Henry VIII, wanted to do even better, and that meant finding the right wife.

### Wife No. 1: Katharine of Aragon

When he came to the throne, Henry was married to Katharine of Aragon. Katharine's family were the up-and-coming Kings of Spain, so marrying her was a major diplomatic coup. She had been married to Henry's brother Arthur, but Arthur died, and in any case, according to Katharine, she and Arthur never consummated the marriage (and she ought to know). Now, strictly speaking, the Bible said you couldn't marry your deceased brother's wife, but Aragon was too good a prize to miss, so Henry had a word with the Pope and the Pope gave him a special dispensation so that Henry and Katharine could get married.

At first, the marriage went well. Katharine trashed the Scots at the Battle of Flodden while Henry was away losing to the French (see the section 'The Stewarts in a Stew' later in this chapter for info on that event). But then she gave birth to a daughter, Mary. Doing that was no good. Henry wanted a son! Even worse, when she got pregnant again, with boys as it turned out, the children always died. Henry wasn't just angry, he was worried: Was God trying to tell him something?

Henry got his Bible out. There the evidence was, in black and white: Thou shalt not uncover the nakedness of thy brother's wife – *Leviticus*. Henry reckoned the dead babies were God's way of punishing him for living in sin. But the Pope had given Henry a dispensation. He had specially put the rule aside. Could the Pope possibly put the rule back again?

### Henry gets a divorce – and a new Church

Henry sent his chief minister, Cardinal Wolsey, to Rome to have a word with the Pope, but when Wolsey got there, he found the Pope had been taken prisoner by Charles V, the Holy Roman Emperor, who just happened to be Katharine of Aragon's nephew. Charles wasn't going to let anyone insult – or divorce – his auntie. Wolsey went home to tell Henry the bad news.

Henry was furious. First, he sacked Wolsey. Then he simply closed down the Pope's Church and opened his own: The Church of England. And this Church gave him his divorce. Some people objected, like the statesman and writer Sir Thomas More and the Bishop of Rochester, John Fisher, but they got their heads cut off, so few others came forward.

# Cardinal Wolsey

Wolsey was the man everyone loved to hate. He was a cardinal, an archbishop, and Lord Chancellor of England, but he wasn't a noble – his father was a butcher, and the people at court didn't forget it. Wolsey was good. He organised Henry's war with France, for example, and he got a good peace deal out of it, too.

Some people see Wolsey as the last of the old-style prince-bishops. He certainly lived in state and had a great palace built for himself at Hampton Court. Someone even wrote a poem asking which court you ought to go to, the king's

court or Hampton Court? Others see Wolsey as a great moderniser, a sort of patron saint of civil servants. Whatever. Wolsey's accomplishments and riches didn't save him when he couldn't get Henry his divorce. He tried everything. He even offered Henry Hampton Court. Henry took it but sacked Wolsey anyway. Wolsey was on his way down to London for the chop when he died, at Leicester Abbey. 'Had I but served God as diligently as I have served the King,' he is supposed to have said, 'he would not have given me over in my grey hairs' – nice thought, but a bit too late.

## Wife No. 2: Anne Boleyn

Henry was crazy about Anne. Couldn't resist her. He'd spotted her when she was lady-in-waiting to Katharine of Aragon and he couldn't take his eyes off her. As soon as he got his divorce from Katharine he married Anne in secret, and nine months later, he got his reward: A healthy baby. Another girl. This one named Elizabeth. He wasn't pleased.

From that point things went downhill for Anne. She had enemies at court, and try as she might she didn't produce a boy. Three years after her glittering coronation Anne's enemies struck. They had her arrested and charged with adultery – with her own brother, Lord Rochford, if you please. Henry sent for a special executioner all the way from France, who could cut Anne's head off in one go with his sword, instead of hacking at it the way those axemen used to do. Wasn't that a kind thought?

## Wives Nos 3–6: A Jane, an Anne, and two more Catherines

**Jane Seymour** was a lady-in-waiting to both Katharine of Aragon and Anne Boleyn. They were both dead by the time Henry married her so no problem existed about whether or not the marriage was valid. It was Jane who finally gave Henry the son he'd been hoping for for so long, Edward. Edward was a sickly child (he'd probably inherited Henry's syphilis), but he lived. Jane didn't. She died giving birth.

**Anne of Cleves** was a German princess. You can blame Henry's marriage to her on Henry's chief minister and staunch Protestant, Thomas Cromwell. At the time it looked like war with the Catholic Holy Roman Emperor Charles V, so scheming Thomas suggested to Henry that they should link up with the German Protestants. The best way, he said, was for Henry to marry a German princess, Anne of Cleves. To judge by Holbein's portrait, Anne was a bit shy, but not bad looking. Henry, however, found her completely unattractive. 'Good God, she's like a Flanders mare,' he said, but he went through with the wedding anyway, all the time thinking, 'this had better be worth it.' Then the emperor changed his mind about attacking England. Henry had got married for nothing! He was the perfect gentleman. He divorced Anne and gave her a nice house and an income. Then he cut Cromwell's head off.

**Catherine Howard** was a cousin of Anne Boleyn's, which you would have thought might have taught her something. She was twenty and Henry was forty-nine when they were married: The typical older-man-falling-for-pretty-young-thing scenario. Catherine, however, had been in love before she married Henry and, silly girl, she carried on seeing her old lover, Thomas Culpeper, after her marriage. While Henry was away fighting the Scots, Catherine and Thomas saw each other openly. Stupid! Henry was bound to find out, and he did. He was so upset he had them both executed.

**Catherine Parr** was the postscript wife, the one who survived and about whom not much is said. But, in fact, she was a highly ambitious lady, determined to make England a Protestant country. She was the first queen since Katharine of Aragon to run the country while Henry was away. She didn't get everything she wanted, but she managed to pass some of her Protestant ideas onto her stepdaughter, Elizabeth.

## Edward VI, Queen Mary . . . and Jane Grey?

Little Edward VI was Henry VIII's son by Jane Seymour (see the section 'A Jane, an Anne, and two more Catherines' earlier in this chapter for information about his mother). Edward VI was only nine when he came to the throne, and he wasn't at all well. He was too young to do any governing, so the 'Protector', his uncle, Jane Seymour's brother, the Duke of Somerset, handled that side of things.

The Duke of Somerset was very popular with the ordinary people – they called him the 'Good Duke' because he tried to protect them from nobles who were fencing off the common land – but he had lots of enemies at court. And 1549 was a very bad year for the Good Duke: He faced two big rebellions, one in Devon and Cornwall about religion, and one in East Anglia against all those enclosures of common land. (See Chapter 12 to see what the religious problems were all about, and Chapter 14 to discover what was wrong with enclosures.) One rebellion may be counted a misfortune; two in the same year looked like carelessness – even by Tudor standards. Somerset's enemies moved in for the kill, so Somerset grabbed the young king and ran off to Hampton Court. This action came too late. He had to come quietly and hand power (and the little king) over to his arch-rival, the Duke of Northumberland.

Northumberland wanted to make England more Protestant (see Chapter 12 for more details on what this meant) but when Edward VI died (and the way he was coughing, he could keel over any day), Katharine of Aragon's daughter Mary would become queen. Mary was a loyal Catholic, so not only would she get rid of the Protestant religion, there seemed a real danger that she would get rid of the Protestants – like the Duke of Northumberland – too.

So Northumberland hatched a plot to stop her. He married off his son, Lord Guildford Dudley, to Lady Jane Grey, who was a sort-of-Tudor (grand-daughter to Henry VIII's youngest sister, if you really want to know – have a look at Figure 11-1). When Edward VI died in 1553 (he was only 16), Northumberland moved fast and put Jane on the throne. But Mary played her cards just right. She claimed the throne as her father's daughter, rode into London and had the whole lot of them, Northumberland, Jane and Guildford, packed off to the Tower. Jane had been queen for just nine days.

Queen Mary (no, not the ocean liner) is best known for putting Protestants to death, though, as Chapter 12 shows, that portrayal isn't really fair. Like every other Tudor, she was desperate for an heir, but she chose the wrong husband: King Philip II of Spain. Officially, Philip's marriage to Mary made him King of England (you can find them both on the coins), which went down like a lead balloon with the people. Sir Thomas Wyatt led a big rebellion in protest, and he got to London before they stopped him. Spain was at war with France, so Mary joined in, too, and that's how she came to lose Calais.

Calais had been English since Edward III's day (see Chapter 9 for details), and losing it seemed like a disaster. Mary was so distraught by the loss she said that after she died you'd find 'Calais' engraved on her heart.

But the cruellest twist for Mary was when she thought she was pregnant. She had cancer of the stomach. And it killed her.

The religion question – Is England Catholic or Protestant? – and the subsequent battles between the two groups were huge issues shaping the reign of many of Britain's monarchs. You can find out more about all this religion stuff – who did what to whom and why – in Chapter 12.

## The Auld Alliance

The English spent a lot of time fighting the French and Scots. Fighting them both was no coincidence. The French and the Scots had a special relationship and would always try to act together against the English. The Scots called this relationship the Auld Alliance. The English called it a wretched nuisance. But the alliance could be a nuisance for the Scots, too. The French got far more out of it, and Scottish Protestants didn't like fighting alongside French Catholics against fellow Protestants, even if they were English. The Scottish also hated being told what to do by the French ultra-Catholic Guise family, the most fanatical anti-Protestants in France. Scotland was going through even more serious problems than England (see the section 'Stewarts in a Stew'), and the Auld Alliance was making them worse.

# The Stewarts in a Stew

Three years after Richard III lost his throne at Bosworth (see the earlier section 'Enter Henry Tudor – and a succession of pretenders' for details), King James III of Scotland lost his throne at the battle of Sauchieburn. Scottish rebels, led by James's own son (who, to his credit, had told the rebels not to harm his father), found him after the battle and did him in. At James III's death, his son became King James IV.

## James IV attacks the English – and loses

James IV was a tough customer: He brought the rebellious Scottish clan chiefs under royal control, encouraged scholars and printers, and set up a rich and glittering court. He married Henry VII's daughter, Margaret, though that wasn't going to stop him from taking on the English. In 1513, with Henry VIII off fighting the French, James IV marched south – into disaster. He ran into an English army led by the Earl of Surrey and Katharine of Aragon (Henry VIII's first wife) at Flodden Field, in Northumberland. The English cannon blew the Scots to pieces, and when the Scots charged with their long spears, the English used their *halberds* (spears fitted with axeheads) to chop the spearheads off. The event was a massacre. The English took no prisoners. Nearly 12,000 Scots died that day, and James IV was one of them.

## A new king and another power struggle

When James IV was killed at Flodden (see the preceding section for details), the new king was his son, James V, a wee bairn of 17 months, which meant that power in Scotland was up for grabs. And the two opposing sides were led by

 ✔ **Queen Margaret:** James IV's widow and Henry VIII's sister, Margaret, who was now married to the Earl of Angus. She led the pro-English party.

 ✔ **The Duke of Albany:** He wouldn't have minded seizing the throne for himself. He led the anti-English (and therefore also the pro-French) party.

The power struggle raged back and forth between them. First Margaret held power, then Albany took over, then Margaret and Angus staged a coup and pushed Albany out again, then she and Angus divorced, and Angus kept hold of James V and refused to give him up (you are following this, aren't you?) until in 1528 James decided it was time to remind everyone who was king. He escaped from Edinburgh, gathered an army, and put the Earl of Angus under arrest. James V had grown up. He was 16 years old!

But which way would James go? Would he be pro-English or anti-English? James hadn't forgiven his English mother or the Earl of Angus for the way they had kept him confined – so, no pro-English line for him. The Auld Alliance, the special pact between France and Scotland that said they'd work together against England, was back with a vengeance, and James wanted to seal it by marrying a French princess. His first French queen died within weeks of arriving, but in 1538, he married the powerful, very anti-Protestant, Mary of Guise. James V and Mary had a daughter, also called Mary. She'd only just been christened when James went to war with England. The war didn't go well for the Scots. The English destroyed the Scottish army at the Battle of Solway Moss. James V was stunned. They say he lay down, turned his face to the wall, and died. (It was probably cancer, but the bad news can't have helped matters). His last words (just before he said "Urgh") were: "Adieu, farewell. It came with a lass and will pass with a lass". The first lass was James's great-great-great-great-great granny Marjorie Bruce, the royal who had first married into the Stewart family and brought them near the throne. The second lass was James's baby daughter – only a week old – who was now Mary, Queen of Scots.

# _Bad ideas of the sixteenth century – No 2: Marrying Mary, Queen of Scots_

Everyone seemed to want to marry Mary. Henry VIII wanted her for his son, Edward, and when the Scots played hard to get, Henry sent an army to invade them. The Scots called this event the _rough wooing_, and had to sign a treaty agreeing to the betrothal, though they quickly denounced it. Once Edward was actually on the English throne, the English came back and won yet another victory at the Battle of Pinkie, but they still didn't get Mary for their king. The Scots weren't going to give in. They got French reinforcements and packed Mary off to safety in France. She was going to marry the Dauphin, the eldest son of the King of France, and the English would just have to get used to it.

Mary loved life in France. She lived at court like a French princess. But she was in line for a lot more than that: Mary stood to inherit three thrones:

- **Scotland,** obviously.

- **France,** because she had married the heir to the French throne.

- **England,** because the English were running out of Tudors, and Mary was next in line.

Mary's claim to the English throne was more complex than simply being next in line. According to Catholics, Henry VIII's marriage to Katharine of Aragon had been valid and above board; his marriage to Anne Boleyn, on the other hand, had been false. And that fact meant that Anne Boleyn's child, Elizabeth, was illegitimate. And if Elizabeth was illegitimate, she had no right to be queen. So Mary should be. Not later, when Elizabeth died, but *now*.

At first, Mary seemed unstoppable:

- **In 1558,** Mary married Prince Francis of France.

- **In 1559,** Francis became King Francis II, and Mary became Queen of France.

And then it all started to go wrong:

- **In 1560,** Francis II died. No longer Queen of France, Mary had to go back to Scotland.

Mary's reign in France was short but sweet, and she hated Scotland: It was cold, damp, and scary. Worse, thanks to a gloomy old thunderer called John Knox, Scotland had become Protestant while she'd been away, meaning that Mary would have to keep her religious beliefs private.

Mary married a distant cousin, also in line to the English throne, Henry Stewart, Lord Darnley. At first Darnley was charming, and soon a little prince was born. The child was called James (named after his grandfather. And his great-grandfather. And his great-great-grandfather. And his great-great-great-grandfather . . .). But then Darnley changed. He was a drunken, violent brute. Mary was desperately unhappy and made friends (and it may only have been friends) with her Italian music teacher-cum-secretary-cum-shoulder-to-cry-on David Riccio. One night, Darnley and his mates burst into Mary's chamber, dragged Riccio away from her, and murdered him. And then things really hotted up:

1. Darnley was lured to Kirk o' Field House by Mary's close, er, 'friend', Lord Bothwell.

2. Kirk o' Field House blew up.

3. Darnley's body was found in the garden – strangled – and the chief suspect was Lord Bothwell.

4. Mary married Lord Bothwell.

Well! Talk about scandal! This sequence of events was just too much. The Scottish lords rose up in rebellion. Bothwell fled (he ended up going mad in prison in Denmark), and the lords took Mary prisoner. They searched Bothwell's house and found a casket full of letters from Mary planning Darnley's murder (in fact, these letters are almost certainly forgeries – 'and wen we ave dun him in, I will mary you' sort of thing – but who was going to believe that?). Mary managed to escape, but where could she go? France? Too far. No, she decided to hop over the border to England and throw herself on the mercy of her cousin, Queen Elizabeth.

Elizabeth immediately locked her up. Apparently, Bad Idea No. 3 of the sixteenth century was throwing yourself on the mercy of Queen Elizabeth. Now is the time to meet Queen Elizabeth.

# The First Elizabeth

Elizabeth I was Anne Boleyn's daughter and nobody's fool. Her sister, Queen Mary, had put her in the Tower because she thought Elizabeth was plotting against her. Elizabeth, therefore, knew all about how dangerous sixteenth-century politics could be. When she became queen, she needed to see to three things straight away: Religion, security, and getting married.

**Religion** was urgent, and Elizabeth and Parliament set up a not-too-Protestant Church of England that she hoped (wrongly) both Catholics and Protestants could go to (head to Chapter 12 for more on the religion issue).

**Security** was always a problem – the Tudors knew all about people trying to seize the throne. The best way to guard against danger was to have an heir, and that meant that Elizabeth needed to find a husband. Here were her options:

- ✔ **King Philip of Spain:** No kidding: he did offer. The English couldn't stand him, and – more importantly – if Elizabeth married him, England would become some sort of Spanish province. No thank you.

- ✔ **A French prince:** This made political sense. It would mess up France's alliance with Scotland and set the King of Spain's nose out of joint. The French king sent his son the Duke of Anjou over, and Elizabeth seemed very interested. Danced with him, called him her 'frog', and kept him hanging on. And on. Until in the end, he gave up and went home.

- ✔ **Robert Dudley, Earl of Leicester:** Ah, Elizabeth liked him! He was her 'Robin'. But a problem existed. He was already married, to a lady called Amy Robsart – at least he was until they found poor Amy lying dead at the foot of the staircase one day. Very fishy. After that incident, no way could Elizabeth marry her Robin. Just think of the scandal.

Whoever Elizabeth chose, there'd be trouble: Either protests, or her husband would try to take over. So she decided not to choose. She would remain a virgin, married only to her people, and not share her power with anyone. Not an easy decision to make.

## *The Virgin Queen vs. the not-so-virgin Mary*

Elizabeth didn't like talking about the succession, but other people had to. She'd only been on the throne for a few years when she nearly died of small-pox. She might not be lucky enough to survive the next illness. Her closest adviser, Sir William Cecil, was desperately worried and with good reason. First was the threat of Mary, Queen of Scots who was already saying that she was the rightful Queen of England and having the royal arms of England put into her own coat of arms. Second, but even worse, was the major blow that fell in 1570 when the Pope excommunicated Elizabeth. Like it or not, she was now in serious danger.

Excommunication was the most dire punishment the Catholic Church could issue. This punishment meant casting someone out of the Church, with no hope of salvation after death unless they performed a very big act of penance. In the case of a monarch, like Elizabeth, excommunication could also mean that they had no right to be on the throne, and that loyal Catholics were allowed – supposed, even – to overthrow her.

## *Catholic plots against Elizabeth*

The following are the Catholic plots to kill Elizabeth and put Mary, Queen of Scots on the throne:

- **Revolt of the Northern Earls, 1569:** Earls of Northumberland and Westmorland stage a major rising to rescue Mary. Revolt defeated; earls flee to Scotland; hundreds of their followers executed.

- **Ridolfi Plot, 1571:** Florentine banker Roberto Ridolfi and the Catholic Duke of Norfolk plan a coup with help from Philip II of Spain and the Pope. Plot discovered. Both plotters executed.

- **Jesuits, 1580:** Jesuit missionaries Robert Parsons and Edmund Campion arrive secretly in England and are suspected (wrongly) of plotting against the queen. Campion is arrested and executed; Parsons escapes to Spain.

- **Throckmorton plot, 1584:** Catholic Francis Throckmorton arrested and tortured. Reveals plot with Spanish ambassador to murder Elizabeth and stage a French invasion. Throckmorton executed, ambassador sent home.

These plots are getting more serious. Cecil and Secretary of State, Sir Francis Walsingham, decide to play dirty. Mary is kept in ever-closer confinement in England, and they keep a close watch on her. In particular, they read all her letters, especially the secret ones hidden in kegs of ale – which reveal that she is up to her neck in the Babington Plot.

## *The Babington Plot (1586) and the end of Mary*

Catholic Anthony Babington plotted to murder Elizabeth, and he got Mary, Queen of Scots to agree to it. That's when Cecil and Walsingham, who'd been reading Mary's correspondence, decided to pounce. They had Mary just where they wanted her.

## *Off with her head!*

Even before the Babington Plot came to light Cecil was desperate for Elizabeth to put Mary to death. Keeping her alive was far too dangerous – well, you can see why. But Elizabeth wouldn't hear of it. First, Mary was her cousin (well, first-cousin-once-removed). Second, Mary wasn't an English subject, so how could you accuse her of treason? And third, but most important, Mary was a queen and so was Elizabeth. Start putting monarchs on trial and executing them and heaven knows where it'll end up.

But even Elizabeth couldn't ignore the Babington Plot. So Mary, Queen of Scots went on trial, and the court found her guilty. All they needed was a death warrant, and all that needed was Elizabeth's signature. Elizabeth didn't want to sign the warrant, so her secretary put it in the middle of a lot of other papers that needed signing so that Elizabeth could 'pretend' she hadn't known it was there. (This ruse nearly cost the secretary his life: Elizabeth tried to make out that she hadn't known anything about it and had the poor fellow sent to the Tower. If Cecil hadn't stepped in, he'd have been executed.)

Mary went to her execution in a black velvet dress. She whipped it off to reveal a blood-red dress underneath. Everyone was in floods of tears. It took three gos to chop her head off, and when the executioner finally held her head up by the hair for everyone to see, the head fell out – her fine 'hair' was a wig. Even after death, Mary could upstage them all.

## English sea dogs vs. the Spanish Armada

During Elizabeth's reign is when the English first really started messing about in boats. There were two main reasons: One was adventure, and the other was money. You could try and make your fortune finding a way round the top of Canada (the 'Northwest Passage') to the wealthy spice islands of Asia, or you could just steal from the Spanish.

The Spanish were sitting on gold and silver mines in their colonies in South America, so sea dogs like John Hawkins and Francis Drake simply sailed to the Spanish colonies, opened fire, took what they could, and ran – and very wealthy this enterprise made them. Drake even sailed all the way round the world to show the Spanish that they could run from him, but they couldn't hide. Hawkins found a nice lucrative market supplying the Spanish colonies with African slaves. All this experience was to be very useful for the English when Spain decided to turn the tables and attack England.

By 1588, King Philip II of Spain had had enough. Not only were Drake and Hawkins and Co. attacking his ships, but Elizabeth was knighting them for it. England needed to be taught a lesson once and for all. And so Philip put together the largest fleet in history, the Great Armada, and sent it against England. And the result was a total disaster.

Everything went wrong. Philip's best commander died, so he had to put the Duke of Medina Sidonia, who had never fought at sea and suffered from sea-sickness, in charge. Then Drake suddenly appeared at Cadiz and burned the still harbour-bound fleet – 'singeing the King of Spain's beard' Drake called it. Finally in 1588, the massive Armada set sail up the Channel in a tight crescent shape that the English weren't able to break. What the English did instead was to prevent the Spanish from landing in England. The Spanish, kept on the move, had to put into Calais, which meant that they couldn't pick up the powerful Spanish army in the Netherlands. Then the English sent fire ships –

think floating bombs – into Calais harbour. Panicking, the Spanish scattered any which way, enabling the English to pick them off one by one. Then fierce storms forced the Spanish to keep going north, round Scotland and Ireland, where many of the ships sank. Less than half of Philip's Grand Armada limped back to Spain.

# The seeds of an empire

Henry VII started the practice of sending English expeditions overseas when he sent John Cabot to the New World to see what he could find (see Chapter 19 for more about the New World) – and he found Newfoundland. But Newfoundland seemed dull, and not until Elizabeth's reign did the English have a serious go at settling in North America. In the 1580s Sir Walter Raleigh set up a colony at Virginia, but it didn't take off. The English had better luck trading in Russia and the Baltic. In 1600 the queen granted a charter to the East India Company, which went on to lay the foundations for the British Empire in India and the east. See Chapter 19 for the full story.

# Protestants in Ulster

By the end of her reign, Elizabeth's troubles were really mounting up. She was arresting Protestant dissidents now, as well as Catholics (see Chapter 12 to find out what was going on), and Parliament was giving her grief about trading monopolies, and the succession, and heaven knows what else. And then in 1594 a serious rebellion broke out in Ulster. She sent the dashing Earl of Essex over to deal with it, but he proved hopeless and came tearing back to England to plan a coup – he had mad ideas of marrying Elizabeth and ruling the country. She soon dealt with him – had him arrested and cut off his head – but that still left the Irish rebels, and by now they were getting Spanish help. She found a much better general in Lord Mountjoy, who ran rings round the rebels and forced their leaders to flee.

Then the English had a clever idea. Why not 'plant' Protestant settlers in Ulster? Then they could control Ireland and make sure that country didn't cause any more trouble. So they did. They started sending strong, anti-Catholic Scottish Protestants to go and settle in Ulster. They're still there: The Protestant Loyalists of Ulster. Anyone today who claims to be "Scots-Irish" is descended from these original Ulster Protestants.

## Sir Walter Raleigh: An Elizabethan gentleman

Sir Walter Raleigh didn't need to go round the world or rob Spanish ships to get his knighthood: He was a genuine Elizabethan gentleman, a courtier, an MP, and a soldier, as well as an explorer. That story about him laying his cape over a puddle for the queen to walk over is probably just a story, but it shows how he liked to be remembered, as a chivalrous royal courtier. He spent a small fortune trying to make a go of his colony in the New World, which he named Virginia after the Virgin Queen (you can't beat flattery!), but it didn't work: Too many colonists died, and no one was really interested in the tobacco and potatoes he brought back. But Raleigh did help to start a different sort of colony: Planting English Protestants in Catholic Ireland. You can read more about that in the section 'Protestants in Ulster'.

## *Don't let the sun go down on me*

Elizabeth hated the idea of getting old. She plastered herself with make-up and hid her thinning hair under a great red wig. Artists had to use a stencil of her face, which showed her as a handsome young woman. Even when she was dying, Elizabeth was still a prince and proud of it. When her chief minister, Lord Robert Cecil (son of old Sir William – they were a family on the up) told her she must rest, she turned on him: 'Must! Is must a word to be addressed to princes? Little man, little man! Thy father, if he had been alive, durst not have used that word.' Ouch!

As death approached, Elizabeth was carried to the throne room and laid down on the steps of the throne. Almost her last words were to say who should succeed her: King James VI, the son of Mary, Queen of Scots. Henry VII had married his daughter Margaret to the King of Scotland and now a king of Scotland was to inherit his throne. The Tudor wheel had come full circle: How would the Stewarts fare? Find out in Chapter 13.

# Chapter 12

# A Burning Issue: The Reformation

## In This Chapter

▶ Understanding the role of the Catholic Church and the impact of the Reformation on Britain

▶ Getting to know the reformers: Martin Luther, John Calvin, and John Knox

▶ Breaking with Rome: By Henry VIII

▶ See-sawing between Churches in England

▶ Picking Protestantism in Scotland

*T*o modern eyes, the sixteenth century can seem obsessed with religion. People agonised over what would happen to them after they died, whether or not they should read the Bible – and if so, in what language – what happens at Communion, what priests should wear and whether they ought to marry, and a whole host of other things. If all this religious angst sounds a bit like worrying about how many angels can dance on the head of a pin, remember this: Some of these people died for their faith, and they were prepared to kill for it, too. Religion was central to the politics, not just of the Tudor period, but of the Stuart period which followed it. In fact you can see religion playing an important part in public life in Britain all the way up to the Victorians and beyond. This chapter explains how not one, but at least two, Protestant churches appeared in Britain, how some people stuck to the Catholic faith, and the terrible things people can do if they think God wants them to.

## Religion in the Middle Ages

If you're going to have any hope of understanding what happened to religion in Britain during the Reformation, you've got to first understand religion in the Middle Ages. (You may find it useful to have a look at Figure 12-1 here, but stick to the Catholic part of it for the moment.)

**Figure 12-1:**
Catholic and Protestant theology.

# *The role of the Catholic Church*

The Catholic Church always claimed that it had been founded by Jesus Christ himself, and that St Peter was its first head. From small beginnings, Catholicism had grown by the Middle Ages into a huge international organisation based in Rome and headed by the Pope. The popes saw themselves almost as successors to the Roman emperors, and in terms of the extent of their power and influence they were.

At the top of the Church was the Pope. The Pope was a senior churchman elected in a secret meeting by other senior churchmen known as cardinals. (The theory was that the Holy Spirit guided the cardinals' choice, but in reality it was guided by hard-nosed power politics.) The Pope had enormous authority: He could make pronouncements about Catholic belief and doctrine, he could appoint (and sack) bishops, archbishops and cardinals, and he could excommunicate – throw out of the Church altogether – absolutely anyone, even the most mighty king or emperor. He could even impose an interdict – a sort of mass excommunication – on a whole country. (England had received an interdict once; see Chapter 8 for details.)

The Pope was also the head of a large central Italian state, and popes were up to their necks in all the usual political skullduggery and fighting just like any other rulers. They led armies into battle and fathered children, and then appointed them to top jobs. Pope Leo X, who was elected in 1513, decided to remodel the Vatican as a fantastic, luxurious palace for himself. Raising the funds for it, however, led – somewhat unexpectedly – to the Reformation.

Bishops, archbishops, and cardinals were senior churchmen appointed by the Pope to help run the Church. Because they were usually highly educated, kings and emperors also appointed them to high offices of state, which is why medieval monarchs were so keen to have a say in how bishops got appointed. A huge battle raged over the appointment of bishops – it was one of the reasons for the quarrel between Henry II and Thomas à Becket (see Chapter 8 for more info on this). Some churchmen even claimed that the Pope had the right to decide who could and could not be king. For this reason, the Pope backed William the Conqueror against King Harold in 1066 (discussed in Chapter 7), and in 1570 Pope Pius V felt he had the right to excommunicate Queen Elizabeth I and invite Catholics to overthrow her (see the section 'The Catholics strike back and strike out' for more about this. You might also like to look back at Chapter 11).

At grass-roots level were the ordinary priests who said Mass and heard confessions for ordinary folk in the local parish church. But even they had great power and influence. Priests were often the only people in the community who could read and write, and they could issue a stern penance – a punishment or act of atonement for sin – on any wrongdoers. The people of the parish had to give the Church a tenth, or a tithe, of anything they earned or produced, and the Church had to build some massive tithe barns to store it all. Priests were meant to lead lives of humility, poverty, and especially chastity. Some did, but a lot didn't.

In addition, the Church ran all the schools and universities, all the hospitals and hospices, it had its own courts and its own codes of law, and it could force the civil authorities to impose punishments – even capital punishment – on anyone who stood up to it. All in all, you didn't cross the medieval Church if you could avoid it.

### Getting saved the Catholic way

Medieval people put up with this powerful Church because it seemed to be the only thing that could save them from eternal torment. According to the Catholic Church, once you died, you went through a selection process in Purgatory before the recording angel decided whether you went to Heaven or Hell. Purgatory wasn't some sort of celestial doctor's waiting room: It was where you got your sin burnt away. The more sin you had, the longer you spent in Purgatory, and woe betide you if you still had some of those deep-down stains when Judgement Day came. (If this process sounds tricky, have a look at Figure 12-1.)

How could you keep your time in Purgatory to a minimum? Ideally, lead a blameless life, but only saints manage that. Alternatively, you could do things that would earn you time off for good behaviour (or grace to give this notion its proper title) and the Catholic Church had a whole set of suggestions:

- **Go to Mass on Sundays:** The Mass was (and still is) the most important ceremony in the Catholic Church. Central to Mass is the Eucharist, also known as Holy Communion. This is where the priest offers up bread and wine and, according to the theory, they become the actual body and blood of Christ. He then gives the bread to the people to eat (see the later section on 'God's on Our Side! – the Protestants and Edward VI' to see why they didn't get the wine). If you didn't receive the bread, the Church said, you would never get to heaven.

- **Pray to a saint:** Doing this was fairly easy – statues of saints were available in every church to help you – but some saints had more clout than others. Best of all was praying over a saint's relic – you know, St Andrew's toenail or a feather from the Angel Gabriel.

- **Do a good deed:** The better the deed, the more Grace you racked up.

- **Go on a pilgrimage:** How much Grace this earned you depended on where you went. Travelling to a major shrine, like the one of St Thomas at Canterbury or the famous one of St James at Compostella in Spain, carried serious Grace.

✔ **Go on a Crusade:** At this rate, you might only be in Purgatory for the weekend. If you had the good fortune to die on a Crusade, you got to bypass Purgatory altogether and proceeded straight to Heaven.

✔ **Get an indulgence:** An indulgence was a Get Out of Purgatory Free card, issued directly by the Pope.

Crusades were over by the sixteenth century, so to bypass Purgatory altogether, you needed an indulgence. Normally you had to do something to earn it, but a Dominican friar called John Tetzel had just appeared in Germany selling indulgences. For cash. And not just for you, madam. These New Improved Papal Indulgences work for people who are already in Purgatory! As Tetzel put it: 'Put a penny in the plate; a soul springs through that Pearly Gate!'

## Enter the reformers

Previous churchmen had protested against the wealth and corruption in the church, like John Wyclif and the Lollards (see Chapter 10 to find out more), and a Bohemian reformer called Jan Hus, but the precedents weren't encouraging. Hus had been burnt at the stake.

### Martin Luther in Germany

Martin Luther (1483–1546) was a Catholic monk who didn't believe that you could just buy your way into Heaven. If only some wayward priest was selling indulgences, Luther might not have been so dismayed. The real trouble was that Tetzel wasn't working on his own. He had the Pope's backing (the money was for Pope Leo X's St Peter's Restoration-in-the-Latest-Renaissance-Style fund). If Luther was right, and you couldn't buy your way into Heaven, that meant the Pope was wrong. So Luther sat up late into the night in the tower of his Augustinian monastery trying to work this puzzle out. If the Pope was wrong about Salvation, then who on earth was right? What Luther came up with out of his agonising would turn Europe upside down:

✔ **You don't need to do anything to get to Heaven:** You just have to believe in Jesus.

✔ **You don't need to go on pilgrimages or pray to saints (including the Virgin Mary):** Everything you need is in the Bible. (Luther thought letting ordinary people read the Bible for themselves was a good idea.)

✔ **Priests (and that includes the Pope) don't have special powers:** They can't change water into wine – or bread and wine into the body and blood of Christ. And while we're at it, nothing exists in the Bible to say priests can't get married if they feel like it, either.

Luther's ideas got him into serious trouble. Without the intervention of his local prince, he would've been put to death by order of the Pope and the Holy Roman Emperor (who wasn't Holy or Roman but was Emperor of Germany). Some German princes who were on Luther's side *protested* against the way the emperor was attacking Luther's supporters, and so they all became known as Protestants.

### John Calvin in Geneva

Important events were also happening in Switzerland. A French lawyer called John Calvin (1509–64) had been appointed minister of the city church at Geneva, and he was coming up with some very interesting new ideas about how to get to Heaven. 'It's easy,' he said. 'Some people are predestined to go to Heaven, even before they are born, and some people are predestined to go to Hell. The lucky ones are the Elect, and the unlucky ones are Suckers. If you're very strict with yourself, pray lots, read the Bible every day, and generally have no fun, then that's a pretty good sign that you're one of the Elect; but if you drink or gamble, then you are Damned.' (See Figure 12-1 to get an idea of how Calvin's ideas worked out.)

Here are John Calvin's rules for How to Run a Church:

- ✔ **Each congregation elects its own ministers.** No priests with special powers.

- ✔ **No bishops in silly hats. Ministers elect a group of Elders to run the church.** (However, Elders may also wear silly hats.)

- ✔ **Ministers wear a simple black gown to preach in.** No, repeat no, fancy vestments.

- ✔ **Pictures, candlesticks, altar rails, statues, and stained-glass windows are evil and should be smashed.** Whitewash those walls.

- ✔ **No special altars.** Just a plain communion table for the bread and wine.

Here's a very important postscript: Calvin's followers worked out an idea which they called the *Doctrine of Resistance*, which said that, if you had an 'ungodly' monarch ('ungodly' means 'disagrees with Calvin'), you had the right – nay, the duty – to resist him. Or her. Even, if necessary, to kill him. Or her. This idea didn't go down well with European monarchs – Catholic or Protestant!

### John Knox

John Knox (1514–72) was a remarkable man. He, like Luther, started out as a Catholic priest, but he changed his mind when he met George Wishart, a Scottish Reformation leader, and he was deeply shocked when Scottish Cardinal Beaton (the Archbishop of St Andrews) had Wishart burnt at the stake. Knox thought it only fair when Cardinal Beaton got murdered later by an angry group of Scottish Protestant lords (see the section 'Scotland Chooses Its Path' for more info on the Reformation in Scotland): 'These things we write merrily!' Knox wrote.

When the Catholic French attacked St Andrews, Knox ended up as a prisoner in the French galleys, until Edward VI (Henry VIII's son) got him released. But Knox had to hot-foot it for Geneva when Mary, Henry's Catholic daughter, came to the throne. In Geneva, Knox was wowed by John Calvin (see the preceding section) and started spreading Calvin's word among English exiles in Germany. He also wrote a famous pamphlet against women rulers, *The First Blast of the Trumpet Against the Monstrous Regiment* (that is, *Rule*) *of Women*. Bad timing. Knox was writing about Mary Tudor and Mary of Guise, but the pamphlet appeared just when Elizabeth became Queen of England. Knox sent her a grovelling letter saying, 'Of course I didn't mean you, Your Majesty....' Elizabeth wasn't convinced.

Back home in Scotland, Knox also met Mary, Queen of Scots – five times. He didn't stand on ceremony; he lectured her the same way he would anyone else. He called her a slave of Satan and compared her to wicked Queen Jezebel in the Bible, meaning Scots should resist her before she dragged the whole country down to Hell. When Mary's husband Darnley was murdered at Kirk o' Field and Mary married the chief suspect (see Chapter 11 for the details of those events), Knox said he wasn't surprised and he thought that she should be executed. He didn't live to see Mary's death, however. He died in 1572. You can bet he wasn't expecting to bump into Mary in the afterlife.

# Back in England with Henry VIII

Henry VIII took a deep interest in theology, and he couldn't stand Martin Luther. He even wrote a book pointing out exactly where he thought Luther had got his faith wrong. The Pope was so pleased that he gave Henry a special title, *Fidei Defensor* – 'Defender of the Faith'. You can still see the letters FD on British coins today. Yet despite Henry's book and feelings about Luther, English scholars were getting interested in Luther's ideas, and his books were beginning to find their way into Oxford and Cambridge, where the next generation of priests were being taught.

Henry's problems with the Pope weren't about theology; they were about what was termed *The King's Great Matter*. Henry wanted the Pope to give him a divorce from his queen, Katharine of Aragon, so that he could marry Anne Boleyn (see Chapter 11 to find out more about why Henry wanted rid of Katharine and why his other marriages didn't turn out too well either). When the Pope wouldn't play ball, Henry decided to break away from the Roman Church and set up an English Church, with himself at its head.

## Breaking with Rome

At first, all Henry wanted was a Church that would give him his divorce. To get that Church, he needed to cut the Pope out of the picture. So he started in 1532 with a set of laws to stop anyone from appealing to Rome and to stop any orders from the Pope coming into England. The laws also laid down that all of Henry's subjects had to take an oath accepting Henry as head of the Church. Some people objected. Sir Thomas More and Bishop John Fisher of Rochester, for example, both refused to take the oath, and Henry had them both executed for it. The monks of the London Charterhouse also refused to take the oath, and Henry had them hanged, drawn, and quartered. Unsurprisingly, most people went along with him.

Henry then struck out at one of the most popular pilgrimage cults in England: The shrine of St Thomas of Canterbury. This saint was Thomas à Becket, the archbishop who had backed the Pope against King Henry II and become a martyr when King Henry's men killed him in Canterbury Cathedral (see Chapter 8 if you want the details of that event). Slightly uncomfortable parallels for Henry VIII, wouldn't you say? So Henry had the shrine destroyed, and told everyone to do the same to any pictures or statues of St Thomas they may have.

## Closing the monasteries

By 1536 Henry VIII was low on cash, and Thomas Cromwell, a Protestant and Henry's chief minister, had an idea for getting some: Close down all the monasteries. Monks were meant to be poor, but their monasteries sat on huge sums, some of it in land and some of it in treasures like gold and silver chalices. Henry's eyes lit up. But they couldn't just close the monasteries like that, so Cromwell sent his men out to investigate them and dig for dirt – which they duly delivered.

According to Cromwell's men, you could hardly move in the cloisters for bags of gold and monks ravishing maidens. This information was good tabloid stuff, just what Cromwell needed to give the orders to shut the places down and turn the monks out into the world to go and earn an honest living. His men even stripped the lead from the roofs, which is why to this day you can see those stark but beautiful ruins of great abbeys at Fountains and Riveaulx and Tintern in the green of the English and Welsh countryside. Closing the monasteries down provoked the most serious challenge Henry had to face in the whole of his reign: The *Pilgrimage of Grace*.

## The Pilgrimage of Grace

Don't be misled by this name. The Pilgrimage of Grace was an armed rebellion, the biggest and most serious that Tudor England ever faced. The rebellion started in Lincolnshire and then spread to Yorkshire, where a local landowner called Robert Aske became its leader. The rebels were angry about lots of things: They didn't like the new taxes Henry had introduced, and they didn't like it when local lords enclosed the common land (see Chapter 14 for more about what the problem with enclosures was all about). But above all, the rebels hated what Thomas Cromwell was doing to the Church. They wanted Cromwell out and their monasteries back, and they thought Henry would listen. Yes, it was a bit naive.

The Pilgrims had a great banner showing the five wounds of Christ (the ones inflicted on the cross), and they said prayers and sang hymns as they went. Henry sent an army north under the Duke of Norfolk to confront the rebels, but when the Duke got there he found he didn't have enough men. So he stalled. He told the Pilgrims that if they all went home, the king would pardon them and give them what they wanted. The poor saps believed him. Norfolk got a few more men together and then struck. Dawn raids. Aske and some 250 of the Pilgrims were strung up on city walls and on village greens to show what happened if you dared so much as raise your little finger against King Henry VIII.

## The Church of England: More Protestant or More Catholic?

So what sort of a Church was Henry's new Church of England going to be? That was the big question, and even Henry didn't seem to be all that sure.

### Swinging toward Protestant ideas . . .

Henry got rid of the Pope, banned pilgrimages, and ordered pictures and statues of saints to be destroyed. He closed down monasteries. Most importantly, he agreed to publish an English Bible. If you've been reading this chapter from the beginning, this idea may sound slightly familiar. By Henry's actions, he seemed to be doing just what Martin Luther had said everyone ought to be doing.

So was Henry VIII's Church going to be Protestant? Henry's chief minister, Thomas Cromwell, was a Protestant, as Anne Boleyn had been and Anne of Cleves (Henry's current wife by 1536) was. When Henry issued the *Ten Articles*, which explained what his Church believed in, he appeared to be Protestant, too. And then, quite suddenly, he seemed to change his mind.

## Translation troubles

You wouldn't think just translating the Bible into English would cause much trouble, but you'd be wrong. The Catholic Church, which didn't approve of ordinary people reading the Bible anyway – it wanted to keep that to priests – had been using a Latin translation called the *Vulgate*, until Erasmus, a top Renaissance scholar, found it was full of mistakes – a point that didn't go down well in the Vatican, I can tell you! William Tyndale came up with a New Testament in English that anyone could read, but he got into trouble with Henry VIII for doing it (this was in Henry's I-hate-Luther days) and he had to flee abroad, and even then the Dutch put him to death at Henry VIII's request. 'Oh Lord!' Tyndale is supposed to have said, 'Open the King of England's eyes!' Maybe he did, because when Miles Coverdale produced a full English Bible a few years later it became Henry's 'official' Bible, distributed to every parish. It even had a cover picture of Henry VIII giving the Word of God to his people. When Henry's Catholic daughter, Mary, came to the throne, English Protestants headed for Geneva where they produced their own *Geneva Bible* (also known as the 'Breeches Bible' because it said Adam and Eve got hold of fig leaves and made themselves breeches, which would suggest they had sewing machines in the Garden of Eden!). Soon a rival Catholic English Bible was produced, too! In the end it was King James I who got all the scholars together to produce the definitive *Authorised Version*, or *King James Bible*, which was so beautifully written even Catholics couldn't really complain.

### Swinging back toward Catholic ideas . . .

When Henry VIII's marriage to Anne of Cleves fell apart (see Chapter 11 to find out why), it turned him off both Thomas Cromwell and his German Protestant friends. When the bishops came up with a book (called – not very imaginatively – *The Bishops' Book*) with all sorts of ideas for making the Church of England Protestant, Henry didn't like it one bit. Henry even had second thoughts about people reading the Bible. He stopped giving out copies and told people to leave Bible-reading to priests. Finally, in 1539, Henry got Parliament to pass the *Act of Six Articles* to say exactly what this Church of England believed in:

- **Transubstantiation:** The bread and wine change into the body and blood of Christ when the priest says the words.

- **People should only receive the bread at Communion, not the wine:** This was very much a Catholic idea.

- **Priests should not marry because God says so:** Another Catholic idea.

- **Private Masses (ones people paid for, often for the sake of souls in purgatory) were okay:** Which was not at all what Protestants thought.

✔ **Widows may not remarry:** Henry was supporting (Catholic-style) vows of celibacy.

✔ **Everyone needs to go to Confession:** And the penalty for denying this? Death!

A word exists for what Henry was doing, and the word wasn't Protestant. A lot of English Protestants got out while they still could and headed for Geneva. Once there, it was just a question of waiting – for Henry VIII to die.

# God's on Our Side! – the Protestants and Edward VI

English Protestants were very relieved when Edward VI came to the throne in 1547. Although he was only nine, he had been taught all about the Protestant religion. The Archbishop of Canterbury, Thomas Cranmer, was becoming more Protestant, too. He got married, for a start, and he banned statues and pictures of saints or the Virgin Mary. But during Edward's reign a more important question needed tackling: Did the bread and wine at Mass really become Jesus's body and blood or not?

The question of what happened to the bread and wine was crucial. The Catholic Church said that the moment the priest spoke the words 'This is my body, this is my blood' the bread and wine became the actual body and blood of Christ. This idea was called *Transubstantiation.* Luther more or less went along with that idea, though he thought they became a sort of mixture of bread-and-body and wine-and-blood, which got called Consubstantiation. But Calvin rejected the whole idea because it made it look as if priests had special magic powers. So Protestants held that the bread and wine remained bread and wine, and you took them in memory of the Last Supper, and nothing more.

One extra point. Because the Catholic Church believed the wine became Jesus's blood, it was absolutely vital not to spill it, so to be on the safe side only the priest drank the wine – everyone else had to make do with the bread. In time the Catholic Church began to speak as if only its priests were *allowed* to drink the wine, and it became yet another thing for Protestants and Catholics to argue about.

So when Cranmer sat down to write the *Book of Common Prayer* or *Prayer Book* in 1549 (the actual words and liturgy that would replace the Catholic Mass in English churches), he had to be very careful in the bit about the bread and the wine. He fudged the details. Deliberately.

The text didn't actually say that the bread is the body and the wine is the blood, but on the other hand it didn't actually say that they're not either. But Catholics weren't having this ambiguity. As soon as the Prayer Books started appearing a huge Catholic uprising occurred in Devon and Cornwall that took a huge army to put down. (See Chapter 11 for the political consequences of this uprising.) Meanwhile Cranmer was having second thoughts. Protestant thoughts. So in 1552, he had another go at writing the book.

The message in the second round was clear: The bread is bread and the wine is wine and nothing else. But within a year, Edward VI died and his Catholic sister Mary was on the throne. No more prayer books or articles. The Mass was back, and so was the Pope.

# We're on God's Side! – the Catholics and Queen Mary

Queen Mary has had some of the worst press in history. Okay, not as bad as Jack the Ripper, but not a lot better. For years historians said that Mary forced the English to become Catholic and burned hundreds of Protestants while she was at it, so she became known as Bloody Mary. They even named a cocktail after her.

Now historians reckon that most English people were quite happy being Catholic until well into Elizabeth's reign. They didn't like Henry VIII's changes, and they hated the Prayer Book of 1552, though that only lasted a year. So when Mary came to the throne and restored the Catholic Church, a general sigh of relief went up.

## A good beginning, then a few bad decisions

Mary had some very able bishops to help her, especially her new Archbishop of Canterbury, Cardinal Pole. Pole wasn't a jumped up butcher's boy like Cardinal Wolsey (see Chapter 11), he was a proper toff, of royal blood. People took out their old Mass books and dug their holy statues out of the attic. Then Mary made some very silly decisions:

- ✔ **Marrying King Philip II of Spain:** It was bound to be unpopular, and it was.

- ✔ **Burning Protestants:** Not quite as unpopular as you may think – this was an age when you could be disembowelled in public, don't forget.

But people didn't like it when the victim was poor or when groups of Protestants were burnt together.

✔ **Going to war with France:** Normally the English were only too happy to fight the French, but this time, they were only dragged into it to help Philip, and then Mary went and lost Calais. They never really forgave her.

## Come on Mary, light my fire

Mary's reign is best known for her policy of arresting Protestants and burning them at the stake.

Catholics and Protestants didn't just think the other side was wrong, they actually thought they were evil and had to be stopped. But you also had a Christian duty to save them if you could. So, first Protestants had to Come Out ('Hi. I'm Bob. And I'm an – an … Anglican.'). Then they had to repent. Finally, they had to be burnt because, through burning there was just a chance that the fire might purify their soul – the old Purgatory idea (see the section 'Getting saved the Catholic way'). The most famous burnings took place in Oxford, when Thomas Cranmer (the one who had worked so hard on the *Book of Common Prayer*) was burnt, as well as Anglican bishops, Hugh Latimer and Nicholas Ridley.

Historians argue about what to make of the burnings. Some point out that Mary's persecution was mild compared to persecution on the continent, which is probably true but wouldn't have meant much to English people at the time. Others say that she turned many people against the Catholic Church. What historians do generally agree on is that Mary and Cardinal Pole, her Archbishop of Canterbury, were very successful in getting the Catholic Church up and running again. Had they lived a bit longer, England could very well have stayed a Catholic country. But they didn't. They died the same day in 1558 and Elizabeth came to the throne. The Catholics had missed their chance.

# Elizabeth Settles It . . . or Does She?

Religion was high up on Elizabeth's list of priorities when she came to the throne. Luckily for her, all Queen Mary's bishops resigned, so she could appoint new ones who would go along with what she wanted. And what she wanted was Protestant – with Catholic bits:

✔ **Elizabeth was to be Supreme Governor of the Church,** not Supreme Head like Henry VIII. Governor meant that the real head of the Church was God.

✔ **Her Church of England was to have proper bishops,** silly hats and all.

✔ **Priests in her Church were to wear vestments.** The vestment only needed to be a white cotton surplice worn over a black cassock, but it had to be worn. Elizabeth wanted her priests to look like priests.

✔ **Some saints' days and feast days could stay.** Elizabeth knew a crowd-pleaser when she saw one.

✔ **Thirty-nine articles summed up what the Church of England believed.** A lot of Calvin appears in the Articles – Article 17 is all about predestination – but a lot of Elizabeth's in there, too. Article 21 stops the Church holding a Council without the monarch's permission, and Article 35 stresses the authority of the queen and her magistrates.

✔ **There would have to be another new prayer book.** As for the thorny problem of the bread and wine (see the earlier section 'God's on Our Side!' – the Protestants and Edward VI' for details on this dilemma), they came up with a very clever solution phrasing the text in such a way as to imply that the bread and wine both are and aren't the body and blood of Christ.

That last point's called having it both ways, my friends! But if Elizabeth thought her settlement was going to win everyone over, she could think again.

## The Catholics strike back and strike out

In 1570 Pope Paul V excommunicated Elizabeth, which meant Catholics were allowed to plot against her. He also started sending Catholic missionary priests into England. Elizabeth responded:

✔ She made it treason even to bring a copy of the excommunication bull into England.

✔ Harbouring a Catholic priest was made illegal. Catholics had to hide the priests in secret priest holes.

✔ Catholics who refused to take communion at their local Anglican church paid a hefty *recusancy* (or 'refusal') fine.

By 1580 recusancy fines had gone through the roof, and Catholics could go to prison just for attending Mass. Imprisoned Catholics had to answer the *Bloody Questions*, like 'Do you obey the Pope?' and 'So if the Pope told you to kill the Queen, would you do it?' Even to be a Catholic priest was treason, and in 1580, the government set up a huge manhunt to catch the first Jesuit missionaries. (Jesuits were members of the elite Catholic order the Society of Jesus.) Jesuit priest Edmund Campion and two others were caught in a secret hideaway. Campion was tortured and executed.

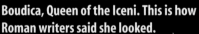

Boudica, Queen of the Iceni. This is how Roman writers said she looked.

King Kenneth I Macalpin. He united the Picts and Scots but he wouldn't have looked anything like this much later portrait.

The Synod of Whitby, AD 664, tied England to Rome for 900 years.

The breathtaking Norman nave of Durham Cathedral.

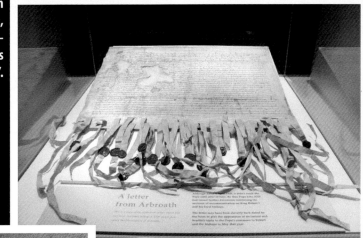

The Declaration of Arbroath, 1320 – Scotland's 'Magna Carta'.

The Black Death. Many people turned to the Church for comfort.

The saintly King Henry VI. His incapacity for ruling led to the disastrous Wars of the Roses.

The romantic beauty of Beaumaris Castle, Anglesey

King Henry VII. Many people had a better claim to the throne and he knew it.

King Henry VIII – a highly dangerous man, as this much later portrait makes clear.

The English engage the Spanish Armada, 1588. The English claimed their victory was the work of God.

King James IV – Scotland's Renaissance Prince.

Queen Elizabeth I. The artist has used the official stencil of her face, making her look much younger. The serpent on her sleeve means wisdom and she holds a rainbow symbolising peace.

The Gunpowder Plotters, 1605. Had they succeeded, England would almost certainly have been plunged into civil war.

The Authorised Version of the Bible – King James I's most enduring legacy.

The seventeenth-century House of Commons. It defeated Charles I but was closed down by Cromwell.

'Freeborn John' Lilburne – champion of the rights of ordinary people through the years of civil war.

The massacre at Glencoe, 1692, tarnished the reputation of King William III.

The Battle of Blenheim, 1704. The Duke of Marlborough defeated the French and established Britain's reputation as a major military power.

The British take Fort Ticonderoga, 1759. Within a generation, Britain's American empire was lost.

Chatsworth House, Derbyshire. The stateliest home of England.

Olaudah Equiano – former slave and anti-slave trade campaigner. He married a Cambridgeshire girl and settled in East Anglia.

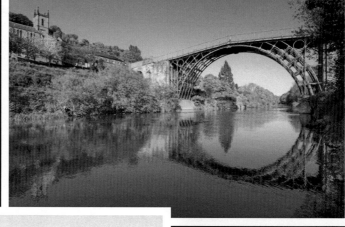

Abraham Darby's elegant iron bridge over the River Severn. Modern Britain starts here.

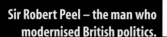

Sir Robert Peel – the man who modernised British politics.

Desperation and starvation in Ireland during the Famine of the 1840s.

A Victorian cathedral to science and progress – the Crystal Palace and the Great Exhibition, 1851.

After the massacre at Amritsar, 1919. The killings sealed the fate of British India.

Winston Churchill in 1945 – the year he won the war and lost the General Election.

The Beatles get the sixties swinging, 1964.

A nice cup of tea. What could be more British?

## The Puritans

*Puritan* is a tricky word. We tend to think of Puritans as wearing large white collars and tall black hats, but only the really serious ones did that. Strictly speaking, no one group called Puritans existed: The term was one of abuse used against Protestants who criticised the Church of England. Some were out-and-out Calvinists, who wanted to get rid of bishops and parishes, and even the queen, but most just wanted to change some of the most Catholic features of her Church, like vestments or decoration in church buildings. Either way, they saw themselves as normal Protestants and everyone else as the oddballs who had got things wrong.

## And the Protestants aren't happy either

English Protestants weren't any happier with the Church of England than English Catholics were. In fact, they thought the Church of England was too Catholic, with its vestments and bishops and candles and what have you.

Archbishop of Canterbury, Edmund Grindal, refused to wear vestments or tell his priests to wear them, so Elizabeth suspended him (from office, not from the window). Some Protestants gathered in small illegal prayer groups called *prophesyings*, where they could elect their ministers and wear plain black, just as Calvin had said they should. For Elizabeth, the religious issue was a question of authority. She was Supreme Governor of the Church; she had laid down the law. Elizabeth had these Puritans, as she called them, arrested and executed.

# Scotland Chooses Its Path

While Henry VIII was deciding what religion he wanted for the Church of England, in Scotland Cardinal David Beaton, Archbishop of St Andrews, knew exactly what he wanted, and it wasn't Protestants. He hunted Scottish Protestants down mercilessly and burned them at the stake.

## Protestant uprising

In 1545 Cardinal Beaton arrested and burned a very popular Scottish Protestant preacher called George Wishart; Wishart's death was the final straw for the beleaguered Scottish Protestants. A group of Protestant lords burst Beaton's door down and hacked him to pieces (you could say he was Beaton to death!). But they had reckoned without the French.

The French had virtually been ruling Scotland ever since James V died and handed over to his baby daughter, Mary, Queen of Scots (see Chapter 11 for the low-down on this). The Regent was James V's ultra-Catholic widow, Mary of Guise. The Scots quickly got tired of being ruled by Mary of Guise, especially as more of them became Protestant, while their French rulers remained staunchly Catholic.

Mary of Guise wasn't going to sit around and see cardinals being murdered. She got her troops together and marched to St Andrews. The Protestants had to surrender, and the French put the prisoners, including one John Knox, in their galleys as slaves.

The Protestant lords weren't quelled, though. A group of them, calling themselves the Lords of the Congregation, signed a covenant rejecting the Pope and all he stood for and dared the French to do their worst. Then John Knox (who'd been freed from galley duty by Edward VI) arrived back in Scotland from Geneva where he'd been lapping up Calvin's ideas. He became minister of St Giles's Cathedral in Edinburgh and immediately started stirring up trouble for the French. The Lords of the Congregation forced Mary of Guise to step down as Regent, and in 1560, Scotland formally broke away from the Catholic Church. And that situation was how things stood when Mary, Queen of Scots came home from France (to find out what she was doing in France and what happened when she returned to Scotland, see Chapter 11).

## Mary's return to Scotland

Mary, Queen of Scots was a Catholic and proud of it, but she knew she could not hope to defeat Knox and the Lords of the Congregation. She sided with the Protestants – if you can't beat 'em, join 'em – and, when a Catholic rising occurred, she crushed it. Her efforts didn't help her much, however: The Protestants still turned against her after all that business with Lord Darnley and Lord Bothwell (see Chapter 11 for details) and forced her to abdicate.

## James VI steps in and muddies the waters even more

With Mary gone, her baby son, James VI, became Scotland's king. Soon Scotland's religion was looking even more confused than England's:

- ✔ **The Church of Scotland (known as the Kirk) was strictly Calvinist, or Presbyterian as they called it (after presbyter, a good biblical name for a priest).** It had elected ministers, who all wore plain black gowns and long beards, and elected the General Assembly to run the whole thing.

- ✔ **Scotland also had lots of Scottish Catholics, especially in the Highlands.** They were on Mary, Queen of Scots's side and wanted her back.

- ✔ **In 1584 the Edinburgh Parliament made King James Head of the Kirk.** According to Calvin's rules, however, you couldn't have a monarch at the head of a church. And King James didn't much like the Presbyterian Kirk anyway. He preferred having bishops (he could control them). He was certainly having no truck with that Calvinist Doctrine of Resistance, explained in the section 'John Calvin in Geneva' earlier in this chapter.

So Scotland was a Presbyterian country headed by a king who didn't like Presbyterians. Tricky, eh? Made trickier by the fact that when James became King of England on Elizabeth's death in 1603, he also became the Supreme Governor of the Church of England, which Presbyterians said was virtually Catholic (although Catholics didn't think so; see the earlier section 'Elizabeth Settles It . . . or Does She?' for the details). Handling all this religious politicking was going to take tact and intelligence. King James VI didn't do tact or intelligence.

# Chapter 13

# Crown or Commons?

*In This Chapter*

▷ Coming south: The Stuarts and James I's reign

▷ Introducing Charles I: Bad beginnings that culminated in civil war

▷ Becoming a republic: Cromwell's England

▷ Returning of the king: Charles II and his uneasy alliance with Parliament

The seventeenth century is the century that made Britain different. And because this was also the century when the British began to settle in America in large numbers, it made America different, too. At the start of the century, England was like any other kingdom, with an all-powerful king, but by the end of it the English had toppled two kings and put one of them on trial. Even more importantly, they had overturned the monarchy itself and turned England into a republic under Oliver Cromwell. Cromwell's republic didn't last, but it certainly changed things. England was going to be a Parliamentary monarchy quite unlike other European states, and Scotland and Ireland were going to have to live with it (and in it) whether they liked it or not.

## The Stewarts Come South

James VI was only a baby when Mary, Queen of Scots had to abdicate and flee to England (see Chapter 11 to find out why) leaving him behind to become King of Scotland. Everyone wanted to be Regent, of course, so initially the Scottish court saw some fine old to-ing and fro-ing between the Earl of Lennox, the Earl of Mar, and the Earl of Morton. All this quarrelling wasn't just about who was going to run the country, it was also about religion (no surprise there; if you are surprised, refer to Chapter 12 to find out why you shouldn't be).

James was brought up by strict Presbyterians who were always worrying that he was going to rebel and become a Catholic like his mother. And these Presbyterians didn't like James getting friendly with the French Duke of Lennox, Esmé Stuart, one bit. In 1582 a group of Protestant lords kidnapped James and held him prisoner until he condemned Esmé to death. James, pluckily, refused. He wasn't a Catholic, and he wasn't going to become a Catholic, but he wasn't going to be told what to do either.

James became Head of the Church of Scotland and reintroduced bishops, which he really enjoyed because it annoyed the Presbyterians so much. But above all, he was keeping a close eye on England. Elizabeth had made England a major European power, much richer and stronger than Scotland, and soon England would be his, all his! James couldn't wait for Elizabeth to die. He wrote to her regularly and was regularly disappointed when she wrote back. Finally, in January 1603, the news arrived: Elizabeth was dead. King James VI of Scotland was now King James I of England. The Scots didn't see James for dust.

England had conquered Wales and Ireland in the Middle Ages (see Chapters 8 and 9 to find out how) but the Kings of England had never quite managed to become Kings of Scotland, so when James became King of England, it was the first time the whole of the islands – England, Wales, Scotland, and Ireland – had ever had the same ruler. James even called himself King of Great Britain, but the name didn't catch on, mainly because his kingdoms were still very different. He also dropped 'Stewart' for the more English 'Stuart'.

James assumed the English Parliament would work much the same way as the Scottish Parliament (which was essentially there to pass any laws the king happened to want). Boy, was he wrong!

James believed in a new theory called the Divine Right of Kings, which held that kings could do what they liked and were answerable only to God. He even said that 'Kings are justly called gods', which was news to the English. James certainly didn't look like a god. He had long spindly legs, and his tongue always hung out, which made him stammer even when he was telling dirty jokes (which he did often). He seemed almost paranoid about being assassinated and wore extra padding in case anyone tried to knife him.

## Know your Puritans

Elizabeth had cracked down on Catholics and Puritans (see Chapter 12 to find out why), so both sides were looking to James to give them a break. The Puritans even hoped James would go a bit further and introduce a few changes into the Church of England. Some hope. James loathed Scottish Presbyterians, and he thought Puritans were just Presbyterians with posh voices.

## The *Mayflower*

Many people know the fine, stirring tale of the Pilgrim Fathers: The small band of God-fearing Puritans who took ship in the *Mayflower* and sailed from Plymouth to Cape Cod (actually they'd been aiming for Virginia but they took a wrong turn) and founded a settlement they called Plymouth Plantation. However, they only survived their first winter in the New World thanks to the help and hospitality of the native tribes. At this point millions of Americans go dewy-eyed and feel a lump in the throat while the rest of the world wonders what all the fuss is about.

Okay, let's get real here. Firstly, less than a third of the settlers were Puritans. Secondly, although New England had an elected governor, it was one of the most intolerant societies of its day. Puritans certainly believed in their own freedom of worship, but they didn't believe in anyone else's. Many people in England were only too pleased to see them go.

Although similar in many ways (they both followed John Calvin's teachings, for example, and they both hated bishops), English Puritans weren't quite the same as the Scottish Presbyterians. An important difference between the two groups was that Scottish Presbyterians didn't believe that a king or queen could be head of the Church; English Puritans, on the other hand, accepted the monarch as the Supreme Governor of the Church of England.

James called a big meeting of Puritans and bishops to Hampton Court in 1604 to try to sort out all these religious problems. The bishops were pretty cross about this meeting. They couldn't see why they should have to sit down with the Puritans at all. They soon cheered up, however, when the Puritans said they wanted to get rid of bishops, and James told them simply, 'No bishop, no king' – and sent them packing. His Archbishop of Canterbury, Richard Bancroft, promptly started hunting down Puritans and forcing them out of the Church. No wonder some of them thought they'd be better off on the other side of the Atlantic and hired a ship, the *Mayflower*, to take them there.

## *Boom, shake the room – the Gunpowder Plot*

If James thought the Puritans were a problem (see the preceding section), he hadn't yet met the Catholics. James was as good a friend as the Catholics were likely to get. He made peace with Spain and even tried to marry his son Charles to a Spanish princess. He certainly preferred Catholics to Puritans, but he couldn't risk appearing soft on popery by removing all Elizabeth's anti-Catholic fines and penalties (the English had executed his Catholic mother, don't forget: James never did). So he allowed his chief minister, Lord Robert Cecil, to re-impose heavy fines on Catholics and banish Catholic priests. Most Catholics simply went and put new sheets on the camp bed in the priest-hole (see Chapter 12), but a hot-headed fool called Robert Catesby decided to get more pro-active. He planned one of the most famous terrorist attacks in history: The Gunpowder Plot.

Catesby, and a group of conspirators, planned to blow the king and the whole of Parliament sky-high. Had they succeeded, the explosion would have destroyed everybody with any claim to sovereignty throughout the islands, and what would have followed hardly bears thinking of: Almost certainly civil war, quite possibly foreign invasion, and very likely sectarian massacre.

The government got wind of the plot (the plotters were filling the cellars under the House of Lords with large barrels and lots of firewood – it would've been hard not to get wind of it) when someone, presumably one of the plotters, sent a note to a Lord Monteagle warning him not to go to Parliament on the 5 November. Lord Monteagle promptly showed the note to Lord Robert Cecil, who sent guards down to the cellar. They found Guy Fawkes, another conspirator, surrounded by barrels of gunpowder, with a fuse in one hand and a match in the other, trying to convince them he'd just come to check the plumbing. They took him away and tortured him, while the rest of the plotters gave themselves up after a gun battle with government troops. The nation breathed an almighty sigh of relief.

The English have got quite fond of the Gunpowder Plot and don't take it too seriously nowadays. The Plot's a good excuse for a big fireworks display each 5 November and a line of jokes about Guy Fawkes being the only honest man to go into Parliament. Of course, there was nothing funny about it at the time.

# *James 1 fought the law and . . . who won?*

Ironically, James was probably a better King of Scotland while he was in London than he had ever been while he was at Holyrood in Edinburgh. He set up a system of nobles, bishops, lawyers, and Scottish MPs to keep Scotland on an even keel while he was away, and by and large his system worked. It was in England that he hit trouble.

The English soon came to despise James, especially when he started relying on favourites – never a good idea. First it was Robert Carr, Earl of Somerset, and then it was George Villiers, Duke of Buckingham. The English didn't like his peace with Spain or his attempt to get England entangled in Europe's Thirty Years' War (if you want to know what the Thirty Years' War was all about, and I know you do, see *European History For Dummies* (Wiley)). But above all, they couldn't take his Divine Right of Kings idea. Lord Chief Justice Sir Edward Coke said James was going against English Common Law. James tried to tell Parliament to stop banging on about human rights, but Parliament said that if James wanted any money out of them, he would have to put up with it. So James decided to do without Parliament and get money by other ways instead.

## Witch crazed

James I was obsessed with witches. He wrote a book called *Daemonologie* about how to spot if your neighbour was a witch and what to do about it if she was (which was, essentially, to hang her). Most people believed in witches, and Elizabeth even had her own personal magus, Dr John Dee, who knew all about the occult. But James's level of interest was something new. While he was still in Scotland he accused the Earl of Bothwell of trying to kill him by using witchcraft to raise up a storm at sea – imagine trying to defend yourself in court against a charge like that! – and Bothwell virtually had to stage a coup to get the charges dropped.

The English soon cottoned on to their new king's interests. Shakespeare wrote witches into *Macbeth*, and a zealous magistrate in Lancashire looked into a suspiciously large number of cases of deliberate healing by old women at the town of Pendle – and hanged them.

To fund his projects, James borrowed; he forced people to lend him money; he sold trading monopolies; and he even invented a new hereditary title, baronet, which he sold to hundreds of eager buyers – social climbing's not a new idea. But all his efforts weren't enough. James had inherited a rich court, and he wanted to make the most of it, commissioning new buildings and paintings in the latest baroque or *Jacobean* (from Jacobus, Latin for James) style. By the time he died in 1625, he had no credit at the bank and not much in Parliament either.

# Charles 1

If ever a man asked for every bad thing that came to him, that man has got to be King Charles I, James I's son. He was arrogant, untrustworthy, and, above all, utterly blind to the reality of what he was up against. James I had left a very tricky political and religious situation to his successor. Charles (who only became king because his elder brother Henry died unexpectedly) made it a whole lot worse.

## Buckingham's palace?

We'll start with George Villiers, Duke of Buckingham. He was James I's great favourite, possibly even his lover. But Buckingham very sensibly took care to make friends with James's heir, too. He took Charles on a madcap jaunt to turn up unannounced in the chamber of the Infanta, the King of Spain's eldest daughter, and demand her hand. Presumably Villiers and Charles thought this act was a lark, but the Spanish were incensed. When the two got back to England, Charles married a French princess, Henrietta Maria, instead.

Out of sour grapes, Buckingham persuaded James to declare war on Spain. Now was the time for Buckingham to demonstrate his capacity for military genius – or rather his genius for military incapacity:

- **Netherlands, 1625:** *Plan:* English troops land on Dutch coast and liberate the Protestant Netherlands from hated Spanish rule. *What actually happened:* Buckingham forgot to pack any food for them, so the men died from hunger and disease.

- **Cadiz, 1625:** *Plan:* Buckingham leads a Drake-style attack on Cadiz to capture the Spanish treasure fleet. *What actually happened:* Buckingham's men got so drunk they couldn't fight; the fleet mutinied; and the Spanish treasure fleet sailed safely home, no doubt baring their buttocks at the English as they went. Parliament discussed impeaching Buckingham. Instead, Buckingham stirred up trouble with France.

- **La Rochelle, 1627:** *Plan:* Brave Buckingham liberates the French Protestant stronghold of La Rochelle. *What actually happened:* The Protestants (Huguenots) wisely refused to let him in, so he landed on the Ile de Ré instead. But he forgot to bring reinforcements, so the French simply crossed over and massacred his men.

- **Portsmouth, 1628:** *Plan:* Buckingham descends on La Rochelle, kicks Catholic butt, saves the world for the Protestant religion, and throws Cardinal Richelieu into the Seine. *What actually happened:* Buckingham got stabbed at Portsmouth by an officer called John Felton, who'd walked all the way from London specially to do it. So much for Buckingham.

## Dissolving Parliament

Parliament spent the first part of Charles's reign complaining about Buckingham, and from the preceding section you can see why. They were also unhappy at the way Charles was using forced loans and ancient legal technicalities to pay for the war. In 1628 the House of Commons managed to get Charles to accept the Petition of Right, promising to respect his people's ancient rights and liberties and not to imprison people without trial, billet troops in people's homes, or raise taxes without Parliament's consent. So far so good, but Parliament's actions didn't stop there.

The leading figure in Parliament at the time was a hot head called Sir John Eliot. He got Parliament to agree only to let Charles I raise the traditional customs duties known as tunnage and poundage for one year. (Elizabeth and James I had had them for life, and Charles expected the same.) Eliot also bitterly attacked the changes Charles was making to the Church. Charles sent his messenger, Black Rod, down to the House of Commons to dissolve (dismiss) it, but Eliot and his supporters shut the door and held the Speaker of the Commons down in his chair by force while Eliot got the House to pass

Three Resolutions saying, in effect, that what Charles was doing was treason. Only after the Three Resolutions were passed did the MPs agree to the dissolution. Charles had had enough. He decided to show that he could rule perfectly well without Parliament, and for the next eleven years he did just that.

Looking at all these events as the House of Commons standing up for the rights of the English people is easy, but in fact, a lot of people thought Eliot and the Commons had gone too far. Some MPs and Lords were so shaken by what happened that they switched sides and became loyal supporters of the king. The most important of these was 'Black Tom' Wentworth, who had actually helped draw up the Petition of Right, but now reckoned that Parliament was a greater threat to law and order than the king was. Charles made Wentworth Earl of Strafford, in effect his royal strong-arm man. He sent him to sort out the frontier – Ireland.

## *Ireland, under Strafford's thumb*

The Tudors never really controlled Ireland except for the Pale, a fenced-in area around Dublin where the 'Old English' settlers had been living for centuries (see Chapter 8 to find out how many centuries). 'Beyond the Pale' still means 'wild, outside the law'. When Tudor England turned Protestant, the Gaelic Irish stayed fiercely loyal to the Catholic Church, and in the Nine Years' War (1594–1603), the Gaelic chieftains Hugh O'Neill, Earl of Tyrone, and Rory O'Donnell, Earl of Tyrconnell, fought to drive the Protestant English out of Ireland. They failed, and in 1607, they fled to France in what's known as the Flight of the Earls. (You can find out more about this crucial period in Ireland's history in *Irish History For Dummies* (Wiley)).

Elizabeth I and James I brought in Scottish Presbyterians to drive the Catholics off the best land and settle it themselves, but the Protestants stayed mainly in Ulster. Most of Ireland was still controlled by the Gaelic tribal chiefs.

Two groups already lived in Ireland: The native Gaelic tribes, who lived under tribal chiefs and had remained Catholic, and the Anglo-Irish, who were descended from the old Anglo-Norman knights who'd come over in the twelfth century. The Anglo-Irish belonged to the Church of Ireland, the Irish branch of the Church of England. These new Scottish Protestants who had settled in Ulster therefore made a third group.

In 1632 the Earl of Strafford arrived in Ireland. Strafford managed to turn everyone – Gaelic, Old English, and Scots – against him, and he couldn't care less. He reckoned Ireland had a lot more money than the king was getting, and he created and enforced a tough policy, called Thorough, to find it. He forced the Old English to pay more taxes; he said the Crown would confiscate lands unless landowners, Old English or Irish, paid protection money;

and when King Charles went to war with Scotland, he made the Ulster Scots swear loyalty to the king. These actions didn't win Strafford any friends, but they worked: Ireland gave Charles no trouble while Strafford was there. But when Strafford came home to England, all hell broke loose. See the section 'Civil War: Battle Hymns and a Republic' for details.

## Getting tough with Puritans – again

Charles had got very busy with the Church of England. Like his father, Charles had no time for Puritans, and he found just the bishop to get rid of them. William Laud was an up-and-coming clergyman who wanted to remind the Church of England of its medieval (that is, Catholic) heritage by bringing back things like crosses and candlesticks and having altars at the east end of churches. Any Puritans who objected soon found themselves out of a job or even hauled up before the dreaded – well, all right, resented – Court of High Commission. Most books tell you that the English hated what Laud was doing, but in fact, he had quite a lot of support. Only when he tried to do the same thing in Scotland did he hit serious trouble.

### Say it with stools!

Charles was head of the Scottish Kirk and in 1635 he gave Laud free rein to do what he liked with it. Laud reintroduced bishops, turned St Giles's Church in Edinburgh into a cathedral, and insisted that the Scots use the same Prayer Book as the English – candlesticks, altar rails, and all. The Scots, er, didn't like these changes. When the minister tried to use the English Prayer Book at St Giles's, one of his parishioners, Jenny Geddes, sprang up and threw her stool at him. The situation got so bad that one bishop kept a pair of pistols with him in the pulpit (presumably in case Jenny turned up with a sofa).

### The Bishops' War

In 1638 the Scots drew up a National Covenant telling Charles and Laud to keep their hands off the Scottish Kirk or there'd be trouble. This declaration was mutiny on a grand scale, but Charles didn't have the money for an army to deal with these Covenanters (he was ruling without Parliament, remember). He had to make do with a couple of men with nothing better to do and a very half-hearted dog. This event was called the Bishops' War, but there wasn't even a battle.

Charles's army got fed up and went home, and the Scots nearly ruptured themselves laughing. At this point, Charles decided he could do with some help and sent for 'Black Tom' Strafford. Strafford told him to call Parliament.

# Parliament: It's back and shows who's boss

Calling up Parliament after having dissolved it eleven years earlier wasn't as crazy an idea as it may sound. You can't fight a war without money, and Charles simply didn't have enough. He'd been living off forced loans and illegal taxes for the past eleven years (with a special Court of Star Chamber dealing with anyone who complained), but it was a very chancy business. Take Ship Money. This tax was supposed to pay for a fleet to protect the coast. Very sensible when Algerian pirates could sail up and down the Bristol Channel kidnapping people in Devon villages and carrying them off as slaves. And it raised a lot of money. But then folk discovered that Charles was using the money to support the Catholic Spanish against the Protestant Dutch, so the English stopped paying it. Landowner John Hampden became a national hero when he went to the pillory for non-payment. So getting Parliament's consent for any new taxes was only sensible.

But when Parliament met in 1640 it was just as bolshie as it had been before Charles had dissolved it. This time, John Pym led the troublemakers. Charles dissolved the recalled Parliament after only three weeks (which is why it became known as the Short Parliament) and Strafford had to make do with press-ganging an army to fight the second Bishops' War. Result? The English soldiers mutinied and the Scots occupied a great swathe of northern England, including Newcastle, and then presented Charles with a bill for expenses at £850 a day. At 1640 prices. Charles was going to have to call Parliament again. This next session became known as the Long Parliament, and it lasted a lot longer than three weeks.

This new Parliament told Charles to:

- ✔ Arrest Laud
- ✔ Arrest Strafford
- ✔ Abolish Ship Money
- ✔ Abolish the courts of High Commission and Star Chamber

Some MPs even wanted Charles to abolish bishops, but the Commons couldn't agree on that one, so Pym advised them to drop it.

## Some very uncivil battles

The trouble with English Civil War (or, more accurately, the British Civil Wars) is all those costumes. Grim-faced Roundheads and swashbuckling Cavaliers galloping around: The vision's a day out for the tourists. In fact, the war was appallingly traumatic, with whole-sale killing and murder, and communities and families split down the middle. At Colchester Castle, the Parliamentary army took the two royalist commanders, put them against a wall, and shot them. Basing House, now a Berkshire stately home, became a deadly killing ground. Each side believed they were doing God's work. Cromwell's soldiers even went into battle sing-ing hymns. And of course even as they did all this killing, each side blamed the other for caus-ing it. Things don't change much!

Arresting Strafford, Charles's most loyal supporter, was the one thing every-one – Parliament, Scots, and Irish – agreed on. Turns out Charles agreed to this demand as well. Pym and Co. tried impeaching Strafford (basically, trying him in Parliament) but they didn't have enough evidence, so the Commons passed a law instead. The law, called an Act of Attainder, said that Strafford was guilty of treason. And Charles signed it. Poor old Strafford was executed. 'Put not your trust in Princes,' he said bitterly. Well, not in this one at any rate. And Archbishop Laud? They put him in the Tower to rot. Charles agreed to that, too. With friends like Charles I . . .

# Civil War: Battle Hymns and a Republic

The trouble leading to civil war started in Ireland. In 1641 the Catholics rose up against all those Protestant plantations in Ulster (see the earlier section 'Ireland under Strafford's thumb') and started massacring everyone they could find. At Portadown, for example, a hundred Protestants were thrown off the bridge and then shot down in the water. Charles needed troops to restore order, and he needed them fast, but Parliament wasn't sure it could trust him. What if he then used these troops against Parliament?

Pym and Hampden drew up the *Grand Remonstrance* which said, in effect, that Charles couldn't govern for toffee and would have to let Parliament take over, but the bill only passed by eleven votes: Several MPs thought Pym was pushing things too far, especially when he started talking about impeaching the queen. Then, just as things looked as though they might swing Charles's way, Charles went and ruined it. He marched into the House of Commons with a troop of soldiers to arrest Pym, Hampden, and three others. The five men had been tipped off and weren't there. When the king asked where Pym, Hampden, and the others were, the Speaker replied, 'If it please your Majesty, I have neither eye to see, nor tongue to speak here, but as the House is pleased to direct me.' Which was a very polite way of telling Charles to get lost. Charles left London that same day. He was going to re-take London by force; Parliament prepared to resist him. The result was Civil War.

## War stories

Initially, the war was a shambles. No professional army existed, so both sides told landowners and towns to raise volunteers. Parliament put two noblemen, the Earl of Essex and the Duke of Manchester, in charge of its army; Charles had his German nephew, Prince Rupert of the Rhine – one of the best cavalry commanders of the day. Rupert ran rings round Essex and Manchester's men at Edgehill, the first battle of the war.

Nothing stood in the way to stop Charles taking London – so he didn't. He got cold feet and set up camp at Oxford instead, while his army wasted time besieging Parliamentary strongholds like Bristol and Gloucester. Figure 13-1 shows the major comings and goings through the war. One Parliamentary officer, a certain Oliver Cromwell, was deeply impressed with Prince Rupert's cavalry and set about training professional cavalry to fight for Parliament. His 'Ironsides' made their debut when they crushed Prince Rupert's men at the Battle of Marston Moor. Parliament completely reorganised its army along the same lines, and it was this *New Model Army* under Cromwell and Sir Thomas Fairfax that finally defeated Charles at the Battle of Naseby. The unthinkable had happened: The King had lost the war.

## Can we join in? Enter the Irish and the Scots

The Irish quickly realised (quite rightly) that Parliament and the Puritans were much more of a threat than the king, and so they decided to fight on Charles's side. They did very well helping to drive the Covenanters (the Scottish MPs whose National Covenant was telling Charles and Laud to leave the Scottish Kirk alone; see the section 'Getting tough with Puritans – again' for details) out of the Scottish Highlands. Charles always hoped that the Irish would save him from the English. Dream on, Charles.

The Scots were a very different matter. They had an alliance with the English Parliament – they didn't want Charles's Prayer Book, remember (see the earlier section 'Say it with stools!') – but not all the Scots were happy about the alliance. Charles reckoned that if he played his cards carefully he could use this fact to his advantage. So after the Battle of Naseby, when Charles lost to Cromwell's army, he deliberately surrendered to the Scots, not the English; then he sat back to watch the fun. Only events didn't quite work out the way Charles was expecting.

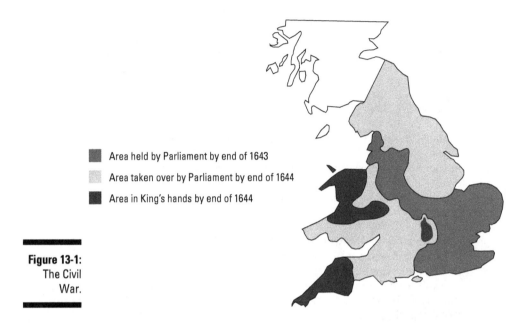

Area held by Parliament by end of 1643

Area taken over by Parliament by end of 1644

Area in King's hands by end of 1644

**Figure 13-1:**
The Civil
War.

The Scots said they'd be happy to put Charles back on his throne if he agreed to close down the Church of England and make England a Presbyterian country like Scotland. Charles didn't say no, but he sure didn't say yes either. This was his own church they were talking about. The Scots lost patience with him. 'Have it your own way,' they said, and handed him over to the English. 'Hello Charlie,' said Parliament. 'Welcome home.'

## *The only good Stuart is a dead Stuart*

More than enough killing had taken place in the Civil War and no one wanted any more: All anyone wanted was to work out some sort of settlement that would leave Charles on the throne but stop him messing everything up. But finding a solution was never going to be that simple:

- ✔ **Parliament was split.** Only Puritans were left: The majority were Presbyterians who wanted to make England a Presbyterian country like Scotland, and the minority were Independents, who didn't.

- ✔ **Parliament and the army were split.** The Presbyterians in Parliament tried to disband the army because it was full of Independents, so the soldiers, who were already fed up because Parliament hadn't paid them for months, marched on London, seized the Tower, and virtually took Parliament prisoner.

✔ **The army was split.** Cromwell and Fairfax were in favour of negotiating with the king, but their soldiers were against it. Many of them had joined a radical group called the Levellers who believed that everyone should be equal and that England should be a republic. The army held a series of discussions about this issue at Putney church. These discussions were known as the Putney Debates, and they turned Cromwell and Fairfax firmly against the Levellers.

## Negotiations galore and a second Civil War

How did all this wrangling affect the king? Simple: Each side tried to use him against the other. Parliament was trying to cut a deal whereby they'd put Charles back on the throne if he promised to turn the Church of England Presbyterian. Cromwell and Fairfax promised Charles could stay on the throne if he promised to allow complete religious freedom (except for Catholics, of course) and also promised not to have any more of Archbishop Laud's silly ideas.

But you couldn't trust Charles. He was constantly writing to the Scots to get them to rescue him, and then he did a bunk and turned up on the Isle of Wight. Which was a silly move really, because the Governor of the Isle of Wight turned out to be a staunch Parliamentarian and just locked him up in Carisbrooke Castle.

But Charles's imprisonment on the Isle of Wight brought the Scots charging down to the rescue, and that started a second Civil War, which had only one big battle, at Preston. Cromwell cut the Scots to pieces. Cromwell decided the time had come to deal finally with Charles Stuart, 'that man of blood'. He was to stand trial for treason.

## Heads you lose

Parliament put the king on trial. The Presbyterians in Parliament had wanted to keep Charles on the throne, but Cromwell had the lot of them arrested, leaving only a non-Presbyterian group called *Independents*, who reckoned a good Stuart was a dead Stuart. Cromwell believed in many things but respect for the sovereignty of Parliament wasn't one of them.

Charles's trial in Parliament was a spectacle to savour. A people putting their king on trial: It had never happened before. This act showed that the people, not the king, were sovereign. You can see why Charles I refused to recognise that the court was in any way legal and sat in dignified silence throughout the trial. Doing so didn't save him. The court found Charles guilty of treason, and Cromwell himself signed the death warrant, along with 59 other MPs.

On a cold January morning in 1649, Charles I stepped out of the window of his father's great Banqueting House in Whitehall onto a scaffold and laid his head on the block. A terrible groan was heard as the axe came down, and people rushed forward to dip their handkerchiefs in his blood – were they after a holy relic, or just a souvenir?

# Oliver!

Oliver Cromwell was a Puritan and a gentleman landowner from Huntingdon. He sat in the Long Parliament (see the earlier section 'Parliament: It's back and shows who's boss') as MP for Cambridge. He wasn't all that prominent until he proved a superb cavalry commander in the Civil War. Cromwell trained up the New Model Army (see the earlier section 'War stories'), and from then on he was right at the centre of events.

## Levellers levelled and Scots scotched

After Charles I had been dealt with and dispatched to the great beyond, Cromwell and Fairfax turned on the Levellers, a group who wanted to destroy all differences of rank. The army commanders (gentlemen landowners to a man) sent the Leveller leaders to the Tower.

The Scots were outraged that the English had executed their king (Charles I was King of Scotland too, don't forget) without so much as a by-your-leave. So, to teach the English a lesson, the Scots defiantly crowned Charles I's son as King Charles II in Edinburgh. That action brought Cromwell charging north with an army. He defeated the Scots at the Battle of Dunbar (only just, which convinced Cromwell that he must have had God on his side) and saw off the rest of Charles II's men at the Battle of Worcester. Charles II, who was no fool, had to run for his life. Cromwell even put a price on Charles II's head and issued a description (WANTED: One tall, dark featured man. Goes by the name of King Charles II). According to one story, Charles II once had to hide up an oak tree while Cromwell's men were searching the bushes underneath. Charles II managed to escape into exile on the continent. In England, Oliver Cromwell took charge.

## England becomes a republic

This fact often comes as a surprise to people who think of England as a monarchy, but England under Oliver Cromwell became a republic.

Parliament abolished the monarchy and the House of Lords, and decided that all this hereditary power was 'unnecessary, burdensome, and dangerous to liberty'. Henceforth England was a commonwealth – a republic to you and me. But the republic wasn't very democratic. The MPs of the 'Rump' Parliament, which was all that was left of the Parliament that had been elected back in 1640 (we're in 1653 by now), were trying to keep hold of their seats for life. So, in 1653 Cromwell closed down the Rump Parliament. He marched in and drove them all out with the famous words 'you have sat too long here for any good you have been doing. Depart, I say, and let us have done with you. In the name of God, go!'

Almost three hundred years later, in 1940, those words were quoted across the House of Commons at Neville Chamberlain, after the Germans had invaded Norway and Denmark (see Chapter 21 for more on this). Chamberlain took the hint and resigned, and Churchill became prime minister.

Cromwell replaced the Rump Parliament with a blatantly rigged affair known as the Barebones Parliament. This parliament offered Cromwell the crown, but he preferred the army's offer (the army was doing all the real day-to-day governing in England by now): To be Lord Protector. 'Cromwell is our king,' one Englishman explained to a German visitor, and when he was made Lord Protector, the ceremony certainly looked suspiciously like a coronation, which meant that both the (real) royalists and the republicans hated him. However, Cromwell went to war with Holland and Spain and beat them both; he unified Scotland and England into one country with one Parliament, which gave the Scots free access to English markets; and above all, he kept the peace. No mean feat for the seventeenth century.

## No ball games or Christmas or fun

You could have a fine time in Cromwell's England as long as you didn't want to sing, dance, go to the theatre, or generally get out a bit. Okay, maybe that description's a bit unfair, but it is true that many Puritans disapproved of 'frivolous' music and pastimes, and the government certainly closed the theatres on public health and decency grounds. They also banned Christmas because they reckoned it was a pagan festival, which had nothing to do with the birth of Jesus. And Cromwell allowed the Jews back into England (see Chapter 9 for info on why they needed to be allowed back in the first place). Cromwell was surprisingly tolerant of people of different religions, (even Catholics) as long as they kept their faith to themselves. But he was merciless with radical religious sects whose beliefs threatened public order, like the Ranters, who appeared to preach that Sin was Good, and the Quakers, who completely turned their backs on conventional worship. Cromwell had the Quaker preacher James Nayler whipped and branded, and a hole bored through his tongue.

## Ireland: The Curse of Cromwell

The Irish had put their rebellion (the one where the Irish Catholics rose up against the Protestants; see the section 'Civil War: Battle Hymns and a Republic') on the back burner, but Cromwell hadn't forgotten it. In 1649 he came over to Ireland looking for revenge. He marched straight for Drogheda, which had played no part in the rebellion but was commanded by English royalists. Cromwell's men besieged it, took it, and massacred everyone they could find. They battered the commander to death with his own wooden leg. Then they marched on Wexford and massacred the people there. Finally Cromwell confiscated any land still in Catholic hands and gave it to his officers. The native Irish were banished to 'Hell or Connaught', and Connaught was worse.

Cromwell genuinely believed he was doing God's work. He saw the Catholic Irish as dangerous savages, serving a religion he believed to be the work of the devil (compare it with nineteenth-century European views of Africans or American views of the native tribes on the Western Frontier). Ireland took centuries to recover from the 'Curse of Cromwell', but then, that was the idea.

# Restoration Tragi-Comedy

Cromwell died in 1658. His son Richard became Lord Protector (what was all that about rejecting the hereditary principle?) but he proved a bit clueless and, crucially, he couldn't control the army. Over in the Netherlands, Charles II (still in exile; see the earlier section 'Levellers levelled and Scots scotched') announced that if the English took him back he'd offer a free pardon, freedom of religion, and he'd pay the army. An officer called General Monck decided this was too good an offer to miss. He marched down to London from Scotland with an army, got a new Parliament together, and persuaded it to take Charles II up on his offer. They invited him to come home and he came. They called this event the Restoration.

## Charles II comes to England

Wild cheering broke out when Charles II came home. Suddenly everyone had been a secret royalist all along, as Charles did not fail to notice. He very sensibly decided not to inquire too closely as long as they hadn't actually signed his father's death warrant. But he never really trusted Parliament, and it's hard to blame him. Instead he negotiated a secret deal with King Louis XIV of France and, in effect, lived off French money. He even went to war with the Protestant Dutch on Louis's behalf, although his loyalty to Louis didn't do him any good because the Dutch won.

## Double whammy – plague *and* fire

The occasional outbreak of plague was an occupational hazard in the seventeenth century, but the outbreak that hit London in 1665 was special: Nothing like it had been seen since the Black Death. Thousands died, and infected houses had to be sealed up with the people inside them. No one had a cure because no one really knew what caused it. The next year, the city burnt to the ground in a terrible fire that started with an overheated baker's oven, though people at the time blamed it on the Catholics. Or the French. Or both.

Charles II himself had to take command, ordering houses to be blown up to deny the fire the chance to spread. By the end the city was a smoking ruin, including the great Cathedral of St Paul. The fire gave the chance for a complete rebuilding programme, of course, which is where Sir Christopher Wren came in with his famous designs, but at the time, it seemed like yet another blow from an angry God on a country that had suffered enough.

## *Some relief for Catholics and Puritans alike*

In 1672 Charles issued a *Declaration of Indulgence*, allowing complete freedom of worship to everyone, even Catholics (Charles wasn't a Catholic, but his wife and his brother were). The Declaration was too much for Parliament to swallow, and Charles had to grit his teeth and agree to the Test Act, which said that only members of the Church of England could serve in the armed forces or Parliament or go to university. But he bided his time.

Titus Oates was a clergyman and professional liar who in 1678 claimed that a huge Popish (Catholic) Plot existed to kill the king. It didn't, but the claim provoked a huge panic, and Catholics soon found themselves under arrest. The Archbishop of Armagh, Oliver Plunkett, was among twenty-four Catholics who were actually put to death; many others died in prison. Parliament even tried to get Charles's Catholic brother James excluded from the succession to the throne. When the truth came out – no such Popish Plot existed – Charles pounced. He dissolved Parliament and ruled without it, living off money from his good friend Louis XIV. When some old Cromwellians really did hatch the Rye House Plot to kill Charles, he had them arrested and executed. He was still firmly in control when he died in 1685.

# *So, Who Won – the Crown or Parliament?*

These wars that were fought during this period were as much about running Scotland and Ireland as they were about the Crown and Parliament, which is why some historians speak of the British Civil Wars. The army won the Civil War, but Charles II came out on top in the end, though he had to play his cards very carefully to stay there.

# Chapter 14

# Old Problems, New Ideas

. . . . . . . . . . . . . . . . . . . . . . . . . . . . . . . . . . . . . . . . . . .

*In This Chapter*

▶ Turning old ideas on their heads: The English Renaissance

▶ Sympathising with the English poor: An old problem that only got worse

▶ Introducing ground-breaking ideas: Thinkers, philosophers, theorists, scientists, and mathematicians

. . . . . . . . . . . . . . . . . . . . . . . . . . . . . . . . . . . . . . . . . . .

*W*hen you look at the Tudor and Stuart times they look, well, historical – all those ruffs, doublets, gadzooks, and what have you. So learning that historians see this period as the start of the Modern period comes as a surprise. These people may look old-fashioned, but some of the things they were thinking and doing were surprisingly close to our own way of thinking. Starting off with the English Renaissance in the sixteenth century, by the time Charles II came home (1660) Britons were well into the Scientific Revolution, with the Enlightenment just round the corner. Modern government? Thank the Tudors. Modern art and music? Start with the Renaissance. Theatre as we know it? They knew it, too. Modern science and medicine? Look no further. Democratic government and communal living? The Stuarts knew all about it. This chapter explains the ideas that started the modern world and made us the people we are.

# *The Renaissance: Retro chic*

If you went to school anywhere in Europe in the Middle Ages, you were given a book by one of the great names of the past – Aristotle for philosophy, Galen (Greek physician to the Roman Emperors Marcus Aurelius and Commodus) for medicine, or St Augustine or Thomas Aquinas for theology – and you sat down and you learned it. You might debate exactly what the great thinker meant, and you might speculate about what they would say now, but these were the Great Books by the Great Minds, hallowed for many centuries: You didn't question what they said, even when you only had to cut open a corpse to see that Galen's ideas about anatomy were completely off the wall (unsurprisingly, since Galen based his ideas on animals).

Then something strange began to happen in Italy around the end of the fourteenth century. Scholars started looking in cupboards and attics and finding lots of ancient Latin and Greek manuscripts they hadn't known about. They found Hebrew manuscripts, too. In this newly discovered treasure trove were works of philosophy and theology, including the works of Plato whom no one had really read before. So scholars started learning Greek and Hebrew (they'd been using Latin translations) and found, for example, that Plato had some very different things to say from Aristotle, and that some of the Church's important Latin documents were actually forgeries. Suddenly unearthing ancient classical writings was the thing to get into. People called the study of the ideas found in these new texts *humanism* because they reckoned they were getting a clearer understanding of what being human actually meant; later on, historians called the studies of this period a rebirth of the Classical world, or in French, the Renaissance.

No one at the time called this period a Renaissance – that word's a nineteenth century label. Nor was it the first big revival of interest in classical literature – a Renaissance occurred in the ninth century and another in the twelfth century. The people of the Renaissance we're talking about had nothing but contempt for the art and architecture of the preceding years – they were the ones who came up with the term 'medieval' or 'Middle Ages' to describe it. They were suggesting the idea of a great gulf of dross between the glories of the Classical world and its revival in the fifteenth and sixteenth centuries. This description's a gross libel on the Middle Ages, but the Renaissance people got their way. Look at the way we use 'medieval' to mean primitive or barbaric today!

## *Sweet music and palaces in air*

Although the Renaissance started in Italy, the spreading of Renaissance ideas across Europe didn't take long, thanks to the new printing press. Oxford and Cambridge both took to the New Learning, and John Colet, Dean of St Paul's, even founded a school especially to spread it. One of the greatest Renaissance scholars, Erasmus of Rotterdam, settled for a long time in England because he found the country so congenial and open to new ideas, and Sir Thomas More, author of *Utopia*, was one of the most important Renaissance intellectuals in Europe. In some ways, however, England was behind its neighbours. Italian artists like Michelangelo or Raphael were studying Greek and Roman sculpture and architecture and reproducing its proportions and dynamism in their own sculptures and paintings. But where, Henry VIII wanted to know, was the English Leonardo or Raphael? With Francis I of France and the Holy Roman Emperor Charles V building themselves swanky new palaces in the latest styles and hiring Renaissance painters to do the walls, Henry was determined not to be left out. He wanted an English Renaissance, and he wanted it now.

### Nonsuch city limits

Henry was a real Renaissance prince: He was just as happy discussing theology or philosophy as he was jousting or wrestling with the King of France (though not usually all at the same time). He had palaces at Greenwich and Richmond, and later on, he got Cardinal Wolsey's palace at Hampton Court (see Chapter 11 for more about Henry and Wolsey) but Nonsuch was the great palace Henry built to wow the world. We don't know exactly what Nonsuch looked like – nothing is left of it except the foundations, and the only drawings we have show the outside – but by all accounts, visiting it was a breathtaking experience. Henry thought big and brash, and historians reckon that all those nice red brick Tudor buildings with their wooden beams were originally hideously garish, with lots of bright colours and gold paint. (Discovering what ghastly taste people in history could have is always a shock.) We can get some idea of what Nonsuch may have been like by looking at Hampton Court, but Nonsuch was a very different sort of place, so we have to rely heavily on the famous paintings of Hans Holbein.

Hans Holbein painted all those famous images of Henry standing with his hands on his hips and his feet planted firmly apart. How good his likeness of Henry – or Nonsuch – was, you can't be sure, as you always have to treat portraits with a lot of care. The purpose of a royal portrait was not just to record what the sitter looked like but also to send a message. So Henry is always shown looking strong and manly, which meant (a) this is not a man to be messed with, (b) he'll quickly start producing sons, and (c) if all else fails he'll make a superb bouncer at a nightclub.

### Thank you for the music

Henry was a keen musician, and music proved to be one branch of the arts the English were good at. They tended to specialise in church music: Thomas Tallis wrote an amazing anthem called *Spem in Alium* for 40 solo voices – it was Wall of Sound long before Phil Spector. His pupil William Byrd became organist to Elizabeth's Chapel Royal, which was a tricky position to be in because Byrd was a secret Catholic, and some people say you can detect Catholic messages in some of his music. English music wasn't all anthems, though. John Dowland wrote some of the most beautiful lute and guitar music, still regularly performed, and Henry VIII himself wrote a popular ballad called *Pastime with Good Company* and may – may – have written *Greensleeves*.

# Shakespeare: The good, the bard, and the ugly

Toward the end of Elizabeth I's reign English theatre suddenly took off. Actors had always travelled the country putting on plays in inns or market squares, rather like circus or fairground troupes nowadays, and people reacted to them in much the same, rather sniffy way. But then permanent theatres began to appear on London's South Bank – the Rose, the Curtain, the Theatre, and the famous Globe – and great nobles like the Earl of Leicester became their patrons. Shakespeare's company had the Lord Chamberlain as their patron, and Queen Elizabeth herself was a fan: Shakespeare wrote *The Merry Wives of Windsor* especially for her. His plays can tell us a lot about his time: Not just about the language they spoke and the jokes they enjoyed, but about what people believed, what they admired, and what they feared:

✔ **Isn't England wonderful?** *This royal throne of kings, this sceptr'd isle, this earth of majesty, this seat of Mars, this other Eden, demi-paradise . . .* That line's John of Gaunt describing England in *Richard II*, in case you're wondering. A lot of Shakespeare's plays have a patriotic ring to them: Just think of *Henry V*. Shakespeare added an Irishman, a Welshman, and a Scot to suggest the idea of the whole nation uniting behind the king. Mind you, even Shakespeare didn't think much of English weather: See *King Lear*.

✔ **Beware of the Pope!** Shakespeare kept the big religious issues of his day out of his plays, which was probably wise since a good chance exists he was a closet Catholic. But apart from Friar Lawrence (who's a sweetie in *Romeo and Juliet*), when Catholic priests do appear, they're nearly always bad guys. Cardinals are arrogant (Wolsey in *Henry VIII* and Pandulph in *King John* both try to bully the king), and even the priest in *Hamlet* won't give Ophelia a proper burial.

✔ **Don't rock the boat!** The Tudors were great believers in law and order. God chose the rulers, and if you challenged them or tried to subvert them, chaos would reign. This idea comes up a lot in Shakespeare. If you kill the king, like in *Macbeth* or *Richard II*, you get rebellion and civil war. Don't do it.

✔ **If the king is no good, however, things become a bit trickier.** Overthrowing Richard III is fine, because he's a murderer and, in any case, that was the official Tudor line. But don't get ideas: In *Julius Caesar* Brutus is good and noble but killing Caesar only leads to trouble, and Brutus loses in the end. Even weak kings like Richard II or Henry VI are put on the throne by God.

✔ **Did I tell your majesty how wonderful you are? Let me tell you again . . .** Shakespeare was no fool, and he put a lot of royal flattery into his plays. *Henry VIII* is about Queen Elizabeth's father and includes a speech about Elizabeth herself, saying how happy England is going to be when she grows up and becomes queen (no point in being too subtle about it!). When James VI came down to London from Scotland, Shakespeare wrote *Macbeth* with lots of witches in it just for him.

Shakespeare's plays dealt with ideas about mortality (Hamlet's 'To be or not to be' soliloquy is all about that); madness and reason (*King Lear*); racial prejudice (*The Merchant of Venice* and *Othello*); fathers, sons, and daughters (*Henry IV* and *King Lear*); and the eternal war of the sexes (*As You Like It*, *Measure for Measure*, *The Taming of the Shrew* – you name it). Medieval plays told bible stories; but Elizabethan theatre looked at questions of life and death and the whole nature of human experience. Theatre was philosophy with greasepaint. (If you want to find out a bit more about Shakespeare and his world, have a look at *Shakespeare For Dummies* (Wiley)).

# It's No Fun Being Poor

What to do about poor people? This issue's one of the oldest problems in the book, but in Tudor times, the problem was a lot worse because there were so many of them. No one quite knew why, though they had some ideas:

- ✔ **Sorry, lads, you're out of a job.** In the Middle Ages every self-respecting nobleman had a great crowd of retainers, all wearing his colours (known as *livery*) and armed to the teeth, just like all those nameless security men in *Star Trek* who only come in so they can get killed. But Henry VII had wanted to put an end to all the fighting at the end of the Wars of the Roses (have a look at Chapters 9 and 11 for more about this), so he banned nobles from keeping retainers. Suddenly all these men-at-arms were out of a job.

- ✔ **Call this a shilling?!** No one quite knew why, but prices started going up. Unfortunately, no one got a wages hike to go with it, so inevitably some people went hungry. The government thought issuing more coins would help, so they cut down on the gold and silver content, mixed in other metals like copper or tin, and started minting like crazy. But when people found that the silver in their coins was starting to rub off and they could see copper underneath, they lost confidence in their money, and merchants put their prices up still more.

- ✔ **It's all these sheep.** Sheep meant money. A flourishing export trade in wool operated but sheep need a lot of grazing land. Canny landowners began enclosing fields with huge hedges and converting them to sheep pasture. Which was fine for the landowners but not so good for people who had their houses knocked down and found themselves turned off the land. In 1549 a series of rebellions against enclosures occurred, and it took a military expedition to put them down. (See Chapter 11 for how this expedition affected the already troubled politics of the time.)

## Crime and public punishment

People had the idea that people charged with a crime should have a fair trial with an impartial judge, but they also thought that the community should play a part in the punishment. For this reason, criminals got sent to the stocks or the pillory. This form of punishment was like being 'named and shamed', and it gave the community the chance to get its own back. Hangings and burnings were done in public partly to deter others and partly so that everyone could *see* justice being done. Afterwards, the body was left to hang in chains by the roadside or over a gateway as a warning.

## *The Poor Laws*

All these changes and the accompanying rise in unemployed and home-less people resulted in a massive crime wave. You could hardly move in Tudor England without running into great crowds, even armies, of beggars. People were used to blind or crippled people begging, but these were sturdy beggars, able-bodied and armed to the teeth. Something had to be done about the situation. Vagabonds could be sent to workhouses and Houses of Correction, which were a sort of sixteenth-century boot camp, but these measures weren't enough. So in 1601 Parliament brought in tough new Poor Laws.

These laws said that poor people had to stay in their parishes, where those who really couldn't work could get some charity. If they went wandering, they could be whipped or branded V (for 'Vagabond') with a red-hot iron on the forehead. The laws stayed in force until Victorian times. The problem of whether to offer benefits or work to the poor is still troubling us today.

## *Crime or class war?*

Avoiding getting caught was critical if you were a criminal in Tudor and Stuart times. Punishments were severe. Stealing or smuggling merited hanging, and you could count yourself very lucky if you got away with being publicly flogged. Parliament kept passing laws to deal with crimes against property (like thievery and poaching), and the punishment was usually death.

Most of the people who were executed were thieves or poachers, and they were often poor and hungry. The judges who sentenced them were landown-ers, protecting the interests of other landowners. You can see why some his-torians see the whole question of crime as a sort of class war.

# New Ideas

Seventeenth- and eighteenth-century Britain produced some of the most important thinkers and scientists in Europe. Hold on tight: Deep Ideas coming up!

## Let's talk about religion . . .

Believe it or not, this discussion of religion and politics isn't about Catholics and Protestants; the man of his particular moment is Galileo, an Italian who, as far as we know, never gave Britain and its problems a moment's thought. Nevertheless, this story starts with him.

### Pointed observations

Galileo observed the heavens and noted down what he saw, which led him to a very important conclusion: The earth moves round the sun and not vice versa. This observation got him into serious trouble with the Pope and the Inquisition, but that's another story (which you can find in *European History For Dummies* (Wiley)). What we need to take note of is how Galileo knew. Simple. He observed, he noted down what he saw, and he drew reasoned conclusions. That exercise may sound fairly obvious, but at a time when the Church expected people to accept its teachings without question, working things out like that was dynamite.

At the same time in England, a statesman-philosopher called Francis Bacon was arguing something similar. Knowledge, he said, doesn't come from books, it comes from observing or experiencing things, thinking about them, and then drawing out some general principles. The posh name for this gleaning of knowledge is *empiricism*. The big question – and I mean big – was, can we observe and deduce the existence of God?

### 1 think, therefore 1 am very confused

Everyone's theory of government, whether it was the Stuarts and their Divine Right of Kings, or Cromwell as Lord Protector (see Chapter 13 for details on these people) was based on the idea that God had said, 'That's how you should be governing.' But now people (well, scholars and deep thinkers, anyway) were beginning to wonder was there a God? And if so, how could anyone be certain of what he was saying?

Now, nothing either Bacon or Galileo said suggested that God didn't exist, but a French thinker, René Descartes, seemed in some doubt. Descartes said that what you need to make sense of life, the universe, and everything else isn't faith, but reason. After all, for all we know, the whole world could be a trick created by the devil. The only thing we can be completely sure of is that we exist, and we only know that because we can think – 'I think, therefore I am,' as he famously put it.

So if (a) we exist and (b) we know we exist, these things might indicate that there is a God who created us in the first place. But the point is, we can deduce there is a God instead of just believing it because the Church says so.

But what sort of God is he, and what does he want? Charles I said the answer was quite simple: God wanted everyone to obey the king. Others said on the contrary, God wanted them to get rid of the king. Cromwell thought massacring the Irish and imprisoning Quakers was God's will. The Quakers thought God wanted them to stay silent in church; others thought God wanted them to walk around shouting about him at the top of their voices. You can see why John Milton, who was a Puritan and a big Cromwell supporter, felt moved to write a long epic poem, *Paradise Lost*, to try to impose a bit of order on things and explain how God operated.

## A little bit of politics

Tom Hobbes (1588–1679) took one look at the times he was living in, what with enclosures and beggars and civil war and massacres and religious nutcases, and he decided that, all in all, life sucks: 'Solitary, poor, nasty, brutish and short,' was how he described most people's experience of life. The only way to keep these selfish, untrustworthy brutes from tearing each other to pieces, said Hobbes, was to have a strong government with absolute power over everyone. Ideally, this government ought to operate with the consent of the people (be fair, the guy was a republican), but Hobbes reckoned that the people wouldn't keep their side of the bargain, so it was probably best to rule them by force. He wrote his ideas down in a great book called *Leviathan*, the first book named after a great sea monster until *Moby Dick*. Every ruler had a copy (of *Leviathan*, that is, not *Moby Dick*).

If you think Hobbes was being a tad pessimistic you may prefer to hear what John Locke had to say. Locke had fought in the Civil War and he witnessed all the debates that followed about who should have power and what to do with a bad king, and so on. He did some deep thinking, and he had some very important things to say:

- ✔ **Babies have no sense of right and wrong:** Locke said that when we're born, we have no built-in moral purpose; that all comes later. We're all of us like a blank sheet – a *tabula rasa*, as he called it. No preconceptions (and no Original Sin either), just an open mind, an open mouth, and a full nappy.

- ✔ **People learn and act by observation:** This idea is empiricism again (see the section 'Pointed observations' earlier for a more complete discussion). Locke believed that we become good or bad, great or small and winners or losers by our own actions and not by anything we are born with. The world is at your feet, my friend. Seize the day!

✔ **People are born equal.** No one is born 'better' than anyone else. So no lords or kings, and no hereditary Lord Protectors either. Locke believed that all government was by consent of the people, and the people had a right to get rid of a bad ruler. The English liked this idea.

Locke's democratic ideas had a big influence in America and would help cause the American Revolution in due course. By contrast, Cromwell's one-man rule as Lord Protector (see Chapter 13 to see what this was all about) was a big disappointment to Locke. The Levellers were the ones who really lived out Locke's ideas (refer to Chapter 13 to find out what Cromwell did to them), and even more so Gerard Winstanley's little commune of Diggers on St George's Hill in Surrey, the first (and last) time anyone has ever managed to set up a communist cell in the Home Counties.

## Even science gets political

The English, it seemed, were really taking these new ideas of equality to heart, so unsurprisingly they started applying these democratic notions to science and medicine. When scientist William Harvey worked out (by careful observation, of course) that the heart pumps blood around the body, it created quite a stir. People had thought of the heart as a sort of king ruling the body politic, but Harvey showed – not just speculated, mind, but actually showed – that the heart was simply a tool with a job to do like any other part of the body.

---

### Bewitched?

Before you get too taken up with belief in reason and scientific observation, bear in mind that this time in history was also the heyday of the witch craze. While the Civil War was still raging, Matthew Hopkins, the 'Witchfinder General', toured East Anglia accusing people, usually harmless old women, of witchcraft and hanging scores of them. Defending yourself against a witchcraft accusation was very difficult – after all, how do you prove that you didn't fly through the air one night? Any wart or body mark could be taken as the 'third teat', which witches were supposed to have for the devil to suckle.

People didn't spend their whole lives in fear of witches, but every now and again there'd be a sudden flare-up of cases, as with Hopkins in the eastern counties, or the famous Salem case in Massachusetts. Gradually the sort of reasoned argument that the scientists and philosophers were developing did see off belief in witches, but the process took a long time and people can still be seized with a sudden irrational belief in mystic powers. How else do you explain *feng shui*?

---

## Halley and the comets

The one thing everyone knows about Edmond Halley (yes, spelt like that, and the name's pronounced *Haw*-lee) is that a comet is named after him, which is a shame because there's a lot more to him than his comet.

Halley (1656–1742) was a good friend of Newton – he even helped pay for publishing Newton's *Principia* – and he was a brilliant astronomer in his own right (it helped that he came from a wealthy family and could afford the equipment). Halley observed a comet in the heavens and then used Newton's laws to calculate when it would come back – and he was right (that's how Halley's comet got its name). As a student at Oxford, Halley wrote to Flamsteed, who was then Astronomer Royal, pointing out ever so politely that some of Flamsteed's figures seemed to be wrong. He was right about that, too.

Halley made his name by sailing to the South Seas and mapping the stars visible down there, even though it meant he had to drop out of Oxford to do it. He got into an argument with the Church by pointing out that the earth had been around a lot earlier than 9 a.m. on Sunday 23 October 4004 BC, which was when Archbishop Ussher said the Creation had happened. He became a Captain in the Royal Navy, a diplomat (and secret agent), Professor of Geometry at Oxford, and he succeeded Flamsteed (who couldn't stand him) as Astronomer Royal. Oh, and he was quite a ladies' man, too – must've been all those heavenly bodies he was always looking at.

All these ideas about God and empiricism, and government led people to start investigating the natural world systemically, empirically, by careful observation. This period's what we call the Scientific Revolution.

## *The appliance of science*

A lot of empirical thinkers were kicking around Britain, including Robert Hooke, Robert Boyle, and a certain Isaac Newton and in 1660, the year Charles II came back (see Chapter 13 for info on this), a group of them got together to found a scientific society. Two years later the king gave this society a royal charter, since when it has been known as the Royal Society. The group was planning to meet together, swap ideas, and show off their latest experiments.

### *Studying Natural Philosophy*

These men didn't make the strict distinctions we do today between, say, chemistry and physics: They saw themselves as investigating Natural Philosophy, the rules by which the earth and the universe work. Engaging in this type of study and still believing in God was quite possible, and most of them did. Just look at the sheer range of their work:

✔ **Gas and air:** Next time you hoover up, thank an Irish aristocrat called Robert Boyle. He demonstrated the world's first vacuum pump, and he also worked out Boyle's Law about how, if you heat a gas, the molecules all start whizzing around like headless chickens, but if you lay off the pressure, they all close up again. All this experimenting with gases led people in interesting directions. A Frenchman called Papin even dropped in on the Royal Society to show how you could use steam pressure to cook yourself a cordon bleu supper. They gave him two stars.

✔ **A map of the heavens:** People had been studying the stars for centuries, but that study had always been dominated by astrology. John Flamsteed was the man who first produced a reliable map of the heavens, showing where each star was and when. He set up the Royal Observatory on a hill overlooking the Thames at Greenwich, and Charles II made him the first Astronomer Royal. The Observatory was designed by Christopher Wren, who was also an astronomer when he wasn't busy designing churches. For a maritime nation like Britain, this sort of work was very important. Charles knew what he was doing by giving the Observatory the royal seal of approval.

✔ **Navigation tools:** Setting sail with a good map of the heavens was all very well, but you needed to be able to see where you were going and to take readings from what you could see. Step forward Robert Hooke. This useful chap designed a proper telescope and quadrant for use at sea, though many years passed before John Harrison perfected the chronometer for measuring longitude.

✔ **Mathematics:** You want to know the key to understanding the natural world and, therefore, the mind of God? Mathematics. Yes, folks, these people could see the beauty of a quadratic equation and the elegance of algebra. Sad, isn't it? They loved the form and symmetry of the natural world and of the heavens, and they liked the way you could reproduce those patterns and proportions in architecture. The Great Fire of London was a wonderful opportunity for architects like Christopher Wren and Nicholas Hawksmoor, and that so much of their time was taken up with designing perfectly proportioned churches makes a lot of sense. The dome of St Paul's was a mathematical masterpiece, and it seemed to echo the perfect spheres of the heavens. It still does, if you whisper too loud inside it.

## Newton

The British don't really appreciate what they have in Isaac Newton. All most of them know is a silly story about an apple falling on his head, and that tale's only half true. This guy was quite simply the greatest scientist in the world. Ever. Full stop.

## Newton's Laws of Motion

Since scientists are always complaining that people don't know Newton's three Laws of Motion, here they are, especially for you:

**Law 1:** Every object that is at rest stays at rest, or every object that is moving carries on moving at the same speed and in the same direction, unless something comes along and whacks it. (A baseball bat isn't needed: It could just be friction or the wind.)

**Law 2:** How much a moving object accelerates depends on how much force is applied to it. If you push a car on your own, it moves a little, slowly; if you get a bulldozer to do it, it moves a lot – fast.

**Law 3:** To any force an equal and opposite reaction exists. For example, if you push against a wall, the wall pushes back just as hard, which is why it doesn't fall over. Of course if you hit someone bigger than you, you also get an opposite reaction but I can't promise it will be equal.

Ironically, Newton was lucky to get an education at all. His father didn't see the point of this reading and writing lark, but luckily Papa Newton died before baby Newton was born. Newton managed to get into Cambridge, which was not exactly at the cutting edge in European science at the time: The university was still wary of these not-very-new-fangled ideas about the earth going round the sun. So Newton shut himself up in his room (he was the original absent-minded professor) and managed to invent differential calculus (and if you're expecting me to explain that to you, think again) and to work out that 'white' light is actually made up of all the colours of the rainbow.

When the plague struck, Newton had to move out of Cambridge, and he spent his time away thinking about why planets stay in orbit and don't just head off in their own sweet way. At this point, the apple comes in. He saw an apple falling from a tree (he saw it, it didn't fall on his head) and he thought, 'Wait a minute. That's a pretty tall tree. If the force that made that apple fall could get up that far, why shouldn't it reach as high as the moon?' Which is not something that occurs to everyone who goes apple picking, you've got to admit. So Newton didn't exactly 'discover' gravity, but he's the one who concluded that gravity applies everywhere, in space, in your back garden – hence, gravity's a universal law.

Newton tended to keep his ideas to himself: It was Edmond Halley (of comet fame; see the sidebar 'Halley and the comets') who persuaded him to start publishing. His greatest work was his *Principia*. Don't rush out and buy this book unless your Latin is really good – like all scientific works at the time, it was written in Latin. In *Principia*, Newton laid down his three *Laws of Motion* (if you want to know the laws, head to the sidebar 'Newton's Laws of Motion').

Not content with coming up with the basic laws governing the universe (and no one would challenge them until Einstein, and even then his ideas only apply if you're travelling on a beam of light or if you're out in deep space), Newton became a Fellow of the Royal Society, Professor of Mathematics at Cambridge, and defended the university against both James II and Judge Jeffreys. (Read Chapter 15 and you'll find out why doing so took some courage.) He also found time to study theology and criticise the Church of England's doctrine of the Trinity (he was a mathematician: Three into one just won't go), and to reorganise the Royal Mint. And his work at the Royal Mint got him his knighthood – the British always got their priorities right!

# Part V
# On the Up: The Eighteenth and Nineteenth Centuries

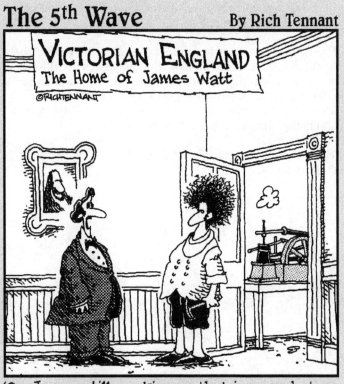

The 5th Wave          By Rich Tennant

VICTORIAN ENGLAND
The Home of James Watt

©RICHTENNANT

'So, James- still working on that improved steam engine idea of yours I see.'

## In this part . . .

In the eighteenth century, the English did a new and extraordinary thing: They created a new nation, 'Great Britain'. Its people were to be no longer English or Scots or Welsh, but 'Britons'. Not everyone was convinced: Britain's American colonies rose in revolt against what they saw as a corrupt government that had lost sight of its own most basic principles.

Even greater changes were afoot: Britain came to lead the world in industrial technology, building miles of railways and canals, and turning little villages into vast industrial cities. Simultaneously, the British were spreading their ideas and their rule across vast dominions in India, Africa, and many other countries around the world.

This was the age when the British helped to shape the modern world.

# Chapter 15

# Let's Make a Country

*In This Chapter*

▶ Understanding why only a Protestant monarch would do

▶ Signing up to a union with England: Scotland

▶ Paying for backing a series of royal losers: Ireland

▶ Fighting the French: Why the English couldn't stop

▶ Creating a whole new nation: How the English did it

*W*hat makes a country? Up until the seventeenth century, four 'countries' made up the British Isles: England, Scotland, Wales, and Ireland. Each one had its own separate sense of identity, its own history, even its own language. If you had asked folk at the time of the Civil Wars (1642–49, but see Chapter 13 for the gory details) what nationality they were, they probably wouldn't have understood the question. If they had, they'd have said 'English' or 'Scottish' or whatever. But by the end of the eighteenth century you'd have heard people using a new term: 'British', or 'Britons' rather than 'English', 'Scots', and so on. You may have heard a new song (*Rule, Britannia*), seen a strange new flag (a mixture of the red and white cross of St George, the white-on-blue St Andrew's cross, and after 1801, a diagonal red cross for Ireland) with an unusual name. Not the 'English' flag, or even the 'British' flag, but the Union flag, or Union Jack. Something decidedly odd was going on.

## No Popery! No Wooden Shoes!

Far and away the most important point about the eighteenth-century English was that they were Protestant and proud of it. (For a quick run-down of the difference between Protestants and Catholics, see Chapter 12.) This definition wasn't just a question of religion; being Protestant meant standing for things like liberty, free speech, and protection by the law. If you look back to Chapters 11 and 13, you'll see that England's experiences of Catholic rulers, whether home-grown like Mary Tudor, or foreign, like Philip II of Spain (the one who sent the Armada), had not been very happy. In any case, the English couldn't understand why anyone would choose to be Catholic. In their view, all those statues and all that incense just kept people poor and subservient while their priests gorged themselves and got up to no good behind convent walls. Catholic rulers, like the King of France or the Pope, were the worst sort of tyrants they figured, locking innocent people up or handing them over to the dreaded Inquisition.

The English felt quite sorry for the French. They saw them as poor, half-starved creatures, who wore clogs because they couldn't afford anything decent to put on their feet. Whenever the English felt in danger of going the same way, the cry went up: 'No popery! No wooden shoes!'

These anti-Catholic protests had such a deep effect on British culture that they're still remembered today. Take a look at the famous Lewes bonfire parade in Sussex each 5 November, and you'll still see banners reading 'No popery!' – though clogs seem to be okay.

# 1688: Glorious (?) Revolution (?)

Anti-Catholic feeling (see the previous section) came to a head when King James II assumed the throne in 1685. James II was the younger brother of Charles II, but he didn't have any of his brother's political skill. Even more importantly, James was a Catholic. Attempts had already been made to exclude him from the throne even during Charles II's reign (Chapter 13 explains how all this had happened), but when James did succeed his brother in 1685, initially he seemed prepared to let bygones be bygones. But then things began to go badly wrong.

- ✔ **1685: Monmouth's rebellion.** James, Duke of Monmouth and illegitimate son of Charles II, lands in Dorset and claims the throne. His main platform: He's a Protestant. Monmouth gathers support in the West Country, but his men are heavily defeated by James II's army at the Battle of Sedgemoor. Victory for James, but then he goes and spoils it.

- ✔ **1685: The 'Bloody Assizes'.** James II sends Lord Chief Justice George Jeffreys (often known simply as 'Judge Jeffreys') down to deal with Monmouth and his rebels. Monmouth is executed (very clumsily – the deed took five blows of the axe and the executioner had to finish the job with a carving knife). Then Jeffreys starts trying the ordinary people who'd taken part in the rising. He bullies and screams at them, and sentences some three hundred people to death, with hundreds more being flogged or transported to the West Indies. The country is appalled; James II is very pleased.

✔ **1686:** James II starts appointing Catholics as army officers and to important posts, like Lord Lieutenant of Ireland and the heads of Oxford Colleges, and sacking anyone who protests. He also reintroduces the Catholic Mass into Presbyterian Scotland (and see Chapter 11 if you want to see why this act was so inflammatory).

✔ **1687:** James II issues – without consulting Parliament – a Declaration of Indulgence. In theory this declaration offers freedom of religion to all. In reality it is designed to promote the Catholic Church. Churchmen or civil servants who oppose it are sacked.

✔ **1688:** James II's attempt to prosecute seven Anglican bishops for opposing the Declaration of Indulgence fails when they are acquitted amidst huge rejoicing. So James tries to get the anti-Catholic Test Act repealed (see Chapter 13 for more about the Test Act) and sets about the wholesale rigging of the next elections in order to get a Parliament that will do it.

The final straw for Protestants came when James II's Catholic queen, Mary of Modena, gave birth to a healthy baby boy, named James Edward after his father. James II already had two grown-up Protestant daughters, Mary and Anne, by a previous marriage, but as a boy little James Edward took precedence. That meant another Catholic king (since little James Edward would certainly be brought up as a Catholic) and probably another one after that, and so on. The prospect didn't bear thinking of. The time had come to act.

## Going Dutch

On 5 November 1688 (5 November was an auspicious date for Protestants because it was when the Gunpowder Plot was foiled – see Chapter 13 for more about this) the Dutch ruler, Prince William of Orange, landed in Devon with an army to overturn James II. Immediately leading English nobles started joining William. When James's army deserted to William, James knew his reign was over. He fled to France, taking his wife and little James Edward with him. (Actually, James got caught at the coast and beaten up by some fishermen, so to avoid putting him on trial, which would have been highly embarrassing, not to mention constitutionally tricky, William had to 'allow' James to 'escape' again!)

William was James II's son-in-law – he'd married James's daughter Mary. He was also one of the leading Protestant princes in Europe. In fact, the main reason he landed in England was to make sure the English joined in the war he was planning with King Louis XIV of France.

## Revolution? Are you sure?

Why call the routing of James II a revolution? Okay, the result was a change of kings, but it wasn't anything like as revolutionary as the Civil War (and if you're not sure what was so revolutionary about that, have a look at all the shenanigans in Chapter 13). But for years the English called this event the 'Glorious Revolution', or even just *The* Revolution. What they meant was a revolution in the sense of a wheel coming full circle. They believed that after centuries of fighting for their liberties, going all the way back to William the Conqueror in 1066 (who? See Chapter 7 to find out), they'd finally regained the liberties which they fondly believed the English had enjoyed in Anglo-Saxon times. The wheel had come full circle – hence, Revolution. (See Chapters 5 and 6 for a slightly less rosy view of Anglo-Saxon times, and the rest of this chapter for a less rosy view of the Revolution!)

Parliament decided that by running away James had in effect abdicated and it declared William and Mary joint monarchs – King William III and Queen Mary II – in his place. (They also declared William king of Scotland, too, which figures in events later. Head to the section 'Making Great Britain: Making Britain Great?' if you can't stand the suspense.) And if you're wondering about little James Edward, Parliament said that he wasn't really the heir because he'd been smuggled into the queen's bed in a warming pan. Well, some people believed that story.

## The Bill of Rights

To the English, one of James II's worst crimes was the way he'd tried to rule without Parliament. They were going to make sure that no monarch – not even a Protestant one – ever tried to do that again. Parliament said that William and Mary could only become king and queen if they agreed to a Bill of Rights, which said that they had to summon Parliament frequently, and that Catholics could not be king or queen or hold any official post.

But if William and Mary thought they could relax, they were wrong. The very next year, James II was back. All those English politicians had forgotten the Catholic Irish. James hadn't.

# Ireland: King Billy of the Boyne

Although all technically 'Irish', three main types of Irish were around in the seventeenth century (have a look back to Chapters 11 and 13 to find out why):

- ✔ **The Catholic Irish:** These were the original inhabitants. The English saw them as dangerous savages – and Catholic savages at that.

- ✔ **The Scots-Irish:** These were Scottish Presbyterians – *really* strict Protestants – who'd been 'planted' in Ulster in Elizabeth and James I's time to displace the Irish Catholics. These Scots were heavily financed by the City of London, which is why they also renamed the old city of Derry 'Londonderry'.

- ✔ **The Anglo-Irish:** Not so many of them but they owned nearly all the land worth owning in Ireland. They attended the Church of Ireland – the Irish branch of the Anglican Church – and they were the ones who voted in elections and sat in the Irish Parliament in Dublin. But don't be fooled: These people were Irish, not English, and very proud of it.

The Catholic Irish had always been loyal to the Stuarts, so when a French ship brought James to Ireland in 1689 they flocked to join him. But when James's apparently unstoppable force met the immovable object of the staunchly Protestant City of Londonderry, events took a wrong turn. The Londonderry apprentice boys (the Scots-Irish) shut the city gates in his face and declared 'No Surrender!' James had to throw a barrier across the river and besiege the city, which took months and simply gave William time to get things ready in England. Terrible starvation raged inside Londonderry, but things weren't much better in James's army. Finally ships arrived from England with supplies, broke through the boom and lifted the siege. James had to turn back.

But by now William was in Ireland with a huge army and a lot of money. In 1690 he caught up with James on the banks of the River Boyne and blew James's army to pieces. James ran, all the way back to France.

James spun out the rest of his life in the Chateau of St Germain near Paris, dreaming of the day he'd be welcomed back to London. His exile was very sad, said Louis's courtiers, but you only had to meet James to understand why he was there.

## The Orangemen

Those people you see banging drums and marching down the streets wearing bowler hats and orange sashes are members of the Orange Order, set up in memory of William of Orange – or King Billy, as they call him – after a battle with the Catholics in 1795. The Order was a bit like the Freemasons, and it was set up to defend working-class Ulster Protestants against attack by the Catholics. But the order also existed to mark out Protestant territory and remind the Catholics who was in charge. The biggest parades each year are still held on 1 July, the anniversary of the Battle of the Boyne, and many Protestant banners and murals proudly proclaim 'No Surrender!' or 'Remember 1690!' Ulster is one land where history still lives – and that's the problem.

## *Bad heir day*

Even with James II out of the way, William and Mary had a problem. No mini William or Mary existed to take over when they died. Mary's sister Anne wasn't much help either. Although she got pregnant 18 times (don't even go there), only five of her children were born alive and four of them died in infancy. Anne's only surviving child was the little Duke of Gloucester, and in 1700, he died, too. The situation wasn't just sad – it was urgent.

If William, Mary, and Anne all died without an heir, the next in line would have to be James II's son, James Edward Stuart. But the Bill of Rights said Catholics weren't allowed to be kings or queens. So the royal genealogists had to get busy finding a Protestant with a claim – any claim – to the English throne.

The genealogists found what they were looking for: Back in 1613. James I's daughter had married a German prince (now dead) and their (now dead) son's wife was still alive . . . and she was a Protestant. (And you thought that soap opera scripts were far fetched.)

So in 1701 Parliament passed the Act of Settlement, saying that the throne would pass in due course to the Electress Sophia (the living Protestant wife of the dead German prince whose mother was James I's daughter – do try to keep up) and her heirs and successors, and must never ever go to a Catholic. This law is still in force today. The Act of Settlement came just in time because suddenly everyone started dying:

✔ **Queen Mary II** died in 1694.

✔ **James II** died, still in exile in France, in 1701.

✔ **William III** died in 1702.

So now Anne was queen. But she had no living children and was not likely to have any more. Over in France, James II's son, James Edward Stuart (now grown up), kept his eyes and ears open for any news from London. Meanwhile, even further away, in Hanover, the Electress Sophia sat waiting impatiently for Queen Anne to die.

## *Marlborough country*

You don't hear much of him nowadays, but in his day, and Queen Anne's reign was his day, John Churchill, first Duke of Marlborough was *the* big star: A military hero and a political leader all rolled into one. He's still generally regarded as one of the greatest military commanders ever. Marlborough was the son of Sir Winston Churchill (no, not that one!) and he made his name fighting for James II, though he changed sides quickly when William of Orange landed in 1688 (see the earlier section 'Going Dutch').

William made Marlborough his Commander-in-Chief, which was good timing, because Europe was just about to go to war. The reason for this war was because the King of Spain had died in 1701, and Louis XIV saw a chance to put his son on the Spanish throne. Doing so would have created a sort of Catholic superstate of France and Spain ('The Pyrenees no longer exist!' exclaimed Louis, gleefully) and no way were the European Protestant states standing for that.

So an English Protestant army set off for Europe with the Duke of Marlborough at its head. The French wouldn't know what had hit them.

Marlborough's greatest weapon was speed. He could move his troops across huge distances much faster than anyone thought possible, and he knew how to make good use of his cavalry. In 1705 Marlborough marched in record time from the coast right into the heart of Germany, and cut the French and their allies to pieces at the Battle of Blenheim. England went mad with joy. Parliament voted him a big house (called Blenheim, naturally) in the middle of a magnificent park. Marlborough went on to beat the French again at Ramillies, Oudenarde, and the very bloody and close-run battle of Malplaquet.

Where Marlborough went wrong was in getting involved in politics. He and his wife were ambitious, and they were strong supporters of the Whigs (see the later section on 'Whigs and Tories' for more info on these people), which was fine to start with because the Whigs were in power. However, Queen Anne was getting tired of the Whigs and was also beginning to fall out with Marlborough's wife so, after the bloodbath at Malplaquet, Anne thanked Marlborough very much for yet another famous victory and then sacked him.

# Making Great Britain: Making Britain Great?

England and Wales had been united as one country since Tudor times (see Chapter 11), but Scotland and Ireland were still separate kingdoms, with their own parliaments and laws. The following sections explain the reason why they both agreed to join England in a new United Kingdom and the battle over how united they were going to be.

## England and Scotland: one king, two kingdoms

England and Scotland had had the same king since James VI became James I of England in 1603 (see Chapter 13 for the background to all the events in this section). But once the Stuarts got on the English throne, they seemed to lose all interest in Scotland.

James I used to talk about being King of Great Britain, and from 1608 Scots were officially English citizens, but no one looked seriously into uniting the two countries until Oliver Cromwell did it by force in 1652. The Scots had never accepted his action.

Even Charles II, who was crowned King of Scotland before he became King of England, steered clear of Scotland once he got back to London. If the Scots had thought that getting the Stuarts on the English throne was going to help them, they could not have been more wrong.

That 'Glorious Revolution' of 1688 (see the earlier section) was deeply worrying for the Scots, because the English Parliament had also made William III King of Scotland. If the English were going to start deciding who was and who was not King of Scotland, then what was the point of having a parliament in Edinburgh? Maybe it was time, thought the Scots, to remind the English and the world that Scotland was a proud and independent nation. And the best place to do the reminding seemed to be – wait for it – the Isthmus of Panama. The plan went disastrously wrong: See the aptly named sidebar, 'Disaster in Panama'.

## Disaster in Panama

The Scots asked themselves: 'Why is England so rich and powerful?' They realised that the answer was partly because she was bigger and partly because of all those English colonies in the New World. 'So,' they said 'why not get a colony for ourselves?' They couldn't go to North America or the Caribbean because the English, French, and Spanish had taken it all, but Central America looked promising. Central America was in Spanish territory, but, hey, this is colonialism. In 1698 a small fleet of would-be colonists set off to found the Scottish empire at Darien in Panama.

Here's a tip. If ever you decide to settle on a swampy, fever-ridden coastline with hostile neighbours and slow communications, do your homework properly before you set out. Darien was a disaster. Everything went wrong. The first fleet set off with 1,200 people, and 200 of them were dead by the time they got there. The settlers had hardly built a fort when they started dying, too, first from fever and then from malnutrition as the food began to run out. They sent an urgent text back to Scotland to warn them not to send anyone else to this appalling hellhole, but text messaging went by ship in those days, and by the time the message arrived in Scotland, the second fleet was already on its way. The folk from the second fleet found the colony deserted, the fort in ruins, and the Spanish closing in. Then they found they hadn't brought the right sort of tools or enough food, but they did have plenty of warm woollen clothing. Very useful in the tropics, I don't think.

The English colonies in the West Indies refused to help them, and the colonists started dying – in large numbers. As the Spanish moved in for the kill, the Scots decided to call the adventure a day. They got into three ships and sailed for home. All three ships sank on the journey. Put all that together and you've got what I call a disaster.

## *Glencoe – death at MacDonald's*

The regime change in 1688 (you can read about that earlier in this chapter in the section '1688: Glorious(?) Revolution(?)') brought one further tragedy to Scotland. The Scottish Protestants didn't like James II (or James VII as he was to them) any more than the English did, but the Catholics in the Highlands did. When the English threw James out of England, these Catholics staged a rising against William and actually beat William's men at Killiecrankie. Of course, their victory didn't change anything, but the Highlanders were about to pay a terrible price for that piece of defiance.

Once William was safely on the throne, he decreed that all the Catholic areas of Ireland and Scotland had to swear an oath of allegiance to him before a magistrate by 1 January 1692. The MacDonald clan left swearing the oath late, partly out of cussedness but mainly because getting an entire clan to up sticks and move across country takes a bit of time. The MacDonald clan got to Fort William in time, but were then told they were in the wrong place and needed to be at Inverary – sixty miles away. They made it to Inverary and took the oath six days late. (Try the journey by train nowadays and see if you can do any better.)

A month later, a party of government soldiers under orders signed by King William, and led by Captain Robert Campbell, arrived at the MacDonald camp at Glencoe. The Campbells and the MacDonalds were old enemies, always stealing each other's cattle, but this animosity didn't stop the MacDonald clan from welcoming their visitors and putting them up for twelve days. Early on the morning of 13 February, the Campbell men set about systematically massacring their hosts. They lined them up, shot them and then gunned the elderly clan chief down as he was getting up.

King William was horrified: He'd signed the order without realising what it was. The MacDonalds put the blame on the Campbells, and the feud runs deep to this day.

## Act Two of Union: Scotland

The reason that Union finally happened was not so much because Scotland needed it (which it did) but because *England* did, to prevent a Stuart come-back. And the English had good reason to fear a return of the Stuarts.

The Scots had been very worried in 1688 about England dictating who was to be their king. Well, in 1701, the English repeated this folly. The Act of Settlement said that the throne would pass to the Electress Sophia of Hanover and her heirs (see the section 'Bad heir day' above). The Scottish parliament refused to agree to this arrangement and even passed an act saying nothing prevented England and Scotland having separate kings again. Which was an obvious hint that they might invite James Edward Stuart to become King of Scotland. Over in France, James Edward Stuart was very interested in this development. Very interested indeed.

The English were alarmed. No way would they allow 'James III' to become King of Scotland. They needed to get talking with the Scots, and fast.

Don't get the idea that this struggle over the succession was a straight English vs. Scots business. England was much richer and more powerful than Scotland, and plenty of Scots saw huge advantages in union. All those impor-tant posts in Whitehall or in the English colonies would be open to Scots. The Scots who supported union thought the anti-English Patriot party were simply trying to keep Scotland in the Middle Ages. And above all, most Scots did not want a Catholic king any more than the English did.

## Jacobites

James II's son was called James Edward Stuart (or King James III if you're a Stuart fan) so their supporters were called Jacobites from *Jacobus*, the Latin for James. The English called him the Old Pretender, to distinguish him from his son, Charles Edward Stuart, the Young Pretender. Many people think of the Jacobites as Scots, but in fact there were plenty of English politicians who kept in close touch with the 'King over the water'. If you fancied making a discreet Jacobite toast (which was treason, remember) you simply raised your glass to 'The King' while passing it over a handy finger-bowl full of water. And you just hoped no one else saw you do it. Sneaky, heh?

In any case, the Scottish Dukes of Argyll and Queensberry bribed so many Scottish MPs with gifts and posts to get the Act of Union passed that the result was a foregone conclusion. Furious anti-Union riots occurred in the streets outside the Scottish parliament building, but in 1707 the Act of Union received Queen Anne's royal assent. With this act, Scotland lost her parliament and her independence (though she kept her own legal system and lots of separate laws) and became part of a new country, to be called Great Britain.

# Rebellions: The '15 and the '45

James Edward Stuart's chance of becoming King of England came in 1714 when Queen Anne died. He had waited 26 years for this moment. And he blew it.

Sophia was dead by the time Anne died, so it was her son, Georg (George in English – you can read more about him and some other Georges later in this chapter), who crossed over to England. He didn't like England, and the English didn't like him. Here at last was James's chance to grab the throne – but he wasn't ready! By the time he'd got his act together it was too late: George had appointed a government, and the English were getting used to him. James finally landed in Scotland in 1715 – the wrong place and the wrong year. And, of course, he was still the wrong religion.

Two major Jacobite rebellions occurred. They were both based in Scotland, and they both failed.

### The '15

This rebellion was so called because James Edward Stuart landed in Scotland in 1715. The Scottish Jacobites lost the Battle of Sheriffmuir. More importantly for James, the English Jacobites lost the Battle of Preston. James had to go back to France and George I could breathe easy. But for the Scots, the worst was yet to come.

## Rob Roy

Most of the great Jacobite stories don't come from the eighteenth century at all, but were invented or embellished a hundred years later, usually by the nineteenth-century Scottish novelist, Sir Walter Scott. Rob Roy MacGregor is a case in point. Yes, he did exist, and yes, he was a Jacobite. He fought for James II in 1688 and for 'James III' in 1715. And he did have to escape from the wicked Marquis of Montrose.

But then, one of Rob Roy's men had run off with a lot of the Marquis's money. Rob Roy was almost certainly a cattle thief, like most of the Highlanders. But he wasn't fighting for Scottish independence or anything like it. If you like your Scottish heroes clean and patriotic, read Sir Walter Scott or watch Liam Neeson on DVD, but keep clear of the history books.

### The '45

By 1745 James Edward was getting a bit old for campaigning, but his son, Charles Edward Stuart, the Young Pretender, landed in the Highlands in 1745 to claim the throne for his father. Charles caught the government completely on the hop. He gathered a large army, took Edinburgh and Carlisle, sent asmall government force packing at Prestonpans, and invaded England. Just like his father, Charles was interested in England, not Scotland. But the English were not interested in him. Hardly any English Jacobites joined him, and by the time Charles had reached Derby, it was clear that his mission to win English hearts and minds was getting nowhere; Charles had no choice but to turn round and go back. But by now he was being stalked by the Duke of Cumberland, with a very large, well-equipped English army.

The two armies met at Culloden Moor, near Inverness. The English had worked out how to deal with wild Highlanders, and doing so consisted mostly of blowing them to pieces with cannon or ripping their guts out with bayonets. Charles had to run for his life, and the English took terrible revenge. They hunted the Highlanders down and killed them; they destroyed whole villages, rounded up the people, and either shot them or put them on ships to be transported. They banned highland dress and highland customs. This terrible revenge was effectively eighteenth-century ethnic cleansing.

This story has a strange epilogue. Culloden was a big shock to both sides, and for years the English absolutely hated the Scots and everything Scottish. But towards the end of the century, they started to change and made a conscious effort to integrate the Scots more into English life. More and more Scots joined the British army or went out to administer the colonies, and Scottish regiments were even allowed to wear the kilt and the tartan with their red coats. Soon English and Scots were used to standing together in battle against the French. As if to seal these congenial relations, George IV – great-great-grandson of George I – went to Edinburgh and wore a kilt. He looked foul, and a painting exists to prove it, but apparently his gesture went down very well with the Scots. Oh, and before you ask the obvious question: He wore flesh-coloured tights.

## Ireland: Penal times

After the Battle of the Boyne (see the earlier section on 'King Billy of the Boyne'), William III made peace with the Irish in the Treaty of Limerick, which might have gone something like this:

> The Treaty of Limerick said:
> We won't put a price on your head.
> We want to be friends,
> If you'll just make amends,
> Drop James, and take William instead.
>
> But the English went back on their word
> For the Ulstermen thought it absurd
> Any Irish RC
> Should get off scot-free
> For treason to William the Third.
>
> They said: 'We need laws and decrees
> Stopping Catholics from being MPs.
> They mustn't own land,
> And they must understand
> Now we've won we shall do as we please.'

So William III and the Irish Protestants brought in a series of penal laws stripping Catholics of their human rights. Under these laws, Catholics were forbidden to:

- Vote or sit in Parliament
- Own or inherit land or even lease it for more than 31 years
- Go to university (even a foreign one) or be lawyers or teachers
- Own any weapons or a good quality horse

In addition, a very close eye was kept on all Catholic priests. And the penal laws worked. They kept the Catholic Irish so poor and powerless that they took no part in all those Scottish Jacobite risings.

## Bonnie Prince Charlie

If ever a man was luckier than he deserved, that man was Charles Edward Stuart, known to history and to tourists buying shortbread as Bonnie Prince Charlie. He became a Scottish folk hero, mainly because the Highlanders sheltered him after Culloden and smuggled him out of the country. In fact, Charles Edward (he would have *hated* being called Charlie) couldn't stand Scotland, and he certainly didn't think of himself as a Scot: He was half Polish, and he'd lived all his life in very comfortable exile in France. By no means did all Scots support him, and plenty of Scots joined the government army to fight against him. Peter Watson's 1964 TV documentary *Culloden* gives a pretty good picture: 'Aye, run you cowardly Frenchman,' one of his officers shouted at him as he did just that. Bonnie Prince Charlie spent the rest of his life leading a complicated love life in France and Italy, while he slowly but surely drank himself to death.

In fact, the laws were so harsh that they were in effect making Ireland a nation of paupers, which didn't help anyone. Even the Protestant Anglo-Irish began to demand Catholic emancipation, which meant allowing Catholics to vote and to sit in Parliament but London wasn't interested.

When the American War of Independence broke out in 1775 (see Chapter 17), the Anglo-Irish raised a military force called the Irish Volunteers in case the French landed. The leading Protestant Anglo-Irish MP, Henry Grattan, more or less told London that if they didn't give Catholics the vote, the Irish Volunteers just might stage a rebellion. With the war in America going from bad to worse, London had to submit.

Getting the vote wasn't quite as big a deal as it looked. Without landed property – and thanks to the penal laws Catholics weren't supposed to have any – no one, Catholic or Protestant, was allowed to vote. (See Chapter 17 for more on eighteenth-century Britain's interesting idea of voting rights.) Moreover, Catholics still weren't allowed to sit in either parliament – Dublin or Westminster.

## Act Three of Union: Ireland

Despite the promising actions started by Henry Grattan (see preceding section), some Irish people thought Ireland's only hope would be to pull away from England. When the French Revolution broke out in 1789, the French said they would help the Irish to break away. In 1796 a young Irishman called Theodore Wolfe Tone arrived in Bantry Bay at the head of a French army; he was turned back by bad weather! Two years later the Irish staged a massive rebellion against the British. At least, the rebellion was meant to be against the British, but it quickly became a rising against all Protestants, English, Scottish – or Irish. The French didn't turn up, so the British, who had spies in the rebel camp, got their forces together and crushed the rebels without mercy. Just when the rebellion was all over, the French arrived, and had to sail away again.

London was badly shaken, and prime minister William Pitt decided to tread carefully: He'd grant full Catholic emancipation, but the Irish would have to give up their parliament in Dublin and accept direct rule from London. At first the Protestants were against the idea, but when Pitt said they wouldn't get any government posts unless they agreed to it, they soon changed their minds. So in 1800, a second Act of Union was passed, creating yet another new country, the United Kingdom of Great Britain and Ireland. (And Catholic emancipation? George III vetoed it.)

# George, George, George, and – er – George

It wasn't actually the law that eighteenth-century British kings had to be called George, but you could be forgiven for thinking so.

Politicians had to be really careful. They had to keep in with the king if they wanted to get anywhere, but if they thought the king wasn't going to last long, they needed to schmooze the Prince of Wales (the heir to the throne). The problem with doing so was that none of the Georges liked their fathers (or sons) much, so you were in deep trouble if you got the schmoozing wrong. Being politicians, they even invented a term for coping with this dysfunctional family – *reversionary interest*.

## The one and only, the original, George 1

George I (1714–27) was quite happy being Elector of Hanover, which he was until he became King of Great Britain in 1714. He didn't like England: He never bothered to learn the language and he spent as much time as he could back in Hanover. He was no fool. The English only tolerated him because he was Protestant, and he knew it. He was en route to Hanover when he died and you'll need to go there to visit his tomb. If you really want to.

## Just when you thought it was safe to go back to the water – George II

George II was a lot more interested in Britain and British politics than his father had been, and with good reason – his reign was when Britain really became a world-class power. George didn't always get his way in politics, but he got Handel to settle in England, and he's responsible for people having to stand up for the Hallelujah Chorus. George was a good soldier, and he was the last British king to lead his troops into battle, at Dettingen in 1743 (and he won, as well).

In keeping with Hanover family tradition, George II hated his eldest son, Frederick, Prince of Wales, and Fred hated his father right back. But then Fred died, and George's grandson, another George, became the new Prince of Wales. Suspense! Would young George hate his grandfather, the king? And the answer was . . . yes, he did! Well, at least someone was maintaining tradition.

## The badness of George III

George III was British born and bred, and very proud of the fact. Poor old George has had a very mixed press ever since he came to the throne. Politicians at the time said he was trying to undermine the constitution and Americans blamed him for driving them to declare independence (see Chapter 17 for more about what went wrong in America). But more recently, historians (British ones at any rate) have been more sympathetic. They say George III was trying to bring the crown back into the centre of politics, but always by working closely with the prime minister, not by trying to take power away from Parliament.

George became very unpopular after the American fiasco, but when his famous madness set in a big wave of sympathy was felt for him. He spent the last years of his life completely blind, out of his wits, wandering around a deserted Windsor Castle. Very sad.

## Completing your set of Georges

George IV was fat, vain, and lazy. As Prince of Wales, he married a Catholic widow, Mrs FitzHerbert, in secret and then lied about doing so. He spent ten years as Prince Regent, supposedly governing the country while his father was ill, but in reality spending money on himself while the country was going through the first period of serious industrial hardship and unemployment in its history. If you really want to know more about this appalling man, you can find the shameful details in Chapter 17.

# *Whigs and Tories*

While the Scots and Irish were rising up or having Acts of Union forced on them, the English were forming the world's first Parliamentary monarchy.

The Glorious Revolution and the Bill of Rights were a good start (you can read about them earlier in this chapter). Neither William III nor George I would have been king if Parliament hadn't said so. Once George I was on the throne, Parliament became even more important, because George I wasn't all that interested in English politics and he went to Hanover for as long as he could. At first, English politicians were a bit annoyed about this lack of interest, but gradually they began to realise that his absence might not be such a bad thing after all. If George didn't want to play, then they could govern the country without him. So they did.

Two political parties operated in eighteenth-century Britain:

- ✔ **The Whigs** who believed in the Hanoverian succession, Parliament, and equal rights for all Protestants, especially non-Church of England ones, called dissenters.

- ✔ **The Tories** who believed in the Crown, freedom of religion for all (as long as they were in the Church of England), and horsewhipping dissenters. In addition, many Tories secretly wanted to bring the Stuarts back.

Of course, they could all agree on some areas. For instance, they all believed in the God-given right of all landowners to hang poachers, to set whatever rents they liked, and to hold on to their land tax-free. And they all hated Catholics.

After the South Sea Bubble (see 'The South Sea Bubble' sidebar), the Whigs were so powerful that for most of the century they *were* politics. They split into warring factions and competed for very lucrative government posts – especially the ones that didn't involve any work – which all made for plenty of corruption and skullduggery.

The master Whig politician was Sir Robert Walpole. Walpole managed the House of Commons so effectively that people said Britain had become a 'Robinocracy' or a 'Whig oligarchy' ('oligarchy' means rule by a small clique). Officially, Walpole was First Lord of the Treasury, but increasingly people called him First or 'Prime' Minister.

## The South Sea Bubble

In 1711 the Tories decided to launch a little money-making venture. The Whigs were doing very well out of the profits of the Bank of England, which they controlled, so the Tories responded by forming the South Sea Company, which won the contract for supplying slaves to the Spanish colonies in South America. Unfortunately, the company got over-ambitious and offered to take over a substantial chunk of the National Debt, paying it off from what it confidently expected would be huge profits. With government encouragement, everyone rushed to invest their money, either in the South Sea Company or in one of the other similar companies that suddenly started appearing. Just like on Wall Street in 1929, many of the schemes turned out to be scams. A crash was inevitable, and it came in 1720 – investors were ruined and tales of corruption and scandal involving ministers and even George I's mistresses abounded. The Tories got the blame, and the Whigs got the benefit: They were in office for the foreseeable future.

Walpole's policy was easy – make money, not war. But that policy didn't always go down well, at least the second part didn't, and in 1739 Parliament went to war with Spain because of a Captain Jenkins (who said he'd had his ear cut off by the Spaniards and brought the ear – or what he said was his ear – with him to prove it!).

This war was one of a whole series of showdowns with the French, outlined in the following section.

# Fighting the French: A National Sport

Lots of wars broke out in the eighteenth century, but one detail was easy to remember: The British and the French were always on opposite sides. Since these wars can get a bit confusing, especially when they start merging into each other, here's a handy guide to the fighting.

## Round 1: War of the Spanish Succession 1701–14

- **Supposed to be about:** Who's to be King of Spain.
- **Really about:** Is the King of France going to dominate the entire continent of Europe or is someone going to stop him?

- ✔ **What happened:** This is the war where Marlborough won his victories at Blenheim, Ramillies, Oudenarde, and Malplaquet (see earlier in this chapter).

- ✔ **Result:** Britain got handy bases at Gibraltar and Minorca, plus most of North America.

# Round 2: War of Captain Jenkins's Ear 1739

- ✔ **Supposed to be about:** Whether or not the Spanish have the right to cut an English sea captain's ears off. The English think, on the whole, not.

- ✔ **Really about:** Whether or not the British should be allowed to muscle in on Spain's monopoly of South American trade. The Spanish think, on the whole, not.

- ✔ **What happened:** It gets overtaken by Round 3.

# Round 3: War of the Austrian Succession 1740–48

- ✔ **Supposed to be about:** Who's to be Emperor – or Empress – of Austria.

- ✔ **Really about:** Is the King of France going to dominate the entire continent of Europe or is someone going to stop him (see Round 1)?

- ✔ **What happened:** George II defeated the French (himself, in person) at Dettingen in 1743. The following year they actually get round to declaring war! Good news for the Hanoverians at Culloden (see the earlier section 'Rebellions: the '15 and the '45') but bad news at Fontenoy, where the French courteously invite the British to fire first, and then hit them for six.

- ✔ **Result:** A draw.

# Round 4: The Seven Years' War 1756–63

- ✔ **Supposed to be about:** A German invasion of part of Poland (sound familiar?).

- ✔ **Really about:** World domination (but British or French, not German).

- ✔ **What happened:** British Secretary of State *William Pitt the Elder* thinks globally, and fights the French in India and North America, as well as in Europe.

- ✔ **Result:** The British take Quebec, Guadeloupe, drive the French out of India, beat the French at the Battle of Minden and sink the French fleet in Quiberon Bay. All in all, a good war for the British.

## Pitt the Elder

The first William Pitt made a name for himself by opposing Walpole and saying rude things about Hanover. Pitt didn't like fighting wars in Europe, but he was a great believer in creating a British trading empire, and he was happy to fight in Canada or India in order to get it. Or rather, to send other people to fight in Canada or India in order to get it.

People didn't quite know what to make of him. When Pitt was made Paymaster-General of the forces, he didn't take the opportunity to embezzle large sums of public money. He became known as the Great Commoner because he believed in the House of Commons and wouldn't be bribed with a peerage. He had virtually created the British Empire by the time George III came to the throne, but George was determined to negotiate peace, even if doing so meant handing back many of the areas Pitt had won.

George III never liked Pitt, though he did make him Earl of Chatham. Pitt supported the Americans in their dispute with Britain until the revolutionary war broke out, but by then he was a sick man, and he collapsed and died rather dramatically in the middle of a speech in the House of Lords. You can still see people in the House of Lords today who seem to have done the same thing.

# Chapter 16

# Survival of the Richest: The Industrial Revolution

*In This Chapter*

▶ Advancing in farming procedures

▶ Waterproofing roads and building bridges for boats

▶ Industrialising the cloth industry

▶ Picturing life and work in the factories

▶ Relating the British sweet tooth to the African slave trade

**P**eople like learning about kings and queens, and, with a bit of luck, you can win them over to finding out about politicians and revolutionaries, but mention the invention of the spinning jenny and their eyes glaze over. Follow that invention up with the water frame and Crompton's mule, and then throw in the factory system and the principles of steam power, and – well, you're already thinking about skipping this chapter aren't you?

Yet this chapter includes things like child labour and the exploitation of the poor and helpless, famine and cruelty, breathtaking beauty and elegance – yes, I am talking aqueducts here – and remarkable inventiveness and enterprise. In short, my friends, this chapter is about how the British created the Modern World in all its glory and splendour, and misery, squalor and vice. It details wealth beyond dreams and poverty beyond nightmares. It also describes how a land was transformed and a people was created. And yes, this chapter's also about the spinning jenny.

## Food or Famine?

In the end, kings and generals don't matter much. What matters are things like food and clothing. The story of how Britain became the first industrial superpower in history begins with these basics. In the eighteenth century attempts were made in England to get a bit more food on the market.

## Problem: Fertiliser; Answer: Turnip

The first problem to overcome so as to increase food production was fertiliser, and in those days, that meant animal dung. Traditional English farming techniques involved leaving fields empty or fallow for a year. In the eighteenth century Dutch experts introduced a more efficient technique. The technique was called crop rotation, and it was all based on turnips. Here's how it worked:

- **Year 1:** Get the wheat harvest in.
- **Year 2:** Plant turnips; pull up turnips; feed turnips to sheep, pigs, and children; swear never to look at another turnip.
- **Year 3:** Sow barley, clover, and grass in the same field. The barley grows; you harvest it. The grass and clover grow up through the barley stubble; you let your cattle and sheep in to eat the grass and clover. They poop all over the field, thus fertilising it.
- **Year 4:** Back to Year 1.

A former Foreign Secretary, now retired, called Viscount Townshend introduced crop rotation on his estate (and got nicknamed 'Turnip Townshend' for his pains), and he spread the word, which helped the method catch on. What also helped was a new machine for planting seeds properly instead of just throwing them around and hoping. Jethro Tull invented this machine, and if you listen carefully, you can just hear him shouting out 'No, not the 70's rock band!' from his grave.

### The luck of the English

In one sense, the English were better off than the Scots or Irish, because they didn't really have any peasants, people who are effectively tied to the land and can't move elsewhere. In England, most of the people in the countryside were tenant farmers or labourers, who sold their services each year at what were called hiring fairs (because people got hired there).

The English also had all those rather lovely country estates you can visit at weekends but which in those days had English nobles sitting in them who, rather unusually, actually took an interest in farming. While Marie Antoinette was playing shepherdesses in Versailles, George III had a proper experimental farm on the royal estate at Windsor.

## Clearing the Highlands

Scotland experienced the worst example of land clearance. Scottish clan chiefs, or lairds, decided that the Highlands would look even better without Highlanders so they started evicting them by force. The Duke and Duchess of Sutherland were the worst perpetrators, who added insult to injury by forcing their few remaining tenants to put up a huge statue to the duke in 'gratitude'. (The lairds wanted the land partly for sheep and partly for grouse shooting.)

The Highlanders had to move out to tiny crofts crowded along the coast, which were virtually impossible to farm. The only option left for many people was to get on a ship and leave Scotland for good. Which is why so many Scottish communities exist around the world, in Canada and Australia and South Africa and the States. They reckon that more 'Scots' reside outside Scotland than in it.

The forced evictions were so successful that hardly any trace of Highland settlements has survived. What happened in Scotland has been compared to ethnic cleansing, and with reason, except that this act was done by the Highlanders' own clan chiefs. So next time you admire the empty beauty of the Highlands, remember that its beauty was bought with cruelty, injustice, and violence. And ask yourself why the landscape's so empty.

## *Baa baa black sheep, that's a lot of wool*

Seventeenth-century animals were all bone and very little meat. So the English, being an inquisitive lot, started dabbling in genetic engineering. Or selective breeding, as they called this technique. The big name in the field was Robert Bakewell, who found that if you chose your sheep carefully, you could end up with massive sheep. Monster sheep. He called these animals New Leicesters and they were very, *very* fat.

With selective breeding, ordinary horses now became giant shire horses, great equine monsters who could pull huge cartloads of turnips (sorry, kids). Even better were the huge pigs and cows the English started to breed, because you could eat them. These animals became superstars. People came from all over Europe to marvel at them.

## *Reaching (en)closure*

All the great farming ideas described above would only work if you had a nice big farm. But most farmers didn't have nice big farms. They had bits of different land spread across all the different fields in the village. So if you wanted to get anywhere with agricultural improvements, you had to go and rearrange who had which land. *Enclosures* resulted, and the process happened like this:

- ✔ **Step 1:** A group of local landowners got Parliament to pass a local Enclosure Act saying they can start juggling around with their neighbours' property.

- ✔ **Step 2:** Parliament sent down two- or three-man commissions to check who owned what, and they wanted written proof. No paper; no land.

- ✔ **Step 3:** The commissioners drew a big map giving all the best land to the local bigwigs; smallholder families who had been farming for generations lost their lands and were forced to become hired labourers.

- ✔ **Step 4:** The big landowners put up lots of fences and hedges round their new lands with signs like 'Keep Out' and 'Trespassers Will be Hanged at the Next Assizes' to keep the neighbours out.

You can look at the establishment of enclosures as blatant robbery by the land-owning classes. And they certainly appeared that way at the time to many of the people forced from their land. On the other hand, Britain had to go through this process if it was going to produce enough food to feed the people in those growing industrial cities. How Britain's industrial revolution could have happened without enclosures is hard to envisage, and many people would probably have had to go very hungry. Enclosures were a classic case of balancing the individual against the common good. Just be glad you're not the individual.

# Getting Things Moving: Road Work

English roads were so bad in the eighteenth century that you could hardly get anywhere. If you did find a bit of highway, the chances were that you'd find a bit of highway robbery, too. Although we like to think of highwaymen as romantic Dick Turpin types, the reality was very different. I don't suppose you like the idea of someone pulling a gun on you and taking your wallet and cards, and people in the eighteenth century didn't like the experience either.

Sometimes, villages clubbed together to pay for road mending and then got the money back by charging tolls; you paid the toll at a tollhouse with a spiked gate, called a turnpike, which discouraged horses from jumping it. Turnpike roads were better than most roads of the time, but we're not exactly talking Route 66 here.

If you think building a road is just a question of clearing a path through the grass, think again. Firstly, you need to work out how to drain the thing; otherwise, you'll be driving through a quagmire the first time it rains. A Scot, John Loudon Macadam, solved the problem. He worked out how to use a layer of small stones on the top to allow the water through. He also decided that the best way to waterproof the roads was a coating of tar – they called it *tarmacadam* or *tarmac* in his honour. Macadam's fellow Scot, Thomas Telford, built so many miles of beautifully straight roads and canals that they nicknamed him the 'Colossus of Roads'. Geddit? Go and see his elegant Menai Bridge linking North Wales with the Isle of Anglesey: The construction's a masterpiece.

# Trouble Over: Bridged Water

Francis Egerton, fifth Duke of Bridgewater, was a rich man hoping to get richer. The Duke had coal by the bucket load on his estate at Worsley, and folks wanted it down in Manchester and Salford. The question was how to get the coal there? The Duke decided on a canal, so he got in an engineer called James Brindley to build it. The Duke had been thinking in terms of a fairly short canal down to the river, but he and Brindley quickly decided to go for something rather bigger: A canal all the way from Worsley to Manchester, which could link up with another canal Brindley was working on between the Trent and the Mersey. And that could connect up with more and more canals until the whole country was covered in canals!

The problem with this plan? A river was in the way. A canal can't cross a river, now can it? But a canal can cross a river if you build an aqueduct. Which just happened to be Brindley's speciality. The aqueduct (oh, all right, strictly speaking the thing's a viaduct) was beautiful, and the sight of a boat crossing the River Irwell at Barton Bridge was the must-see of the age.

# Revolutionising the Cloth Trade

Go into any house in eighteenth-century England, even a very poor one, and you'd almost certainly see a big loom taking up most of the space. The man of the household sat down to work there when he came in from the fields. Then there'd be a spinning wheel, where his wife would turn raw wool into thread for the big loom. This 'cottage industry' as they called it made some very useful extra income for the family, and the work was well worth the effort, because English cloth was good. And then all those inventors came along and changed the whole system.

See the big beautiful churches of East Anglia. All paid for by wool (which is why they are still called cloth or wool churches to this day). Think of the big city companies in London, like the Mercers or the Merchant Taylors. Think of Harris Tweed or Saville Row or posh English gentlemen talking about their tailors and you've got a handle on just how big the cloth trade always has been for the English. The Chancellor of England took his seat in the House of Lords on a big sack stuffed with wool, still called the Woolsack, a symbol of what had made the country rich.

## The spinning jenny has landed

You'd be forgiven for thinking that you could hardly bung a brick in the eighteenth century without hitting some clever inventor just itching to come up with a new machine for making more and more cloth and making it faster, like these people who saw particular problems and solved them:

- **Problem 1: Weaving is a laborious business,** and you can't get cloth wider than a man's arms, because otherwise he can't reach to weave it. 'I know!' says one John Kay, 'why not have a special gadget to move the warp for you? And faster, too?' Good idea. He calls it the flying shuttle.

- **Problem 2: Flying shuttles go too fast,** and are unfair to the women, who do all the spinning. 'How can we possibly keep up?' the women complain to their husbands. The sheep aren't too pleased either. 'I know!' says a weaver called James Hargreaves. 'Why not have a spinning wheel that spins more than one thread?' – a solution so simple, you wonder why no one had thought of it before. His model, called the spinning jenny, could spin 8 threads off one wheel, and by the time he died, people were using them to spin 80. (Saying that he called the wheel the spinning jenny after his daughter would be nice but probably untrue. Jenny or ginny was just a shortened form of 'engine', which was what people in Lancashire called machines in them days.)

- **Problem 3: The thread the spinning jennies make isn't very strong** – nowhere near strong enough for warp. 'I know!' says a canny Lancashire wig-maker called Richard Arkwright. 'We'll have a machine that can both spin the threads and spin them together to make a tougher thread.' The machine he built was too big to work by hand, so Arkwright decided to power the machine, which he called the water frame, by water. And this idea led to Problem 4.

- **Problem 4: Arkwright's water frame had to be by a river but people still worked from their homes.** And that was when Arkwright had his big idea, the one he should be remembered for but usually isn't: Bring the workers to the frame. He called this idea of working a factory and it made Arkwright's name – he even got a knighthood out of it – and his fortune. (Next time you get stuck in rush hour traffic on your way to or from work, think of Arkwright and give him his due.)

Just because a machine was invented didn't mean that suddenly it was being used all over the country within the week. Most of these machines took a long time to get taken up, and not all of them even got patented. For the most part they were used in one or two places and only gradually began to catch on as other people in the trade noticed that one mill or factory seemed to be producing a lot more cloth than normal. Even then, the way in which they spread was very patchy, so you get a fully working factory system in one area and handloom weavers still working away in another. Later on, historians would look at all this period and call it an Industrial Revolution. At the time, however, whether this revolution affected you directly depended very much on where you lived.

## *Things speed up even more*

Rather like the waterwheel, which carried on turning as long as the current flowed, Arkwright had started a process that couldn't be stopped. A fiddler called Samuel Crompton worked out an even better spinning machine, with some bits from the spinning jenny and some bits from the water frame. He called his machine a mule – which was the last little joke he made. Crompton was happy for other people to build their own mules but he expected them to pay him properly for his ideas, and he was taken aback when they didn't. He even presented Parliament with a census he'd undertaken of the wool industry which revealed just how many of his machines were in use (this document is an invaluable source of information for modern historians) but he never did get properly paid for his efforts.

With all this speed-spinning going on, someone was going to have to invent a way of speed-weaving. That someone was a clergyman called Edmund Cartwright, who hit on the idea of attaching a loom to a steam engine. Now weaving could keep pace with spinning and the whole industry could take off. It didn't do poor Cartwright much good, though. People kept pinching his workers to operate their own power looms and he had to spend years in legal battles to prove his patent in the courts.

# *It's (Not So) Fine Work, if You Can Get it: Life in the Factories*

Using steam to power the machines crucially meant that now your factory no longer needed to be next to a river: You could build it anywhere, which in effect meant in the middle of a town. Or, more accurately, you built your factory and a town sprang up around it. With a steam engine, you also didn't need to switch off at night; you could keep going 24 hours a day (not 24/7 because you needed to give everyone time off on Sundays), working in shifts. The workers had to live with a factory hooter and a factory clock telling them when to get up and when to go home, and generally regulating their lives in much the same way that the Church had done in medieval times. Except that they led a very different sort of life.

## *Trouble at t'mill*

Like the young scientist in the old Alec Guinness film who invents an indestructible fibre for making cloth but discovers, to his dismay, that other people aren't as excited by his idea, the inventors of the eighteenth century had to deal with the, shall we say, less than supportive reactions of others.

## New Lanark: New Labour?

Robert Owen was a Welshman and a factory owner who, in 1800, tried out an experiment at his mill at New Lanark in Scotland. Owen provided his workers with decent houses, schools, and shops, and he set reasonable working hours. To his competitors' surprise, New Lanark made a handsome profit. Owen was demonstrating that people work better if you treat them properly. Owen hoped he was starting a new trend, especially when other manufacturers made a beeline for New Lanark to find out how he did it. While they were always very impressed, no one really took up his ideas.

Some people were just jealous of the new inventions, like those who attacked James Hargreaves and smashed his stock of jennies. But jealousy soon gave way to sheer anger when people realised that all these machines were going to put them out of work. Hand-loom weavers hated Crompton and his wretched mule, for example, and in 1790 they attacked his factory and torched the place. Yet more and more factories began installing mules, and more hand-loom weavers were thrown out of work.

By the 1810s, it was the turn of the croppers – skilled workers who produced the fine finish on the cloth. When a new machine appeared to do their work for them, the men met in secret to plan attacks on the factories, and they became known as Luddites – we don't really know why, though it may have been after someone called Ned Ludd who is supposed to have broken a weaving frame. We can all sympathise with the Luddites – haven't you ever wanted to smash up a computer? – but they were never going to stop the spread of Arkwright's factory system. Which was a shame, because the system had developed in ways no one, least of all Arkwright, had predicted. (Given their violent tendencies towards machinery, I suppose you could call the Luddites a splinter group.)

## *It were grim in them days*

Some factory owners became like medieval barons, controlling their workers' lives just as a lord of the manor had controlled the lives of his serfs. The factory owner built the workers' houses, which were cheap and cramped, with no sanitation. Workers used a factory shop, where they paid with tokens provided by the factory. Children worked in the factory, crawling in and out beneath the moving machinery. If you tried to set up a trade union you'd be out of a job. And if you went on strike, what would you live on? No strike pay existed, and no unemployment benefit either.

The workers earned a tiny wage, just enough to pay for a small terraced house which might be ankle deep in filth. These towns had no sewers and no running water – they were just asking for disease, and they got it. This squalid life was the underside of all those beautiful artefacts that you can find in antique shops and on bric-a-brac stalls today.

All those inventions had created two new classes of people, the factory owners and the factory workers, and the workers were discovering just how powerful the owners really were. And they seemed unable to redress the balance.

# All Steamed Up

James Watt did not – repeat not – invent the steam engine. Nor did he ever claim that he had. A Cornishman called Savery designed the first steam pump back in 1698, but you took your life in your hands if you used it because no safety valve existed. Then another Cornishman, Thomas Newcomen, decided he could improve on Savery's pump, which he did. Figure 16-1 shows you how Newcomen's engine worked.

James Watt comes into the story in 1763 when he was working as an instrument maker at Glasgow University. Someone brought him a broken model of Newcomen's steam pump and asked if he could fix it. Watt had a look at the thing and thought 'Ping! I know what this wee fellow needs.'

What Watt recognised was that the Newcomen engine was inefficient because the piston was moved by first heating and then cooling the single cylinder.

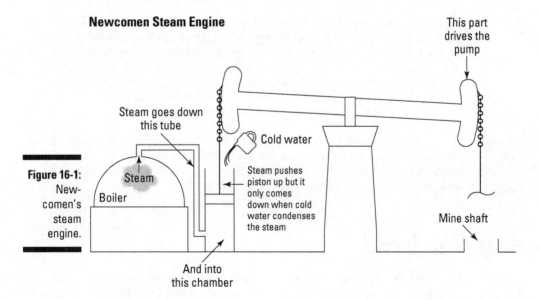

Figure 16-1: Newcomen's steam engine.

What this thing needs, thought Watt, was a separate condenser, which would let the steam out of the hot cylinder to cool somewhere else.

Watt's engine made the steam engine faster, more efficient, more reliable, and more economical to run. It created a demand for coal, which in turn created an entire new deep-shaft mining industry. It stimulated a demand for high quality iron, and thus stimulated that industry, too. Watt's engine became efficient enough to be used for powering vehicles to run on metal rails, thus inaugurating the Age of Steam and leading eventually to fully grown men keeping model train sets on large layouts in their attics.

## Do the Locomotion

James Watt did very well marketing his steam pumping engines with his partner, Matthew Boulton. It didn't take very long before someone looked at these highly efficient – and very expensive – Boulton and Watt pumping machines and applied them to locomotion. In 1814 William Hedley came up with a locomotive for pulling coal wagons. He called the engine *Puffing Billy*, and a great ungainly monster it was too. But it worked.

In 1825 George Stephenson designed the world's first proper railway locomotive, the *Locomotion*. It ran on the world's first proper railway line, from Stockton to Darlington, and on its maiden journey it reached 15 mph – bear in mind that a galloping horse might hit six or seven if it was lucky and not too tired.

In 1829 the Directors of the Liverpool and Manchester Railway offered a £500 prize for the fastest engine, which turned out to be another Stephenson, product, Robert Stephenson's (son of George) *Rocket*. Tragically, the day of the trials was marred by the world's first railway accident. A leading politician, William Huskisson MP, misjudged the *Rocket*'s speed (not his fault: Nothing had ever travelled at that sort of speed before), hesitated – and was lost. Or rather, crushed and mangled. Nasty.

Note to purists: Actually, the first steam engine to run on rails was called *Catch Me Who Can*, and Richard Trevithick, a Cornish wrestler, built it. But it only ran on a circular track as a fairground attraction, and in any case the track kept breaking, so his engine never came to anything.

## Any Old Iron?

One thing, they say, leads to another, and never was this expression more true than with all these inventions. Mules and jennies and steam engines and railway tracks and boilers and condensers, and so on – all had to be made out of metal. Which, for the most part, meant iron. Smelting iron in those days involved heating it on a slow charcoal fire in the middle of a forest. Hopeless. Until a remarkable family came along, mad keen on iron – and every one of them called Abraham Darby.

Granddad Abraham worked out how to get sheet iron from a very pure form of coal called coke instead of charcoal. Abraham No. 2 found a way of refining the coke so you can get wrought iron. Abraham No. 3 used this new wrought iron to create the world's first iron bridge. This construction's still there; over the River Severn as beautiful and elegant as the day Abraham Darby III opened it.

# Tea, Sympathy, and the Slave Trade

The British, like other Europeans, developed a sweet tooth in the eighteenth century, and the people who could supply the country with sugar stood to make a fortune. The sugar was harvested in the Caribbean, which is why the British were so keen to get hold of West Indian islands during the long wars with France (see Chapter 15 for more about these wars and why they went on for so long). The harvesting of sugar was done by slaves.

The slave trade was called a *triangular trade*, because it consisted of three legs:

- ✔ Shoddy quality trade goods were shipped from Britain to Africa and exchanged for slaves.

- ✔ The slaves were packed into slave ships and carried from Africa to the West Indies.

- ✔ The slaves were sold and the money used to buy sugar. This sugar was then shipped back to Britain.

## Beauty and the beastliness

The Industrial Revolution wasn't all grimy factories and smoky chimneys; this period's also a story of craftsmanship and beauty. Skilled Sheffield cutlers known as little mesters were working in small workshops producing fine cutlery long after Henry Bessemer produced his famous converter for turning iron into steel.

In the pottery towns of Staffordshire, which became known as the Black Country because of all the grime and soot, Josiah Wedgwood based his designs on those of the ancient Greeks and Romans – beautifully elegant designs, with simple figures against a rich blue background. Wedgwood called his potteries *Etruria* after the area of ancient Italy that produced some of the finest pieces he was imitating. He virtually invented the modern science of marketing and advertising in order to sell his wares to fashionable people down in London, and doing so made him a lot of money. Pots of money, you could say!

# Fighting slavery

Remembering that slaves did fight against slavery themselves is important – risings occurred on slave ships and black speakers against the slave trade did exist. But fighting the institution of slavery was obviously a lot easier for whites. One of the earliest voices against the slave trade was the seventeenth-century woman writer, Aphra Behn, in her novel *Oroonoko*. Later the Quakers and evangelicals took up the issue. One of the most remarkable campaigners was a clergyman called John Newton: He'd been a slave ship captain himself, so he knew what he was talking about. But in the end only Parliament could abolish the slave trade. William Wilberforce, MP for Hull, an evangelical Christian and good friend of the prime minister, William Pitt, spent his life bringing forward bills against the slave trade, and he just lived long enough to see slavery outlawed in the whole British Empire in 1833.

On the ships, the slaves were crammed into lower decks sometimes so close together that they could only lie on their sides. They were chained together, and only let out for exercise in small groups. This exercise usually consisted of leaping out of the way of a whip aimed at their feet. On the bunks they had to eat and soil themselves where they lay, so that many died of disease. No wonder some preferred to leap overboard, while in some cases the slaves rose up and tried to take over the ship.

But most slaves had to live through the horrors of the middle passage as best they could until they reached the slave markets of Barbados. Here they were sold to the highest bidder and put to work on the hot and back-breaking work of cutting sugar cane so that the British would have something to put in their tea. The money from the slave-and-sugar trade – and there was lots of it – was often invested in the very industries which produced the goods that paid for the next shipload of slaves. So the triangle came full circle.

Most people in Britain didn't think much about the slave trade one way or the other, but exceptions existed, and one of them was a music critic called Granville Sharp. In 1771 he boarded a ship in London armed with a writ of habeas corpus and demanded the release of a black slave called James Somerset. James's owner, a Mr Stewart of Boston, Massachusetts, protested and the case went up to the Lord Chief Justice, Lord Mansfield. Mansfield wasn't usually particularly liberal, but on this occasion he came to a remarkable and momentous decision. He freed James Somerset on the grounds that the air of England is so pure that no one may breathe it and remain a slave. In other words, slavery is, in effect, illegal in England, and any slave who sets foot in England is, by definition, free.

Despite Lord Mansfield's judgement, overcoming the planters' resistance and getting the slave trade abolished took until 1806, and even then, slavery itself remained legal in British colonies until 1833. Nevertheless, the British did take a leading role in outlawing the international slave trade: They forced other countries to abolish it after the Napoleonic Wars, and the Royal Navy spent much of the nineteenth century patrolling the African coast hunting down slavers.

# Why Britain?

No one around at the time talked of an 'Industrial Revolution', but people did have a sense that things were changing and changing fast. Artists painted pictures of the new industrial towns and of the new types of people to be found there, like anthropologists stumbling on a new tribe. And undeniably all of this industrial activity was making certain parts of the country, and certain people, extremely rich. Everyone bought British, even Napoleon. When he invaded Russia his soldiers' coats were made in England. But what was so special about Britain?

Britain's being an island helped. No foreign armies were marching all over the place, which is always bad for business, and having lots of rivers and ports – and canals – meant getting all these manufactured goods out to the people who wanted to buy them was easy. Lots of iron and coal was available as well. Britain was also helped by all those lords and nobles who didn't mind mucking in and getting their hands dirty. But whatever the reason, the Industrial Revolution started in Britain, and Britain – and the world – would never be the same again.

# Chapter 17

# Children of the Revolutions

*In this Chapter*

▶ Clarifying what they meant by 'revolution' in the Age of Revolution

▶ Understanding why a civil war broke out in the British Empire in North America – and why it's not called that in other books

▶ Working out why the British welcomed the French Revolution – at first

▶ Describing why the British fought Napoleon for so long

▶ Discovering how the British feared – and hoped – they were next for a revolution, and what they got instead

Somewhere around the second half of the eighteenth century, historians get their rulers out and start drawing dividing lines: The Modern Age begins here. They do so mainly because of the big changes in politics, economics, and society that took place at that time, which are usually termed 'Revolutions': The American Revolution, the French Revolution, and the Industrial Revolution.

This chapter looks at how these big events affected the British. How did they end up fighting a long and bitter war against their own colonists in America, and how did they cope with losing it? Why did the British feel the need to fight the French yet again when the French seemed perfectly capable of fighting each other? Consider that this was the time when the whole way of life in Britain was changing as people started working in factories and mills and moved from the countryside to the big cities. (See Chapter 16 to find out more about how Britain became the world's first modern economic power.) A lot of people thought that after America and France, Britain's turn was next for a revolution. What they got was a reform of Parliament, but in its way, that was something of a revolution, too.

# Revolutions: Turning Full Circle or Half?

Strictly speaking a revolution is a complete turn of a wheel so that you end up where you started, and that was how the British used the term in the eighteenth century. When they spoke of 'The Revolution,' they meant the Glorious Revolution of 1688, which had turned the wheel full-circle back to the liberties that they genuinely believed the English had enjoyed in Anglo-Saxon times (see Chapter 15 for the Glorious Revolution and Chapter 5 for the Anglo-Saxons). The Americans meant more or less the same thing when they spoke of their 'Revolution', only this time they meant recovering the freedom they had enjoyed before George III started interfering.

When the French overthrew King Louis XVI a few years later, that theirs was a very different sort of revolution was quickly evident. The French had no idea of restoring anything; the French Revolution was more about turning things upside-down, so that those who had been at the bottom of society under the old regime were now on top – a half-turn of the wheel, to be precise.

# A British Civil War in America

Firstly, get rid of the idea that the American Revolutionary War was between the 'Americans' and the 'British'. Eighteenth-century 'Americans' regarded themselves as fully British, and the thirteen colonies as extensions of England, so declaring independence in 1776 was a real wrench. Throughout the war, many 'Americans' continued to regard themselves as British, while in Britain, many people were profoundly unhappy at going to war against fellow 'Englishmen'. So how had the situation gone so badly wrong?

If you want the patriotic American angle on this, you can find plenty of films (*Revolution* with Al Pacino and *The Patriot* with Mel Gibson are just two examples) showing the Americans as stout-hearted, freedom-loving, and heroic, while the British appear as little better than red-coated Nazis. If you like your history that way then you'd better stick to the films (though the TV mini-series *John Adams* got it about right); the truth is a bit more messy.

---

## Pontiac's rising, 1763

Chief Pontiac of the Ottawa united the Indian tribes and tried to drive the British out of America. He captured nearly every important British fort and settlement in the west except for Detroit and Pittsburgh. He even laid siege to these, but without artillery, he had to withdraw and the British regained control. But his actions had scared the British (and the colonists) and no one could be sure that the Indian tribes wouldn't rise up again.

---

# No taxation without representation

No taxation without representation was the idea, supposedly from Magna Carta, that taking money in taxation is theft unless it is done with the people's consent, through their representatives. The Americans used this argument as a basis for objecting to the Stamp Act because no American MPs were in Westminster. Of course, you could say that taxation is theft whether done through consent or not!

## *How the trouble began*

The end of the Seven Years' War, in 1763, was the start of the trouble in America. For the British, this event was a moment of glory – they'd trounced the French on three continents and ended up with control of most of India and North America. But when the celebrations died down, they faced the small matter of how exactly to defend and pay for this empire.

Like all governments after a major war, London was looking to economise where possible, and asking the American colonists to contribute some of the cost of what was, after all, their own defence seemed reasonable. The problem was how.

✔ **Tax sugar** (or, to be precise, molasses). Tried: 1764.

Sugar was *the* big money crop of the age, but the government got precious little revenue from it because it was so easy to smuggle. In fact, the government reduced the duty on molasses, but this time it was going to be enforced properly. That was why the colonists complained about it.

✔ **A stamp tax** (a duty on legal documents, newspapers, playing cards, and other printed material). Tried: 1765.

The British were used to stamp taxes, but the idea was new to America. As a result, massive protests occurred, and I mean massive, not just against the tax but also against the idea that Parliament had the right to tax America at all. Result? Stamp Act repealed – but the government also passed a Declaratory Act which said, in effect, 'Just Because We're Giving Way On This One, Don't Think We Can't Tax You Any Which Way We Choose, Alright Mate?'

✔ **Tax other commodities** (like paper, glass, paint, and tea). Tried: 1767.

These were the 'Townshend Duties', named after the minister who introduced them. No one denied that Parliament could regulate trade, but the Americans argued that these duties were nothing to do with trade and all to do with asserting Parliament's authority over them. Result? Events took a turn for the worse.

## The Boston Tea Party

The Boston Tea Party had very little to do with the tax on tea. The British East India Company was badly in the red, so London had given special permission for a consignment of Indian tea to sail straight for Boston without having to go via England. Doing so made the tea *cheaper*, not dearer, but the local merchants didn't want to be undercut, so they arranged the famous raid. The Boston Tea Party looked very symbolic and patriotic, but really it was all about profits.

## *Things get nasty: From Boston to Concord*

By 1770 the British were in a very difficult position. They'd given way on the Stamp Act, and now they repealed all of the Townshend Duties – except the one on tea. Well, they had to save face somehow. But they could not appear to be giving in to violence. The colonists had made violent assaults on Stamp Act officials, and in 1770, troops in Boston fired on a mob who'd been attacking a sentry – the Boston Massacre. Two years later, colonists attacked and burned a British revenue cutter, the *Gaspée*. In 1773 came the turn of the ships carrying tea into Boston harbour, sailing into the most famous tea party in history. A gang of Bostonians, loosely dressed up as Mohawk Indians, raided the ships and poured the tea into Boston harbour. Thus, as Mr Banks puts it in the film *Mary Poppins*, rendering the tea unfit for drinking. Even for Americans.

In fact the other colonies thought that Boston had gone too far, but then the British turned on Boston, closing the harbour and imposing direct rule on Massachusetts. Now the other colonies were worried that what happened to Boston today could happen to them tomorrow. They decided to stand by Boston. So, when the British commander in Boston got wind of an arms dump at nearby Concord and decided on a search and destroy expedition, he found the locals prepared to fight – on the village green at Lexington. Someone – we don't know who – fired a shot. And that shot began the war.

The British made it to Concord and destroyed the arms cache, but they were decimated on the way back by deadly accurate American sniping from behind trees and stone walls. By the time they got back to Boston, the British knew they had a war on their hands, and the fighting wasn't going to be easy.

## *Declaring independence*

Once the fighting had started, the Americans met in Congress at Philadelphia, set up a Continental Army under George Washington, and promptly launched an unsuccessful invasion of Canada. At just this point, with passions aroused and both sides appalled at the bloodshed, Tom Paine (British philosopher and author) came on the scene with one of the most influential pieces of writing in history. Called *Common Sense*, Paine's writing pointed out that, instead of faffing around trying to work out what the king and Parliament could or could not do, just declaring independence made much more sense. And on 4 July 1776, Congress did exactly that.

The Declaration of Independence placed the blame for the trouble fairly and squarely on the shoulders of King George III, not because he'd actually taken the lead in American affairs (he hadn't), but because being independent meant being independent of the king. Declaring independence, however, was one thing; winning independence was another matter altogether. The British had a huge army, and they were prepared to use it.

## The fight's on

People often think that the Americans were bound to win, but the situation did not seem that way at the time. The Americans were thirteen separate colonies who had a record of not being able to agree on anything except what day of the week it was. They had no professional soldiers, no allies, no navy, and their Commander-in-Chief, George Washington, had never held any military post higher than a junior rank in the Virginia militia. The Americans were up against a large and professional British army, reinforced by large numbers of German troops from Hesse. The British had won the Seven Years' War – the first world war in history – including victory in North America. No eighteenth-century bookies were offering odds on an American victory, and the first year of fighting suggested they were very wise not to do so. The following are some highlights of the war:

---

## Tom Paine

Tom Paine has become something of a hero on two continents, though he wasn't generally regarded like that in his lifetime. He was a corset-maker by trade, and his enemies made sure no one forgot that fact. He came from Norfolk, and in 1774, he set sail for America where he wrote *Common Sense* and fought in the American army against the king. When the French Revolution broke out Paine was elected to the French National Convention, the revolutionary 'Parliament', but he fell foul of the Jacobins, the extremist party, for voting against the execution of Louis XVI and he was lucky to escape with his life. He returned to America, where he'd always been appreciated and where he died in 1802. His enemies regarded him as little better than the antichrist; more recently he has been recognised as a true Radical, one of the most important political writers and thinkers Britain has produced.

- ✔ **1776: The British take New York.** Britain's General Howe launches a massive amphibious assault that catches Washington completely on the hop. New York remains in British hands until the end of the war.

- ✔ **1777: British surrender at Saratoga.** Britain's General Burgoyne launches a huge three-pronged attack to cut the United States in two. Howe defeats Washington again, but Burgoyne is cut off and forced to surrender at Saratoga thanks to swift action by the American general, Benedict Arnold.

- ✔ **1778: The French come in.** The British surrender at Saratoga encourages the French to declare war on the British because the situation suggests they might be on the winning side for once. The British get out of Philadelphia. And can you blame them?

- ✔ **1779: The British take Savannah** and drive off French and American counter-attacks.

- ✔ **1780: The British land in the South,** take Charleston and rout US General Gates, who's been sent South by Congress specifically to prevent this happening.

At this point, Benedict Arnold, who was by then far and away the most successful American commander, turned traitor and nearly handed the British the whole of New York state. How the British could not have won the war had Arnold handed the state over is difficult to envisage.

But he didn't. His British contact, Major John André, was captured, in civilian clothes, behind American lines, and with plans of Fort West Point hidden in his boots. Arnold was rumbled and fled to the British lines; André was hanged. America's War of Independence could resume.

## George Washington

Where was George Washington while all this fighting was going on? In 1776, the American commander launched a daring attack on the Hessians while they were all legless after a boozy Christmas dinner at Trenton, New Jersey, having crossed the Delaware River (though almost certainly not standing up in the boat as you see in the famous painting, at least not if he had any sense). He also saw off a British counter-attack at Princeton.

These defeats were a nasty shock for the British and showed that that the Americans were still very much in the war. But the fact remains that Washington was much more successful as an organiser of his army than as a field commander. He was defeated far more often than he won; by contrast, the British General Howe never lost a battle. Washington's greatest achievement was to hold the American army together, especially through the notorious winter of 1778, when it was camped at Valley Forge, Pennsylvania, and drilled remorselessly into shape, until the British finally over-reached themselves. Any general can win a battle; Washington showed that it takes a great leader to win a war.

## Revolution or War of Independence?

The most accurate term for what happened between England and its colonies in America is a civil war, but that view has always been more British than American. Suggesting that not everyone was keen on independence goes against the American patriotic grain (as Alistair Cooke once pointed out, the sort of people who commemorate the Revolution nowadays would almost certainly have been on the British side). To Americans, the conflict has long been the *Revolution* or the *Revolutionary War*, in Britain, until recent years, it was generally referred to as the *War of American Independence*.

These terms are not just a matter of semantics: An important difference of interpretation exists here. To Americans, overturning a king and establishing an independent republic with an elected president was a revolution both in the modern sense of the word and in the older sense of a return to a state of liberty that had been lost. British historians, however, were less convinced. Compared with genuinely revolutionary movements like the French or Russian revolutions, the American experience looked pretty tame: No purges, no Terror, no massacres or dictatorship. Although the term 'American Revolution' is in more common use in British textbooks now, the basic British view of this war has not changed.

## Calling it quits: The world turned upside down

The British attack in the South began to run out of steam as Washington regrouped his forces, and eventually in 1781 British General Cornwallis found himself trapped between Washington's army and the French fleet on the Yorktown peninsula. He surrendered. His bandsmen played a tune called 'The World Turned Upside Down', because in a world where colonists could beat their masters (and the French could beat the British!), that is how the situation seemed.

# The French Revolution

In 1789 unexpected and exciting news arrived from France. The people of Paris had risen up and stormed the Bastille. This event was like the fall of the Berlin Wall exactly two hundred years later. The Bastille was a sinister fortress and prison, widely believed to be full of innocent victims of a cruel and repressive regime. In fact, the Bastille held only seven inmates when it fell, but, hey, feel the symbolism.

The French declared the *Rights of Man* and set up a constitutional monarchy, not unlike the British one, but then found that you cannot just import forms of government wholesale, like cloth or brandy. Some leaders didn't want a monarchy, constitutional or otherwise: They wanted a republic, and in 1792, a republic is just what they got.

## The nutshell version

Since the French Revolution had a profound effect on events on the other side of the Channel, here's a brief outline (and if this tempts you on to the full version of events, have a look in *European History For Dummies*).

### Phase 1: Risings 1789–91

In 1789 the French monarchy, under the kindly but inept King Louis XVI, went bankrupt. In an effort to raise money, Louis summoned the ancient Parliament of France, the Estates-General, to Versailles. When the Estates-General met the deputies wanted much more far-reaching changes. When the king refused to play ball the deputies declared themselves the National Assembly, representing the People of France. In Paris, the people took the opportunity to attack the symbol of royal power, the Bastille. The National Assembly declared the *Rights of Man and the Citizen* and set up a constitutional monarchy, with Louis XVI at the head, ruling according to the rules. In theory.

### Phase 2: Republic and Terror 1792–94

Louis XVI did not co-operate for long, and in 1791 he fled, trying to reach the Austrian frontier and lead an Austrian army into France. Unfortunately (for him) he was caught, put on trial, and guillotined. France became a republic, and immediately went to war with its neighbours. The war began badly, so the radicals, led by Maximilien Robespierre and the Jacobins, declared a Reign of Terror, with 'suspects' sent to the guillotine on the flimsiest evidence.

### Phase 3: War 1794–99

In 1794 Robespierre's enemies decided enough killing was enough – especially as they were next on the list – and had him arrested and guillotined himself. The war went on, though the news was generally good for the French thanks to a gifted young commander, General Bonaparte. In 1799 Bonaparte returned from an unsuccessful campaign in Egypt to seize power in France.

## Sounds good to us . . . we think

At first the British liked what they heard from France. The Whig leader (and Chapter 15 will fill you in on what one of those was), Charles James Fox, described the French Revolution as the greatest event in history. One of Fox's closest friends, Edmund Burke (who was another Whig politician), disagreed.

His book *Reflections on the Revolution in France* denounced the Revolution and said it would lead to anarchy and military dictatorship. But no one really listened to Burke – his own friends thought he'd gone mad. Until these events made them change their minds:

- ✔ **Wholesale murder in Paris:** Within a month of coming to power, the new French republic had organised a wholesale massacre of people held in all the prisons in Paris.

- ✔ **The French invaded Belgium:** (Officially this country was the Austrian Netherlands, but everyone called it Belgium.) Belgium's ports were a perfect base for invading England, and Antwerp was such a strong potential trade rival to London that it had been closed to trade years before. Only now the French were opening Antwerp up again.

- ✔ **The French executed King Louis XVI:** The British thought Louis XVI had brought a lot of the trouble on his own head, but they didn't want to see that head cut off. A big wave of sympathy was felt for him, and a brisk trade occurred in sentimental prints of his final moments.

- ✔ **The Edict of Fraternity:** The French revolutionary leaders issued a decree saying they would help any people struggling to be free of oppression. The British government assumed they had Ireland in mind, and they assumed right.

## *This means war! Britain and France at it again*

In 1793 the French declared war on Britain, though the British were planning to declare war anyway. The government was led by William Pitt the Younger, and although the war wrecked all his careful plans to return the British economy to the black, he seemed to welcome it with grim satisfaction. The Whigs, led by Charles James Fox, were outraged, and accused Pitt of waging an illegal ideological war – that is, one against an idea rather than against a specific threat. However, as the French grew stronger and more menacing, more and more people came round to supporting Pitt and the war.

### Pitt the Younger and boy wonder

William Pitt the Younger was the son of William Pitt the Elder (later Earl of Chatham) who won a huge empire at France's expense in the Seven Years' War (1756–63) (see Chapter 14 for more on the elder half of this remarkable political family). Pitt the Younger was something of a boy wonder, who studied at Cambridge aged fourteen and won a Double First, and went on to become prime minister and thanks to George III and at the age of twenty-four. Not surprisingly, Pitt the Younger was staunchly loyal to the king.

British landings on the Continent were so disastrous that they are recalled in the children's song *The Grand Old Duke of York* (you get the idea and up the hill, down again, no idea where they were going or what they were doing). Far more effective was the close naval blockade the British imposed on the French coast, which seriously disrupted French trade. Roads were so bad in those days that much internal trade was carried along the coast, so a naval blockade had major nuisance value.

The French were able to defeat their other enemies on land, while the British made the most of their own naval victories, and by 1795, the two sides were so exhausted they came close and but only close and to making peace. In 1796 the French tried a landing in Ireland, which might have worked if not scuppered by bad weather. When the Irish staged their own rising two years later, the British were ready for them. (You can read the gory details in Chapter 14.)

## *Impeached for free speech: Restricting freedoms*

Prime Minister Pitt was as worried about enemies at home as he was about the French. He brought in laws to clamp down on free speech, and anyone calling for changes in the political system risked being charged with treason. Incidentally, reminding Pitt that he himself had supported changes only a few years before was pointless. That was then, he argued; you don't repair your house in a hurricane.

Parliament itself was the only place where you could safely say anything against the government, because you couldn't be arrested for anything said there (though many people think you should be). But all was not lost. When a large treason trial of Radicals was held in 1797, the jury found the defendants not guilty. No such luck for Tom Paine: He'd written a book called *The Rights of Man* as a counterblast to Edmund Burke's anti-revolutionary *Reflections on the Revolution in France* (see the earlier section 'Sounds good to us . . . we think'). He fled to France and was found guilty of treason in his absence. (See the sidebar earlier in this chapter for more on Tom Paine and why he was so important.)

Not content with suspending the freedoms he was supposed to be fighting to defend, Pitt went on to pass the Combination Laws, which made combinations (Trade or Labour Unions to you and me) illegal. So any workmen who complained about their wages or the conditions in factories stood the risk of being sent to prison. No wonder some workers declared they sympathised with the French. (See Chapter 16 to find out why the workers had something to complain about.)

## *Cruising for a bruising – Nelson*

Badly needing a success story, the British milked the Nelson story for all it was worth, making him one of the first media war heroes. Don't get me wrong: Nelson was without question a very fine commander, and he was very, very lucky – no bad thing to be (ask Napoleon, who valued luck in his commanders above actual military ability!) – but he wasn't exactly a good role model for aspiring young officers. One of his most famous actions was to put his telescope deliberately to his blind eye so as not to 'see' a signal from his superior officer telling him to disengage. For anyone else that action would've meant a court martial. Nelson often neglected his duty to spend time with his mistress, Emma Hamilton (with whom he enjoyed a curious *ménage à trois* with her husband, the British ambassador in Naples).

If you're going to be that sort of an officer, you'd better win (the British had shot Admiral John Byng in 1757 for turning away from a battle he had no chance of winning), and fortunately for Nelson, he did:

- ✔ **1798:** Nelson destroyed almost the entire French fleet at anchor in Aboukir Bay in Egypt (this event became known as the Battle of the Nile, which sounded better), stranding Napoleon and his army in Egypt.

- ✔ **1801:** Nelson sailed into Copenhagen harbour when it looked as if the Danes were going to enter the war, and destroyed their fleet, too (this was when the 'blind eye' incident took place).

The British had come to rely more on Nelson for their protection than on the Royal Navy itself.

Britain and France signed a truce in 1802, but neither side expected it to last and it didn't. In 1804 the war began again, and this time Napoleon intended to invade Britain. Nelson's job was to stop him.

## Life in Nelson's navy

For a nation that prided itself on its seapower, the British seemed to have taken remarkably little care of their seamen. The harsh conditions on board His Majesty's ships were notorious, from the poor food and late pay to the floggings with the cat o'nine tails – a nine-thonged leather whip, often with spikes, used on the naked back. Never mind mutiny on the *Bounty* – in 1797 the whole fleet rose in mutiny against their conditions. However, no navy can win battles by terrorising its men, and more recently historians have pointed out that although conditions may horrify us, they were often a lot easier than conditions on land – regular food was on offer, the pay was adequate, and most captains were nothing like Captain Bligh. Nelson himself was universally admired for the care he took to ensure his men were well looked after, and they fought all the better under him.

In fact, Napoleon had already given up his invasion plans in despair at his admirals' reluctance to take on the British when Nelson finally met the combined French and Spanish fleet off Cape Trafalgar in 1805. The British cut the French and Spanish line of battle and destroyed or captured almost all their ships. But they lost Nelson, who was shot by a French bullet. It may have been a French marksman – Nelson was easy to spot because he refused to cover up all his medals – though some modern historians think it unlikely that anyone could have picked him off accurately at that range during a battle. Either way, Nelson lingered on until it was clear that he had won a great victory, and then died. Even though Trafalgar had destroyed Napoleon's naval power, the British were so upset by Nelson's death that they hardly took this victory in. Who was going to save them now?

Napoleon tried Plan B. He used his command of the Continent to close every European port to British trade and slowly starve her into submission. Unfortunately, Europe needed British manufactures so badly that leaks kept appearing in Napoleon's trade wall.

## Bonaparte's Spanish ulcer: The Peninsular War

Britain's chance to defeat Bonaparte on land came in 1807 with a revolt against French rule in Spain and Portugal. When the Spanish managed to defeat a French army, London sent a large army to Portugal under Sir Arthur Wellesley, soon to become the Duke of Wellington.

The war dragged on from 1808 until 1814, and at times seemingly Wellington was being forced to retreat, though in fact he was wearing the French down (not for nothing did Napoleon refer to the war as his 'Spanish ulcer'), tying down badly-needed French troops when Napoleon invaded Russia in 1812 and eventually crossing the Pyrenees into France itself.

The great irony of this Peninsular War (after the Iberian peninsula where it took place) was that it was a war by the Spanish and Portuguese people, helped by the British, against a French-imposed government that was supposed to be governing in their name.

## The Battle of Waterloo: Wellington boots out Napoleon

Napoleon's big mistake was invading Russia in 1812; he never recovered from his devastating retreat from Moscow. By 1814 his enemies had pursued him to Paris, and he was forced to abdicate. While the allies restored the discredited Bourbon Kings of France, Napoleon himself was sent to govern the small island of Elba, just off the Italian coast. Within a year, however, he had escaped from the not-very-close watch that was kept on him and was back in control of France. Rightly expecting that the allies wouldn't let him stay on the throne if they could help it, he decided to get his retaliation in first by attacking the nearest army to him. This happened to be a mixed British and Belgian army – commanded by the Duke of Wellington. They met near the small village of Waterloo.

The Battle of Waterloo was one of the bloodiest battles of the entire war. The French hurled themselves against the British lines for a whole day; the situation was touch and go whether they might break through, when Wellington's Prussian allies arrived and the French had to flee.

The British were obsessed with Waterloo – they named towns and stations after it, and marked Waterloo Day, 18 June, every year until the First World War. Waterloo was a tremendous feat of arms – the British were the first to make Napoleon's famous Old Guard turn and run, and it did bring Napoleon's career to an end. The great man was carried in a British ship to exile on a remote British colony, St Helena, from where even he couldn't escape.

# A British Revolution?

The men who fought at Waterloo (see the preceding section for details) came home to a country that seemed about to stage a revolution of its own. British industry had been growing rapidly, and the growth had been a painful process. The skilled craftsmen thrown out of work by the new machines fought back as best they could by attacking the factories and smashing the machinery. To control these Luddites (see Chapter 16 for a bit more about these men and what drove them), the government had to deploy more troops than Wellington had with him in Spain. Factories meant long working hours, low wages, and a system that hardly cared whether its workers lived or died. And if you and your fellow workers wanted to do anything about the situation – bad news. Under the Combination Laws (explained in the section 'Impeached for free speech: Restricting freedoms'), workers getting together in groups was illegal. Welcome home, lads.

And just when you thought the situation couldn't get any worse, it did. The government put up the price of food.

## Sowing discontent: The Corn Law

The increase in the price of food was due to the Corn Law, so called because it said how much corn could be imported into the country and at what price and what the import duty on it was to be and how much home-grown corn there could be, and at what price – hey, wake up! Yes, I know all these corn details sound even less exciting than a wet weekend in Skegness, but beneath all the economics is one rather important principle: Are poor people going to be able to afford to eat or are they not?

The idea of the Corn Law was to keep foreign corn out of the country, which would help the farmers; unfortunately, the law also meant that farmers and the people who speculated in corn could keep the price high so as to maximise their profits. Expensive corn equals hungry people, and hungry people could equal revolution. The signs already existed.

### Hampden Clubs discuss reforms, 1812

The Hampden Clubs, named after John Hampden, who'd resisted King Charles I (you can meet him properly in Chapter 13), were radical discussion groups set up for workers to discuss reform. The government used the clubs as an excuse for suspending habeas corpus and clamping down on public meetings.

One of the most important civil liberties to emerge from the constitutional conflicts of the seventeenth century, *habeas corpus* (1679) stops the police or the government arresting you just because they don't like your face – or your opinions. Governments have often tried to suspend habeas corpus in times of emergency. Tony Blair's opponents said he was doing just that with his security proposals after the London bombings of 2005 (see Chapter 23).

### Spa Fields meeting, 1816

This big public reform meeting in London was stirred up into a riot, and the crowd raided a gunsmith's shop. The government feared this event could have been Britain's storming of the Bastille.

## The Prince Regent

Poor old George III finally went mad in 1810 and had to be locked away in Windsor Castle where he hung on for another ten years. Meanwhile his eldest son, George, Prince of Wales (also called 'Prinny', though not to his face), ruled as Prince Regent. Prinny was fat, lazy, and utterly self-obsessed. He and his dandy friends like George 'Beau' Brummell spent a fortune on gorging and drinking themselves senseless each night and rising each day as early as one or two in the afternoon to face the challenges of the morning. Yes, I know, this description sounds more like the life of a student than the Prince Regent.

Prinny conceived the idea of building himself a pleasure dome in Brighton, a tasteless piece of ostentation that can't even decide whether it's meant to be Chinese or Indian. The regency style was very elegant – think *Pride and Prejudice* and those elegant Nash terraces in London – but there was nothing elegant about the man who gave his name to it.

### March of the Blanketeers, 1817

The March of the Blanketeers was meant to be a massive march of workers from Lancashire to London (the blankets were to sleep in) to present a reform petition to Parliament. The army stopped the march and arrested the leaders.

### Pentrich Rising, 1817

This event was an armed rising by the men of a small Derbyshire village called Pentrich. Unfortunately for them, the organiser turned out to be a government agent known as Oliver the Spy, and the leader of the rising was hanged.

### 'Peterloo' and the Six Acts, 1819

In 1819 a huge meeting of people from all over the North-West of England was held in St Peter's Fields in Manchester to demand reforms. The local authorities panicked and sent in Yeomanry cavalry, who charged at the unarmed crowd with sabres. Over 400 people were wounded – and you should see what a cavalry sabre can do – and eleven were killed. One of the men killed had been fighting for his country at Waterloo only four years earlier. People were so disgusted that they nicknamed the incident 'Peterloo' (that's irony, 1819-style). The Prince Regent, on the other hand, was delighted and sent a message of congratulations to the cavalry.

The government responded to Peterloo by introducing a set of six laws to reduce free speech, restrict public meetings, make newspapers more expensive, and give the authorities greater powers to search private property.

### Cato Street conspiracy, 1820

The Cato Street conspiracy was a plot to kill all the members of the Cabinet as they sat down to dine. The plan was discovered in time because one of the plotters was a government agent. Having an inside agent always helps.

## What the protestors wanted

What did they want, all these people protesting against the system? Well, of course they wanted things like better wages and a modicum of safety at work, but the main thing they were calling for was what is known in the trade as Parliamentary Reform. Not only did they want the vote: They wanted the whole parliamentary system reformed.

### Small Cornish fishing villages: 2 each; Major industrial cities: nil

When King Henry III summoned the first Parliament back in 1258 (you can read all about this in Chapter 9), the map of England looked a bit different.

Places like Manchester or Birmingham were little villages; the big towns were cathedral cities and towns in the cloth trade. So these were the places that sent MPs to Parliament. By the nineteenth century, though, Birmingham and Manchester were major industrial centres, and the places that had been big in 1258 were now small market towns and Cornish fishing villages. The size of the towns and villages didn't make any difference: They still had two MPs each, and the big cities had none.

### No pot? No vote!

Then the little question of who had the vote was significant. Apart from no women having the vote anywhere, the rules were different in each constituency. The main types of voters were:

- **Householders.** This was the basic qualification, but different rules applied according to how much your house was worth. In some places, you got the vote if you could prove your hearth was big enough to hold a large cooking pot, and you claimed your right to vote by taking your pot along to the hustings. (So when you voted you took pot luck!)
- **Members of the City Council.**
- **Everybody!** Two places existed, Preston (Lancashire) and the borough of Westminster, where pretty much everyone had the vote as long as you had spent the night before in the borough and were (a) adult and (b) male.

### You think that's bad? Wait 'til you hear about the corruption

No secret ballot existed. Electors declared whom they were voting for in front of a large crowd. With so few voters, bribing them was easy, especially when they were the tenants of the local landowner. Voting was usually rigged by buying up the local inn and providing free food and drink for the duration of the election, which in those days could be a week or more.

---

## The rottenest boroughs

Boroughs with very few voters were known as 'rotten boroughs'. The rottenest were:

- *Gatton* (Surrey): Number of voters (er, no they didn't actually *live* there): 6; Number of MPs: 2.

- *Dunwich* (Suffolk – well, *near* Suffolk because in fact it had fallen into the sea):

Number of voters: 0; Number of MPs: 2. Number of fish: 4,000.

- *Old Sarum* (Wiltshire): Number of voters: 0; Number of inhabitants: 0; Number of houses: 0 – yes, folks, it was a grassy mound! Number of MPs: 2.

## Rotten boroughs: Rotten system?

No one argues that the old political system didn't need changing, but historians have disagreed about just how bad it was. Obviously, the system offends against all our democratic principles; on the other hand, the oddest thing about it was that, by and large, it did work. Some of Britain's greatest statesmen, including William Pitt and Sir Robert Peel, came up through the old, unreformed system, and an able young man without much money could get into Parliament with the help of an obliging patron. Not all patrons tried to dictate what 'their' MPs said and did, and even when they did, plenty of independent-minded constituencies had no truck with patrons and their 'pocket' MPs.

Some boroughs were so completely controlled by the local lord that they were known as pocket boroughs and meaning that the borough was effectively in someone's pocket. Pitt the Younger's pal Henry Dundas had twelve seats in his pocket and effectively controlled the whole of Scotland. (For details on Pitt the Younger, see the sidebar earlier in this chapter.)

In many boroughs, no elections were held, because the local lord just nominated whom he wanted elected and that person got in unopposed.

In effect the system kept the landed classes in power which was why the Radicals and the people who wanted change and argued for a reform of Parliament as a first step before changing anything else.

## *The Great Reform Act*

So did the protestors get what they wanted? Not at first. In the years after Waterloo, anyone arguing for parliamentary reform got locked up, but gradually things calmed down. The landowners eventually realised that they really ought to do something for the big industrial cities. By 1830 almost the only two people opposed to some sort of reform were King George IV (who had been Prince Regent, see earlier in this chapter for more on him), and he died, and the Duke of Wellington, who was prime minister at the time – and he was turned out of office anyway. After an epic battle, in 1832 Parliament finally passed the Reform Bill, which became known as the Great Reform Act. This Act modernised the parliamentary system, bringing it kicking and screaming into the nineteenth century and only thirty-two years late!

# Was THAT the British Revolution?

Okay, the Great Reform Act wasn't very revolutionary. It standardised and helped to geographically balance the voting system, but the Act certainly didn't give the vote to the working people. The people who gained most from this legislation were the middle classes: They could now organise as a political force to be reckoned with. But the Act did change the system, and it did break the old landowners' hold on power, and above all it was passed.

In the centre of Newcastle, a magnificent column stands with a statue on top. This statue's not another one of Nelson, but Earl Grey, the man who got the Reform Bill through Parliament. In his way, Grey was every bit as important as Nelson: If Trafalgar saved Britain from a French invasion, the Great Reform Act saved Britain from violent revolution. Britain was going to change, and the change would indeed be revolutionary, but it would come through Parliament. That fact was what made Britain different as she entered the Victorian age.

# Chapter 18

# Putting On My Top Hat – The Victorians

*In This Chapter*

▶ Meeting Queen Victoria and important members of Parliament

▶ Covering major events of the era, from the People's Charter to the Great Exhibition

▶ Giving the Victorians their due (and telling the truth about piano legs)

*T*ravel back in time to 1837 – the year Victoria came to the throne – and you're in a costume drama. The men are in breeches, and the ladies in bonnets, and you're in a scene from the *Pickwick Papers*. But fast forward to the end of her reign and you get an eerie feeling: This environment looks like home. Okay, the lighting is gas and horses are still on the streets, but the men wear shirts and ties and jackets, and take the train in to work each morning. A telephone sits on the desk and a secretary works at a typewriter and the messages are arriving by email – well, telegraph, but the idea's the same. The newspapers are the same – the *Times*, *Daily Telegraph*, and *Daily Mail*, as well as a large tabloid press – printing the same stories: Politics, sex, and scandal. Sound familiar?

Modern times. Our world. The Victorians placed science and technology on a pedestal to go alongside religion. They invented the city as we know the concept, with its suburbs, town hall, parks, libraries, buses, and schools. They invented the seaside and the seaside holiday, and even 'the countryside', at least as somewhere to go and enjoy. Yes, they sent boys up chimneys, but they also stopped sending boys up chimneys, as they also stopped the slave trade and cock fighting. The Victorians were full of contradictions, but they made our world, they framed our minds, and ultimately, they made us.

# Queen Victoria

Okay first up, the lady who gave her name to these people and the age in which they lived. Queen Victoria. She was only eighteen (and still asleep in bed) when she came to the throne and she had a lot to learn. Her reign had a rocky start: Her coronation was a shambles – one lord, nicely called Lord Rolle, tripped on his cloak and literally rolled down the steps of the throne.

Young Vicky thought that, as queen, she could do as she liked, and quickly had to learn that she couldn't. First, Victoria found to her dismay that she couldn't keep her Whig Prime Minister, Lord Melbourne, when he lost his majority in Parliament. (See Chapter 13 for the origins of the Whigs and Tories.) Then she found she couldn't keep her ladies of the bedchamber, because they were political appointments; when the government changed, they changed, too. Victoria dug her heels in on that issue, the result being that the in-coming Tory prime minister, Sir Robert Peel, refused to come in, which left poor old Lord Melbourne struggling on with a wafer-thin majority. In fact, Victoria was losing popularity fast, which was a bad thing to do in the 1830s because monarchs who lost popularity could lose their thrones as well – just ask the French. What saved her was a handsome young cousin who came over from Germany and swept her off her feet. Albert. Very sensible, very practical, very serious, no sense of humour (he only liked puns), but to Victoria he was a Greek god. With brains.

The Victorians thought Albert was a bit stuffy and more than a bit German, but on the whole they recognised that his heart was in the right place. He came up with the idea for the Great Exhibition, one of the defining events of the century (see the later section 'Crystal Palace's Great Exhibition'), and he was an enthusiastic patron of science, technology, and education. The Albert Memorial and the Royal Albert Hall stand in the middle of the museums and institutes he founded in South Kensington. Above all, for many years, Albert was credited with having kept Queen Victoria on the straight and narrow and drawn her away from her ideas about doing as she liked. More recently, however, historians have tended to view Albert's role slightly differently. He wanted the monarchy to be above party, but only so that it could play a more active role in politics, not less.

Albert was a great admirer of the Tory leader, Sir Robert Peel, and he told Victoria that next time Sir Robert came into office and wanted to make some changes in her household, she should let him change anything – though maybe not the carpets – but she should keep hold of him. Because if Sir Robert left office the Whigs would come in and Albert didn't think much of them. By now Victoria was so completely under Albert's spell that she took his advice, so when Sir Robert did return to power, this time she didn't cause any fuss.

Albert never really persuaded Victoria to stay neutral. He wanted the Crown to play an important part in politics, and he died in 1861 while playing a crucial part in keeping Britain out of the American Civil War.

After his death, Victoria was so distraught that she virtually retired from the world and had to be coaxed back into public life by Disraeli. The queen admired Benjamin Disraeli, the leader of the Conservatives, and made no secret of the fact that she loathed his Liberal opponent, the venerable Mr William Gladstone. But although she could drive Gladstone up the wall – and often did – she sometimes helped things to happen even though she had very little power. (To find out more about Disraeli and Gladstone and their famous feud, head to the section 'Bill and Ben: The Gladstone and Disraeli show' later in this chapter.)

Queen Victoria's reign spanned sixty-four years, from 1837 to 1901. She presided over an age when Britain changed almost beyond recognition, and by the time she died most of her subjects couldn't remember any other monarch.

# Prime Ministers and MPs of the Age

The nineteenth century was the great age of Parliament. This period produced some great speakers and statesmen, and many dramatic battles were fought out on the green benches of the House of Commons or the scarlet benches of the House of Lords. Here are some of those great Victorian statesmen.

## Sir Robert Peel – tragedy of a statesman

Sir Robert Peel, who was prime minister twice, 1834–5 and 1841–6 was, quite simply, one of the greatest prime ministers of the nineteenth century. As Home Secretary, he created the modern police force, unarmed and in blue so as to be as unlike the army as possible. As prime minister, he single-handedly financed Britain's economic expansion, and he did so by cutting import duties. He also came up with a new tax, which he thought would only last a few years: Income Tax. Nice idea; shame about the timescale. Peel's career, however, was brought to a sudden end by the Irish Famine.

---

## Trade without frontiers – bread without tears

The Victorians believed in free trade as a way for nations to get on in peace and harmony. Free trade would mean prosperity and freedom and love and peace, and universal happiness. You won't be surprised to learn that the people who came up with this idea were the very manufacturers and industrialists who were making the goods that would be traded. Some of their opponents did point out that the workers didn't seem to be sharing in much of this prosperity and happiness.

The free traders set up a huge lobby group called the *Anti-Corn Law League* because the best examples of restrictive trade were the laws governing the corn trade. These Corn Laws allowed farmers and landowners to make money by forcing the poor to pay through the nose for bread. So the fate of the Corn Laws became a sort of conflict between industrialists (who didn't want them) and farmers (who did). Thanks to Peel, in 1846 the Corn Laws were repealed, and thanks to Disraeli, Peel was essentially repealed, too. Nevertheless, Peel was right: Free trade did make Britain very rich and very powerful. In the League's home city of Manchester, citizens raised money for statues not to generals, but to the men who led the Anti-Corn Law League.

## The Irish Famine

In the 1840s a million people in Ireland and Scotland starved to death. The disaster began when the European potato crop was destroyed by disease. In most countries, this crop destruction caused hardship but not famine, but the Irish and the Highland Scots were kept so poor that potatoes were the only things they could afford to eat. As famine began to take a hold in Ireland, the authorities' reaction seemed to make a terrible situation even worse:

- The government provided work, usually road building, so the people could earn enough money to buy food. Unfortunately, heavy labour isn't the best thing to give people already desperately weak from hunger.

- The Church of England set up food stations, but they sometimes tried to force people who came for food, most of whom were Catholic, to agree to become Protestants – they reckoned it was being Catholic which kept them all so poor and backward in the first place.

- People in Britain gave thousands of pounds in donations for famine relief, but after a while 'compassion fatigue' set in, rather as it still does with big charity appeals today.

What Sir Robert Peel would not do was just give out free food. He reckoned that would wreck the fragile Irish economy and just produce even worse poverty. When he finally relented and allowed in some emergency supplies of American maize, this foodstuff turned out to need too much preparation before it could be eaten.

Was the Irish Famine a case of genocide, as some people have said? No evidence whatsoever exists to support that idea. Genocide means setting out specifically to exterminate an entire people, like the Nazis' war on the Jews; the British may have disliked, and they certainly despaired of, the Irish but they didn't set out deliberately to kill them. The government simply had no idea how to cope with an unprecedented situation. (However, for a genuine example of genocide, look at the case of Tasmania, outlined in Chapter 19.) Remember that if you want to know more about the Irish Famine, take a look at *Irish History For Dummies* (Wiley).

## Peel forgets to check behind him

Peel calculated, quite rightly, that the trouble in Ireland was not lack of food but lack of money. Therefore, he believed, the best way out of famine would be to free up trade in order to allow more money to circulate in Ireland. In the long term, he was probably right, but the policy wasn't going to help the Irish who were starving in the fields. In any case, his party wanted nothing to do with Peel's idea. They liked the old system, which kept the farmers and landowners (who mostly voted Tory) in money. When Peel, who never took too much heed of his own party at the best of times, proposed repealing those great symbols of protection, the Corn Laws (you can find out about these highly controversial measures in Chapter 17), his MPs turned on him. Young Benjamin Disraeli saw a chance to make a name for himself and tore into Peel mercilessly for 'betraying' his own party. Peel got the Laws repealed, but his party deserted him, and he had to resign. This incident was a sad end to a very distinguished career. Peel died in a riding accident shortly afterwards, so he never lived to hear Disraeli and the other rebels a few years later admitting that he'd been right all along about free trade.

## Lord Palmerston – send a gunboat!

Lord Palmerston was in Parliament from 1806 until his death in 1865 and for most of that time he was a minister. He was prime minister twice, 1855–8 and 1859–65, but he's best remembered for his energetic approach to the subtleties of international diplomacy. His speciality was sending a small fleet to an opponent's port (and if it happened to be the capital city, even better) to blow it to pieces. This approach, which became known as 'Gunboat diplomacy' worked with the Chinese, the Dutch, and the Egyptians in the 1830s and 1840s. In fact, 'Pam', as he was affectionately nicknamed, only really got into trouble when, as Foreign Secretary in 1850, he tried this form of diplomacy on the Greeks.

The Greek government had got into a long and complex legal dispute with a shady character by the name of Don Pacifico, who happened to have been born at Gibraltar, which meant he was technically a British subject. As a British subject, Pacifico claimed protection from the British ambassador. The ambassador got onto London, and the next thing anyone knew, a large British fleet appeared off Athens making an offer on Don Pacifico's behalf that the Greeks really couldn't refuse: Give in or we blow your city to pieces.

Calling in the Royal Navy over a personal legal dispute was a bit much even for the Victorians, and Palmerston had to come and explain himself to the House of Commons. The British, he said, were like the ancient Romans: They were entitled to protection anywhere in the world, and if anyone stood in their way they'd have Lord Palmerston to deal with. The public loved this notion. Britain was to be the world's policeman, patrolling the seas and keeping the peace, or *Pax Britannica*.

## Don't send a gunboat

Palmerston's *Pax Britannica* idea didn't always work. On one occasion a British sailor called Bowers went ashore in a foreign port and was promptly arrested in flagrant breach of international law. Everyone expected Palmerston to act – send a gunboat! – but this time, he didn't lift a finger. You see, the country was the United States, the port was Charleston, South Carolina, and poor Mr Bowers's 'crime' was being black.

## *Bill and Ben: The Gladstone and Disraeli show*

The Victorians loved Punch and Judy, and in the 1860s and 1870s they got their very own political knockabout with two political leaders with real star quality. In the blue corner, Conservative leader Benjamin Disraeli (prime minister 1868 and 1874–1880, also known as Ben, Dizzy, the Earl of Beaconsfield), and in the yellow corner, Liberal leader William Ewart Gladstone (prime minister 1868–74, 1880–4, 1886 and 1892–3, also known as the People's William, the Grand Old Man, Mr Gladstone, or just That Madman). The two men had been rivals since Peel's day (see the section 'Sir Robert Peel – tragedy of a statesman' earlier in this chapter) and they couldn't stand each other. Someone asked Disraeli once for a definition of the difference between a misfortune and a catastrophe. 'If Gladstone fell in the river,' he replied, 'that would be a misfortune. If anyone pulled him out, that would be a catastrophe.'

Gladstone believed in God and in sound finance, and he was pretty sure a connection existed between the two. For Gladstone politics was a mission: To bring peace to Ireland or to provide free education for all. If other people didn't agree with him, the situation was quite simple: He was right and everyone else was wrong, even when he changed his mind.

Disraeli didn't do missions. He didn't even do principles, really. He was a popular novelist living well beyond his means, and he only went into Parliament because MPs couldn't be imprisoned for debt. He didn't know much about finance, and his time as Chancellor of the Exchequer in the 1850s and 1860s proved it. But Disraeli did know about social – and political – climbing. He married a rich heiress, and when he finally became prime minister he declared he'd 'reached the top of the greasy pole'.

Gladstone wanted to give the vote to working people who'd earned it, but not to those who hadn't; Disraeli didn't really believe in giving the vote to anyone, but in 1867 he did give it to a whole section of the working class so he, instead of Gladstone, could get all the credit. Nor was Disraeli particularly interested in the Empire, but he reckoned there were votes in it and that Gladstone probably disapproved of it (he was right on both counts). So, in 1872 Disraeli suddenly announced that the Empire was good and right, and that the Conservative Party would stand up for it through thick and thin. Gladstone went red then purple then red again with rage and frustration at Dizzy's cheek – but then, that was Disraeli's plan.

Everyone took sides. Newspapers, cartoonists, and songwriters all joined in the Disraeli–Gladstone knockabout. In some pubs, you could even get beaten up for supporting the wrong party! Gladstone kept preaching at the queen, which she couldn't stand; Disraeli flattered her shamelessly and even managed to get her an exotic new title: Empress of India. She loved it. Mind you, when he lay dying and she sent a message asking if he'd care for a visit, he said, 'Better not: She'll only want me to take a message to Albert.'

# Troubles at Home and Abroad

Although the Victorians liked to stress how stable Britain was compared with its European neighbours – or the United States – they did have some serious problems to contend with. These were some of the most urgent issues of the day.

## The People's Charter

When Queen Victoria came to the throne, working people didn't have the vote – any of them. Remember that these were the people who did all the work, which made Britain the great industrial giant that she was (refer to Chapter 16 for information on the Industrial Revolution). So a group of working people in London got together and decided to do something about the issue. In 1838 the Chartists drew up what they called the *People's Charter* (which had a nice ring of Magna Carta about it; see Chapter 9 for info on that) to demand the vote. But not just the vote – the Chartists had thought a bit more deeply than that. They wanted the following:

- **The vote:** Well, obviously. And some of them even wanted women to have it, too.

- **Equal electoral districts:** Otherwise, the middle classes could fix the boundaries to their own advantage.

- **No property qualification for MPs:** At the time, you had to own property to become an MP. And since not many workers could afford houses or land, not many workers had been able to become MPs.

- **Payment for MPs:** Without pay, how was a working-class MP to live? At the time, most MPs were against being paid, but more recently, however, they've become much more keen on the idea.

- **Secret ballot:** No more of that getting up in front of a large crowd and declaring your vote in a loud voice – so handy for any local landowner wanting to intimidate his tenants.

- **Annual Parliaments:** These would've meant an election every year: A bit drastic, but remember that the acid test of democracy is not whether you can vote someone in, but whether you can vote them out. If you get the chance to elect someone every year, they'll soon learn who's boss.

Despite what their opponents said, the Chartists weren't revolutionaries (though the German political philosopher Karl Marx, founder of communism, who was in London at the time, rather wished they would be!). But if you look again at their six demands you can see a fully working democracy with power in the hands of the people. Maybe the middle classes had a point: The Chartists were more revolutionary than they realised.

### Petitioning Parliament

The Chartists got two massive petitions together: The first had over a million signatures, and the second had three million. That petition took some organising: No computers or databases in the 1840s, remember. But Parliament wouldn't even look at the petitions. Not surprisingly, trouble broke out. The Chartists organised a national strike and a big riot occurred at Newport in Wales. In 1848 they tried again with an even bigger petition. Parliament, more nervous this time because of revolutions on the Continent, called in troops and cautiously agreed to have a look at the petition. Which was fine until they started looking at the signatures and found that, er, some of them were false. Unless, of course, Queen Victoria, the Duke of Wellington, and Mr Punch really had signed it – at least seventeen times. The MPs fell about laughing and the Chartists had to creep away.

So, were the Chartists important? Well, if the question is: 'Did Parliament grant them their demands immediately?' the answer is no. But if the question is: 'Did they have an impact?' the answer is yes. The Chartists formed a national movement organised by ordinary, often ill-educated working people who managed to run a national newspaper and maintain a vast political campaign, complete with meetings, posters, processions, pamphlets, speakers, and petitions. They ran an education scheme, a land scheme, even a teetotal movement. The Chartists created the biggest working-class political movement before the Labour Party.

### Labour days?

After all the political shenanigans, how much power actually went to the people? Some of the better-educated skilled workers got the vote, mainly thanks to Disraeli (see the earlier section 'Bill and Ben: The Gladstone and Disraeli show' for information about him), but most working men – and all women – still didn't have the vote by the time the queen died in 1901.

Workers may not have had the vote, but plenty of trade unions existed that were showing their muscle. A long and bitter strike occurred in the London docks in the 1880s, which the strikers won. The girls who made matches at Bryant and May even organised a strike – striking matches! But even strong trade unions were no substitute for a voice in Parliament. The first 'Labour' MP was Keir Hardie, a shrewd Scot who made a point of not wearing the smart top hats and frock coats that other MPs wore. In 1900 the labour movement finally got its own Labour Party. No one knew if Labour would last, and no one predicted that it would go on to become one of the two leading parties in the land, and that it would be solidly entrenched in power in time for the Millennium in 2000.

## The Crimean War – not Britain's finest hour

Even the most gung-ho combat fan would have difficulty justifying the Crimean War (1854–6). Officially, it was fought to resolve a big dispute over which group of monks should have the keys to the Church of the Nativity in Bethlehem (I promise you I'm not kidding) and whether or not the Russians had the right to tell the Turks how to govern their own country (and other people's). In reality, the war was about safeguarding the route to India (which was British) that lay through Egypt (which wasn't), whether the Russians should be allowed into the Mediterranean, and whether Romania and Bulgaria should be free.

The war began when the Russians invaded Turkish territory (no doubt crying out 'Support our monks!') and the British and French governments declared war – mainly because the British and French press decided they should. Never having fought the Russians before, the Brits weren't too sure of the rules, and they started off by sending a fleet to the Baltic. When they found it was nowhere near the Mediterranean or Turkey, they had another look at the map, noticed a big Russian port called Sevastopol in roughly the right area, and decided to attack it.

The war was a shambles from start to finish. The British commander, Lord Raglan, kept forgetting that the French were his allies (he'd been at Waterloo, you see) and had to be reminded not to attack them. The allies won every battle, but capturing Sevastopol still took them almost three years because after each battle they could never decide what to do next. Tennyson's famous poem *Charge of the Light Brigade* was inspired by the Crimean War. Five regiments of cavalry found out that if you charge against cannons – especially if they're on three sides of you – you tend to get blown to pieces. And all this slaughter occurred because Lord Raglan couldn't word a message clearly.

# Lady and the Lamp

Florence Nightingale is probably the best-known Victorian woman – possibly the best-known Victorian – after the queen herself. Not only did she go out to the Crimea to nurse the soldiers, but she took on the whole bureaucracy of the military high command and won. Soon children were learning stories of the gentle, warm-hearted 'Lady with the Lamp' going round the wards at night while the soldiers kissed her shadow as she passed.

If you imagine Florence Nightingale like that, forget it. Sure, she took on the doctors, but she wasn't particularly gentle. She was a tough cookie, and she got her way by being even harder-nosed than the doctors were. She wouldn't listen to people who disagreed with her, and she was quite happy to ignore inconvenient evidence. She refused to believe that bacteria spread disease and insisted that it was carried by miasma in the air. She was a chronic hypochondriac and spent most of the second half of her life propped up in bed. She designed hospitals and other communal buildings, like barracks and prisons, and set herself up as an expert on India, even though she never set foot in the place. Some books still claim that every Viceroy of India dashed round to see her as soon as he was appointed. That claim's a complete fiction invented by her admirers. She was totally intolerant of anyone she saw as a rival. She got other nurses sent home from the Crimea and only met her match in an equally feisty Catholic Mother Superior. She was totally dismissive of 'old Mother Seacole', a very popular Jamaican nurse who was actually a great admirer of hers. Florence Nightingale certainly deserves the credit for creating the modern nursing profession – no mean feat. Just be thankful you never had to work with her.

A lot of people died in the Crimean War, and most of them did so because the people in charge couldn't organise a day out for an infants' school. Only two people really emerged with any real credit: Florence Nightingale (read more about her in the sidebar 'Lady and the Lamp') and the *Times* reporter William Howard Russell who told the story to his readers like it was. Because that story needed telling.

## Did the upper classes really have the upper hand?

At first sight, it might seem that the upper classes were in control of everything, but this picture isn't really accurate. True, Victorian Britain had no shortage of lords and ladies, and they all lived in those lovely stately homes you can pay to visit, but these houses were hideously expensive to maintain, even in those days, and land didn't pay the way it used to. The lords who did well were those who moved their money – or married – into industry or finance. In politics, the House of Lords was gradually becoming less important. At the start of the nineteenth century, having a lord as prime minister or Foreign Secretary was the norm; by the end of the century, you still got some prime ministers in the Lords – Lord Salisbury was prime minister four times, for example – but the situation was becoming more unusual. You certainly didn't get Cabinets full of Lords as you'd done earlier in the century. In fact, the Lords were getting a reputation for being more interested in huntin', shootin', and fishin' than in high affairs of state. Gilbert and Sullivan had great fun poking fun at rather dim members of the House of Lords in their operetta *Iolanthe*. (You'll be pleased to hear they were just as harsh on the House of Commons, too.)

# How Victorian Were the Victorians?

You can easily get the wrong idea of the Victorians. We think of them as uptight characters, deeply religious, terrified of sex, and constantly forcing children to work up chimneys. But is that image the whole story? Is it part of the story at all? Here are a few of the more common misconceptions that people tend to have about the Victorians.

## Were the Victorians really so cruel to children?

Small children were certainly employed as chimney sweeps in Victorian England but don't forget that children had always been expected to work as soon as they were old enough. The lucky ones got apprenticed in a trade, the less lucky ones worked on the farm or helped with the spinning. When new types of work appeared with the development of industry and factories, using children for work that adults couldn't do seemed perfectly natural: Crawling underneath machinery or sitting in coal mines to open and close the ventilation doors.

The point about the Victorians is not so much that they did employ children, but that they were the first people to ask whether doing so was right and to introduce laws saying what you could and could not expect children to do. The Victorians came up with the idea that all children should go to school, and they checked to make sure the schools were up to scratch, too. They were the first people to develop a whole school of literature specifically for children – Lewis Carroll's *Alice* books are the best known. In many ways you could say that the Victorians invented the idea of childhood, as we know it today.

## Were the Victorians really scared of sex?

Sorry to disappoint you, but contrary to a widespread myth, the Victorians did not cover up curvaceous table legs in case they found them a turn-on, and no, Victorian women did not just lie back and think of England to get them through the unpleasant necessity of having sex with their husbands. All the evidence we have – and we have a lot of it – suggests that the Victorians enjoyed sex every bit as much as we do. Sex did rest uneasily with their religion and the big emphasis they put on church-going, that is true, but you only have to look at the size of Victorian families to realise that they knew something about the facts of life.

Prostitution and sexually-transmitted diseases were a huge problem in Victorian Britain. The government tore its hair out about the rate of venereal disease in the army and navy and in 1864 introduced the highly controversial Contagious Diseases Acts which gave the police powers to inspect any woman found hanging around near barracks or docks, whether she was a prostitute or not.

Corsets and stays worn by Victorian ladies were designed to show off the body to maximum erotic effect. Crinolines defined a sort of exclusion zone where men were not permitted, but they often wore them with off-the-shoulder tops that encouraged men to have a go. In fact, the Victorians had such an appetite for sex that they were rather amused by people they thought exhibited more hang-ups about it. Like Americans, for example, who they thought were so afraid of sex that they covered up their table and piano legs in case they found them a turn-on. It wasn't true of the Americans either. (Canadians, maybe . . .)

## Were Victorians really so religious?

Clearly Victorians took their religion very seriously. Look at all those churches they built, the hymns they wrote, and the prayer books they carried. Look at the Salvation Army and *Barchester Towers* and all those missionaries in Africa.

If the Victorians weren't religious, what were they? In 1851 Parliament ordered a religious census of England and Wales and counted everyone who was at church on a particular Sunday. The figure was so low – over five million people didn't go – that they never held another one.

Most Victorians believed in the literal truth of the Bible, and churches ran Sunday schools for children and mission hostels for the poor. Evangelical Christians campaigned against alcohol at home and slavery abroad. Anglican clergymen ran the best schools and all the Oxford and Cambridge colleges. The Church of England seemed to be almost as important and powerful as Parliament itself – but it wasn't, for a couple of reasons. First, a lot of other churches existed. Non-conformist chapels were very big, especially in Wales and the north of England, and in 1850 the Catholic Church re-established its network of bishops and dioceses in England and Wales. A lot of working people went to chapel or to Mass rather than to the Church of England. Second, the belief in science and technology was gaining ground. In 1851 the Great Exhibition was held, a celebration of science and technology, and in 1859 Darwin went to press with *The Origin of Species*. New university colleges were springing up, which weren't run by the Church of England, and from 1870, a whole network of state schools existed, where Religious Education was optional.

## Did the Victorians oppress women?

We tend to think of Victorian Britain as a male-dominated place, where the husband and father (a really posh word exists for him – *paterfamilias*) comes home from his important job in the City, stands warming his coat tails against the fire while his wife sews and says 'Yes, dear' and his children are seen and not heard, and after dinner, he retires to his club. And to be fair, that image is how the Victorians liked to think of themselves. But relations between men and women were never as simple as that.

Legally, for example, until 1870, a woman's property became her husband's as soon as they married, but from the large number of legal arrangements existing between husbands and wives clearly this was more a legal technicality than a fact of everyday life. Nevertheless a huge amount of male prejudice existed, and some women had a massive fight to get accepted into 'male' professions. The first women's colleges at Cambridge opened in 1875, but women were still not allowed to take a full university degree. When Sophia Jex-Blake tried to study medicine at Edinburgh, the professors used every legal trick they could find to stop her, and the students virtually beat her up. Nevertheless Sophia won, and she had a huge amount of support, from both men and women. By the end of the century, young women were working in offices, department stores, and telephone exchanges. They could even vote and be elected in every type of election except for Parliament, and plenty of moves were happening to change that situation, though not until 1918 did most women finally win the Parliamentary vote (see Chapter 20 for more about the long fight for female suffrage).

# Things Can Only Get Better

The Victorians believed strongly in progress and that the British were slowly but surely making the world a better place to live in. Some of these improvements came about because of reforms in the number of hours people could work or how low a ship was allowed to be in the water, but much of the progress was happening through science and technology. And Britain led the way.

## Crystal Palace's Great Exhibition

We'll never see anything quite like the Great Exhibition of 1851. Plenty of international exhibitions have been staged since – the Eiffel Tower was left up after the Paris exhibition of 1889 – but they were pale imitations of the original. The Great Exhibition was housed in a magnificent palace of glass, called the Crystal Palace, a huge greenhouse designed by Joseph Paxton, who supervised the gardens at Chatsworth House. The Exhibition was a sort of statement of faith in what mankind could achieve, from heavy industry to the latest gadgets for the home, and it was phenomenally popular. People came from all over the country to marvel at the wonders of technology. The Exhibition included stunning displays from all over the world, but over half of the exhibits came from British designers and British engineers. If the Victorians believed in Britain, you can easily see why.

## Two giants: Brunel and Darwin

If ever a man deserved to be commemorated in the latest technology, it was Isambard Kingdom Brunel (1806–59). The man was a technological genius. He built the Great Western Railway from London to Bristol and designed every detail, from the bridges and tunnels to the decoration in the stations. He built a great glass cathedral of a station at Paddington and a sort of railway-station-cum-parish-church at the Bristol end. His Clifton Suspension Bridge over the river Avon is still one of the most beautiful sights in England. He designed the *Great Britain*, the first steam ship to make regular transatlantic crossings, the *Great Western*, and the vast *Great Eastern* – a huge monster of a ship, the largest in the world. When he accidentally swallowed a coin (during a magic trick for his children that went wrong) and it got stuck in his gullet, he quickly designed a special choking-man-upside-down-turner-and-coin-shaker-out machine, and that worked, too. Brunel didn't always get his own way. He wanted his trains to run on wider tracks, but the other railway companies defeated him: Every train derailment since is a reminder that Brunel was right.

Charles Darwin (1809–82) never intended to become a scientist. He studied theology at Cambridge though he didn't want to be a priest. He joined HMS *Beagle* on its round-the-world voyage in 1831 to keep the captain company, and he collected animals and plants as a hobby to pass the time. Only as he was classifying his specimens did he begin to think about the nature of species. Putting his ideas down on paper took him years, and he only finally rushed into print in 1859 because someone else was about to publish a book saying more or less what he was going to say. Even then, most scientists already agreed about evolution: Darwin was merely the first to talk about natural selection, how different species adapt to their environment and only the strongest survive. Darwin had been afraid his ideas would cause a storm, and he was right. The Church was up in arms because, it claimed, Darwin was challenging the story of Creation as told in the Book of Genesis, even though Darwin's book didn't actually say anything about the origins of humankind. Church leaders denounced him as the antichrist. 'Is it through his grand-mother or through his grandfather that Mr Darwin claims descent from a monkey?' asked one bishop in sarcastic mode, but the Church was fighting a losing battle: Opinion in Britain gradually swung behind Darwin.

# Novel contemplation

Dickens, Thackeray, Trollope, Thomas Hardy, Charlotte Bronte, Emily Brontë, Anne Brontë, George Eliot, Mrs Gaskell – shall I go on? Victorian novelists, all of them. But not only the writers mattered: So did the readers. The Victorians were obsessive, compulsive readers. Their newspapers and magazines, even the ones for children, were printed in close-typed columns, and people read them through avidly. Ever wondered why Victorian novels are so long? Because they appeared as monthly serials in magazines, and the writers got paid by the yard. The public loved sensation and mystery: Sherlock Homes and Dracula were both Victorian creations. They loved sentiment and romance – cue *Jane Eyre* or Tennyson's poems of King Arthur. They read sermons, history, and science, as well as fiction – one British commander was reading Darwin and Trollope in-between blowing the Chinese Imperial Army to pieces. But above all, the Victorians enjoyed novels with good story-lines, lots of suspense, and strong characters. They've been called the soap operas of their day. They weren't. They were better.

# Chapter 19

# The Sun Never Sets – But It Don't Shine Either

### In This Chapter

▶ Creating an empire without meaning to: How the British did it

▶ Building empire in America, India, Australia, New Zealand, China, and Africa

▶ Understanding what went wrong in India and South Africa

A historian once said that the British got their Empire in 'a fit of absence of mind', as if they'd gone out to the shops one day and come back with a huge Empire without any recollection of having bought it. There is some truth in this idea. The point is that no one ever sat down and said, 'Right, this Empire then. Which bits of the world are we going to need?' Empire building was much more haphazard, and the British often opposed it. After all, if you take somewhere over, you've got to defend it and maintain it, and doing so costs money. And ultimately, money was one of the main things British imperialism was all about.

Figure 19-1 shows the Empire at the peak of its expansion in 1920. Many of the countries in the Empire at this time had been taken from Germany at the end of the Great War (see Part VI for more on the later history of the Empire); other countries – such as the American colonies – would have featured on an earlier map, but had long since been independent by this time (see Chapter 17 to find out why).

Anyone writing about the British Empire nowadays has a problem. On the one hand, the Empire was an appalling story of greed, cruelty, massacre, genocide, theft, and pretty cynical self-interest by white Europeans exploiting weaker people all over the world. But Empire was also a tale of high hopes and dreams, of enormous energy and enterprise, of people who really did believe they were making the world a better place and helping those less fortunate than themselves. The Empire spread huge technological and political advantages all around the globe, but it did so at a terrible and shameful cost in human suffering. For historians, getting the balance in the story right can be tricky.

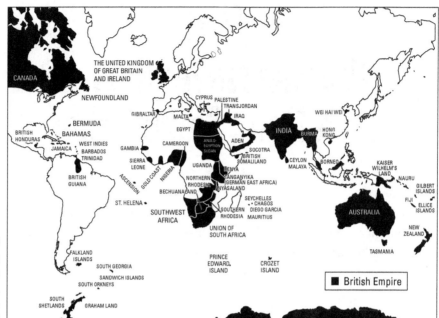

**Figure 19-1:**
The British
Empire,
1920.

# New World Order

To understand how the British Empire got started, you have to go back to the
sixteenth century and Tudor times – doublets and hose, and men with doilies
round their necks (see Part IV to find more about these people). An Italian
sailor called Giovanni Caboto arrived at the court of King Henry VII. Would
the king be interested in stumping up the cash for a voyage to the New World?
Now, a few years earlier Henry had turned Columbus down, and he didn't want
to make the same mistake again. So he said yes, and John Cabot – the English
couldn't cope with his real name – sailed west until he hit 'New-found-land'. He
didn't know it, but he was also founding the British Empire.

Newfoundland proved very good for fish, which was big business in those days
– no meat allowed on Fridays or in Lent, so demand was high – but what the
English really wanted was to get into the highly profitable spice trade with the
East, and to do that they needed to get past the New World and on to Asia, if
they could only find the way through. But they couldn't. One group did try to
settle in the New World in Henry VIII's reign, but found so little food there, they
ended up eating each other. So by Elizabeth I's time, the English had come up
with a much better way of making money out of America: Robbery.

Imperial Spain was *the* world superpower, thanks in part to her South American
gold and silver mines. The Spanish forced the locals to mine it and then shipped
it off to Spain. The English simply ambushed the ships (see Chapter 11 for more
about these English sea dogs).

# Colonies in the New World

In Elizabeth I's reign (1558–1603) the English had their second go at setting up a colony in America.

In 1584 Sir Walter Raleigh found a site at Roanoke in Virginia (named after Elizabeth, the 'Virgin Queen'), but the colony only lasted a year. By the time a second colony was set up at Jamestown in 1607 King James I's anti-smoking drive had reduced the demand for tobacco. Virginia collapsed. In addition, the colonists tried to swindle the local tribes, so they massacred the colonists.

The failure of the Virginia colonies would've been the end of the story of British colonialism had it not been for all the religious strife back in England. (Have a look at Chapter 13 to see what this was all about.) The Pilgrim Fathers, the most famous religious refugees in history, hired the *Mayflower* in 1620, sailed to the New World, landed in Massachusetts, and set up another colony. That this group made it through the first winter was a bit of a miracle – and solely due to the local tribes who stepped in and lent a hand – but the colony survived. In 1630 John Winthrop led another group of Puritans to Massachusetts, and two years later Catholic colonists arrived in Maryland. The Scots decided to join in with a Scottish colony at what they called Nova Scotia (New Scotland), and this might have worked had it not been for politics: Charles I lost a war with France, and as part of the peace deal, he agreed to hand Nova Scotia over to the French.

By the end of the century, the English had enough colonies in the New World to rival the French and the Spanish.

## Hey, sugar sugar

Initially, the English didn't really know why they wanted the colonies. When the government asked the Pilgrim Fathers what they intended doing in the New World once they arrived, the Pilgrim Fathers looked a bit embarrassed and mumbled something about maybe doing a bit of fishing.

Once the English got to the New World, of course, they found all sorts of useful things to sell. They found furs – European winters were getting a lot colder then, so these were very welcome – tobacco, fish, and potatoes. But the king of all products, the one that brought the pound signs to the eyes, the one that really mattered, was sugar.

Sugar made all the travails of colonisation worthwhile. You could eat it, shape it, use it to sweeten anything from cakes to drinks, and sugar tasted good! But harvesting sugar took a lot of hard work – which is why this British Empire in the New World was based so heavily upon slavery. To see the sordid connection between the sugar and slave trades, refer to Chapter 16. The crucial fact to know here is that the slave trade made the sugar islands rich, so rich, in fact, that the British seriously considered giving Canada back to the French in return for just one sugar island in the Caribbean. Even ports that never saw a slave made money out of the slave trade. Bristol and Liverpool were small seaside towns: The slave trade made them the richest ports in Britain.

After many years of arguing about the slave trade, the British finally abolished it in 1807 and abolished slavery throughout the British Empire in 1833. By then they'd worked out a way of growing sugar beet at home, so there was less need for slave labour in the Caribbean colonies anyway.

# India Taken Away

The story of the British in India begins on the very last day of the sixteenth century, when a group of merchants met in London to set up the East India Company to conduct trade with the East. The first Englishman to go out, Sir Thomas Roe, worked out a very good deal with the Mughal Emperor which gave the English a trading base in Surat on the west coast. Then King Charles II (you can find out more about him in Chapter 13) married a Portuguese princess called Catherine de Braganza, and she gave him the Indian port of Bombay (Mumbai) as a wedding present!

Gradually the English, like the French and the Portuguese, who also had trading bases in India, got sucked into the violent and unpredictable world of Indian politics, which basically meant taking sides in a series of very complex and bloody civil wars. These European trading companies began to set up their own armed forces of Indian soldiers under European officers, and by the eighteenth century the British East India Company (we can call it British by the eighteenth century – see Chapter 15 to find out why) had a full-scale army with which to square up to the French East India Company – and its own full-scale army. In 1751 the British Company's army, under its rather wild young commander Robert Clive, defeated the French Company army at Arcot and more or less drove the French out of southern India.

## Black Hole in Calcutta

In 1756 the British heard disturbing news from Bengal: The Nawab of Bengal had attacked the British garrison in his capital, Calcutta, beaten them and taken many of them prisoner. He locked them up in a small cellar overnight, but the night was stiflingly hot, and in the morning many of the prisoners had died. This cellar became known as the Black Hole of Calcutta.

The 'Black Hole of Calcutta' is important, because it was one of the main reasons the British gave for taking India over, and for years British children learned about the incident as a terrible atrocity and a sure sign that Indians weren't to be trusted. Exactly how many people died is a matter of some dispute. The British claimed that 146 men were locked in and only 23 survived, but historians dispute this, and in any case whether the deaths were intended is by no means clear. As so often in history, what actually happened isn't what matters so much as what people thought had happened. The British were convinced that the Nawab killed the men deliberately, and they set out for revenge. And that revenge meant regime change in Bengal.

Clive headed north and met the Nawab and his French allies at Plassey in 1757. Clive had 3,000 men, British and Indian; the Nawab had 68,000 Bengali and French troops. Think of that ratio as 3 against 68. Yet Clive won. How? Easy. He cheated (mind you, with odds like that, who can blame him?). Clive made a secret deal with the Nawab's relative, Mir Jaffir. If Mir Jaffir would keep his troops out of the battle, the British would put him on the throne of Bengal. Which they did, though much good being on the throne did him. After Plassey, the Mughal Emperor handed Bengal over to the British, so Mir Jaffir was no more than a puppet controlled by a British governor. He was the first of many.

## The Battle of Warren Hastings

Everyone knew what went on in the East India Company: Shady dealings, back-handers, and chaotic accounting. By the 1770s the company was nearly bankrupt (think Enron). Clive was hauled back to England to face corruption charges. The man sent out to India to clean things up was Warren Hastings. He'd studied Indian culture and languages, and he was very good at admin. Unfortunately, Hastings was also very difficult to get on with. He was embroiled in bitter arguments with the three-man council he was supposed to work with and even wounded one of them in a duel, which didn't help. During his time in office a terrible famine also hit Bengal, which killed five million people – a third of the entire population.

Hastings's enemies had friends in London, and they got him recalled to face a long list of charges. The trial was held in Parliament with some of the leading Whig politicians heading up the prosecution (see Chapter 15 to find out about who the Whigs were). The trial dragged on for years. Eventually Hastings was found not guilty, but his career was in ruins. The government decided leaving India to be governed by a private company was no good, and it started gradually taking over India itself.

## Great game, great game!

After Warren Hastings (see the preceding section) the British took a new line in India. Instead of trying to fit into the Indian way of doing things, they would make the Indians do things the British way: British laws and British education. They stopped bothering to learn Indian languages and Indian history and even let Christian missionaries in. But the British were worried about the Russians moving in, too – if you look at a map, you'll see that idea wasn't completely silly. So the Brits sent spies and secret agents up to the North West Frontier to keep an eye on the Russians. They called this intriguing the 'Great Game'. India's neighbours were going to join in the game, whether they liked it or not:

- ✔ **Afghanistan, 1839–42:** The British were afraid that the Russians were going to invade India through Afghanistan, so they sent an army into Kabul and put their own man in charge, a hapless character called Shah Sujah. The Afghans knew a British puppet when they saw one. They started shooting British soldiers in Kabul and took command of the narrow passes through the mountains, so the British were cut off. When the British finally did retreat, the Afghans shot them to pieces. Then they did the same to Shah Sujah.

  Invasions of Afghanistan have a habit of going badly wrong. The British imposed another puppet government in 1878 and the Afghans overthrew that one, too. The British had to launch a Second Afghan War and even after that conflict they still didn't have much control of the country. In 1980 the Soviet Union invaded Afghanistan and installed a pro-Russian government, but after eight years of guerrilla fighting they too had to pull out. An American and British coalition invaded Afghanistan in 2001 in retaliation for the 9/11 attacks on New York and Washington, which had been backed by the Afghan Islamic regime, the Taliban. Just like the British in the nineteenth century, the coalition forces conquered the country fairly easily and then found themselves fighting an ever larger and fiercer guerrilla war. Afghanistan is one area of the world where knowing your history is well worth the effort!

- ✔ **Sind, 1843:** British commander Charles Napier took the North West Indian state of Sind basically in revenge for what had happened in Afghanistan the year before. You could call the attack unprovoked aggression, and you'd be right. According to legend, he even sent a joke message – *Peccavi!*, which means 'I have sinned' in Latin. Get it?

- ✔ **Punjab:** This Sikh kingdom was falling into chaos after its great ruler Ranjit Singh died. The Sikhs invaded British territory, and after two tremendously bloody campaigns (1845–6 and 1848–9), the British drove them back and took over.

- ✔ **Burma:** The British attacked Burma three times (1824–6; 1852; 1885–6) and finally took the whole country over. Why? Mainly so the French couldn't have it. No-one asked the Burmese for their opinion.

## *This is mutiny, Mr Hindu!*

What, you may ask, did the Indians think of what the British were doing? The British hardly seemed to wonder. They assumed the Indians were happy and that everything was hunky-dory. Boy, were they wrong. In 1857 India rose in revolt, for three main reasons:

- ✔ **The 'Lapse' rule:** This was an interesting system the British came up with for when an Indian ruler died. If no heir existed according to British rules, then the succession 'lapsed' to Britain –that is, the British took it over. The fact that an Indian heir existed according to Indian rules didn't count!

- ✔ **Greased cartridges:** Indian soldiers, or sepoys, were issued with new bullets that were coated in grease. According to the rumours, the grease was either cow fat, which Hindus couldn't touch, or pig fat, which Muslims couldn't touch. Whatever the truth was, the British told the sepoys to stop grumbling and use the bullets.

- ✔ **An old prophesy:** An old story said that British rule would end a hundred years after the battle of Plassey in 1757. Now it was 1857. Spooky!

In 1857 the sepoys at Meerut in northern India refused to use the bullets, killed their officers, and started a huge rising against British rule. They dragged the old Mughal emperor out of his happy retirement and told him he was to lead them; various Indian rulers seized the chance to get their kingdoms back; and the British found themselves cut off in towns like Cawnpore (Kanpur) and Lucknow.

Make no mistake: This rebellion was very bloody. At Kanpur, the Indians cut the bodies of British women and children up and threw them down a well. The British sewed captured Muslims up in pig skins, hanged prisoners from trees without any sort of trial, made Indians lick blood up from the ground, and used an old Indian practice of tying prisoners to cannons and blowing them to pieces. Afterwards, both sides were deeply shocked by the violence. The British government took over completely from the old East India Company and tried – very reluctantly – to give Indians more of a say in governing the country. The Indian Mutiny, as the British insisted on calling this event, was a terrible warning of what could happen if they got governing India wrong.

# Cook's Tour: Australia and New Zealand

While the British were busy conquering India (see the preceding section), some very different empire building was going on further south. The British had got keenly interested in the possible uses of exotic plants, and the Admiralty sent out ships, like HMS *Bounty*, to go and find them. We all know what happened to the *Bounty*, but Captain Cook on HMS *Endeavour* was rather more successful. In 1770 he sailed into such a rich collection of plants that he called the place Botany Bay (in what is now New South Wales, Australia), and claimed it for Britain before going on to explore the rest of the Pacific. The people who actually lived at Botany Bay had tried to stop Cook and his men from landing. And they weren't the only Pacific islanders who smelt trouble when the British arrived – Cook was killed by islanders in Hawaii – but the British weren't going to let his murder stop them.

The British were used to sending prisoners over to the American colonies – it was cheaper than looking after them in prison – but after America became independent, they had to look elsewhere. 'How about Botany Bay?' asked some bright spark. 'It's on the other side of the world, so if they do survive, there's a good chance they won't come back.' The first shipload arrived in 1788.

The convicts were treated like animals, even though the only crime some of them had committed was stealing a loaf of bread to feed their family at home. When these prisoners were released, they simply pushed the Aborigines off their land. But the situation was much, much worse in Tasmania. Tasmania's a small island with lots of poisonous snakes, so the British thought it was the ideal place to dump their hardest criminals. These *bushrangers*, as they were called, hunted the Aborigines for sport – with official encouragement. Within seventy years the Aborigines were dead. All of them. If you want an example of genocide, British Tasmania is a good place to start.

New Zealand didn't escape. The Maoris were luckier than the Tasmanians – the Brits had a habit of recognising some peoples as 'noble savages', normally based on how well they fought, and they reckoned the Maoris fitted the bill. By the 1840 Treaty of Waitangi, the Maoris handed the country over to the British and the British nobly refrained from wiping them out. Instead, they flooded New Zealand with European settlers and simply drove the Maoris off their land. Depressingly familiar scene, isn't it?

# Opium? Just Say Yes: China

With all of the wars the Brits fought to secure land and routes throughout the world, a pretence could at least be made that the British were trying to promote trade or good government or something. But even at the time, the British themselves couldn't come up with much of an excuse for the opium wars with China.

## A Franklin's tale

One thing the Brits never gave up on was the idea that a way must exist into the Pacific round the north of Canada. (A way does exist, but so far into the Arctic Circle that it's hardly worth bothering about.) In 1845 Sir John Franklin, a naval commander, Trafalgar veteran, and former governor of Tasmania, set off with two ships, HMS *Erebus* and HMS *Terror*, to find that wretched North West Passage. And he probably did find the passage, but he never came back to tell the tale. The two ships got trapped in the ice, and the men tried to get home over land. Even though they had the latest tinned food, none of them made it home. In the 1980s some of the bodies were found, perfectly preserved by the cold. They'd died from lead poisoning from the tins.

The East India Company found that it could make a packet by exporting opium to China, despite all the Chinese government could do to stop it. When the Chinese raided the drugs ships and warehouses in 1839, the British Foreign Secretary, Lord Palmerston (Palmerston and his highly original approach to international peace and harmony is covered in Chapter 18), sent a fleet of gun-boats to Canton and opened fire. The Chinese had to give up Hong Kong, agree to let the British pump them as full as opium as they liked, and not to stop honest British drug peddlers ever again. But the Chinese did try to stop the dealers. In 1856 the Chinese arrested a British ship for piracy; the Brits invaded China again. Invasion was even easier this time because a civil war was going on in China and the British had the French on their side. They took Beijing and forced the Chinese to open even more of their ports to British trade.

In the twentieth century, the Chinese called all these nineteenth-century agreements 'unequal treaties' and refused to consider themselves bound by them. This refusal is what lay behind the Chinese government's determination to get Hong Kong back from Britain in 1997 – which it did.

# Wider Still and Wider: Scrambling for Africa

You may not guess this detail from everything so far, but until the 1880s, the British weren't actually all that interested in getting colonies. They cost a lot of money for no very obvious return. But in the 1880s, something changed. Suddenly the British became really keen on their Empire. They didn't just like their Empire, they believed in it. They started calling it 'The Empire on which the sun never sets' – a name with two meanings: One, the Empire was spread so far around the globe that the sun was always shining on some part of it, and two, that it would go on for ever. They called their Empire one of the greatest forces for good the world had ever seen. And they started taking over more and more of the world's surface, especially in Africa.

For a long time, the Victorians didn't really 'do' Africa. They thought of Africa as the 'Dark Continent', full of jungle and disease and – well, no one really knew. The man who changed the popular opinion of Africa was David Livingstone, the Scottish physician and missionary who first went out there in 1841. Everyone loved reading his reports. And they began to dream. Maybe there was more to Africa than they thought? Like gold? Or diamonds? Or power . . . ?

## Zulu!

Okay, you've seen Michael Caine and the gallant Welsh holding off the entire Zulu army – *thahsands* of them. But what really happened? This story is about two empires, one British, one Zulu. The Brits come into the story when they took the Cape of Good Hope – that area's the bottom bit of South Africa – off the Dutch in 1795, during the French Revolutionary Wars (see Chapter 17 to find out what these wars were all about). The Cape of Good Hope was such a handy base to have, halfway between Britain and India, that the British decided to keep it. The Dutch didn't like losing the Cape, and they liked it even less when the British abolished slavery in 1833. The Dutch lived by slavery. So they upped sticks and set off on the Great Trek to get away from the British and find some new Africans they could enslave.

The Dutch set up two states, called the Transvaal and the Orange Free State; while the British were left thinking 'Wouldn't it be a good idea if we could take over the Dutch areas?' but not doing anything about it. Yet.

Meanwhile, a small local tribe called the Zulu was doing rather well for itself under its – shall we say, totally ruthless? – king, Shaka and setting up a large empire which even made the Dutch very nervous. In 1879 the Dutch asked the British for help and the British Governor of Cape Colony, Sir Bartle Frere, came up with a Cunning Plan. 'Why not help the Dutch by picking a fight with the Zulu (who had no quarrel with the British) and wiping them out? The Dutch will be so grateful, they won't notice when we take their land over as well.' Not a great exponent of moral philosophy was Sir Bartle Frere. So in 1879, without any provocation, a British army under Lord Chelmsford invaded Zululand. And immediately hit trouble.

The Zulu wiped out an entire British army column at Isandhlwana. The British had guns, but they couldn't open the ammunition boxes because they hadn't brought the right spanners! The Zulu went on to attack the small base at Rorke's Drift – the battle re-enacted in the film *Zulu*, and yes the British (only a few of whom were actually Welsh) did hold them off, though by rifle fire rather than massed Welsh male voices singing (though that tactic would've done just as well). Bartle Frere's little plan was going badly wrong.

## Dr Livingstone, I presume?

In a story with precious few heroes, David Livingstone does stand out as a good guy. Everyone liked him – except slave traders. He was a doctor and a missionary, and he went to Africa to spread the gospel, heal the sick, and find out a bit more about the place. He managed all three. Unlike the people who came after him, Livingstone respected the Africans and didn't seek to disrupt their way of life. A tale exists that he once found some diamonds but threw them away because he knew what would happen if other people found them. He would have been horrified if he'd been able to see what would happen as a result of his reports. He got a taste of future events when he met Henry Morton Stanley, the Welshman sent out by the *New York Herald* to 'find Livingstone'. (Livingstone wasn't actually lost; it was just that everyone else wanted to know where he was.) Stanley was an appalling man, dishonest and a sadist to boot – thinking of anyone less suited to working with Livingstone is difficult. Livingstone died loved by all and was buried in Westminster Abbey; Stanley went on to help King Leopold of the Belgians set up a brutal tyranny in the Congo. He got a knighthood (a British one).

Ultimately, the British won: Even Lord Chelmsford couldn't lose a whole campaign with rifles and cannon against spears and shields. But even worse events were to come.

## The wild Boers

Two years later, the British marched into the two Dutch republics (see the section above). They thought the Dutch Boers (farmers) would be only too pleased for British protection, but they weren't. The Dutch fought back, and these farmers proved deadly accurate marksmen: They slaughtered the British at the Battle of Majuba Hill. The Brits pulled out of the Transvaal as fast as they could run. (For the second round of these Anglo-Boer wars, see the section 'The Anglo-Boer War: A hell of a lesson and a hell of a shock' a bit later on in this chapter.)

## One for you and two for me – cutting up Africa

After being cut to pieces by the Zulu and by the Boers, you'd think the British would have had enough of Africa, but you'd be wrong. Within a year they were back, this time in Egypt. Egypt was important to Britain because of the Suez Canal – easily the best way to Britain's colonies in India and the Far East, and the canal was run by the French and British governments. So, in effect, was Egypt, which is why an Egypt-for-the-Egyptians movement got going. So Gladstone, of all people (and see Chapter 18 to see why this detail was so surprising) sent in a military force under Sir Garnet Wolseley to deal with the insurrection. Which he did, though the British now found they were lumbered with all Egypt's problems, whether they liked it or not.

### Khartoum capers

Egypt's biggest problem was the Sudan, which was ruled by Egypt but didn't want to be. A big Muslim fundamentalist rising was going on in the Sudan, led by the Mahdi (a sort of Muslim Messiah). The government in Cairo sent an army into the Sudan to deal with the Mahdi under a British officer called Hicks, but Hicks and his men got wiped out (this was becoming a habit). Gladstone decided enough military disasters had occurred in Africa, and that Cairo (which was now controlled from London, don't forget) pulling out of the Sudan altogether would be best. Some Egyptian civil servants and Europeans still resided in the Sudanese capital, Khartoum, so in 1884 Gladstone sent General George Gordon to get them out. Bad choice.

Gordon was another religious fanatic, but this time a Christian one. He wanted a trial of strength with the Mahdi, so instead of evacuating Khartoum, he fortified it. He didn't have many troops but he hoped that Gladstone would send him some. Gladstone thought Gordon should have stuck to his instructions, and refused to send him any reinforcements – even though the press and the queen were screaming at him to do so. By the time he finally gave in and sent a force out to Khartoum, it was too late: The Mahdi had taken Khartoum and Gordon was dead. Public opinion in Britain was outraged (they changed Gladstone's nickname G.O.M – Grand Old Man – to M.O.G – Murderer of Gordon) but Gladstone thought Gordon deserved everything he'd got.

The other countries in Europe didn't see why the British should have all the fun in Africa. So the French started taking over North and West Africa, the Italians moved into Tripoli (Libya) and Ethiopia (though they moved out again pretty sharpish when the Ethiopians whipped them), and the Germans moved into East Africa. King Leopold of the Belgians took over the entire Congo basin as a sort of private estate and ran it as a massive slave labour camp. The period was a mad scramble – the Scramble for Africa.

The British, of course, didn't like all these foreigners moving in on 'their' area, so they started taking more land, too. Sometimes they set up companies, like the Royal Niger Company which created Nigeria by drawing straight lines on maps right through different tribal areas. This arbitrary creation is why Nigeria fell apart in civil war in 1967 and why Nigeria remains a deeply divided country to this day.

Cecil Rhodes, the gung-ho British prime minister of Cape Colony, dreamed of running a railway on British territory all the way 'from Cairo to the Cape'; unfortunately, the French had a similar idea, only they wanted French territory across Africa from West to East. Someone was going to have to give.

### Welcome to the Middle of Nowhere

The big showdown between the British and the French in Africa happened at a tiny place called Fashoda in the Sudan. There was nothing to see at Fashoda. Nobody wanted it, probably not even the Fashodans. But in 1898, Fashoda hit the headlines when it was the meeting place for two very different military expeditions:

- ✔ **The British, heading North to South:** A large British army under General Hubert Kitchener had set out to conquer the Sudan and to get revenge for what happened to Gordon (see the preceding section, 'Khartoum capers').

- ✔ **The French, heading West to East:** A small French expedition consisting of Captain Jean-Baptiste Marchand, three bearers and a dog, but with a very big French flag, was out to claim the Sudan for la Belle France.

Kitchener's men won the battle of Omdurman against the Sudanese due to them having taken the precaution of stocking up on machine guns for mowing the enemy down in large numbers. Just as they were settling down to their post-massacre tea and biccies, French Captain Marchand arrived and, after much bowing and saluting, told them, in a very high voice, to kindly get the hell off French territory – *Zut alors!* General Kitchener told the little chap that he admired his courage but that he had ten thousand British troops at his back plus a large number of cannon and, if Captain Marchand didn't turn round and march back the way he'd come pretty sharpish, he'd feel the imprint of some of their boots on his backside. 'Zis means war!' fumed Captain Marchand, as he sat down to write a very stiff postcard to Paris. And, unbelievably, the incident nearly did cause a war.

The French took *l'affaire Fachoda* very seriously (they still do). When the British had stopped laughing, they gently reminded the French that, at that stage, the French had only one friend in the world and that was the Russians, and they weren't going to lift a finger to help. The whole situation blew over. No, my friends, when it came to fighting wars in Africa with the whole world lined up against you, no one could touch the Brits. (You can see this British characteristic in the section 'The Anglo-Boer War – one hell of a lesson and one hell of a shock', later in this chapter.)

# The Colonies Grow Up – As Long As They're White

If you'd asked British people in the nineteenth century what their Empire was for, they'd say that they were governing all these people until they were ready to govern themselves. And if you asked when that might be, they'd point proudly to colonies that were doing just that:

- ✔ **Canada:** The French Canadians couldn't stand the English, English couldn't stand the French, and the whole place had had to be divided in two back in the eighteenth century. By 1867 the country's all joined together again and allowed to govern itself.

- ✔ **Australia:** Complete shambles, especially after the gold rush of 1851. Proper government introduced state by state until, in 1901, the Aussies are ready to rule themselves. We taught them to play cricket too. Bad mistake.

- ✔ **New Zealand:** Economy doing well. Lots of sheep. Gold there, too. More sheep. Ready to govern itself by 1907. Did I mention the sheep?

If you happened to point out that this steady march to self-government seemed a tad white, you'd get a lot of talk about how, of course, coloured people weren't so well advanced, and would take longer to be ready to govern themselves, and it wasn't in their nature, and so on and so on. And if you persisted, you might learn about the riots in Jamaica, which the British took as proof that some people (read that as non-white people) needed British rule (read that white British rule) for their own good. For the details about the events in Jamaica, see the sidebar 'Rum goings-on in Jamaica'.

## Rum goings-on in Jamaica

Jamaica's economy collapsed when Britain got rid of slavery in 1833 and didn't think through what to put in its place. By the 1860s the blacks in Jamaica were desperately poor and asked the government to reduce their rents. When the government said no, a group of women marched into Kingston and stoned some sentries. All hell broke loose. Very serious rioting broke out, with sickening violence. One man had his tongue torn out, another was thrown into a burning building, a third was literally hacked to pieces – and then Governor Edward Eyre took a hand.

Eyre hunted the rioters down and shot or hanged them without even stopping to inquire if they had had anything to do with riots. He even made the rioters hang each other. He had

a thousand homes burned to the ground and 600 people flogged, often with wire whips. He reckoned the trouble had all been caused by the Reverend G. W. Gordon, a member of Jamaica's House of Assembly – the Jamaican Parliament – so he had him arrested and hanged, and no, he didn't bother with a trial. The Reverend Gordon was black, you see.

What happened to Eyre? He was sacked and recalled to face trial. Some people thought he was a murderer, others thought he was a hero. The trial found him Not Guilty. One last point, though. Before the trouble, Jamaica had at least given black people the vote. Now they lost it. Hardly worth abolishing slavery, was it?

# Lion Tamers

A lot of people will tell you that the British won their Empire by using cannon and machine guns against people armed with spears and clubs, but that view is by no means always true. In many cases – India is a good example – they were up against people every bit as well armed and trained as they were. There were always people who were ready to stand up to the British and tell them where to get off.

## What about the Irish?

The Irish were very active in the Empire, but they didn't see why they should be treated as a colony at home. Despite the Act of Union (see Chapter 15 to see the shenanigans when *that* was passed), a British colony was more or less what Ireland was, with thousands of Irish tenants kept in utter poverty by landlords who often couldn't even be bothered to come and visit their own estates. So the Irish decided to initiate some changes.

They campaigned for a fairer system of rents – you know, a system that didn't involve them being evicted and having their cottages demolished by the local constabulary. The campaign got nasty: Landlords who evicted tenants were boycotted – completely shunned, as if they'd got the plague – and if that tactic didn't work they often got shot. Gladstone's government gave the police special powers to lock people up, but in the end, Parliament had to tackle the rent question, and it did, quite successfully. (If they'd tackled the problem to start with, they'd have saved everyone a lot of bother.)

By then, however, the Irish had moved on to the question of Home Rule, which didn't quite mean being independent, but did mean getting the Irish Parliament back (see Chapter 15 for why they'd lost it in the first place). The leader of the Home Rule League was an Irish Protestant MP called Charles Stuart Parnell (pronounced *Par*nul), and he knew just how to drive Prime Minister William Gladstone up the wall. He obstructed parliamentary business by just talking for hours on end (and when his throat gave way another Irish MP took over) until he forced Gladstone to do something about Home Rule. Parnell's own role had to stop when his love affair with Kitty O'Shea – er, *Mrs* Kitty O'Shea – became public knowledge, but by then Gladstone had decided that he'd always believed in Home Rule anyway. Unfortunately Parliament didn't agree: Gladstone split his party and in 1886 his Home Rule bill was thrown out. He tried again in 1893 with a stronger majority, but this time the House of Lords threw the bill out. The Irish were going to have to wait for Home Rule.

## The Anglo-Boer War: A hell of a lesson and a hell of a shock

The Boer republics in South Africa (see the earlier section 'Wider Still and Wider: Scrambling for Africa' for the background to this section) found they were sitting on some of the world's largest diamond mines. The British wanted them. Many British people went to work in the Boer republics, and the British government complained loudly that they weren't allowed to vote, but lack of franchise was just an excuse really. In 1895 London and Cape Town secretly backed an illegal raid into the Transvaal led by a hot-headed adventurer called Dr Starr Jameson – the idea was to spark off a rising by the British settlers, but the Transvaal government got wind of the plan and arrested the raiders. London and Cape Town then desperately tried to deny they'd known anything about the plan. No one was convinced.

The Boers reckoned (probably rightly) that the British would launch a full-scale invasion, so they decided to attack first. In 1899 they invaded British territory. At the Battle of Spion Kop, they slaughtered the Highlanders; they cooped the Brits up at Mafeking, Ladysmith, and Kimberley; and they so trounced the Soldiers of the Queen that the attack was, as Kipling said, one hell of a lesson.

Ultimately, sheer weight of numbers (the British outnumbered the Boers) was bound to tell, but even when the British had taken all the Boer towns, the Boer commandos (guerrillas) took to the veldt and started guerrilla raids. General Kitchener then came up with the idea of concentration camps. The idea was to herd the entire Boer population together where they couldn't hide or supply the commandos. Unfortunately, without proper water, sanitation, or food supplies thousands of people were bound to die in these camps, and they did. And not just white South Africans either: Black camps existed, too. Yes, Britain won the Anglo-Boer War, but she won precious little credit for doing so. The great Imperial Dream was turning into a nightmare.

# Part VI
# Don't Look Down: The Twentieth Century

The 5th Wave    By Rich Tennant

In August of 1939, British codebreakers recieve a stolen German cipher machine called, "Enigma". The machine was used to send coded information between German U-boats and land based command.

'We've pretty much deciphered how this thing works. One thing—we're still having trouble setting the bloody clock. Can't seem to stop it from showing "12:00" all the time!'

# In this part . . .

The assertive confidence of the nineteenth century was destroyed on the battlefields of the Great War. The Second World War seemed to change that self-image back at a stroke. The nation rallied to Churchill's voice, promising victory snatched from the jaws of defeat. When victory finally came, the British could continue for a while in the fond belief that they were still a force to be reckoned with in the nuclear age.

At the same time, Britain seemed a gloomy place after its wartime triumph. The bombsites gave way to dreary tower blocks and British industry was stricken with conflict and strikes. Old certainties were changing: Commonwealth people came to live in Britain, and Britain threw in its lot with the European Union.

The last years of the century saw Britain revive under two political giants: Margaret Thatcher and Tony Blair. Britain entered the twenty-first century as an ultra-modern, hi-tech country, but war in Iraq and Afghanistan sparked off old-style protest and controversy.

# Chapter 20

# The Great War: The End of Innocence – and Everything Else?

### In This Chapter

▶ Charting big changes and challenges happening in Britain before the war

▶ Understanding how the alliances and agreements made in the early nineteenth century came back to haunt Britain

▶ Witnessing the death of Franz Ferdinand and the start of the Great War

▶ Describing horrors on the battlefields

*P*ut simply, you cannot begin to understand modern Britain unless you look at the First World War. Every 11 November, the British wear red poppies and gather at war memorials to listen to words written in memory of the First World War dead. The date is the anniversary of the Armistice in 1918, and the poppies recall the only flowers that grew on the shell-torn battlefields. Schoolchildren regularly visit the cemeteries in France and Belgium where the graves of the dead of the First World War are still lovingly tended. For the story of modern Britain, start here.

## Indian Summer

To get an idea of why the war still matters so much, look at the world it ended. Peruse the pages in any book of old British photographs and you'll see scenes that look as if they've come straight from *The Railway Children* or Beatrix Potter, with tradesmen's horses and carts, pretty thatched cottages, and little girls in petticoats or boys in Eton collars playing in the road with hoops or tops and not a car in sight. The images look very innocent, but of course, more was going on in those photos than meets the eye.

## Go easy on the ice

Take the year 1912. The *Titanic* sank that year. The *Titanic* was the biggest ship afloat, had all the latest radio equipment, was fast, and the absolute height of luxury. Below the First Class cabins and ballrooms were the poky little holes for the steerage passengers, those people who could only afford the cheapest tickets. The *Titanic* represented Britain: Confidence in technology and class, yet felled by one of the oldest and simplest hazards in the book – an iceberg.

The same year another icy tragedy occurred. Captain Scott and his men died after failing to beat a Norwegian expedition to the South Pole. Although Scott became a national hero, in fact he largely had himself to blame. His expedition looked splendid and heroic, but was badly planned. Did Scott's ill-fated expedition also represent Britain – proud and confident, but fatally flawed and heading for catastrophe?

## Not so quiet on the home front

If you'd lived in Britain in the years before 1914, you wouldn't have thought her a very peaceful country. Serious industrial strikes were taking place, Parliament was in turmoil, women were demonstrating for the vote, and civil war even seemed about to break out in Ireland.

### Home Rule for Ireland?

In 1912 Parliament passed a Home Rule bill for Ireland (doing so meant giving Ireland a parliament though not actual independence. If you want to know a bit more about the background to Home Rule, have a look at Chapters 15 and 19). The Ulster Protestants were furious: They signed a Solemn League and Covenant saying they'd resist Home Rule tooth and nail, and they got hold of the guns to do it, too. The Catholics got guns as well, to fight *for* Home Rule (which, don't forget, was actually the law by then). The army was all ready to intervene, except that a number of British officers said they wouldn't fight against the Protestants – which is called taking sides, my friends. In fact, the only thing that stopped these events from becoming a shooting war was when the Germans invaded Belgium and everyone agreed to put that disagreement on hold.

### Gloves off in Parliament

Another hot topic in Britain was the budget. Now, you wouldn't think that a budget could cause so much fuss, but Lloyd George's 'People's Budget' of 1909 couldn't have caused more trouble if it had tried. The Liberal government, which had won a massive majority in the 1906 General Election, had already introduced Old Age Pensions, and the budget brought in the taxes to pay for them. For once, the rich were going to have to stump up most of the money. But the House of Lords weren't having this situation. They threw the budget out. 'Right,' said the House of Commons, 'they want a fight, do they? They can have one.

## Suffering Suffragettes

The Suffragettes showed incredible courage, but they almost certainly harmed their own cause. Most politicians were in favour of extending the vote to women as well as to the rest of the male working population, but they couldn't if doing so made the government look as if it was giving in to violence. The Suffragettes wouldn't see the struggle in those terms. When anyone – including her own daughter Sylvia – dared disagree with Mrs Pankhurst, she threw them out of the movement. (Sylvia's disagreement with her mum? She wanted to get the vote for working-class women: Mrs Pankhurst was more interested in getting the vote for middle-class ladies like herself.) Ultimately, the Suffragettes didn't get the vote for women at all; Mrs Millicent Fawcett's non-violent Suffragists did, and they got it by hard-nosed political bargaining. But they didn't smash windows or run under racehorses, so no one's heard of them.

An election – the Peers vs. the People – was called and the House of Commons introduced a bill saying that the House of Lords could never stop a budget ever again. In fact, the House of Lords would never be able to stop much of anything. A fine old battle ensued. The Lords had a choice: Either agree to the bill, or be swamped with Liberal peers, who'd do what the government said. The Lords gnarled and gnashed their teeth and stamped and said it wasn't fair, but in the end they had to give in. The House of Lords has never had that much power ever again.

### *Votes for women!*

If anyone knew how to behave properly, surely it was nice middle-class ladies having tea parties and asking the vicar if he'd like more sugar. Right? Yet in the 1910s, these ladies were precisely the ones who started smashing windows and heckling government ministers, and generally behaving in a most un-ladylike way. And all this bad behaviour was in the cause of Votes for Women.

Most books tell you that women didn't have the vote because men thought they were too hysterical or too easily swayed to be trusted with the responsibility, but, as with most things, the suffrage issue wasn't anywhere near that simple. For one thing, most men still didn't have the vote either, and for another, not only did women have the vote, but they were being elected in large numbers – in every sort of local election taking place. People had every reason to expect that the vote in Parliamentary elections would be next, if the women and their supporters kept the pressure up. Instead, Mrs Emmeline Pankhurst's Suffragettes seized the headlines by heckling Cabinet ministers at public meetings and getting themselves arrested. The Suffragettes staged demonstrations and bombed postboxes, and went on hunger strike in prison; the authorities used force-feeding – and that tactic isn't forcing your mouth open for a spoonful of casserole, it means ramming a rubber tube up your nose and pumping liquidised food down it. Force-feeding is a form of torture. But by the time war broke out in 1914, all the efforts of the Suffragettes had failed. The government was set against votes for women, and that was that.

# Alliance Building

As if all the problems going on at home weren't enough, things were looking very threatening abroad.

Back in 1870 the Germans had invaded France and within weeks they were shelling Paris (if you want to know why, see the companion volume *European History For Dummies*). Europe was shocked and Europe was awed. What was the Germans' secret?

- ✔ **Get military:** In Germany, *everything* was planned along military lines – schools, politics, police, even the railways. Other countries began to do the same. In Britain they even copied the German school system, with regular drill in the playground – for girls as well.

- ✔ **Get strong:** The French were strong, but the Germans were stronger. The key seemed to be to attack with overwhelming force.

- ✔ **Get fast:** Apart from the siege of Paris, the invasion was over in a matter of weeks. Lesson? If you got A and B right, you could have a short war, march into your enemy's capital and be home in time for tea – or Christmas.

To achieve a successful invasion, teaming up with someone else in an alliance seemed to be the trick. An alliance is basically an agreement that, if you hit me, my friend will come and hit you back. And of course, if your enemy gets an ally, you need to get one, too – preferably more than one. So in the years after 1870, a sort of square dance occurred in Europe with countries signing alliances with each other and then signing alliances with other countries until eventually the whole situation reduced to two big alliances glaring and snarling at each other, while rapidly arming to the teeth: Germany, Austria-Hungary, and Italy were on one side, and France and Russia were on the other.

## Loitering with entente

The British weren't keen on getting dragged into other people's quarrels, so they hung about on the edge in what they liked to call Splendid Isolation, which means they didn't have a friend in the world and pretended they didn't care. But actually, the British did care: Their army had done incredibly badly in the Boer War (Chapter 19 explains what this was all about). What if one of these alliances (the German-Austria-Hungary-Italy alliance or the France-Russian alliance) decided to attack the British Empire? Perhaps Britain needed to make one or two friends.

So the British signed two agreements, one with France and one with Russia. These agreements weren't alliances – the British still didn't like that idea – but they were ententes, 'understandings', clearing up leftover business from the Empire. The French entente sorted out who should have what in Africa, and the Russian entente a couple of years later cleared up the Great Game in Central Asia (if you're not sure what all these colonial problems were, you'll find them all explained in Chapter 19). But even if these understandings weren't officially alliances, when the Germans twice deliberately provoked the French in Morocco, the Brits stood by them so strongly that they might just as well have been.

## Going great guns – the naval race

One of the oddest things about the First World War is that the British had no particular quarrel with the Germans or their allies, and the Germans liked and admired the British. At one time, the British and the Germans looked as though they might have their own alliance – after all, who could've resisted the German army and the British navy? The trouble was the Kaiser. In some ways Kaiser Wilhelm II could hardly have been more English. His mother was Princess Victoria, eldest daughter of Queen Victoria and Prince Albert. (You can meet them properly in Chapter 18.) When his grandma, Queen Victoria, lay dying, he rushed to be with her – she died in his arms. He was an honorary admiral of the Royal Navy and very proud of the post: He even had a desk made of oak from Nelson's *Victory*. (See Chapter 17 for more on Nelson.) But Wilhelm was not English, he was German, and he never forgot that fact. Why shouldn't Germany have a share in England's glory – her 'place in the sun'? In response to that question, Wilhelm II was thrilled when Germany started getting colonies in Africa and he started building up the German navy.

If you really wanted to scare the British, you threatened their naval supremacy. With such a small army, the navy was all the British had to make them feel safe; especially after HMS *Dreadnought* was launched in 1905. Until then, ships could either be fast and light (first on the scene, not many guns) or powerful but slow (big guns, no handbrake turns). But *Dreadnought* had big guns and thick armour plating and it was fast. Suddenly dreadnoughts were all that mattered and the British got building. But so did the Germans.

'What do you want all those ships for?' asked the British government. 'Well, we have colonies, too, and we have a coastline to defend, don't forget,' said the Germans. 'Coastline my foot,' said the British, 'you want to invade us!' Suddenly everyone was reading spy stories like Erskine Childers's *Riddle of the Sands*, all about sinister Germans planning to invade Britain with thousands of boats. Britain must out-build the Germans. Four dreadnoughts now, said the government – which had a big social programme to fund as well – and four later. 'We want eight!' clamoured the public, 'and we won't wait!' So eight dreadnoughts they got. Ultimately, the British did out-build the German fleet, but the idea that the Germans were the Enemy got fixed in the British public's mind.

## Sir Edward Grey and the street lights

On the night that the British ultimatum to Germany expired, Sir Edward Grey, the British Foreign Secretary, stood looking out of the window of the Foreign Office watching the street-lighter going along lighting the gas street lamps with his pole. 'They are putting out the lamps all over Europe,' Sir Edward remarked; 'we shall not see them lit again in our lifetime.' This lovely quote catches the moment perfectly.

Needless to say, some historians have said no evidence exists that he ever said it, and in any case why should the sight of lamps being lit put him in mind of lamps going out? But the truth doesn't really matter. For people like Sir Edward, who had a better idea of what was coming than the ordinary people who would soon be rushing to join up, this moment was the end of an era. And anyway, why shouldn't he have thought of it?

## *Bullets in Bosnia*

And then the world situation exploded, quite unexpectedly, in the glorious summer of 1914. Archduke Franz Ferdinand of Habsburg, nephew to the Austrian emperor and, thanks to a series of assassinations and suicides, the heir to the Austrian throne, was gunned down in Sarajevo by a Bosnian Serb, Gavrilo Princip. The Serbs wanted Ferdinand because they reckoned Bosnia was Serb territory and the archduke had deliberately chosen the most important date in the Serb calendar, 28 June, the anniversary of the Battle of Kosovo – which was also his wedding anniversary – to review what they called the Austrian army of occupation. Plenty of important assassinations had occurred recently, including an American president and numerous Russian ministers, so what was so special about this one that made it the catalyst for the First World War?

- ✔ **The Austrians** were longing for an excuse to hit their old enemies, the Serbs.
- ✔ **The Germans** said they would support the Austrians whatever they decided to do.
- ✔ **The Serbs** knew they could count on their old allies, the Russians.
- ✔ **The Russians** had old scores to settle with the Austrians.

All of these reasons are fine if you're going to have a war between the Austrians and the Serbs, with the Germans and the Russians joining in. But Russia would want its ally, France, to help, and the Germans would be caught in the middle. But the Germans had a Plan.

## General von Schlieffen's cunning plan and Britain's ultimatum

Chief of the German General Staff Count Alfred von Schlieffen had devised a clever strategy, which went something like this:

1. We are going to have to fight the Russians and the French.

2. So why not knock France out quickly and then concentrate on Russia?

Schlieffen reckoned the way to knock France out was to invade through Belgium. No one, not even the French, put up defences against the Belgians.

Unfortunately, a problem was evident in Schlieffen's plan: Britain. The British had helped create Belgium in the first place. Belgium is just the place to be if you're thinking of invading England, so the British reckoned having a small Belgium that couldn't harm anyone was better than having the area controlled by big countries trying to dominate the world. In the past, those big countries meant the Spanish or the French, but in 1914, it meant the Germans.

When the Germans invaded Belgium in August 1914, the British government told them to clear out fast, and when the Germans said Nuts! – or *Nüsse!* – Britain declared war.

# The Great War

No one called the conflict the Great War to start with. The Great Punch-up if you like. All those years of tension, of telling people to beware of the Big Bad Germans or the Russian Menace – now at last the chance had come to have a crack at the other guy and show him what British or French or Serb or Russian or German men were made of.

Everyone thought the war would be over by Christmas. Why? Because so many wars recently had been very short. And with all those modern trains and motor cars everyone thought they'd be in the enemy's capital within a week. No wonder people were afraid they might miss the action. So what went wrong? Two things:

✔ **The Russians got their act together.** Their doing so was a shock because the Russians hadn't been in time for the start of a war since the eighteenth century. But somehow the Russians managed to get their troops into uniform and on the right trains with boots, rifles, and clean vests within three weeks. Which was a lot faster than the Germans had banked on.

> ✔ **The Schlieffen Plan didn't work.** The Germans invaded Belgium all right, but then they ran into the British. The British army was so small it wasn't even called an army, it was the British Expeditionary Force, but it was highly professional, and it held up the Germans long enough to give the French time to rush up from Paris.

And at that point, both sides dug in.

## Your Country Needs YOU!

Someone once said Lord Horatio Herbert Kitchener, the British war hero and Secretary for War in 1914, may not have been a great general, but he made a great poster. You've almost certainly seen the famous one of him pointing and saying that Your Country Needs YOU! But be fair: He was one of the first people to recognise that the war was not going to be over by Christmas and that Britain was going to need a lot more troops. And that need meant getting a million volunteers: Hence the posters.

The Suffragettes also helped the war effort. They organised a campaign of handing out white feathers for cowardice to young men out of uniform – even if it transpired they were soldiers home on leave or in essential war work at home. But women were needed in other ways, too. In 1916 the government introduced conscription, so women had to replace the men in the factories and on the land. To everyone's surprise – including their own, sometimes – women showed they could run machinery or drive tractors just as well as men. The work was dangerous, too: In munitions factories, you could be arrested just for carrying a match – hundreds of women were killed in accidents.

The Defence of the Realm Act (DORA) gave the government emergency powers to take over factories and control production. Pubs had to close early so that the workers could go back to work sober, and the post and press were closely censored. When the Germans started torpedoing supply ships, the government introduced strict rationing and everyone, from the king and queen downwards, started growing food on small allotments. War was now total.

## Death in the trenches

Even though people were feeling the pinch at home, they had no conception of what the men at the front were experiencing. In the west, the trenches went in an unbroken line all the way from the Swiss border to the English Channel. The British manned the trenches in northern France and Belgium, where a bulge, or salient, existed around the town of Ypres. German shelling flattened the town, and the salient was not a popular place to be stationed because the Germans could fire on you from three sides.

The trenches were deep, and they went in a sort of zigzag pattern, offering corners to hide round if the enemy happened to get in. If you weren't actually on duty, you could rest in a dugout – a sort of room buried deep underground (Figure 20-1 shows a cross-section of a British trench). At first, the British soldiers went into action wearing caps, but so many of them got shot in the head peeping over the top of the trenches that in 1916 the army issued them with steel helmets.

Going on patrol into no man's land, the area between the two front lines, was the most common type of action. In some places, the front lines were so close that the soldiers could hear the other side talking. In 1915 the Germans used poison gas for the first time. The British and French complained bitterly, and then started using it themselves. So on top of everything else, soldiers had to carry a gas mask and know how to put it on in seconds. Failure meant a ghastly, choking death.

The generals on both sides were completely thrown by trench warfare. Everything they'd learnt at staff college said that the attackers always had the advantage, so they hurled more and more men at the other side's trenches. You started by shelling – for some reason they thought that would cut the barbed wire – and then your men advanced behind an artillery barrage. In theory, that tactic meant that the shells kept pace ahead of your men, but all too often in practice the men were blown to bits by their own barrage. Even more deadly were the machine guns, just one or two of which could wipe out whole battalions, especially if they got stuck on the barbed wire.

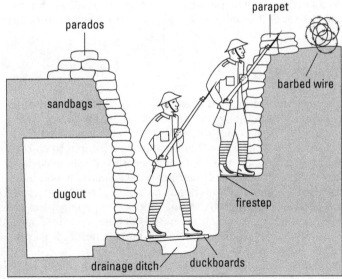

**Figure 20-1:** Cross-section of a trench.

## Death in the Dardanelles

The First Lord of the Admiralty, Winston Churchill, had a nearly brilliant plan: Breaking the trench deadlock by attacking Germany's new ally, Turkey (no one thought much of the Turks as fighters; they were wrong). Then the allies could send troops to help the Russians, squeeze the Germans so tight they'd have to divert troops from the west, and hey presto! The war would be won. Even better, to attack Turkey, you only had to take the narrow entrance to the Black Sea known as the Dardanelles. You know what they say about the best-laid plans.

First the British used the navy. The Turks were caught completely on the hop. This strategy might have worked if one of the ships hadn't hit a mine. So they pulled the navy out and decided to try again, this time with the army. No one at allied HQ seems to have pointed out that they'd rather lost the element of surprise. When the allied troops (consisting of British and French soldiers and a substantial contingent of ANZAC – the Australian and New Zealand Army Corps) did land, at Gallipoli, they found to their amazement that the Turks were ready and knew how to use a machine gun. The allies were never able to move inland from the beaches, and after spending the better part of a year pinned down, losing thousands of men, they pulled out. That withdrawal, at least, caught the Turks by surprise.

If you've seen the film *Gallipoli*, you know that Australians portray this battle as their men dying because of stupid British generals. In fact, all the allied troops suffered, and once the Turks knew they were coming, the allied generals could do very little. The Dardanelles was an attack that either worked in the first surprise, or it didn't work at all. The attack didn't work at all.

## Death at sea

Before the war, the British had been obsessed with German battleships, but German submarines actually proved the most deadly threat. The Germans declared that they'd sink any ship in British waters, even neutrals, and they did. So many ships went down that the government had to start rationing food and the British had to sail in convoys with warship escorts. In 1915 the Germans sank the British passenger liner SS *Lusitania*, which had sailed from New York with a number of Americans on board. The Germans had been tipped off, probably correctly, that the ship was carrying arms, but America was outraged. A couple of small sea battles occurred in the South Atlantic, and the German raider *Emden* did a lot of damage before it was finally sunk.

The only major naval battle of the war was at Jutland, off the Danish coast, in 1916. If you decide who won by the number of ships lost, then the Germans won; if you decide by what happened next, then the British won – because the Germans sailed back into harbour and never came out again except to surrender at the end of the war. Nevertheless, Jutland was a bad day for the

British. Not only did they lose contact with the German fleet at the crucial point, but the Germans found that, when they fired at a certain angle, the lightly armoured British battle cruisers blew up. Just when you don't need it, you discover a design fault.

## Death on the Somme

The Somme made all the difference to the conclusion of the First World War. The battle began in mid-summer and lasted into the autumn, but the first day, 1 July 1916, is what really matters. On this day, the soldiers – most of them volunteers from 1914 taking part in their first big battle – were arranged in pals' battalions, so called because lads who worked in the same factory or lived in the same town were all together in the same units. The plan was to launch a massive attack against the German lines near the river Somme. Because the British commanders were worried that these young, inexperienced soldiers might end up running all over the place, they gave orders for them to walk. One officer even gave them a couple of footballs to kick about, to jolly them along.

The idea of the Somme was that British artillery would flatten the German trenches with the biggest bombardment in history. The bombardment lasted a week, and you could hear it in London. The Germans said the bombardment resembled hell on earth. But their dugouts were deeper and stronger than the British realised: They sat there until the guns stopped, and then they ran back up to the top with their machine guns. There they saw long lines of British soldiers walking slowly towards them. So they shot them down.

Books list the number of casualties as 60,000: As a rough rule, that figure means a third dead, a third permanently maimed, and a third wounded. So 20,000 died, in one day! And thanks to the pals' battalions, some communities lost *all* their young men.

The British couldn't believe the outcome of the Somme. What about all those promises their generals had made? Whose stupid idea had it been to tell the men to walk? Who'd said that shelling could cut barbed wire? The Somme made the British begin to ask some very serious questions about the people at the top.

## Death in the mud

One last nightmare occurred for the British. In 1917 Field Marshal Douglas Haig, the British commander on the Western Front, attacked the Germans in Belgium, near the village of Passchendaele (pronounced *passion dale*). Rain poured down and the shells turned the battlefield to mud. Not football-pitch-mud, or even assault-course-mud. We're talking mud so thick and deep that you sank in it up to your chest – and plenty of men drowned in it. The battle went on for months, and got nowhere. One staff officer, fresh from grappling with the paper clips back at Chateau Comfy HQ, came visiting the front line to see what it was like. He stared in horror. 'Did we send men to fight in that?' he asked. Yes, my friend; you did.

## The war ends

In April 1917, the United States declared war on Germany. The Germans reckoned they had one last chance of winning before the Americans started arriving in large numbers. The Germans were so short of food thanks to the British navy blockading their coast that they could not survive another winter. So in March 1918, the Germans launched their last, huge attack. And that attack worked.

They pushed through the British lines (on the Somme, ironically) and charged on towards Paris. It was like 1914 all over again. Only this time, they ran out of steam, and fresh American troops barred their way. The British recovered and started rolling up the German advance. The allied counter-attack in 1918 was one of the most dramatically successful campaigns in British military history (and if you're interested in knowing the others, see *British Military History For Dummies* (Wiley)). By the autumn, the Germans were in full retreat and asked for a ceasefire, or armistice. The allies agreed, and on 11 November 1918, at 11 o'clock in the morning, the Great War ended.

## Field Marshal Haig – lion or donkey?

Field Marshal Sir Douglas Haig was the British commander on the Western Front. People still argue bitterly about him. Haig was obsessed with winning the war, even if that victory had to be by attrition – killing as many people as you can until there are more of you left than there are of them. The Germans couldn't understand him. They admired the courage of the British soldiers, but thought they were 'lions led by donkeys', as one of them put it.

In the 1960s show *Oh! What a Lovely War*, Haig appears as a bumbling murderer, which is pretty much how most people saw him by then. But soldiers at the time adored him. After the war, he devoted his life to working for the men who'd been wounded in the trenches, and it was the Earl Haig Fund that produced the poppies people wore every November. Historians have begun to rethink Haig. He'd learned his soldiering in the days of red coats and cavalry charges; now he was fighting a new kind of war with tanks and gas and aeroplanes. He needed some time to understand that war, but then who didn't? By the end of the war he'd mastered the new techniques and inflicted a crushing defeat on the Germans. But that wouldn't make a good musical so no-one knows about it. Except you!

# Chapter 21

# Radio Times

· · · · · · · · · · · · · · · · · · · · · · · · · · · · · · · · · · · · · · · · · · ·

## In This Chapter

▶ Considering the troubles that plagued Britain at home and abroad

▶ Introducing Britain in the 1920s, from salad days to the slump

▶ Watching events leading up to the Munich Conference and war

▶ Understanding why Britain fights a Second World War

· · · · · · · · · · · · · · · · · · · · · · · · · · · · · · · · · · · · · · · · · · ·

After the horrors of the trenches, Britain was in a collective state of shock. But even as the British began to create the culture of Remembrance they found that the world wasn't going to stand still. With great empires destroyed and the United States retreating back into isolation, Britain and France had to lead the world, this time through the League of Nations – whether they liked doing so or not. And problems existed at home: Ireland became a bloodbath, and in 1926, the whole country ground to a halt in Britain's first ever General Strike. Not all the news was bad. For many people the 1920s were a prosperous time, but this reprieve was relatively short-lived and left the British ill-prepared when the Crash came. The Depression hit Britain badly, especially the old industrial areas in Scotland, Wales, Belfast, and the north of England. The whole political system seemed to go into meltdown, with a National Government and an aggressive Fascist party: Even the monarchy seemed about to fall. Overshadowing all of these issues was the growing threat of Hitler's Germany.

## Big Troubles

The British had won the First World War, but they had no time to rest on their laurels – or even to catch their breath. Britain was already sending troops into Russia to fight against Lenin's *Bolsheviks* (Communists) and into Turkey to keep the Turks and Greeks apart. And soon they had to deal with serious troubles closer to home.

## Remembrance

Every town and village has its war memorial erected after the First World War. The British talked of a 'lost generation' of young men killed in the trenches, and even if the reality wasn't strictly accurate, the idea was right. The king unveiled the simple and dignified Cenotaph in Whitehall, and for years men would remove their hats in respect when they passed that memorial. In beautiful war cemeteries designed by the architect Sir Edwin Lutyens, the dead lay in neat rows, private soldiers next to officers, each with his own simple memorial stone. Most striking of all, an unidentified soldier was brought back from France and buried with full honours at Westminster Abbey – the Unknown Soldier. You can still see these remembrance ceremonies each year, with their wreaths of red poppies and the trumpeters poignantly blowing the Last Post. Remember these scenes when you wonder why the British were so keen to avoid a second war only twenty years later.

# Ireland – the Troubles

Ireland had been arguing for increased self-government for years (see Chapter 19 for some of the background here). 'England's difficulty', goes an old Irish saying, 'is Ireland's opportunity', and at Easter 1916, with Britain concentrating on the war with Germany, the IRB (Irish Republican Brotherhood) staged a rising in Dublin to demand Irish independence. The Brits put the rising down without too much difficulty: The Dubliners were so angry with the rebels – their boys were fighting in France and here were these IRB stabbing them in the back – that the British soldiers had to protect the IRB prisoners from being torn to pieces by the crowds. Then the Brits blew their position of advantage, by putting the prisoners in front of a court martial and shooting them. One of the ringleaders, James Connolly, was so badly wounded they had to carry him to his execution strapped to a chair. The men became instant martyrs. In the 1918 election, Sinn Fein, which had been a small nationalist party, became the biggest political party in Ireland. But instead of going to London, the Sinn Fein MPs went to Dublin and set up the *Dail Eireann* – the first parliament of an independent Ireland. And that parliament had Michael Collins and his IRA (Irish Republican Army) to defend it.

The fighting that ensued became known as *The Troubles*. This conflict was a very dirty terrorist war. The British brought in undercover agents and auxiliary troops, nicknamed Black and Tans from the khaki and black of their uniforms. These troops shot first and asked questions later. What the British didn't know was that Michael Collins had spies inside British HQ in Dublin Castle. He knew where they lived. The IRA shot policemen and ambushed British soldiers and Black and Tans. On 21 November 1920, 'Bloody Sunday', fourteen top British undercover agents were murdered by Michael Collins's men. That same afternoon, British troops and police opened fire on the crowd watching a football match at the Croke Park stadium in Dublin and killed twelve people.

The Croke Park massacre is one of the most emotive and controversial moments in the history of Ireland's struggle with Britain. Historians – and plenty of other people – still argue about whether the police and army were deliberately taking revenge for that morning's murders of the British agents, or whether it was an operation to grab suspects that went horribly wrong. Either way, the massacre at Croke Park certainly fuelled anti-British feeling in Ireland – and it hardly needed extra fuelling in the first place.

But events didn't all go the IRA's way. In May 1921 120 IRA men were surrounded and forced to surrender at the Dublin Customs House. 'Now,' said British Prime Minister David Lloyd George, 'we have murder by the throat!' He wasn't entirely wrong. Each side was exhausted, and in 1921 Lloyd George offered talks. Eamon de Valera, President of the Dail, accepted but he sent Michael Collins to London instead of going himself. He had an inkling of what the British would say.

Sinn Fein wanted the whole island of Ireland to be independent, but the British would never let them have the Protestant north, and de Valera knew it. Sinn Fein either had to accept partition or go back to war. Collins brought the treaty back to Dublin and told the Dail to accept it; the offer was the best they'd get:

✔ **Six Protestant counties of Ulster** to be given the option to remain part of the United Kingdom (which meant they would).

✔ **Rest of Ireland** to be a Free State under the British Crown. Members of the Dail to swear an oath of loyalty to King George V. No Irish Republic.

The Dail was split down the middle. They voted for the Treaty by 64-57, but de Valera resigned in protest, and the anti-Treaty members walked out. Civil war erupted all over again, the pro-Treaty IRA against anti-Treaty IRA, and this time the fighting was even more savage. The pro-Treaty men won, but Collins didn't live to see that victory. He was shot in the head in an anti-Treaty ambush in County Cork, on his way to try to make peace.

You can get an idea of this appallingly violent period in Ireland's history in two films, *Michael Collins* and *The Wind that Swept the Barley* (though beware: Each film has some important inaccuracies), or you can find out more in *Irish History For Dummies* (Wiley).

Too bloody for you? Grit your teeth; more violence lies ahead.

## India – massacre at Amritsar

By the First World War, a nationalist movement was growing in India, led by the Indian National Congress (or just 'Congress'). Initially, the Congress wanted Indians to have more of a role in government, but by the 1910s, they were getting nowhere – and getting impatient. British women had been given the vote for working in the factories, but thousands of Indians had died fighting for

Britain in the trenches and London still couldn't bring itself to give them a bit of Home Rule. 'Right,' said Congress, at its increasingly big public meetings, 'No more Mr Nice Guy. We want self-rule and we want it now.' The British hit back, locking up anyone who criticised British rule and in April 1919 Congress announced it was going to hold a big meeting in Amritsar in the Punjab. 'Oh no, you don't,' said the State Governor, who had the two main speakers arrested and banned political meetings.

All hell broke loose: Rioting, arson, and five Europeans dead. 'Right,' says the local military commander, General Reginald Dyer, 'it's time someone restored a bit of order round here.' So when he heard of a large gathering in an enclosed courtyard called the Jallianwala Bagh he marched there with 90 soldiers, lined the soldiers up in front of the main entrance, and opened fire. Not a warning shot (Dyer didn't give any sort of warning) but 1,650 rounds of ammunition, repeated firing, into the thickest part of the completely unarmed crowd. The official figure was 379 dead (some battles have fewer casualties than that): The real figure was probably over 500. To get an idea of the scene, you can see Richard Attenborough's 1982 film *Gandhi*.

Dyer's actions didn't exactly restore order: The rioting got worse, the British resorted to public floggings, and Dyer had to face an enquiry. The enquiry was appalled, but the Brits in India (and quite a few of them in Britain) thought Dyer was a hero, giving Congress a lesson it wasn't going to forget in a hurry.

## Problems back home

Back at home, no sooner was the First World War over than the unions came out on strike. In 1919 the railway men downed tools; the following year the miners did so, and the government had to declare a state of emergency. In 1921 a national strike nearly occurred in support of the miners and was only called off at the last minute.

The cause of all the trouble was that people felt that the rich had virtually declared war on the poor: Cutting wages and laying people off work. Then in London in 1921, the rates, taxes levied by local councils for public services, were standardised, which was fine if you lived in Kensington but desperately unfair on the poor people who lived in the East End. In Poplar, one of the poorest East End boroughs, the local Labour council led by George Lansbury (later leader of the Labour Party and grandfather of actress Angela Lansbury) actually went to prison rather than set a rate that they thought was unfair. The country seemed to be sliding into a very polite, civilised, and thoroughly British form of Class War.

### Shady goings-on at Number 10

The prime minister was still David Lloyd George, but he was in a very odd position. He was a Liberal at the head of a Liberal-Conservative coalition, but by 1922, he was the only Liberal left in it. Lloyd George was a brilliant politician – dynamic, passionate (just ask his secretaries), and a man who got things done – but you wouldn't want to buy a used car from him. He had a political fund called the Lloyd George Fund, and in 1922, they found out how he'd raised the money. Lloyd George was selling titles. Fancy being Baron Bloggs? Cost you £80,000, cash in hand. Knighthood? Just for you, £12,000, no questions asked. (Mind you, in 2006 Tony Blair's government was accused of much the same thing. Some things never change.)

For the Conservatives, this revelation was the last straw. Lloyd George had become an embarrassment. At a secret meeting at the Carlton Club, the Conservatives decided to ditch their too-liberal prime minister. They forced an election and won it. But then the Conservative prime minister, Stanley Baldwin, did a very silly thing. In 1923 he called another election. He had his reasons for doing so, but that didn't help the outcome: Labour and the Liberals outnumbered the Conservatives. Baldwin had to go, and Labour took office.

### A message from your friendly Bolsheviks

King George V was worried about having a Labour government, but he needn't have been. Anyone less like Lenin's Bolsheviks than the smartly dressed Labour ministers who went to kiss hands and take tea with the king in 1924 would be difficult to imagine. James Ramsay MacDonald was prime minister, and he wanted better housing and schools, but wasn't going to start staging revolutions. Labour was in a minority, so in October 1924, MacDonald called yet another election to see whether he could get a few more MPs. And a very strange thing happened. The right-wing *Daily Mail* reported a scoop. The paper published a letter from Soviet Foreign Minister Gregori Zinoviev to the British Communist Party saying that now was the time to stage the Revolution in Britain. 'Comrades!' the letter said (or something similar), 'Let capitalist blood flow in the streets of St James's, string up the rich on the lamp posts of Park Lane, and tell everyone to vote Labour.' A reading of 8.7 registered on the Richter Scale as the collective jaws of the middle classes hit the floor, and the blood of retired colonels boiling over caused a sharp rise in atmospheric pressure. In the election, the Conservatives stormed home, Labour was out of office, and the Liberals virtually disappeared. And the letter? It was a forgery – of course.

### A general strike

The class tension climaxed in May 1926 – in the mines. The mine owners wanted to cut wages and lengthen the working day, so the government set up a commission to look into the issue. But when the government, too, recommended lower wages and longer hours, the miners came out on strike, and this time they weren't alone: The Trades Union Congress (TUC) called a General Strike to support them.

The General Strike lasted nine days. The trains, presses, gas, electricity, post – everything stopped. The strike was particularly solid in South Wales and Scotland, so the government declared a state of emergency and sent in troops. Home Secretary Winston Churchill put armoured cars onto the streets, and his newspaper, the *British Gazette*, accused the strikers of planning a revolution. No evidence exists of this plan. Apart from a few violent incidents, the whole event was remarkably relaxed. Middle-class volunteers lent a hand trying to keep services going, driving trains and loading mail bags, and when the police got bored watching the strikers, they challenged them to games of football.

Gradually the men drifted back to work. On 20 May the TUC called off the strike. The miners were furious. They stayed out on strike until the end of the year, when they, too, couldn't afford to stay out any longer. They had to go back to work, and they had to accept the longer hours for less pay. The workers had had their General Strike – and they'd lost.

# The Years That Roared

The decade following the Great War was dubbed the Roaring Twenties. If you had the money – and as Britain slowly recovered from the war, more and more people did – you could have a ball.

## Party time!

The leg-kicking Charleston hit Britain in 1925, just the thing for all those young women known as flappers in their slimline dresses and cloche hats. In 1928 young women over twenty-one even got the vote. In-between dance dates, you could tune into the BBC (motto: Nation Shall Speak Unto Nation) and catch your favourite dance bands on the wireless. Soon people were regularly attending the cinema, also known as the kinema or the Picture Palace, where they could watch some of the biggest Hollywood stars, like Stan Laurel or Charlie Chaplin, who happened to be British. People wanted to pretend they lived in the country, so they built neat semi-detached houses with mock-Tudor beams and gables in leafy suburbs, with front gardens, garages for all those affordable new motor cars, trees planted along the road, and a handy tennis club or golf course. In 1925 Chancellor of the Exchequer Winston Churchill announced that Britain was going back onto the Gold Standard. Yes, for those who were doing well – which tended to mean people in the southern half of England – life in the 1920s felt very good.

## Party's over: The slump

Wall Street crashed in October 1929, and the world's economy slumped. Within weeks, no one was trading with anyone, and firms were going bust all over Europe. By 1930 Britain had two million unemployed people. Labour Prime Minister Ramsay MacDonald set up a commission to figure out how to put Britain back on a solid economic footing, and he didn't like its findings one bit. The commission reported that the only way out was big tax rises plus massive cuts in government spending, including 20 per cent off the Dole. You couldn't ask a Labour government – a *Labour* government – to cut back on help for the unemployed.

The Cabinet refused to accept the commission's recommendations, and MacDonald resigned, but the king said he had to stay. So MacDonald formed a National Government with the Conservatives. Or, as his Labour colleagues would've said, MacDonald sold out to the Tories. In effect, MacDonald was heading a Conservative government. The Labour Party hasn't forgiven him to this day. When Tony Blair's critics accused him of getting too close to the Tories towards the end of his time as prime minister, they even nicknamed him 'Ramsay MacBlair'!

### Hard times

Imagining the despair of the Depression years is difficult nowadays. Looking back, people said the period was worse than the war because at least you knew the war would end one day, but the Depression seemed able to go on forever. The heavy industrial areas – coal mines in Wales and Yorkshire, shipyards in Belfast, Glasgow, and Tyneside – were hardest hit. To get unemployment benefit, you had to submit to the humiliating Means Test in which officials came into your home and probed into every detail of your private life to work out how much help you were entitled to. In 1936 out-of-work shipbuilders in Jarrow decided to march all the way down to London to shame the government into doing something for them. The government didn't take a blind bit of notice.

### Black shirts and black eyes

Oswald Mosley was an up-and-coming Labour MP who got frustrated with MacDonald, and in 1931, he set up the New Party to offer a dynamic new way forward: Massive government spending, work for the unemployed, and a general national revival. And no Irish or Jews. In case anyone hadn't guessed yet, he renamed his party the British Union of Fascists (BUF) and grew a little moustache. He couldn't wear a proper uniform because the government banned them, so he had to make do with a black jumper. In 1936 Mosley led a march into the most Jewish part of the East End – the BUF didn't do subtlety – which started a massive street battle with the Communist Party. The next year, he got hit on the head by a brick. Makes you proud to be British.

# How Goes the Empire?

'How goes the Empire?' is officially what King George V is supposed to have said on his death bed in 1936 (although the other version, 'Bugger Bognor!' sounds more likely, especially if you've ever been there). And the answer to that question was: Not very well.

## The king who never was

When the British finally learned that their new king, Edward VIII, had been going out with Wallis Simpson, who was (a) divorced, (b) married (and about to be divorced again), and (c) American, they found it hard to know which detail was the worst. Although the Church of England had been founded by a royal divorcee, it wasn't keen to be headed by another one. The Bishop of Bradford spilled the beans by saying in a sermon that the king (who was also Head of the Church, don't forget) had a lot of serious thinking to do and that he might take a peek at the seventh commandment while he was at it, which is not the one about making a graven image.

Edward refused to stop seeing Mrs S, but as the prime minister pointed out, no way could Mrs S be crowned as his queen: The Church wouldn't have it, the British people wouldn't have it (even though they didn't really mind him marrying her), and above all the Empire had made it very clear that it would not have it. So Edward had no way out except to abdicate and hand over to his shy, stammering brother, the Duke of York, who became King George VI. So if you come across an Edward VIII coronation mug, keep hold of it because they're very rare. At the time, people were very angry at losing Edward – he'd been a popular Prince of Wales. But Edward was a weak character, and he and Wallis soon fell under Hitler's spell. When war broke out, the government packed him off to the Bahamas, safely out of the way. The royal family never forgave him – or (especially) her.

# Palestine – the double-promised land

In the First World War, the British promised the Arabs, including the Palestinians, independence in return for their help against the Turks.

'Okay, you're on,' the Arabs said, and they started ambushing trains and starring in *Lawrence of Arabia*. Meanwhile, a very influential Jewish group, the Zionists, who wanted to go back home to the Promised Land, asked the British if they'd help and the British, mindful of the Zionists' influence in Washington, said yes. So now the British had promised the same land to two different groups, the Palestinians and the Jews.

Guess what the British did? They broke both promises. They didn't set up a Jewish homeland, and they didn't give the Palestinians independence either. Instead they took Palestine over themselves. They let some Jews in to settle, but when the Palestinians complained of being swamped, they stopped any more Jews from coming. Before long, Jews and Palestinians had started shooting each other – or any British soldiers who tried to get in the way.

# Gandhi

After what happened at Amritsar (refer to the earlier section 'India – massacre at Amritsar'), the Indian Congress wanted the British out, and they wanted them out now. Mohandas Gandhi (known as the Mahatma Gandhi), leader of the Indian nationalist movement, then came up with his idea for how to do gain independence: Non-violence. If the British used violence, as Gandhi knew they would, the Indians would just take it.

The Indians started by refusing to pay their taxes and ignoring the Prince of Wales when he came to visit, but Gandhi also set out deliberately to provoke the British. In 1930, he led a 200-mile march to the sea to gather natural salt, which was a British monopoly. The police beat him and his followers savagely and threw Gandhi into jail. The following year, Gandhi was an honoured guest in London, meeting the prime minister and taking tea with the king. Basically Gandhi held out by refusing to compromise. The only fly in the ointment was whether or not to have a separate Muslim state. Gandhi said no, but some of the Muslims were keen on the idea. The Labour Party came round to Indian independence, but in 1931 the National Government was created (see the earlier section 'Party's over: the slump' for more info on this unusual government), and they weren't going to give up India. So the protests and the civil disobedience went on. When the Second World War broke out, Gandhi told his followers to have nothing to do with the conflict. The British would have to make do without them. So the British locked him up again.

# The Road to Munich

Britain's policy of appeasing Nazi Germany is probably the most controversial and most misunderstood episode in British twentieth-century history – possibly in all British history. 'Couldn't they see?' people ask. 'Why didn't the British stand up to Hitler while they had the chance?' But for many reasons – beyond the claims of cowardice, incompetence, or complicity – appeasement seemed like a viable option:

## Out for a – *duck!*

The British even managed to anger their white colonies, through cricket, of all things. In 1931 the Australians toured England and beat them, thanks to the Australian batsman, Donald Bradman. How to beat him? The English came up with a plan. They would bowl fast (cricket balls are very hard, and a good fast bowler can bowl them at speeds of up to 60 or even 70 mph; the England bowler Harold Larwood was the fastest there was), but they wouldn't aim for the wicket: They'd go for the body. 'Bodyline' bowling worked. Bradman and his team mates had to leap out of the way of the ball, and England won the series. But two Australian players were badly injured. Australians were outraged: 'One team is playing cricket,' stormed the Australian captain, 'and the other one isn't.' Cricket was supposed to embody all that was best about the British Empire – fair play and sportsmanship and all that. Yeah, *right.*

- ✓ **The British believed in the League of Nations.** The League was the idea of US President Woodrow Wilson and the British had come to believe in its philosophy of collective security: Nations acting together to solve problems, instead of conspiring against each other and going to war.

- ✓ **The British people did *not* want another war.** In 1933 the Oxford Union voted not to fight for King and Country, and in 1935 eleven million people signed the Peace Ballot against war. No democratic government could ignore that level of public opinion.

- ✓ **Germany was not necessarily the main threat.** The most direct threat to Britain came from Mussolini, who wanted the British out of the Mediterranean, and the Japanese in the Far East. So the British worked out a long-distance rearmament programme based on ships and aircraft, rather than on a large army suitable for fighting the Germans.

- ✓ **Not everything the Germans wanted was unreasonable.** The British thought the Treaty of Versailles after the First World War was far too harsh on Germany.

- ✓ **The British were in no position to fight a war.** Britain only started rearming in 1936. (Neville Chamberlain financed rearmament by a tax hike on tea: He knew trouble was brewing!) But although the navy and air force were recovering, Britain's army was still small and ill-equipped. Britain had to play for time.

- ✓ **1936 Hitler sends troops into the demilitarised Rhineland.** The British take the line that the Rhineland shouldn't have been demilitarised in the first place. Hitler is 'only moving into his own back yard' as people put it.

- ✓ **1938 Hitler takes over Austria.** Some unease is felt in Britain, but the issue doesn't seem worth fighting over, especially as so many Austrians are clearly delighted by Hitler's arrival.

## The Munich Conference

In September 1938 Hitler demanded the German-speaking Sudetenland area of Czechoslovakia. This issue was serious, because the Czechs had a military alliance with France. If Czechoslovakia was attacked the French were duty-bound to help them. But by 1938 the French were desperate to avoid a war. So Chamberlain took finding a way to let Hitler have the Sudetenland without actually fighting for it upon himself. The deal took three face-to-face meetings with Hitler, but in September 1938 the Sudetenland went to Hitler at the famous Munich Conference.

Everyone had been expecting a war, so this peace settlement was wildly popular in London and Paris. 'You would think,' said one British official, looking down at the crowds cheering Chamberlain, 'that we had won a victory, instead of selling a small country to the Germans.'

For many years historians were very harsh on Chamberlain and accused him of giving far too much to Hitler. Later historians were more sympathetic towards him. They argued that he had very little room to manoeuvre, especially as Britain was so weak. Chamberlain's problem is that he carried on trying to appease Hitler even after Hitler took over the rest of Czechoslovakia. It's difficult to avoid the conclusion that Chamberlain was completely out of his depth and simply refused to see it.

## And then Hitler attacked Poland

When Hitler attacked Poland only a few months later, Britain declared war. In many ways this was a crazy thing to do. Britain couldn't help Poland any more than she could help Czechoslovakia, especially after Hitler and Stalin agreed to divide Poland between them. But by September 1939, people in Britain had changed their ideas about Germany. Hitler had taken over the rest of Czechoslovakia and on *Kristallnacht* (the Night of Broken Glass) the Nazis had smashed up Jewish shops and businesses and sent thousands of German Jews off to concentration camps. The British decided: No more deals with this man. So when the Germans invaded Poland on 1 September 1939, the British told him to get out, and two days later Britain declared war.

# World War Two

The British had already been issuing gas masks and Anderson air raid shelters, which you could put up in your back garden. Now they put their city children on trains and evacuated them out to the country and started calling up men and women to serve in the armed forces. But where were the British troops going to go? They couldn't get to Poland, and in any case the Germans and Russians soon crushed the Poles. So the British sent their small army to France and waited. And waited. And waited. And then the Germans launched their *blitzkrieg* – lightning war.

## Early battles and Churchill's finest hour

The German blitzkrieg came in Denmark and Norway. The British had in fact already mined Norwegian waters – which was illegal – and the Germans lost so many ships that Hitler was put off the idea of any more invasions by sea. But although the British and French did briefly throw the Germans out of Narvik, they soon had to clear out again.

Next the Germans stormed into Belgium and Holland, charged through the Ardennes forest and cut off the entire British army in France on the beaches at Dunkirk. The British had no option but to go home, and for reasons we still don't really know, Hitler told his tanks to stop, which gave the British time to gather a fleet of small private pleasure craft (yes, things were that desperate) to ferry the troops to the waiting ships. The British liked to call this event the 'Miracle of Dunkirk', but since they had had to leave behind just about everything except two pistols and a very sharp stick, there wasn't much miraculous about it. As Churchill, pointed out, 'Wars are not won by evacuations'.

Losing Norway brought down Chamberlain's government and Winston Churchill became prime minister. Not everyone thought he was a good choice, especially when he came out with his famous speech about never surrendering. Britain didn't seem able to do anything else, especially after France had to surrender in June 1940. Yet here was Churchill talking about Victory. The idea seemed crazy – until the Battle of Britain.

## Battle over Britain

After Dunkirk the British had so few guns left that they were reduced to doing their drill with broomstick handles until the factories could manufacture sufficient real weapons. But simply by refusing to make peace, Churchill could keep the war going whether Hitler wanted it to or not. So Hitler told his generals to come up with an invasion plan, Operation Sealion. This plan necessitated destroying the RAF. Hermann Goering, Hitler's commander-in-chief of the Luftwaffe, the German airforce, thought he knew how to do just that.

In the summer and autumn of 1940, the German Luftwaffe took on the RAF in the first proper air battle in history, the Battle of Britain. The Germans tried to destroy the British airfields and very nearly succeeded. Three things saved the British:

- ✔ **Radar:** The British could track the German planes as soon as they took off and be ready to intercept them.

- ✔ **The Spitfire**: The Spitfire was the nippiest plane in the battle. Not only could it shoot down German bombers – anyone could do that – but it could shoot down German fighters, too. This plane gave the British just the edge they needed.

- ✔ **The Blitz:** The Germans were only supposed to bomb airfields and military installations, but when a German bomber got lost and dropped its bombs over London, the RAF hit back and bombed Berlin. 'Bomb my capital, will you?' spluttered Hitler, 'I'll trash yours!' This declaration was bad news for London and Coventry, but a welcome relief for the RAF. If the Germans were bombing the cities they couldn't bomb the RAF's airfields. On 15 September Goering launched the big attack to destroy the RAF and found the RAF ready for him. The RAF were attacking in large numbers now, and the Luftwaffe was shot to pieces. As the German planes limped home, Hitler decided to scrap Operation Sealion. Britain could die another day.

## The Blitz

The Germans bombed the heart out of Britain's cities in the Blitz (Figure 21-1 shows the cities that suffered the most). They bombed the ancient city of Coventry so badly that the Germans coined a new expression 'to Coventry', that meant to destroy something totally. They didn't just target industrial cities like Newcastle or Glasgow either. The Germans bombed the cathedral cities of Exeter, Canterbury, and Norwich, too, after the British bombed the ancient port of Lübeck.

The British liked to suggest that the bombing only made them more united and determined not to give in. When a bomb landed on Buckingham Palace, the queen commented, 'At last I can look the East End in the face.' On the whole, the bombing probably did make the British more united, but that national feeling wasn't the whole story. Riots broke out after very heavy bombing in Plymouth, and both Churchill and the king sometimes got booed when they visited the bomb sites. But at least they went. Hitler never dared.

**Figure 21-1:** Cities bombed during the Blitz.

Glasgow-Clydeside (1,329)

Newcastle-Tyneside (152)

Belfast (440)

Manchester (578)

Hull (593)

Liverpool-Birkenhead (1,957)

Sheffield (355)

Nottingham (137)

Birmingham (1,852)

Coventry (818)

Cardiff (115)

Bristol-Avonmouth (919)

London (18,800)

Southampton (647)

Portsmouth (687)

Principal objectives, with bomb tonnages aimed at them in major raids (100 tons or more) from September 7, 1940, to May 16, 1941

Plymouth-Devonport (1,228)

### *Mr Brown went off to town on the 8:21: Life at home*

If you were too old (or too young) to join the regular army, you could always join the part-time Home Guard, so Hitler wouldn't know what had hit him if he landed at the weekend or after 6:00 p.m. He wouldn't have been able to see much either, thanks to the blackout. Everyone had to put up thick black curtains, and wardens patrolled to make sure no one was guiding German bombers with their bedside lamp.

Rationing existed: meat, butter, sugar, petrol, clothes – anything, in fact, which had to be brought in past the U-boats. While you were waiting, you could 'Dig for Victory', growing food in your back garden or on the local cricket pitch. The government issued special recipes, like Woolton Pie (all veg and no meat), telling people what they could do with their rations, though most people could have told them. 'Is Your Journey Really Necessary?' asked the posters at railway stations. And 'Careless Talk Costs Lives!' warned everyone of the danger of German spies and sympathisers lurking about. One siren warned you that an air raid was coming, and another gave the All Clear. If you got your call-up papers they might not mean you were going to fight: Women were called up to work in the factories, and young men expecting to be in uniform were sometimes sent to work down the mines – just as vital for winning the war.

## *If it ain't flamin' desert, it's flippin' jungle*

In 1940 the British attacked the Italians in North Africa and the Germans had to come to their rescue. For a long time German commander Rommel seemed about to win, but in October 1942, British Field Marshall Bernard Montgomery, commander of the 8th Army in North Africa, defeated him at El Alamein in Egypt. By then the United States was in the war, thanks to the Japanese attack on Pearl Harbor in 1941. The Japanese also attacked British possessions in Asia. They took Hong Kong and Burma, and in 1942, they took the great British island fortress of Singapore. That Singapore was lost was bad enough, but what made the situation worse was the Japanese hadn't even had to fight much of a battle. They attacked from behind down the Malayan peninsula, and not by sea as the British had been expecting. With water supplies running low, General Percival decided resistance was useless and just surrendered. The image of the mighty British Empire had been shattered.

## *Boats and bombers*

Churchill said the only thing in the war that really worried him was the U-boats, which were sinking thousands of tons of shipping and threatening to cut off Britain's food supplies. The British used convoys and underwater radar known as ASDIC, but information was the best weapon. To get that vital information, they set up a secret listening centre at Bletchley Park in Buckinghamshire where top British boffins were able to tap into the Germans' secret codes. But not always, and for several crucial months, the British had to fight blind. Not until the Americans brought in long-range bombers that could cover the whole Atlantic were the Allies able to turn the tables on the U-boats.

Bombing was the only way the British could take the war to the Germans. At first the Germans just shot British bombers down, but once the United States was in the war, the Allies were able to bomb round the clock, the Americans by day and the British by night. The Germans had bombed Britain hard, but the British retaliation was far worse. Whole cities were flattened in terrible fire-storms, and Britons began to question whether their actions were right. The worst case was Dresden, which was destroyed in a terrible raid in February 1945, even though the city wasn't a major military target.

You could argue that bombing was necessary. This tactic kept up the pressure on Germany, disrupted its industry, and kept men and guns pinned down, which might otherwise have been used against the Russians (and let's be quite clear about this: It was the Russian front that won the war for the Allies). On the other hand, people have argued that this sort of bombing was nothing more than murder and a war crime itself.

## D-Day – fighting on the beaches

By 1944 Britain was a vast armed camp, and on 6 June 1944, D-Day, the British, Canadians, and Americans launched the biggest invasion in history on the beaches of Normandy. The invasion nearly came to grief on Omaha Beach, but in the end, the Allies were able to fight their way ashore. Meanwhile the Russians were closing in on Germany from the east. The British came up with a plan to cross the Rhine and dash ahead to Berlin before the Russians got there, but the plan went wrong when the British landed on top of a German panzer division at Arnhem in Holland. Instead, US Supreme Commander General Eisenhower insisted on advancing more slowly, and the western Allies finally met up with the Russians in the spring of 1945.

In February 1945, Churchill, Stalin, and Roosevelt (the Big Three) met up at Yalta in the Crimea to discuss the final defeat of Hitler and to decide who would get what during the postwar occupation, what would happen to the liberated states in Eastern Europe, and more.

## The war with Germany ends

The war with Germany ended on 8 May 1945 – V-E Day (for 'Victory in Europe'). During the Yalta Conference (see the preceding section) the Allies had decided to hold a war-crimes trial of the leading Nazis. Following the defeat of Germany these trials were held in the old courtroom at Nuremberg, about the only public building still standing. But while the Allies were working together to convict the Nazis, elsewhere the alliance was falling apart at the seams. When the Big Three next met, at Potsdam, in the summer of 1945 just outside Berlin, serious arguments occurred: The Cold War was about to begin.

## The war with Japan continues

Japan still needed to be beaten, don't forget. The British fought a long war in the jungles of Burma and India, but their soldiers called themselves the 'forgotten army' because no one seemed to take any notice. Specially trained British, Chinese, and American Chindit units landed behind Japanese lines, blew up bridges, ambushed patrols, and generally created havoc. In 1944, when the Japanese invaded India, the British and Indians defeated them at the battle of Imphal. So this part of Britain's war ended with one last great Imperial battle: The future was going to be very different.

(Don't forget you can find out a lot more about the war in *World War II For Dummies*.)

# Chapter 22

# TV Times

*In This Chapter*

▶ Understanding why Churchill had to go – and so did the Empire

▶ Seeing the State become a nanny – and how nanny got into a state

▶ Swinging through the sixties

*T*his chapter's something of a roller coaster. If you were in Britain not long after the war – and perhaps you were – you'd have seen a pretty drab country, still with rationing and a general sense of gloom. Britain had won the war but was in the process of losing both its Empire and its prestige. But if you'd visited Britain in the sixties you'd have found London swinging and an upbeat sense of a country on the move. Come back to Britain in the seventies and you wouldn't find much moving – or working (for even more strikes, head along to Chapter 23). Not for nothing was one form of industrial action called a *go-slow*. This chapter is about Britain down, then up, then down again. Hang on tight.

## We Are the Masters Now

That statement's more or less what the Labour Party said when it won the General Election in 1945. Its victory still seems a bit difficult to grasp. Churchill (a Conservative) has just led you through the biggest war in history, the Cold War is just beginning – and you choose this moment to ditch the Great Man? Well, yes, and for some very good reasons:

▸ **Churchill completely misjudged the public mood.** People linked Churchill's Conservatives with the unemployment of the 1930s, and their ideas didn't seem to have advanced since then. Instead of saying how he would set about solving social problems Churchill gave a crazy warning that the Labour Party would establish some sort of Gestapo in Britain if they were elected.

▸ **The army had been running a political education service for the troops,** and many of them had become convinced Labour Party supporters.

> ✔ **Labour ministers had served in Churchill's wartime cabinet and had more or less run the home front.** Now the Labour Party said it would bring in the recommendations of the Beveridge Report.

## The Beveridge Report: Fighting giants

During the war, the government set up a special commission chaired by an Oxford academic, Sir William Beveridge, to look into how to create a better Britain after the war. Beveridge talked of five 'giants' that had long plagued Britain:

- ✔ Poverty
- ✔ Disease
- ✔ Ignorance
- ✔ Squalor
- ✔ Unemployment or 'Idleness'

To fight these ills, Beveridge said, you needed free health care, some sort of national insurance scheme, and full employment. Some people wondered where the money for all this social welfare would come from, but most people thought the Beveridge Report was just what the doctor ordered. The ideals of this report were something worth fighting for.

## Going into Labour

People were expecting big things of this new Labour government. Would it be able to deliver? The big match was about to kick off, and the star players were:

- ✔ **Clement Attlee,** the new prime minister. Looked like a bank manager from Croydon. Churchill called him 'A sheep in sheep's clothing', but Attlee proved a lot tougher than he looked.

- ✔ **Aneurin 'Nye' Bevan,** the fiery Welsh minister with the job of bringing in a free health service for all. He enjoyed a fight, and Britain's doctors were going to make sure he got one.

- ✔ **Ernest Bevin,** a bull-faced trade unionist who, to everyone's surprise – including his own – became Foreign Secretary and proved no friend of the Russians. 'My foreign policy,' he once said, 'is to be able to buy a ticket at Victoria Station and go wherever I damn well please'.

# The National Health Service

You know the scene: Poor Victorian family weeps over sick child, but they haven't got the money to fetch a doctor. This image is the stuff of bad drama, and Labour wanted to make sure that was where it stayed. Health care – doctors, dentists, hospitals, false teeth, and specs – was to be free for everyone. The doctors were up in arms about it; it would threaten their livelihoods and they'd have to treat poor people. Nye Bevan (the Welsh minister charged with reforming the country's healthcare system) faced them down and brought in the National Health Service (NHS) in 1948. The NHS was so successful that demand outstripped supply. People wanted to get their money's worth, and they used the NHS so much that it had to expand much more quickly than anyone had anticipated. Soon the government had to start charging for prescriptions, and Bevan resigned in protest. As healthy people lived longer, they ended up using the NHS even more as they grew older. So it got bigger and bigger and more and more expensive, and by the end of the century, NHS funding had become one of the biggest problems facing British governments.

## *Power for the people*

Attlee and the Labour Party believed that instead of leaving everything to private companies – the system that had failed so spectacularly in the thirties (see Chapter 21 for details on what had gone wrong) the State should run the really big basic industries, like coal and steel and the railways, and that the State should provide benefits for everyone. This policy marked a really radical departure from past practice.

### *Nationalisation*

Attlee took coal, steel, electricity, and the railways away from private companies so that they could be run 'on behalf of the people'. The new National Coal Board got off to a bad start when it was hit by the big freeze in its first month and couldn't cope. Nationalising the railways got off to a better start, but running all those pretty little local lines proved far too expensive, and in 1962 British Rail's Richard Beeching axed hundreds of them. Some people in Britain still haven't forgiven him.

### *Welfare State*

Attlee said there'd be no return to the bad old days when, if you were too poor, you just starved. From now on the State would look after people properly, from the cradle to the grave. Free health care and free education would be provided, schoolchildren would get free milk to make them healthy, and *state benefits* – payments – would exist for mothers or for those not working. Sounded good – if this system could be carried through.

## Who was the Third Man?

Carol Reed's film *The Third Man* is set in Vienna just after the war, but in 1951 Britain got its own 'Third Man' drama when two British diplomats, Guy Burgess and Donald Maclean, suddenly did a bunk and turned up a few days later in Moscow. They were revealed to be spying for Stalin, and the police were just going to haul them in when the two men got a tip off. But who was the Third Man, the one who tipped them off? This person turned out to be another diplomat, Kim Philby, who'd known Burgess and Maclean at Cambridge University. The Russian secret service reckoned all these English spies – there were others – were some of the best agents they ever had.

# *You may have won the war, but you can't have any sweets*

When the war ended, every man who'd served in the armed forces got a civilian *demob* (demobilisation from the armed services) suit, free-of-charge, to help get him back into civilian life. But if people thought peacetime was going to be one big party, they were in for a shock. You don't recover from six years of total war overnight, and the Brits had to get used to even tougher restrictions on everyday life than they had experienced during the war:

- ✔ **National Service continued.** Young men were still called up to serve in the armed forces until 1960. Plenty of wars and conflicts still occurred requiring a British military presence and soldiering helped keep the unemployment figures down.

- ✔ **Rationing got worse.** Less butter and margarine was available than in the war, and they even rationed bread. Everything was in short supply – meat, eggs, sweets, chocolate. Clothing coupons were still necessary and no fancy fashions, either: You had to make do with sensible 'Utility' styles. And Utility styles were very, very boring.

- ✔ **The big freeze came.** The winter of 1947 was one of the coldest on record: Just the time to have a national coal shortage. The trains couldn't get the coal supplies through the snow. And when the snow melted huge floods occurred.

The Labour government called all this rationing and tightening of belts *austerity*. Translation? No money's in the pot, so you can't have any fun. But some bright spots did lighten this period. The nation had a party when Princess Elizabeth married the Duke of Edinburgh, and everyone got madly excited when the first bananas arrived – thanks to the war most children in Britain had never seen one. But on the whole, the Brits had had enough of this austerity lark, and when Christian Dior launched his 'New Look' for women, with broad skirts and hour-glass figures, women went for it and to hell with the clothing coupons.

## Discovery and recovery

The 1948 Olympic Games – the first ones since Hitler snubbed Jesse Owen in Berlin in 1936 – were held in London. The event wasn't quite as lavish as Hitler's had been, but who cared about that?

Then some bright spark pointed out that 1951 would be the centenary of the 1851 Great Exhibition (see Chapter 18 to find out about this), and people thought, 'Why not have another Great Exhibition, and this time make it fun as well?' They called this event the *Festival of Britain*. A big bombsite on London's South Bank was cleared to create a Discovery theme park. In the Dome of Discovery, you could find all the latest advances in science and technology; then you could come outside and marvel at the Skylon, which shot up into the sky without visible means of support. When your mind had finished boggling, you could go down to Battersea funfair and discover the dodgems.

These seemed exciting times. In 1953 thousands of Britons watched the new Queen Elizabeth's coronation on a relatively new invention called The Television. On the same day, news arrived that Edmund Hillary and Sherpa Norgay Tensing had climbed Everest – okay, Hillary was a New Zealander and Tensing was Nepalese but the expedition was British. 1953 was also when James Watson and Francis Crick worked out the structure of DNA at Cambridge, and the next year Roger Bannister ran the world's first four-minute mile at Oxford.

# End of Empire

The Victorians liked to say that the sun never set on the British Empire because it was always shining on some part of the globe that was British. Of course, they also liked to think that the Empire would go on forever, but empires don't do that, and the British one was no exception.

The British began to talk less about the Empire and more about the *Commonwealth*. No one was too sure quite what the Commonwealth was – people talked of a 'family' of nations who'd all been part of the British Empire, and the queen was Head of the Commonwealth, which meant that at least you got a good lunch at Commonwealth summits. On the whole the British tend to like the Commonwealth, if only because the Commonwealth Games are the only way they can get a decent haul of sporting medals.

## Sunset in the east . . . and the Middle East

Churchill hated the idea of 'giving up' India, but Gandhi had been campaigning for the British to quit India ever since the Amritsar Massacre back in 1919 (see Chapter 21 for the details on this appalling incident). During the Second

World War Gandhi launched a full-scale campaign to force the British out. Result? The British locked him up, and all the other Indian nationalist leaders they could get their hands on. Some Indians even went over to the Japanese side and fought with them against the British. By the time the war ended in 1945, India was fast sliding out of control – riots and demonstrations took place and the British seemed incapable of restoring order. The Viceroy of India, Lord Wavell, bowed to the inevitable and took India's nationalist leaders out of prison and into government.

Meanwhile, back in Britain Attlee's Labour government had decided the time had come for the British to go home. But a problem existed. Gandhi wanted a single India, with both Hindus and Muslims, but the Muslims wanted a separate country to be called Pakistan. If they got this separate country, where was its border to be? And what about the people who would now be on the 'wrong' side of it? Attlee sent Lord Mountbatten out to India to replace Wavell as Viceroy, with orders to sort things out. Should Britain partition India or not? Mountbatten decided 'Yes, and fast' – he announced that partition would take place in August 1947, a year ahead of schedule. About seven million people had to up sticks and move from one state to another. Trouble was bound to occur, and it did. Almost half a million people were killed in riots against partition, and in 1950 an anti-partition Hindu shot Gandhi for agreeing to it.

The British left many legacies to India – democracy, railways, the English language, and the strange custom of lawyers wearing pinstripe suits under a tropical sun – but they hadn't expected to bequeath a bitter border dispute in Kashmir. India's princes and maharajahs had to choose whether to join India or Pakistan. States along the border normally went with the wishes of the majority, but the Maharajah of Kashmir, in northern India, which had a mostly Muslim population, declared that he was handing his kingdom over to India and not to Pakistan, which is what his people wanted. The Kashmiri Muslims protested, Pakistan invaded, and the result was one of the world's longest-running, and most dangerous, border disputes.

### Emergency in Malaya

The British had rather more success in Malaya than in India. They reorganised the region as a federation in 1948 in preparation for pulling out and going home, but just then a major communist rising started. However, the communists weren't Malays; they were Chinese. The native Malays wanted nothing to do with them and certainly didn't want their country to become a Chinese-dominated communist state. So the British stayed on and fought a highly successful counter-insurgency campaign against the communists, grouping the population in fortified villages and denying the guerrillas access to food or supplies. By 1957 the rising was sufficiently under control for Britain to grant independence to Malaya and pull out.

The war in Malaya is always termed the 'Malayan Emergency'. Why? Because the British rubber planters' insurance policies didn't cover war damage but did cover emergencies. You could say they stretched a point.

## Mountbatten

Historians still argue furiously about Mountbatten's role in Indian independence. The debate was not helped by Mountbatten's own version of events, which was essentially, 'All the best ideas were mine, and all my decisions were right, and everyone else was wrong, but once they realised how right I was we all became firm friends.' Mountbatten was a genuine royal – Queen Victoria was his great grandmother – and a charismatic naval commander in the Second World War, which was just as well because his ship sank. He was Supreme Allied Commander in South East Asia, overseeing operations against the Japanese and he accepted their surrender at Singapore in 1945. Attlee thought that Mountbatten had just the right sort of authority to pull off the British withdrawal from India.

Mountbatten got on very well with Gandhi and Nehru (according to rumour his wife went one better and had an affair with Nehru, though the evidence for it is slim); however, he found Jinnah, the Muslim leader, much harder to fathom. His critics say he rushed India into partition before people were prepared for the idea, and that therefore he was to blame for the violence. That accusation's probably going too far – plenty of communal violence occurred before he arrived and partition was bound to provoke trouble whenever it was done – but it is true that the border had to be drawn and all the practical arrangements made against a hopelessly inadequate timescale. Even his harshest critics cannot have wished Mountbatten's ultimate fate on him – in 1979 he was blown up by the IRA.

The British success against communist guerrillas in Malaya seemed to contrast with the later American failure against communist Viet Cong guerrillas in Vietnam, and some people have argued that the Americans should have studied the British tactics more closely. But in fact the two situations were very different; crucially the Malay people were against the communist guerrillas whereas many Vietnamese supported the Viet Cong. (If you want to know why, see *The Vietnam War For Dummies*.)

### Palestine: Another fine mess

Britain was given Palestine to look after by the League of Nations after the First World War (see Chapter 21 for more on Britain's curiously inept entry into the complex politics of the Middle East). Since then the British had been trying to allow controlled Jewish immigration while at the same time reassuring the Palestinians that they weren't about to be swamped. After the war, many thousands of Jews wanted to turn their backs on Europe and make a new life in Palestine, but that alarmed the Palestinians still more, so the British Foreign Secretary, Ernest Bevin, said no more Jews could enter Palestine at all. Those who tried were locked up in barbed wire camps.

But these people had survived the Nazi death camps, and they weren't going to be so easily dissuaded. Jewish terrorist groups, *Irgun* and the *Stern Gang*, started killing British soldiers. In 1946 they blew up the King David Hotel, which housed the British administrative headquarters: ninety-one people were killed. The British had enough problems without trying to solve the entire Middle East, so they pulled out and handed the whole situation over to the United Nations. The UN set up the State of Israel. And found they couldn't solve the problem either. (To find out more, see *The Middle East For Dummies*.)

# Wind of change in Africa

The British developed quite a taste for all these midnight independence ceremonies, with lots of officials in silly hats nobly hauling down the flag to the tune of *The Last Post*. The first African country to gain its independence was Ghana; one of the VIP visitors at its independence ceremony in 1957 was Dr Martin Luther King, Jr. By 1968 one African colony after another had gained its independence – Nigeria, Sierra Leone, Uganda, Malawi, Zambia, Gambia, Botswana, Lesotho, Swaziland, and Tanzania.

### Trouble brews in Kenya

In Kenya nationalist guerrillas from the Kikuyu tribe, called *Mau Mau*, staged a rising against the British. The British responded savagely, arresting thousands; it has been alleged that the British used torture. Mau Mau also killed fellow Africans – in 1953 they massacred ninety-seven Africans in the village of Lari – and gradually lost the support of ordinary Kenyans. In 1963 Britain pulled out of Kenya and handed power over to Jomo Kenyatta, who'd only recently come out of jail. But by then you couldn't call yourself a true nationalist leader unless the British had locked you up at some point.

Kenya had had an unusually large white population of farmers getting up to all sorts of hanky panky in the White Highlands, or 'Happy Valley' as it was known. When independence came most of them packed their bags and headed home to Britain, but the whites of Rhodesia and South Africa had very different ideas. They enjoyed lording it over the black Africans and they weren't going to give their position up without a struggle.

### Apartheid appears in South Africa

The white South Africans had come up with an idea called *apartheid*, which said that whites should have all the best land, schools, houses, jobs, and so on, and blacks had to keep out unless they came in as labourers for the whites. In 1960 the British Conservative Prime Minister Harold Macmillan went to Cape Town and told the white South Africans that they could not resist black majority rule for ever: A 'Wind of change' was sweeping through the continent. The whites hated it.

A few months after Macmillan's 'Wind of change' speech, the South African police opened fire on an unarmed crowd of black Africans at Sharpeville and killed sixty-seven people, most of them shot in the back as they were running away. Britain's anger over the incident was so great that South Africa decided to declare independence and left the Commonwealth. The Commonwealth responded by imposing sanctions on South Africa – no trade and we're not going to play you at cricket either, so there. Officially the British government supported this line; unofficially, many British firms and banks, and not a few cricketers, ignored it.

### White rebellion in Rhodesia

The whites of Rhodesia decided they wanted to be independent, too. Britain said they could only be independent if they agreed to black majority rule. Or, to put the idea another way, democracy. The white Rhodesians weren't having that situation, so they went ahead and in 1965 declared UDI (Unilateral Declaration of Independence) to defend their right of superiority over black people. Britain said UDI was illegal, and spent the next fifteen years imposing sanctions on white Rhodesia (or rather, imposing them and then turning a blind eye to British companies breaking them). Rhodesia finally got black majority rule in 1980 and changed its name to Zimbabwe, and even then the whites still owned all the best land in the country.

# Losing an Empire, Finding a Role

'Great Britain,' said American statesman Dean Acheson in 1962, 'has lost an Empire and has not yet found a role.' He had a point. Without her Empire, Britain could be one of three things:

- ✔ **A world power,** with the atom bomb and a veto at the United Nations

- ✔ **A leading player in Europe,** rather than the whole world

- ✔ **A small nation which no one took seriously.** (Don't laugh, this situation had happened before. Austria and Spain had both been Great Powers, and have both declined.)

So, which option was it to be? The following sections consider these possibilities.

## A world power or just in de-Nile?

In 1956 the ruler of a large, poor developing country took charge of his country's only major economic asset. The country was Egypt, the ruler was Colonel Gamal Abdel Nasser, and the asset, which had been run by the British and French, was the Suez Canal.

London went ballistic. Conservative Prime Minister Anthony Eden had stood up to Hitler and Mussolini in the 1930s (well okay, he resigned from Chamberlain's cabinet, so there) and he wasn't afraid to stand up to Nasser. Some people thought Eden was right; others thought he'd gone mad.

## Angry young men

A small living room on a Sunday night. A young-ish guy is sitting with no trousers on – his wife is ironing them. 'I suppose,' he says, 'people of our generation aren't able to die for good causes any longer . . .There aren't any good, brave causes left.' This scene is from John Osborne's *Look Back in Anger*, the in-your-face new drama that hit the Royal Court Theatre in 1956 just in time for the Suez Crisis (see 'A world power or just in de-Nile?'). Osborne was one of a number of 'Angry Young Men' who took a look at the drab, bankrupted Country Which Had Won The War and said 'Is that it?' If you like plays about sad, disappointed people with no ideals or illusions left, then you could have a ball in the late fifties. In due course, the Angry Young Men became the Grumpy Old Men of today.

Eden hatched a plot with the French and the Israelis. Israel would invade Egypt and then Britain and France would send troops in to, er, keep the peace while 'accidentally on purpose' taking control of the Suez Canal. The British and French went in on 31 October 1956, and initially events seemed to be going Eden's way – but things aren't always as clear-cut as they seem. Huge protests broke out in Britain, the United Nations told everyone to pull out of Egypt, and US President Eisenhower refused to help the British and French. Investors were all pulling their money out of London, and Britain desperately needed a billion-dollar loan from America. Eisenhower's answer was simple: One (financial) loan for one (military) withdrawal. So Eden pulled out. Result: Total humiliation for the Brits (and French). Britain doesn't sound much like a World Power, does she?

## *Into Europe?*

The British had been fooling themselves for years that they didn't need Europe. True, Churchill helped set up the Council of Europe in 1949, but the Council couldn't actually do anything. Meanwhile the French and Germans had set up a Common Market with Belgium, the Netherlands, Italy, and Luxembourg. Should the British join this market, too? They hummed and they hawed and they even set up their own rival, the European Free Trade Association (EFTA) with six other countries they didn't actually trade with much. Finally, in 1962 Conservative Prime Minister Harold Macmillan decided to bite the bullet and apply to join the Common Market. Except he couldn't because the French vetoed Britain's entry. President de Gaulle thought that Britain was only a stalking horse for the Americans, and he wasn't having that situation in 'his' Europe.

Finally, in 1973, Prime Minister Edward Heath managed to drag Britain kicking and screaming into the European Economic Community (EEC), which was the posh name for the Common Market, and even then the British held a referendum two years later to see if they really wanted to be in it. They voted 'Well-now-we're-in-it-we-might-as-well-stay', which roughly translates as 'Yes'.

Whatever new role the British found for themselves, 'Leaders of Europe' wasn't it.

## Black and British – and brown, and yellow

Black people have been in Britain since Tudor times but people usually put the starting point for really big-scale immigration into Britain at 1948, when the SS *Empire Windrush* brought the first batch of post-war immigrants over from Jamaica.

These people came because they had British passports and because Britain had invited them. British companies advertised in the Caribbean and Indian press for people to come to Britain to do the sort of menial jobs that the white British didn't want to do. So they came.

Some British people were scared the new immigrants would 'take their jobs'. In fact, the new arrivals kept coming up against a 'colour bar', which meant they often couldn't get work or lodgings. Many immigrants had to start up small corner shops or Chinese and Indian restaurants and takeaways. Serious racial fighting occurred in London's Notting Hill in 1958 and race riots at Toxteth (Liverpool) and Brixton (South London) in 1981. In 1993 a black teenager called Stephen Lawrence was murdered in London, and the police investigation was so badly handled that an inquiry was held, which found that the Metropolitan Police was 'institutionally racist'.

That is the bad side of immigration. On the plus side, Parliament passed a Race Relations Act in 1965, which outlawed racist speech and behaviour. Right-wing groups like the National Front or the British National Party have occasionally won the odd seat on a local council, though never for very long (though in 2009 the BNP did win two seats in the European Parliament). Finding mosques in city centres is now quite normal and some of the biggest Hindu and Sikh temples outside the Indian subcontinent are in London. Being complacent about these issues is stupid, but on the whole the immigrant communities have integrated into Britain much more easily than anyone in 1948 could have predicted.

## Rivers of blood

Enoch Powell was a maverick Conservative MP and classical scholar. In 1968 he made one of the most outrageous speeches about immigration ever heard in Britain. If they didn't stop coloured people coming in, he said there would be death, destruction, and civil war. 'Like the Roman,' he said, 'I seem to see the River Tiber foaming with much blood.' The speech went down a storm with racist bigots, few of whom understood the classical allusions. The Conservatives sacked him, so he went and joined the Ulster Unionists. The Thames hasn't foamed with blood yet.

## Horror on the moor

The sixties weren't all about young people having fun and free love. In 1966 the country was stunned by a horrific murder case in the north of England. An arrogant young psychopath called Ian Brady, together with his girlfriend Myra Hindley, had enticed a string of children into their car and taken them out to a stretch of lonely moorland where they abused and murdered them. In court the prosecution played a tape the pair had made of one of their victims screaming for mercy as they tortured her. They were both jailed for life and remained national figures of revulsion for the rest of their lives.

## Yeah yeah, baby – groovy

Just think: Without Britain in the sixties, we'd never have encountered Austin Powers. Suddenly in the sixties Britain, and especially London, became *the* hip place to be seen – if you were young, that is. Britain's new-found popularity started with The Beatles, and soon you could rock to the Rolling Stones, shout with Lulu, or even ask Cliff Richard exactly where he got his walkin' talkin' livin' doll. The BBC was a bit sniffy at first about this new-fangled 'pop' music and tried to keep it off the airwaves, so disc jockeys had to operate from Radio Luxembourg or from 'pirate' stations on ships at sea, like the famous Radio Caroline. But in 1967 the BBC decided to get down with these groovy young people and launched Radio One, Britain's first non-commercial pop station.

British designers seemed to rule the world, whether it was Mary Quant's fashions or the curved corners of the Mini Minor, everyone's favourite car. No wonder one of the most successful British films of the sixties was *The Italian Job*, which ends with a high-speed car chase involving three mini minors coloured – of course – red, white, and blue. While American students were burning the Stars and Stripes in protest at Vietnam – including on one occasion in front of the US Embassy in London's Grosvenor Square – the British were wearing the Union Jack on everything from t-shirts to bikinis. When a group of secretaries from Surbiton decided to do their bit for the economy by working an extra half hour a day for no pay they started a patriotic confidence campaign with badges saying 'I'm Backing Britain!' printed on the Union Jack. You could even back Britain with a Union Jack miniskirt. Oh *behave*.

## What ARE those politicians up to?

Churchill became prime minister again in 1951, but he was too old and ill to achieve anything much. Anthony Eden (prime minister 1955–7) was just itching to take over and show everyone what he could do, which turned out to be very little. Lordly Harold Macmillan (prime minister 1957–63) was more upbeat.

'You've never had it so good!' he declared, and his War Minister (no namby-pamby 'Defence Minister' in those days), John Profumo, took him at his word. In 1963 it transpired that Profumo had been having it good with a nude model called Christine Keeler, who'd also been sleeping with a military attaché at the Soviet Embassy. Profumo hadn't actually been whispering any state secrets over the pillow, but he did lie about the affair to the House of Commons, so he had to go. Mind you, if everyone who told a bit less than the truth in Parliament had to resign we'd be left with the Archbishop of Canterbury and the cleaners.

## *Labour pains*

The Conservatives had been in power since 1951, and they didn't seem to have much to show for it. 'Thirteen wasted years' taunted Labour as the nation went to the polls in 1964, and the country seemed to agree – just. Labour was back in with a majority of four. The new prime minister was Harold Wilson (prime minister 1964–70; 1974–6), who wore raincoats, smoked a pipe, and spoke with a strong Yorkshire accent. No more toffs appeared in Downing Street during his leadership.

Harold Wilson gave honours to The Beatles, and launched comprehensive schools for all and a visionary Open University, using all the latest technology of television and records so that everyone could get higher education. He was even in office when England won the World Cup (see the sidebar, '1966 and all that'), which he reckoned won him the 1966 election. But in other ways, Wilson didn't do so well. Unemployment kept going up, and so did prices, so that in 1967 Wilson had to devalue the pound. 'This will not affect the pound in your pocket!' he declared, but no one believed him – and they were right.

## 1966 and all that

In 1966 England won the World Cup. At Wembley. In front of the queen. And they beat West Germany to do so. The Scots, Welsh, and Irish understandably get rather tired of constantly being reminded of this particular English victory, especially as English newspapers and television mention it so often you could be forgiven for thinking the match has only just happened, but it was a significant event even so.

This victory happened only twenty years after the end of the war and it seemed like a reaffirmation of the verdict of the war, especially as West Germany appeared to have recovered rather better than Britain. Mind you, Germans – and many Scots, Welsh, and Irish – argue that Geoff Hurst's winning goal was offside anyway and shouldn't have been allowed.

## Watching the telly

Everyone started buying TV sets after the Coronation was broadcast in 1953. Initially, you had to make do with the BBC, where they spoke posh and always knew what was good for you. Independent Television (ITV) arrived in 1954; this channel was less posh and it even carried adverts. Harold Wilson was probably the first politician to realise the power of television:

He even appeared on the ever-popular comedy show *Morecambe and Wise.* When TV cameras were finally allowed into Parliament, politicians stopped making eloquent speeches – and sense – and started coming up with snappy soundbites just to get on the telly. Tough on crime, tough on the causes of crime – and tough on the viewers.

Conservative Prime Minister Edward Heath (prime minister 1970–4) changed the pound even more than Wilson had done – by making it decimal in 1971. A miners' strike and a war in the Middle East forced Heath to cut the working week to three days. Sounds good, until you realise you're only being paid for three days as well. Labour didn't fare any better. In 1976 Labour Prime Minister James Callaghan (prime minister 1976–9) even had to apply to the International Monetary Fund for a £2.3 billion loan. In 1979 the whole country seemed to grind to a halt when the public service workers all came out on strike in the Winter of Discontent – that strike meant picket lines at hospitals, no rubbish collections (so it all piled up in the street), and even a strike at the cemeteries so you couldn't even have a grave to turn in. Callaghan faced a vote of No Confidence in the Commons, and he lost it. That defeat meant he had to call a General Election, and he lost that, too. So Conservative leader Mrs Margaret Thatcher moved into 10 Downing Street, and the country held its breath. Breathe out by reading Chapter 23, which gives the low-down on Margaret Thatcher's leadership and plenty more strikes.

# Chapter 23

# Interesting Times

## In This Chapter

▶ Introducing Britain in the grip of the unions

▶ Following Britain and the unions in the grip of Mrs Thatcher

▶ Going into the new millennium – and Iraq – with Tony Blair

*T*he Chinese have an old curse that goes 'May you live in interesting times'. Which may not sound too bad, until you realise that benign curse is wishing everything from war and revolution to civil strife on your head. The last decades of the twentieth century and the first decade of the twenty-first have amassed more than enough wars, revolutions, strikes, economic booms and collapses, not to mention seriously bad fashions, to keep the historians of the future busy for years to come. If you were too busy party-ing, raving, buying shoulder pads or investing in red braces and the dotcom boom to notice, you can catch up here. As you'll see, we've all been living in interesting times.

## Mrs Thatcher's Handbag

Even its proudest citizens would have to admit that Grantham is not one of England's lovelier towns. Grantham's a rather dull place in the flatlands of Lincolnshire where, before the war, a small grocery shop was kept by a very respectable citizen and alderman on the town council called Alfred Roberts. Mr Roberts's daughter Margaret helped in the shop, carefully count-ing the pennies and learning the basic economic facts of life: Pay your debts and don't spend money until you've got it. Margaret married a business-man called Denis Thatcher, so it was as Mrs Thatcher that young Margaret entered the British political scene. She didn't like what she found.

Until the 1970s the two main British parties, Conservative and Labour, oper-ated a form of consensus politics which saw them disagreeing on details but agreeing on the basics of British political and economic life. They both accepted a *mixed economy*, with heavy industry and utilities run by the state and everything else in private hands, and lots of *quangos* (Quasi-Autonomous

Government Organisations, a nickname made up by people who didn't like them) taking charge of different aspects of national life. They also both accepted the power and importance of the trade unions.

## *Union power and power cuts*

By the 1970s the trade unions had grown into massive organisations of awesome power. To people living at the time, the country seemed to be always on strike. Other countries used to talk about militant strikes as 'the British disease'. Strikes didn't just hit the factories where the dispute occurred; workers at other factories, even in completely different industries, would come out in sympathy with their striking brother workers. Sometimes they'd send *flying pickets* to join the original strikers picketing the factory gates, and woe betide any worker who tried to cross a picket line and report for work: Such people were denounced as *scabs* and they and their families were completely shunned by the whole local community. Sometimes they, their families, or their homes were attacked.

The Labour prime minister Harold Wilson tried to keep in with the union leaders: He once invited them to a meeting at Downing Street where he put the traditional dainty tea and biscuits on hold and served them beer and doorstep sandwiches instead. When the Conservative prime minister Edward Heath took over in 1970, he tried to get the unions to agree to limit their wage demands. Bad idea. The National Union of Mineworkers announced a ban on overtime working (they didn't even need a full strike to bring the country to its knees) which cut coal supplies to electricity power stations and meant nightly power cuts to save electricity. All over the country people had to spend the evenings sitting in the dark with only candles for light, which makes a good story to tell the grandchildren but wasn't so funny at the time. Then the Arab world cut off oil supplies to the West after the 1973 Middle East war (see *The Middle East For Dummies* by Craig S. Davis for more on this crisis), so to save energy Heath had to shorten the working week to just three days, which, since it meant only three days' pay, again had the unions up in arms. By 1974 Heath had had enough. He called a general election on the question 'Who runs Britain – government or unions?' And he lost.

The Conservatives were so badly shaken by losing the 1974 election that they turned on Heath and elected his former Education Secretary, Margaret Thatcher, as their leader instead. Heath never forgave her and nursed his hurt feelings in one of the longest sulks in history.

## Some of your prints may be affected by sunlight and all-out industrial warfare

One of the most bitter industrial disputes happened in 1976-7 at a mail-order photo-developing company in North London, called Grunwick. The director sacked a group of Indian women workers who insisted on their right to join a union. The case was taken up by the trade unions and soon mass pickets from all over the country descended on the plant. Violent clashes took place between pickets and police at the factory gate, and when the postal workers refused to handle the company's mail, an extreme right-wing group called the Freedom Association took on the job and the strike collapsed.

### *Now is the winter of our discontent . . .*

The Labour government spent the 1970s fighting a losing battle with galloping inflation. In 1976 they had to ask for a loan from the International Monetary Fund, and the payoff was that they had to limit the unions' wage demands. The unions wouldn't play ball. In 1978 they demanded bigger and bigger wage rises knowing they just had to walk out on strike and their bosses would give in. In the grim, cold winter of 1978–9, while prime minister James Callaghan was away at an international summit in Guadeloupe (why, oh why, he must've wondered, did the summit have to be on a sunny Caribbean holiday island?) the country collapsed into chaos. Goods and fuel dried up because the lorry drivers were on strike, hospitals and schools closed because the nurses and ancillary workers were on strike, and huge quantities of rotting food and rubbish piled up in the streets because the dustmen were on strike. Rats had the best time since the Black Death (see Chapter 10 to find out why), only you couldn't bring out your dead because the gravediggers were on strike, too. People called this period the Winter of Discontent.

### *. . . Made glorious summer for this daughter of Grantham*

When Callaghan flew back from his summit with his souvenirs and a nice tan some reporters asked him what he was going to do about the crisis. 'Crisis? What crisis?' was how they summed up his reply. As soon as the workers had got their pay rises and gone back to work he called an election. The Conservatives seized their chance. 'Labour isn't working' declared their election poster, showing an enormous line of unemployed people, and the country clearly agreed. Labour lost heavily and Mrs Thatcher moved into Number Ten. Now things were set to get bumpy.

Mrs Thatcher liked to stride into battle clutching her handbag. She had a typically robust analysis of what Britain needed:

1. **Ditch consensus politics.** We don't agree with the Labour Party so let's stop pretending we do.

2. **Reduce the power of the unions.**

3. **Stop spending government money propping up failing companies.** If that means the companies go under and workers lose their jobs, so be it.

4. **Reduce the size of the government.** It was too big. Sack some civil servants, close down the quangos, and cut back on local government.

Mrs Thatcher's approach to politics was based on encouraging individuals to make their own way, owning their own homes and even shares in the companies they worked for, instead of relying on the state. Her ideal was what she called a 'property-owning democracy'.

Mrs Thatcher got many of her ideas from an American economist called Milton Friedman and his philosophy, *monetarism*. Monetarism taught that governments should cut taxes, especially on the rich, so as to allow a free flow of money at the top end of society which would trickle down to the lower levels as people set up new businesses that would provide jobs. In the short term, monetarism meant heavy unemployment as unprofitable companies lost their government subsidies and went bust, but so long as workers were prepared to try new ways of working, the economy would recover in the end. So went the theory, at any rate.

Mrs Thatcher started by changing the law to allow people living in council houses to buy their own homes. When the Labour-run Greater London Council objected she closed it down. Next she sold off privatised industries and offered shares in them to everyone. The trouble was that her policies were causing massive unemployment, especially in the north of England where many of the old heavy industries were being undercut by new technology or more efficient working practices abroad. The steel industry virtually had to close down in order to reinvent itself. If you've seen the film *The Full Monty* you'll have an idea of the hardship this policy caused in Sheffield, the centre of the steel industry. But the biggest conflict came over coal.

### The great miners' strike

After centuries of mining, coal stocks were running low and Mrs Thatcher's government was keen to move away from what they saw as a dirty, dangerous, and increasingly irrelevant industry. They also relished the idea of a final showdown with the National Union of Mineworkers (NUM). So did the fiery NUM leader, Arthur Scargill.

When the National Coal Board announced it would close down a large number of pits, Scargill called the whole union out on strike. This time the government had stockpiled coal supplies and arranged for foreign coal imports; it had also passed laws making *secondary picketing* (picketing somewhere other than your place of work) illegal. When vast crowds of angry pickets gathered outside collieries, the police were ready for them. Pitched battles broke out between police and miners, especially outside Orgreave colliery in South Yorkshire. It seemed like civil war.

The whole nation was bitterly divided. Some thought the government was being vindictive, others were appalled at the way Scargill and the miners were prepared to resort to violence. In one of the worst incidents, a group of miners dropped a concrete slab onto a taxi carrying a working miner and killed the driver. People all over the country held collections to support the families of striking miners, but Scargill was also getting money from Colonel Gadaffi's regime in Libya, which leapt at the chance to destabilise a Western country. The Libyans had shot and killed a British policewoman in London a couple of years before, so this Libyan link didn't go down well. Even the Labour Party leader, Neil Kinnock, turned against the strike.

### Divide and fall

After a year of increasingly bitter and violent confrontations, the miners had to give in and go back to work – while there was still work to go back to. Here's why the strike collapsed:

- ✔ **The miners were divided.** Scargill hadn't balloted the miners to check they supported him, and the miners in Nottinghamshire and Derbyshire didn't. They even formed a breakaway union which defended its members' right to carry on working.

- ✔ **The government refused to allow any power cuts.** The winter of 1984 was mild in any case, so people didn't miss coal as much as they had back in 1973.

- ✔ **The other unions didn't support the NUM.** The other unions were angry that Scargill had denounced the Trades Union Congress (TUC) for not giving him enough support. From then on, Scargill was on his own.

- ✔ **Mrs Thatcher refused to give in.** And Scargill blinked first.

## Falklands fight, Hong Kong handover

Mrs Thatcher was getting some of the lowest approval ratings since records began when, in 1982, help arrived in the unlikely shape of a right-wing military junta in Argentina. Argentina had a long-standing claim to the Falkland Islands in the South Atlantic, home to a small population of Britons and a large population of sheep. The Argentinean dictator, General Galtieri, ordered a full-scale invasion and Mrs Thatcher hurriedly put together a military task force to sail south and take them back. The conflict was a close thing, especially when British ships proved horribly vulnerable to Argentinean missiles. HMS *Sheffield* was destroyed by a single missile and in one particularly ghastly incident, a boat full of Welsh guardsmen was hit with heavy loss of life. However, the British managed to get ashore and fought their way overland to retake the capital, Port Stanley, from its garrison of tired, cold, hungry, and scared Argentinean conscripts.

Having fought so hard to keep the Falklands out of the clutches of one dictatorship, Mrs Thatcher proved remarkably compliant about handing Hong Kong over to another. Britain's lease on the New Territories in Hong Kong ran out in 1997. Mrs Thatcher agreed to hand the whole of Hong Kong back to China if the Chinese agreed to maintain Hong Kong's booming financial and capitalist economy and respect its democratic institutions. Since the British had made sure that Hong Kong didn't have any democratic institutions the Chinese didn't see any problem with this agreement, until the new governor of Hong Kong, Chris Patten, suddenly introduced elections. The Chinese called Patten all sorts of rude names until 1997, when British rule over its last profitable colony finally ended. The Chinese then set about raking in the profits from Hong Kong's economy while taking no notice of its democratic institutions. So no change there, then.

## *Very special relationships*

Mrs Thatcher had a bracing way of getting on with other world leaders. 'The eyes of Caligula and the mouth of Marilyn Monroe' was how the French president François Mitterrand described her (he was referring to a mad Roman emperor and an American sex goddess, in case you're not sure). She got her own back anyway by declaring, on its bicentenary in 1989, that the French Revolution had been a waste of time and blood and the French should have copied the English example instead. So there.

Mrs Thatcher got on much better with the US president Ronald Reagan, even allowing him free use of UK airspace for his 1986 bombing attack on Libya. And she was more than happy for him to station as many cruise missiles in Britain as he liked, as the Cold War seemed to hot up in the early 1980s.

### Sink the Belgrano!

On 2 May 1982 a British submarine sank the Argentinean cruiser *General Belgrano*, killing 360 people. Gotcha!' was the *Sun* newspaper's tasteless response. But opinion in Britain began to waver when it emerged that the *Belgrano* had actually been steaming away from the Falklands, not towards them. Mrs Thatcher angrily maintained that this detail made no difference: The cruiser was still a danger to the British task force. But others, led by a Labour MP, Tam Dalyell, argued for years for an inquiry into the sinking, calling it a war crime. The sinking of the *Belgrano* still divides opinion today.

## Protest and survive

The Campaign for Nuclear Disarmament (CND) started in 1958 and grew into the biggest protest movement of the century. It made headlines in the 1980s when American cruise missiles were installed in western Europe. Women maintained a permanent protest against the cruise missiles at RAF Greenham Common. CND made people aware of what nuclear missiles could do, and may – *may* – have given the politicians pause for thought. Or there again, maybe not.

The Russians had disparagingly called Mrs Thatcher the 'Iron Lady'. They thought it was an insult, but her supporters loved it. When Mikhail Gorbachev became the new leader of the Soviet Union in 1985, Mrs Thatcher declared he was a man she could do business with, and her approval helped boost his popular image in the West.

Ironically, Mrs Thatcher's approval ratings in America and Russia soared just when her popularity was on the slide at home. When her end came, she fell over two issues: The Poll Tax and Europe.

# The Lady Vanishes

People either loved Mrs Thatcher or they absolutely loathed her. She won three elections in a row (in 1979, 1983, and 1987), but as the 1980s drew to a close her core supporters were suffering. In 1987 the stock exchange crashed spectacularly. House prices boomed as people bought them not to live in but to sell on again at a huge profit, but then the housing market collapsed and thousands of home owners found themselves stuck in houses which were worth a lot less than they'd paid for them. Just when it seemed things couldn't get any worse, Mrs Thatcher hit the nation with the Poll Tax.

The Poll Tax (officially it was called the *Community Charge*, which sounded nicer but no one was fooled) was a tax to finance local government services. The trouble was that it was set at the same rate for everyone, however rich or poor they were. The last time a poll tax was introduced it sparked off the Peasants' Revolt (see Chapter 10 to find out how). The protests against the Thatcher Poll Tax were the worst since the miners' strike (see the earlier section 'The great miners' strike' to find out about this). Even though war was brewing over the Iraqi invasion of Kuwait, the Conservatives decided she would have to go.

One last drama needed to be played out first, though.

## All alone in Europe

The European Community's first taste of the Thatcher style came when she demanded a rebate on Britain's contribution to the EEC's budget. 'I want my money back!' she demanded, rapping on the desk like an irate customer in her father's shop back in Grantham. She got the rebate, too, but the rest of Europe was rather put off by this strange housewife figure with the formidable handbag, and from then on Britain regularly found itself in a minority of one on major European votes.

Mrs Thatcher hated the EEC's Common Agricultural Policy, which paid farmers for overproducing and led to huge stockpiles of unsold butter, grain, and wine. She did sign up to the Single European Market, which removed all restrictions on trade, but she hated the EEC's socialist-style *Social Chapter*, which guaranteed a minimum wage and the right to belong to a union, and she strongly opposed plans for a United States of Europe with a single European currency. When the Berlin Wall came down in 1989, Mrs Thatcher opposed German reunification, saying that the Germans might take the opportunity to dominate Europe again.

By 1990 her ministers and ex-ministers, especially the pro-European ones, had had enough of Mrs Thatcher. When Sir Geoffrey Howe resigned from the government in protest at her stance on Europe he made a powerful resignation speech, attacking her whole style of government. Her ministers took the cue and trooped in one by one to tell her the game was over; she had to go. With tears in her eyes, Mrs Thatcher left Downing Street for the last time.

## Belfast blows up

In 1968 many people in Britain were bewildered when appalling violence broke out in Northern Ireland. To anyone who had looked at Ireland's history in the twentieth century, this eruption of violence came as no surprise at all.

Most of Ireland had become independent from Britain in 1922 (see Chapter 21 to find out how) but six Ulster counties with a majority Protestant population had chosen to remain part of the United Kingdom. Irish nationalists had never given up hope of bringing them into a united Ireland – whether they wanted to or not.

For most of the 1960s Northern Ireland seemed peaceful enough, but underneath the surface serious problems were growing. In areas with a Catholic majority, like the city of Londonderry, the Protestants were rigging the electoral boundaries (known as *jerrymandering*) so as to keep control in their hands and to make sure their families got the best schools and houses. In 1968 a Catholic civil rights movement started protesting against this but Protestants attacked the protestors with stones and batons while the (Protestant) police stood by and watched. The riots got worse and the next year prime minister Harold Wilson sent troops into Northern Ireland to restore order and protect the Catholics.

The nationalist – and Catholic – IRA (Irish Republican Army) saw their chance to get people interested in a united Ireland again. They started shooting British soldiers (even though the soldiers were there to protect the Catholics). The soldiers started turning angrily against the Catholics, the Catholics turned against the soldiers, and the long, bloody Troubles began.

### The Troubles

The Troubles involved so many ghastly incidents that knowing where to start is difficult. These are just a handful of the most notorious events – many, many more occurred:

- **1972: Bloody Sunday** – British paratroopers open fire on a civil rights protest march in Londonderry and kill thirteen people. The British blame the IRA; everyone else blames the British.

  For many years the British army insisted that the soldiers had only opened fire in self-defence and the official enquiry into Bloody Sunday, chaired by Lord Widgery, largely agreed. The Widgery Report was widely denounced as a whitewash until 1998 when Tony Blair's government set up a second enquiry, chaired by Lord Saville, to find out what really happened. The Saville Enquiry went into so much detail that it wasn't until 2010 that it reported back. Its conclusion? The army had gone in looking for trouble and had opened fire without any provocation at all. It may take time (in this case thirty-eight years) but the truth, as they say, will out.

- **1974: Birmingham** – the IRA bombs two crowded pubs on the British mainland, killing seventeen people. The police have the bright idea of framing a group of entirely innocent people with the crime and keeping them in prison for sixteen years. Which leaves the actual bombers free to strike again.

- **1984: Brighton** – the IRA bombs the hotel where Mrs Thatcher and her Cabinet are staying for their party conference. She escapes death by a whisker.

- **1987: Enniskillen** – the IRA bombs a Remembrance Day parade in the small town in County Fermanagh.

- **1996: Canary Wharf and Manchester** – after a ceasefire breaks down, the IRA place bombs which devastate London's financial centre and Manchester's shopping centre.

The British arrested hundreds of paramilitary suspects and held them without charge in the Maze prison's notorious H blocks (so called because they were in the shape of a letter H). The British interrogation methods, which included sleep deprivation and disorientation techniques, were condemned as 'inhuman and degrading' by the European Court of Human Rights. IRA prisoners demanded political status and went on hunger strike, refused to wear prison clothes, and even smeared their cells with their own excrement in protest when they didn't get it. One IRA prisoner, Bobby Sands, even stood successfully for Parliament from his prison cell. Mrs Thatcher, however, whose

Northern Ireland spokesman, Airey Neave MP, had been blown up by the IRA at the House of Commons, refused to give in; Bobby Sands and the other protesters starved themselves to death without having achieved their aims.

### Searching for peace

In 1976 two housewives, Betty Williams and Máiread Corrigan, started a peace movement which even won them both the Nobel Peace Prize, but it soon fizzled out. The only way to stop the violence was to work out who Northern Ireland ought to belong to. In 1973 the British closed the Northern Ireland Parliament down and started endless talks to work out some way in which the Protestants could share power with the Catholics. Not easy with people who sometimes refused to sit in the same room together. In 1974 the Protestants stopped one attempt at power-sharing by staging a general strike. In 1985 Mrs Thatcher allowed Dublin a tiny little say in Northern Ireland's affairs, but the Unionists responded 'Ulster Says No!' very, very loudly.

In 1993 prime minister John Major signed the *Downing Street Declaration* with the Irish taosaich Albert Reynolds, by which both sides agreed to respect the wishes of the majority of the people of Northern Ireland, and in 1998 Tony Blair negotiated the *Good Friday Agreement* with all parties, including Sinn Fein (the IRA's political arm), which confirmed the 1993 agreement and finally called a ceasefire. The paramilitaries refused to surrender their weapons, but they undertook to *decommission* them – somehow put them beyond use – and a special commission was set up under a Canadian general, John de Chastelain, to make sure they did it.

The people of Ireland, north and south, voted by a massive majority in favour of the ceasefire, but that action wasn't good enough for one group of diehards: On 15 August 1998 the 'Real IRA' exploded a car bomb in Omagh killing 28 people, including children visiting from the Republic and from Spain, and three generations of one family. The bombers were trying to derail the peace process; for once they failed.

---

## The Americans are coming!

When trouble broke out in Ulster in 1968 many Irish-Americans contributed to Noraid, which raised money for the IRA. Public opinion in Britain was deeply offended at the sight of American money bankrolling terrorists and for a long time British governments were wary of letting the American government intervene in Northern Ireland. When Tony Blair became prime minister in 1997 he set up a good working relationship with US president Bill Clinton, who liked to claim he had Irish blood even though he hadn't. Clinton gave the green light for Senator George Mitchell to cross over to Ulster to supervise the peace negotiations between the British and Irish governments and the Northern Irish political parties, including Sinn Fein. After the Good Friday Agreement was signed, Clinton came over to Ulster and addressed a cheering crowd from Belfast's City Hall. And no doubt felt Irish all over again.

Mind you, the situation looked as if the politicians would be able to scupper the peace process all on their own. The first Northern Ireland government under the terms of the peace agreements had a Unionist leader and a Sinn Fein education minister. That government didn't last. Here's why:

Number of weapons decommissioned in Northern Ireland 1997–2000: Zero

In 2000 Tony Blair's government had to suspend the new Northern Ireland Assembly for a few months and reimpose direct rule from London. Nevertheless, without bombs going off every few months Northern Ireland started to recover. Belfast and Londonderry began to develop the sort of café and club culture that other British cities were used to. To everyone's amazement, the Unionists, under their veteran hard-line leader, Dr Ian Paisley, even went into a power-sharing government with Sinn Fein – their deadly enemies. Paisley seemed to get on so well with his Sinn Fein counterpart, Martin McGuinness, that they were nicknamed 'the Chuckle Brothers'. Against all expectations, the peace seemed to hold. End of story?

The basic problem of Northern Ireland hasn't gone away: Ireland is still partitioned. Northern Ireland's troubles have a habit of reappearing in just when you think you've seen the back of them for ever.

# New Labour, New Dawn

Ironically, Mrs Thatcher probably changed the Labour Party even more than she changed the Conservatives. At first Labour responded to her by moving much more to the left, calling for unilateral nuclear disarmament, high taxes, heavy government spending, and the re-nationalisation of everything she'd privatised.

Labour councillors in Liverpool under Council leader Derek Hatton refused to set a legal level of rates. They wanted to soak the rich and they weren't going to let a little thing like the law stop them.

Labour leader Neil Kinnock finally took on the left and expelled the extremists from the Labour Party. He was particularly scathing about Hatton's councillors in Liverpool, who'd plunged the city into such financial chaos that they had had to sack hundreds of their own workers. So Labour was already looking much more balanced, moderate, competent, and electable when in 1994 the party elected a young up-and-coming MP called Tony Blair.

Tony Blair persuaded the party to drop its commitment to the state ownership of industry. To people on the left, state ownership of industry was what the Labour Party was for, but Blair had an answer for them: That was Old Labour; this was *New Labour*.

## Major problems

After Mrs Thatcher's fall (see the section "All alone in Europe" earlier in this chapter) the Conservatives limped on under the luckless John Major. On *Black Wednesday* in September 1992 the pound collapsed in value and Major had to pull Britain out of the European Exchange Rate Mechanism. Most people probably didn't understand the issue, but the crisis made the government look weak and, worse, incompetent.

Major skilfully negotiated a special opt-out for Britain from the single European currency, but the rotating eyeballs brigade within the Conservative Party thought the European Union was the work of Lucifer and continually denounced Major for not being man enough to stand up to it. By 1997 Major's parliamentary majority could be counted on the fingers of one hand, and his party was deeply tarnished by sleaze and scandal. In the General Election that year, Tony Blair trounced him.

## Blair's Britain

Tony Blair's New Labour kicked into action straight away. The new Chancellor of the Exchequer, Gordon Brown, immediately handed over control of interest rates to the Bank of England: No longer would ministers push people's mortgages up or down for their own political advantage. Labour introduced a minimum wage for all employees, passed a Freedom of Information Act, and incorporated the European Declaration of Human Rights into English law.

Mrs Thatcher had hated local government; Blair strengthened it by introducing elected mayors in some of Britain's major cities. The undoubted star was the energetic Labour Mayor of London, Ken Livingstone, who was a more effective critic of New Labour than the Conservatives were and who ignored the grumblers to introduce a Congestion Charge to tackle London's chronic rush-hour gridlock.

Mind you, Blair's embarrassingly empty Dome at Greenwich, built to mark the new millennium, became a national joke, but it was party time in 2005 when London won the right to host the 2012 Olympics. Meanwhile, the countryside was in economic crisis and up in arms about Labour's plans to ban hunting. Blair's was a very urban government.

## Scotland and Wales – sort-of nations once again

Scottish and Welsh nationalists were also putting in a bid to pull out of Great Britain plc. These nationalists called the process *devolution*, which wasn't quite independence, but was a bit more than allowing soldiers to wear kilts or leeks in their hats. The Scots got a proper parliament, with a state opening by the queen, a state-of-the-art new building (eventually – it was late and way over budget) and the power to do pretty much everything except send out ambassadors and declare war. The Welsh got a much more limited assembly in Cardiff. This assembly couldn't do much, and it didn't.

Despite devolution, New Labour proved very keen on developing a sense of national citizenship and devised a ceremony for new British citizens, with a large Union flag and a tape recording of the National Anthem. If you think it sounds a bit like graduation, you're right, because immigrants had a citizenship test to pass as well. It covered just about everything from the political structure of the country down to what to do if you knock over someone's pint in a pub. (Answer: Run.)

## Lording it over the Lords

Blair was keen to reform the House of Lords, or at any rate stop it opposing him. The Lord Chancellor, Lord Irvine – a rather grand man who liked to compare himself to Cardinal Wolsey to Blair's young Henry VIII (see Chapter 11 if you're not sure what on earth that was all about) – negotiated a deal to get rid of most of the hereditary peers. This left almost all of the House of Lords to be nominated by the party leaders, which was just asking for dodgy dealings. Sure enough, in 2005 the police started investigating claims that seats in the Lords had been changing hands for cash.

Like Mrs Thatcher, Blair won three elections in a row (in 1997, 2001, and 2005). He did so by appealing to *middle England*, the sort of middle-class people with a bit of money put by who'd traditionally voted Conservative but who were dismayed by the Conservatives' sleazy reputation and general incompetence. Unfortunately, many people in the Labour Party thought that Blair was so concerned about winning former Tory voters that he'd forgotten his own traditional Labour supporters. Blair kept the privatised industries privatised, and even extended private enterprise into schools and hospitals. For a Labour government, this state of affairs all looked very odd.

## Hold it right there, General. You're nicked.

In 1998 the former Chilean dictator General Pinochet was arrested in London at the request of a Spanish judge. The courts couldn't decide whether the General, as a former head of state, enjoyed immunity or not, but the House of Lords ruled that he didn't. The case against Pinochet rocked to and fro and in the end he was sent back to Chile on, er, health grounds anyway. But the principle underlying the Lords' judgement still stands in international law: even former heads of state can be tried for crimes against humanity.

But nothing dismayed Blair's Labour supporters more than his approach to foreign policy.

# *Shoulder to shoulder with America*

New Labour had learnt a lot from Bill Clinton's success in making the Democrats electable again after the Reagan years, and they shared many of the same attitudes and outlook. Blair, who was always a very dutiful husband and father, even stood by his friend Bill throughout the lurid Monica Lewinsky scandal in Washington.

When George W. Bush was elected president in 2000 he was wary of Clinton's British buddy, but after the *Al-Qaida* (the extreme Islamist international terrorist network) attacks on New York and Washington on 11 September 2001, Blair was quick to declare that Britain stood shoulder to shoulder with America in its hour of need. When Bush ordered a full-scale invasion of Afghanistan to flush out Al-Qaida's bases and the Taliban government that had supported them, Blair immediately committed British forces to fight alongside the Americans (though perhaps he should've checked in this book first to see what happened on previous occasions when Britain invaded Afghanistan. You can, in Chapter 19.)

And then Bush started talking about Iraq.

## *Iraq Round One: 1990–1*

From the 1960s Iraq had been ruled by a brutal, anti-Islamic dictatorship set up by the Ba'ath Party under its leader, Saddam Hussein.

The West supported Saddam in his war with Iran and carefully looked the other way when he used poison gas to murder hundreds of Kurdish people in northern Iraq. But when Saddam launched an invasion of the oil-rich Kingdom of Kuwait in 1990, the West suddenly denounced him as a tyrant and a murderer. A US-led coalition invaded Kuwait and drove the Iraqis out, but did not carry on into Iraq itself and overturn Saddam. Unfortunately, Iraq's Kurdish people had risen in rebellion against Saddam, expecting that the allies would help them. Once it was clear that the allies weren't going to invade, Saddam launched his army against the defenceless Kurds.

John Major sent British troops to Iraq and came up with the idea of *safe havens* and *no-fly-zones* for the Kurds, where the Iraqi government was not allowed to send troops or planes and the Kurds could be safe. Coalition forces policed the no-fly-zones and the system seemed to work. Britain and the US also maintained international sanctions against Saddam's regime.

### Iraq Round Two: 2003

After the invasion of Afghanistan in 2001 President George W. Bush started talking about the threat from Iraq's stash of *Weapons of Mass Destruction* (WMD) He said that the only safe solution was regime change. Which meant invasion.

In London, a quarter of a million people marched against the war in one of the biggest demonstrations in British history. To persuade parliament of the need for war, Blair's government prepared a dossier of evidence gathered from British intelligence. The dossier claimed that Iraq had missiles that could hit British territory in only forty-five minutes. Even though it turned out that some of the dossier had been lifted from a PhD student's thesis on the Internet, Parliament gave the go-ahead and British troops went into Iraq alongside the Americans.

Unfortunately, the coalition forces found no evidence whatsoever of WMD. A BBC journalist reported that a top British weapons inspector had claimed Blair's office had 'sexed up' the intelligence reports to make them look more definite. A furious row then broke out between the government and BBC, when the weapons inspector in question, Dr David Kelly, was found dead, apparently by his own hand. All very fishy.

Soon everybody was demanding public inquiries. The first one, chaired by Lord Hutton, criticised the BBC; the second one, chaired by Lord Butler, former Cabinet Secretary, said Blair's informal 'sofa' style of government meant he'd taken the country into war without proper records being kept of crucial discussions and meetings. And then the war came even closer to home.

# Britons bomb Britain

On 7 July 2005 four young British men took a train to London, boarded the *tube* (underground railway) in four different directions, and detonated bombs in their rucksacks. One of them couldn't get onto the tube because the stations were all being evacuated after the first three bombs, so he got on a bus and blew that up instead. In all, 56 people were killed that day, not counting the bombers. People assumed this was an Al-Qaida attack in revenge for British participation in the occupation of Afghanistan and Iraq and they were right. But the bombers hadn't come from outside: They were British Muslims, born and bred.

Britain was shocked. Blair tried to maintain that the bombings had nothing to do with Iraq, but no one believed him, and soon video tapes from the bombers were released which made the connection quite clear. Two weeks later a second group of British Muslims tried but failed to explode four more suicide bombs. The following day the police shot a young Brazilian electrician,

Jean Charles de Menezes, in the head in front of horrified tube passengers in South London. The police said they thought he, too, was a suicide bomber, but it soon turned out they'd made a horrific mistake.

What was happening to Britain? The government responded to the attacks by bringing in even tougher restrictions on personal liberty, allowing the police to lock suspects up for long periods without charge. The judges ruled that some of these new laws were themselves illegal, and that they denied liberties the British people had fought for centuries before.

## Where was the queen while all this was going on?

When Elizabeth II came to the throne in 1952, everyone said her reign was going to be a 'new Elizabethan' age. It wasn't. The queen has so little power she isn't necessarily needed even when a dead heat occurs in an election. However, she has the right to have her advice listened to and many prime ministers have found her questioning surprisingly sharp. Her Silver Jubilee celebrations in 1977 were a great success, with street parties and acres of red, white, and blue bunting; Prince Charles's wedding to Lady Diana Spencer in 1981 was an even bigger worldwide hit. Diana had genuine star quality and developed a devoted following round the world.

But when the royal dream went sour the tabloids turned on the royals with undisguised glee. In the 1950s when the issue was 'Would Princess Margaret marry divorced Group Captain Peter Townshend?', the answer was no. In the 1960s when it was 'Would Princess Margaret and Lord Snowdon get divorced?', the answer was yes. Then Princess Anne's marriage collapsed and Prince Andrew had hardly brushed the confetti out of his hair before his wife, Sarah 'Fergie' Ferguson, the Duchess of York, was caught on camera cavorting with a Texan millionaire. Could things get any worse? Yes, they could. Diana and Charles were getting divorced, too.

Charles had apparently, it transpired, never really wanted to marry Diana and had been in love for years with Mrs Camilla Parker-Bowles. Diana gave a frank television interview pointing out that with three people in it, her marriage to Charles was rather crowded. Not long after her divorce Diana was killed in a spectacular car crash in Paris, and the public grief had to be seen to be believed. The royals were in deep trouble and they knew it.

Yet, amazingly, the royal family bounced back. Diana's children, William and Harry, were very popular, the Queen Mother's death in 2002 won the royals a lot of sympathy, and against all the odds the Queen's Golden Jubilee in 2002 was a triumph. Public opinion even came round to accepting Charles's marriage to Camilla in 2004. Much of this success was down to the undiminished respect for the Queen herself, who rose to the occasion with some well chosen words when Muslim suicide bombers struck in London in 2005. What will happen after she has gone? Watch this space!

# *You said I could have a go! –*
# *Gordon Brown*

It's always sad when friends fall out, especially when those friends (make that ex-friends) are the Prime Minister and the Chancellor of the Exchequer. As young up-and-coming new MPs Tony Blair and Gordon Brown had shared an office at the House of Commons. Grumpy Gordon was a bit scary and you didn't want to be caught with him at parties, but he was a heavy-hitter, widely tipped to be next leader of the Labour Party. But to everyone's surprise – especially Gordon's – Tony Blair – smoother, flashier, and much easier to talk to – beat him to it. The two old room-mates had reached a deal at a fashionable eatery called the Granita in fashionable Islington: Tony Blair would become leader and (hopefully) Prime Minister first, and then he would hand over to Gordon Brown. And Gordon believed him.

Guess what happened? Tony Blair soon found that he liked being Prime Minister and forgot all about his promise. Gordon sank into one of the biggest sulks of the post-war era. The Labour Party split into Blairites (who thought it was best to keep in with Tony) and Brownites (who were keeping their eye on what they hoped was the future). It wasn't until 2007, ten years after he first became Prime Minister, that Tony Blair finally stood down and made way for Gordon Brown.

Gordon Brown, though, simply wasn't one of history's lucky leaders. Almost immediately he became Prime Minister, everything started going wrong.

- ✔ **Election time! Oh all right, then, not election time.** In 2007 Brown's younger ministers urge him to call a snap election and crush the Tories. 'Bring it on!' say the Tories, trying to be brave. Will he? Won't he? Brown finally decides against it. 'Chicken!' say the (mightily relieved) Tories.

- ✔ **Lock 'em up! Oh all right, then, don't lock' em up.** Brown's proposal to lock terrorist suspects up for 42 days without charge prompts a rebellion amongst Labour MPs who haven't entirely forgotten Habeas Corpus (and nip ahead to Chapter 25 if you have) and gets defeated in the House of Lords.

- ✔ **Referendum time! Oh all right, then, not referendum time.** Blair and Brown promise a referendum on the new EU Constitution, but when the EU makes a few alterations, changes the font, and gives it a new cover, Brown decides he had never seen this document in his life and it doesn't need a referendum. 'Chicken!' say the Tories – again.

✔ **Just put it on expenses!** The press exposes how MPs of all parties have been charging the taxpayer for anything from groceries to duck houses, and even porn films. Some of the worst examples of cynical system-playing – including claiming for phantom mortgages – involved Labour MPs, who were meant to be above that sort of thing.

By 2010 Gordon Brown couldn't delay holding a general election any longer, but his run of bad luck still hadn't ended. He struggled in a series of live TV debates with his highly telegenic rivals, Conservative David Cameron and Liberal Democrat Nick Clegg. And then he forgot to switch off his mike while on campaign and was recorded describing a Labour-voting grandmother as a 'bigot' because she'd asked him about immigration. Tip: If you must insult the voters, don't do it with a live microphone attached to your jacket.

The 2010 election produced a hung parliament, with no overall majority. The Tories and Liberal Democrats did a deal in which David Cameron became Prime Minister and Nick Clegg became his deputy in Britain's first coalition government since 1945.

Interesting times indeed.

# Part VII
# The Part of Tens

# In this part . . .

**T**his part gives you some information to slip into conversation at dinner parties. You know the sort of thing: The talk is flowing, people are blabbing away, and you have to go and say: 'The British? I'll tell you about the British. They've given ten major things to the world, and ten *only*. And if you'll give me a moment to look them up, I'll tell you what they are.'

So here you are. My lists of turning points, documents, people who should be better known, and places to visit that you may not otherwise have thought of. Oh, and those ten things the British have given the world. You may not agree with any of them, but that disagreement is the great thing about history – people think it's about facts but it isn't, history's about opinions. Mine, in this book, but yours too!

# Chapter 24

# Ten Top Turning Points

*In This Chapter*

▶ Important and far-reaching political events

▶ Pivotal military campaigns

▶ The beginning of an island race

Sometimes people know when something happens that the event's really important, that things will never be the same again. Usually, however, how pivotal an event is only becomes clear much later on. When Queen Victoria died in 1901, everyone talked about the end of an era, but now we can see that her passing wasn't nearly as important as the outbreak of the First World War in 1914. Yet when war was declared, no one really took it too seriously. They thought the hostilities would be a short scrap, 'over by Christmas', in the famous phrase. So people living at the time aren't the ones who make 'turning points'; that job's left to historians, who come later and can see what followed. Here's my list of ten points in British history that really did make a difference.

## End of the Ice Age, c. 7,500 BC

You sometimes hear a good story about how a British newspaper once carried the headline: 'Fog in the Channel: Continent cut off.' Okay, the paper was joking, but even so it encapsulates the British and their outlook on the world. Everything hinges on their being on an island, and this is the period when they became one. To read about the early, *early* history of Britain, head to Chapters 2 and 3.

## The Romans Invade Britain, 43 AD

The English felt very proud of having once been Roman citizens and even started talking about being descended from a Roman figure called Brutus: A Roman past set them apart from the Scots and Irish. Later, the Victorians likened their Empire to the Romans': Where the Romans brought aqueducts and the *Pax Romana*, the 'Roman Peace', the British brought railways and the *Pax Britannica*. One Victorian Foreign Secretary even justified using military force against the government of Greece by saying that any British subject could claim military protection from London, just as a Roman citizen could claim Rome's protection anywhere in the world (refer to Chapter 18 for more on this event).

# The Synod of Whitby, 664

Christianity has played a central role in British history ever since it arrived back in Roman times. Christianity comes in many different versions: Which version should the British follow? In 664, the issue was thrashed out at a big meeting at Whitby Abbey in Yorkshire, presided over by King Oswy. On the face of it, the meeting was about whether England was going to stay with the Celtic Church, which was the church in Ireland and Scotland, or whether it was going to join the Roman Church, which had sent missionaries into Kent. But what was really at stake was whether England was going to join the European mainstream, or whether it was going to stick to its own, native way of doing things. King Oswy opted for the Roman Church and for links with Europe. The Synod of Whitby was the point when England finally turned its back on the Celts and squeezed them out, even in their own church. You can find out more about this Synod and life in Anglo-Saxon England in Chapter 5.

# The Norman Invasion of England, 1066

The Norman Invasion is still one of the most remarkable military campaigns in history. The Normans shouldn't have won: They came from a small, second-class duchy, and England was a stable, sophisticated, and wealthy kingdom. But once they had won, everything changed. The Normans made England a European power, not just strong enough to defend itself, which is what the Saxons had done, but able and willing to expand. That capability for expansion is why 1066 matters to the Welsh, the Irish, and the Scots as well. Head to Chapter 7 for more on the Norman invasion.

# The English Invade Ireland, 1170

Only one Pope has been English: Nicholas Breakspear, who reigned as Pope Adrian IV. He was the one who gave the go-ahead for King Henry II to launch an invasion of Ireland. In fact, the King of Leinster, an Irish kingdom, had invited the English in to help him get power, but the English decided to stay and take power themselves. These actions changed England's relations with

Ireland forever and started centuries of misery and bloodshed. (Chapter 8 provides more information on how the English became involved with Ireland.) The English could never control all of Ireland, but as long as they thought they should, there would never be peace. And there wasn't.

# The Battle of Bannockburn, 1314

The Battle of Bannockburn is Scotland's favourite battle. This battle's the big one, when they beat the English and sent them packing. The English had already conquered the Welsh, and they had every reason to think Scotland was going to go the same way. Bannockburn saved the Scots and shattered the idea that the English were somehow invincible. If England had won, Scotland would have become an English province, just as Wales had (Chapter 9 explains this in more detail), and the idea that it had once been a separate kingdom would have become a memory. The fact that Scotland retained its separate identity and history owes a lot to what happened at Bannockburn.

# Henry VIII Breaks with Rome, 1532

Henry VIII's quarrel with Rome may look like a purely English event, but it had huge implications for the whole of Britain. Henry's taking the English church out of the Roman Church gave the green light to a wave of religious change that spread throughout the islands. The Reformation crossed national boundaries – Scottish Protestants felt they had much more in common with English Protestants than with Scottish Catholics – but the English came to associate being Protestant with being English. Their Protestantism was one more thing that separated the English from the Irish, and it became one of the most important differences between them and the French or Spanish. Protestantism helped divide and shape Britain along lines we still see today, and Henry VIII started the process off. Read Chapter 11 for details about Henry's reign and Chapter 12 for the role religion played in the events occurring during the reigns of the Tudor and Stuart monarchs.

# Charles 1 Tries to Arrest Five MPs, 1642

Anyone can stage a rebellion, but defying the king to his face is something else. Even rebels usually protest their loyalty to the king and say they are only angry with his 'evil advisers'. But when Charles I went into the House of Commons to arrest five MPs in 1642, the House told him, in effect, to get lost. Charles hadn't just lost his authority: He'd lost it for all the monarchs who might come after him as well.

The British may tolerate a monarch, may even go all gooey-eyed about a monarch, but after 1642, monarchs were there because the people said so and for no other reason. Charles I, James II, George III, and even Edward VIII all learned this lesson the hard way (by losing – in the order mentioned – their head, throne, American colonies, and throne). Cutting off Charles's head set a powerful precedent for other revolutions to follow: You could say that the House of Commons changed the history of the world that January morning in 1642. Head to Chapter 13 to find out more about Charles I's reign and the tug of war that led to civil war.

# The Great Reform Act, 1832

Time was when everyone learned about Earl Grey and the Reform Act (explained in Chapter 17). Not any more. That omission's a shame, because the Reform Act was as important as any battle, possibly more so. On the face of it, the Reform Act was all about rotten boroughs and different types of franchise, but the Act was more important than the inequities it addressed.

When you consider that just about every other European nation had a revolution and the USA had a civil war, the fact that Britain didn't was no mean feat. The difference was that the British had mastered the art of reform, knowing when and how to change within the system. Ultimately, this mastery meant that the British, without a bloody and violent revolution, could develop a democratic system that would survive through the twentieth century and beyond. Thank the Reform Act.

# The Fall of Singapore, 1942

The British Empire was always based on bluff, and in Singapore, the bluff got called. Everyone thought Singapore was impregnable, the symbol of British power throughout the East. The British were so used to being superior that they assumed that, as Churchill put it, the 'little yellow men' would never dare take on the might of the British Empire. But they did and, in the process, showed that the Empire wasn't so mighty after all. Singapore didn't fall after some desperate last-ditch battle; it fell with hardly a shot. All those proud British officers and men had to surrender to an Asian army. All that sense of racial and military superiority the British Empire stood for collapsed. The British were no more special than anyone else, and the whole world knew it. From that moment on, who won the war didn't matter. The British Empire was doomed. You can find out more about the beginning and end of the British Empire in Chapters 19 and 22.

# Chapter 25

# Ten Major Documents

*In This Chapter*

▶ Pondering political manifestos of the people

▶ Acting on Acts of Parliament and legal documents

▶ Revering religious and scientific works

**D**ocuments are the life-blood of history. They are the most direct way in which we can communicate with the dead and read into their minds. Of course *document* is a wide term: A document may be a great legal charter, or it might just be someone's pocket book. But the important documents don't just tell us about the people who wrote them: They take on a life of their own and tell us about the people who came after.

## Bede's Ecclesiastical History of the English People (731)

Kicking off with a history book may seem strange, but Bede's *History* isn't quite like other history books. Bede was a monk at Jarrow in northeast England, and he set himself the task of describing the story of the English people through their experience of Christianity. And a good story he tells, too. Bede's been called the Father of English History, and he deserves the title. But he's more than that – he's our way into the world and beliefs of Anglo-Saxon England.

## The Book of Kells (800)

*The Book of Kells* is an illustrated copy of the gospels, probably produced in Northumbria and now on view in the library of Trinity College, Dublin. This book shows Celtic art at its finest, with rich colours and intricate patterns, all lovingly created over what must have been many years. You have to remind yourself that these guys were working by hand, and if they made a mistake, they couldn't just screw the page up and start again. *The Book of Kells* isn't just a piece of beautiful craftsmanship, it's a reminder of the rich Christian heritage that once united Britain and Ireland.

# Magna Carta (1215)

Magna Carta (discussed in Chapter 9) is so famous that putting it in perspective can be difficult. Historians like to point out that this document didn't actually transform England into a medieval democratic republic, but so what? The barons who faced King John at Runnymede in 1215 drew up this document, a bill of rights if you like, and they stood over the king until he accepted it. And some of the rights were fundamental, like the right to have a fair trial, or the right not to be taxed without your own consent. But even more important, the barons were forcing King John to accept the principle that the Crown was not above the law: Kings had to obey the law just like anyone else.

# The Declaration of Arbroath (1320)

The Declaration of Arbroath is Scotland's Declaration of Independence. The Scottish nobles under King Robert the Bruce drew the Declaration up and sent it to the Pope. It says that Scotland is an ancient, independent kingdom, with its own people, separate from England and not subject to her. And the Declaration of Arbroath says this in fine, defiant language.

But the Declaration isn't just about who should rule Scotland, or even about Scotland being a separate nation. This document's about the right of any people to fight for the freedom to govern themselves. All Scots learn about the Declaration of Arbroath: Not enough English do. Perhaps things might be different if they did.

# The Authorised 'King James' Version of the Bible (1611)

The English Bible was the single most important product of those busy printing presses during the Reformation, and of all the many versions, the King James version was the finest and most beautiful.

The King James Bible wasn't just a work of literature: This book became an integral part of life. Even the poorest family had a family Bible at home and read it. Inside they often kept a copy of their family tree. Phrases from the King James Bible have passed into the language: a wolf in sheep's clothing, salt of the earth, the apple of his eye, and many more. This Bible became part of the armoury of missionaries, trade unionists, colonists, teachers, and soldiers. A genuine masterpiece.

# The Petition of Right (1628)

King Charles I (refer to Chapter 13) had only been on the throne three years, and already he was putting backs up. The Petition of Right was when Parliament first drew up a list of what the king had done wrong and got him to accept it. As with so many documents about rights and freedom, you have to be a bit careful in interpreting its purpose: No one was trying to introduce universal human rights in 1628. But the Petition did lay down a king's duties towards his subjects, and it did establish that Parliament had a right to discuss these things. The Petition came in very handy when the American colonists were looking for a precedent for their objections to the way King George III was ruling them (see Chapter 17). In that sense, the Petition of Right was sending a warning note out to all monarchs everywhere: You cannot simply do as you please. Not bad for 1628.

# Habeas Corpus (1679)

If Britain is not a police state, thank this Act of Parliament, passed back in the reign of King Charles II. Never mind about the funny Latin title, which is all about 'that you have the body': This Act defines one of the most important and fundamental of all human rights. If the police in Britain arrest you, they have to say why they are holding you by charging you with a recognised offence, and they have to produce you in person before a magistrate (the bit about 'having the body' comes in here) within a couple of days. If you're thinking 'So what?', consider the alternative. Without Habeas Corpus, the police could arrest you for anything at all – your face, your views, your colour – and could keep you for as long as they liked. They could kill you in prison and no one would ever know. Feel a bit different about Habeas Corpus now?

Much of the controversy surrounding the anti-terrorist measures brought in after the London bombings of 2005 was about how far security measures were taking away the ancient right of Habeas Corpus.

# Lord Mansfield's Judgement (1772)

Lord Mansfield was a tough old conservative Lord Chancellor who sat in 1772 in what was known as the Somerset case. A black slave called James Somerset had run away from his master, who was now demanding him back.

Thousands of African slaves were in Britain at the time, but that didn't stop Mansfield coming up with a truly remarkable judgement. He decided that Somerset had to go free, because habeas corpus applied to everyone so, in effect, slavery was illegal in England. Not in British colonies overseas, mind, but in England. Instantly, all those thousands of other slaves in England were free. Lord Mansfield's Judgement began the long legal battle for racial equality that continued through the fight against slavery, through Martin Luther King's fight for black civil rights, and into today. One of the great legal judgements of all time.

# The People's Charter (1838)

In 1838 a group of London working men led by a joiner called William Lovett met together to produce one of the most remarkable documents in British history: The People's Charter. The People's Charter was a manifesto calling for working people to be given the vote. But this document's a lot more than that. Lovett and his fellow *Chartists* had very carefully thought out just how universal suffrage should work: Having the vote without a secret ballot or if the electoral boundaries are unfair is useless. So instead of just demanding the vote, the Chartists put forward a whole political programme, almost a philosophy. In short, they'd worked out how to turn the Victorian political system into a democracy. Did it get them the vote? Well, not immediately it didn't. But the Chartists were proved right in the end. You can find out more about the People's Charter in Chapter 18.

# Darwin's The Origin of Species (1859)

Darwin nearly didn't publish *The Origin of Species* because he was afraid it might provoke a fuss (turns out he was right). Darwin didn't get his ideas about natural selection and survival of the fittest out of the blue: Plenty of other scientists were thinking along the same lines, but no one put the ideas together quite as coherently as Darwin. *The Origin of Species* sold: People knew it was an important book, one they needed to get their head round. The Church of England was outraged, as Darwin had expected, but the tide of opinion in Britain was strongly in Darwin's favour. Darwin's ideas didn't break the Church by any means, but it broke the very literal way of understanding religion, and in that sense, the world was never quite the same again.

# Chapter 26

# Ten Things the British Have Given the World (Whether the World Wanted Them or Not)

*In This Chapter*

▶ Legal systems and civil rights

▶ The Beatles *and* Gilbert and Sullivan

▶ Advances in technology, science, and medicine

▶ The world's first – and many of the greatest – novels

▶ Tea with milk

*H*ow would the world have been different if the British hadn't come along? Here are some examples of great – and maybe not so great – cultural contributions which the world would have missed.

## *Parliamentary Government*

You can't get away from this one. Of course, parliamentary government wasn't always a happy export, but the idea that it *is* possible to have a stable and workable system of representative government was one of the most important ideas the British gave the world. Parliamentary government was an inspiration to the French revolutionaries, and it was never far away from the minds of other Europeans as they manned the barricades in the nineteenth century. We all get fed up from time to time with the 'Mother of Parliaments', but the importance of what it achieved cannot be denied.

# The English Common Law

Alongside Parliament, English Common Law is probably the most influential aspect of Britain's 'unwritten' constitution. It is the basis of legal systems around the world, and it forms an important part of the legal system in the United States: American courts can and sometimes do cite English legal precedents.

The basic idea of English Common Law is that people are tried by their peers on a specific charge and on nothing else. So the issue's not 'Are you a bad person?' – which you may well be – but 'Did you do *this*?' which you might not have done, even if you are a bad person. And you are innocent until proven guilty. Oh, and all those gowns and wigs make a great TV drama.

# Organised Sport

The Victorians had quite a genius for creating sports and exporting them round the globe. The Duke of Wellington said the Battle of Waterloo was won on the playing fields of Eton, where his officers learned about leadership and being part of a team. And look at the list of international sports the British have given the world: Golf from Scotland, rugby from England, football, tennis, badminton, horse racing, and of course cricket. The British didn't just invent these games; they drew up the rules and took them around the Empire. Just think: If they hadn't exported sports, the rest of the world would never have had the chance to beat the Brits at golf, rugby, football, tennis . . .

# The Novel

A bit difficult to call the novel a British invention exactly (though Samuel Richardson's *Pamela* is normally regarded as the first one), but the British very quickly made the novel their own. The Victorians were obsessed with novels and awaited each instalment just like a modern TV audience with the latest soap. Dickens got lapped up on both sides of the Atlantic, and when ships from Britain docked in New York while *The Old Curiosity Shop* was being serialised, people on the quayside yelled out to the people on board, 'Is Little Nell dead?!' As well as producing world-class novelists like Dickens, Jane Austen, and the Brontës, the Victorians also created a whole new genre of children's books, like *Alice in Wonderland* and *The Water Babies*, which has carried through to Enid Blyton, Roald Dahl, and the unstoppable Harry Potter phenomenon.

# DNA

The way James Watson and Francis Crick came up with the DNA double helix was wonderfully British. Yes, I know Watson was American, but he and Crick were working in Cambridge, in a race with Maurice Wilkins and Rosalind Franklin at Imperial College, London. The process was all so gentlemanly and amateurish, and when Watson and Crick finally worked it out, they immediately ran out and announced the news in the nearest pub. You don't get more British than that.

# The BBC

Telecommunications owe a lot to Britain: Marconi, who invented the radio, worked in England, Alexander Graham Bell, who invented the telephone, was a Scot, and so was John Logie Baird, who invented television so you could have something for your telephone to interrupt. The BBC quickly turned radio into an authentically British institution, to go with afternoon tea and crumpets. The BBC radio soap *The Archers*, about the goings-on in a small country village, has been running since the 1950s. Nothing ever happens in *The Archers*, but some people would kill rather than miss an episode.

# The Beatles

The great thing about the Beatles is that they used words. The lyrics matter, which is why you can hardly visit any major tourist attraction in Europe without hearing someone strumming a guitar and singing 'Yezderdeh, oll mah trrbles simmed so feurrh aweh.' The Beatles are a good example of how the British managed to take the pop revolution and tame it. When they first arrived on the scene, the British didn't know what had hit them, but if you looked, all those girls screaming their heads off at London Airport were still wearing their school uniform: Very British. The boys went through their different phases (remember those weird suits with no lapels or collars?), and before you knew it, they'd been awarded the MBE and you had military bands playing Beatles numbers at royal garden parties.

## Tea with Milk

Originally, putting the milk in first meant that your china was so fine – that is, expensive – that, if you didn't, it would shatter; now putting the milk in first is considered not quite the done thing in posh circles. Tea purists look with horror on the British habit of swamping fine oriental teas with cold milk, but you probably just have to accept that the world now has two different tea drinks: Tea as drunk in most of the world, with lemon or sugar to taste, and tea-with-milk as drunk by just about everyone in Britain. And don't forget British builders' tea, which is a large mug of milk with half a pound of sugar added and waved in the general direction of a used tea bag.

## Penicillin

How many times have you had an infection or a cut that's gone a bit septic? Quite a few I expect. Right. For most of history, a good chance existed you'd have been dead by now. Ordinary infections killed millions of people until Alexander Fleming (another Scot – see how many of the really useful advances are made by Scots) discovered penicillin by peering at some mould that had formed on an unwashed petri dish. A long time elapsed before penicillin got into a form where people could take it as a medicine (and that was done by a team working in Oxford) but when it did, it changed history. It's hard to think of anything the British have come up with that has saved more lives and done more good around the world than penicillin.

## Gilbert and Sullivan

They may or may not be to your taste, but these guys deserve a mention here. Their operettas were meant to be fairly light skits on the fashions and fads of their day. *Iolanthe* pokes fun at politicians (who doesn't?), *The Pirates of Penzance* sends up the Victorians' strong sense of duty, and *Patience* was written specifically to have a laugh at Oscar Wilde and all his hideously pretentious chums. Normally satire dates very quickly, but G&S are still phenomenally popular both in Britain and in the English-speaking world precisely because they're good enough to work even without the satire.

# Chapter 27

# Ten Great British Places to Visit

**Y**ou don't need me to tell you to visit the Tower of London or Edinburgh Castle or Buckingham Palace or Stratford on Avon: You're bound to do those places anyway. Here are some other ideas for places to visit if you're looking for a sense of the history you've read about in this book. Maybe they were on your list already, but if they weren't, put them on now.

## Skara Brae

Skara Brae is up in the Orkneys, and putting it down on your travel list is worthwhile for that reason alone – if you haven't been up to the Orkneys, you haven't lived. Skara Brae is a beautifully preserved Neolithic village, one of the most complete examples we have. At Skara Brae you get a real sense of going back in time to the distant dawn of civilisation, when humankind emerged from the grip of the ice and first made inroads into the environment. And that's just the hotel. Stonehenge was for special occasions: At Skara Brae you can see how people lived from day to day.

## Iona

The isle of Iona was the haven of peace where St Columba (see Chapter 5) set up his community of monks, and a religious community still exists there today. The abbey was founded much later on by the Benedictines, and you can find the ancient Kings of Scots all buried there, too. The place still has a sense of quiet and peace: You don't go so much as a tourist as you do a pilgrim.

# Hadrian's Wall

Just reading about Hadrian's Wall doesn't do it justice: You have to experience the Wall for yourself. The best way is to put on a pair of stout shoes and start hiking, but you can visit by bus or car, too. Hadrian was no fool: His wall goes through some of the most beautiful countryside in England, but the cities at either end, Carlisle and Newcastle upon Tyne, are well worth visiting, too. If the weather's wet (which it usually is) think how the Romans would have felt, stuck up there in the cold instead of sunning themselves in Tuscany. (Or, if you prefer, think how you're feeling, stuck up there in the cold instead of sunning yourself in Tuscany.)

# Durham

American writer Bill Bryson was bowled over by the city of Durham and couldn't understand why the British didn't shout about it more. Durham is a World Heritage Site, and seeing why isn't difficult. Durham Cathedral has one of the most dramatic sites you can get, right on top of a cliff with the river Wear running round three sides of it. Then when you come out of the cathedral, you find a castle sitting just next door. Durham's a beautiful medieval town, small but with a proud history. Don't miss it. Oh, and see what you make of the accent.

# Stirling Castle

Stirling Castle is just where a castle should be, high up on a rock where you can pour boiling oil on people's heads. If you wanted to control Scotland, Stirling was more important than Edinburgh, so the castle was forever changing hands between the English and the Scots. Edward I had to take Stirling Castle twice.

The castle has a magnificent renaissance Great Hall built by James IV, and the town's well worth visiting, too. And Stirling Castle's not all. Base yourself in Stirling, and you've got three battlefields all within easy reach: Stirling Bridge (1297, Scots beat the English), Bannockburn (1314, Scots trash the English), and Sheriffmuir (1715, Scottish Jacobites beat pro-English Scots but forget to tell anyone, so everyone thinks they lost). The area also has monuments to William 'Braveheart' Wallace and Robert the Bruce. Pack a copy of Robert Burns before you set off.

# Beaumaris

Beaumaris Castle on the Isle of Anglesey is just how you imagine a castle: Round towers and a moat. Beaumaris has been so well-preserved because, like so many castles, it didn't actually see much action until the English Civil War (see Chapter 13), when those round towers weren't going to be much use against heavy cannon. The castle is right on the sea, so you get lovely views, and the site's just the place for a sailing holiday. You may even learn some Welsh. *Croeso.*

# Armagh

If you haven't been to Northern Ireland, then you have a treat in store. The area is breathtakingly beautiful, and knowing what's best to choose is difficult. See the famous Giant's Causeway on the Antrim coast, or the city walls of Londonderry, and all of Belfast is worth exploring. But the City of Armagh gets the prize because you probably wouldn't think of it otherwise. The city is small enough to 'do' easily, and it has two cathedrals (one Protestant, one Catholic – that's Ulster for you!). Armagh is the ancient seat of the Kings of Ulster, and the famous Brian Boru is buried here. Beautifully elegant Georgian terraces and an eighteenth century observatory can be seen in Armagh, all in the lovely local stone that glows in the sun. You can see Jonathan Swift's own copy of *Gulliver's Travels* and listen to it being read by a twenty-foot giant. But then Northern Ireland has a thing about giants.

# Chatsworth House

You can find lots of mansions in beautiful parkland that will take your breath away with their sweeping drives and their deer parks and lakes, but Chatsworth House in Derbyshire takes some beating. Chatsworth's huge, for one thing, and lies in a gorgeous setting in the Peak District. Chatsworth is the home of the Dukes and Duchesses of Devonshire, including the famous Georgiana who went round at election time kissing the voters. The rooms are superb, and a magnificent eighteenth-century water cascade flows outside that makes the hillside look as if it's dancing. Even the gardeners are famous. Joseph Paxton got the idea for the Crystal Palace (see Chapter 18) from the beautifully elegant Chatsworth greenhouses. If you can only manage one stately home, make it this one.

# Ironbridge

Ironbridge is an amazing place. This site's a beautiful little valley in Shropshire, as well as the birthplace of the Industrial Revolution. If you find yourself switching off at the words 'Industrial' and 'Revolution', think again. You can visit a Victorian town at Blist's Hill or see the amazing things the already pretty amazing Darby family managed to do with iron at Coalbrookdale (head to Chapter 16 for more on the Darbys and other important inventors of the age). Not to mention the elegant iron bridge that gives the town its name. The whole valley is a World Heritage Site and rightly so. The Romantics saw beauty in the sheer elemental power of industry: Go to Ironbridge and you can see what they meant.

# Coventry Cathedral

Coventry was pretty impressive even before the terrible night in November 1940 when it was flattened by the Luftwaffe. The cathedral, founded by Leofric of Mercia and his famous wife Lady Godiva, was the pride of the town. When the Germans bombed Coventry, they were trying to destroy something of England's sense of its heritage and identity. The city was so badly destroyed that the British never forgot it, and the Germans coined a new word, *Koventrieren*, to mean more or less what people would soon mean by Hiroshima or Dresden. After the war, Coventry became a symbol of how Britain was going to pick herself up and face the future. Well-paid jobs were available in Coventry's big car factories, and the city centre was rebuilt in the latest futuristic style. Best of all was what they did with the cathedral. Instead of demolishing the ruins, they left them as a permanent memorial, and built a totally new cathedral next to them. The theme was peace and reconciliation, and Coventry forged strong links with its devastated counterpart, Dresden. Coventry's two cathedrals remain a monument to British hopes for the future.

# Chapter 28

# Ten Britons Who Should Be Better Known

*In This Chapter*

▶ People who stood up to injustice

▶ People who overcame almost insurmountable odds

▶ People who advanced medicine or science to the benefit of humankind

How do you judge how well known someone is? You can try a recognition survey, but the results won't tell you much. In any case, people can be very well known at one time and completely forgotten a few years later. Well, here are some other people you may or may not have heard of, but they're all of them worth knowing about. This is their chance to get into the history books.

## King Oswald of Northumbria

Starting a list of people who should be better known with a king may seem odd, but pretty much all the kings of Anglo-Saxon England deserve to be better known. Oswald (AD 633–42) wasn't on the throne long in comparison with some rulers, but he was phenomenally successful. He came back from exile to liberate his native Northumbria from the fearsome Welsh King Cadwallon and triumphed over him against massive odds. Oswald was a Christian, and he got St Aidan down from Iona to help spread the gospel. He gave Aidan the island of Lindisfarne for his base, just down the coast from Oswald's own castle at Bamburgh, and the two men worked very closely together. Oswald was one of those all-round monarchs like Alfred or Henry VIII, a scholar as well as a soldier. For more information on Oswald, head to Chapter 5.

# Robert Grosseteste

Robert Grosseteste (1175–1253) was a thirteenth-century bishop of Lincoln. He was also a great scholar and theologian, and chancellor of Oxford University, where he taught the pioneering scientist-monk Roger Bacon.

Grosseteste was a genuine scientist: He worked in astronomy and optics, and he showed how you could use lenses to see close up or at a great distance, as well as how light refracts in water. He was also a genuinely good bishop: He cleared up all the abuses in Lincoln diocese and saw to it that his parish priests did their jobs properly. Grosseteste wasn't afraid to stand up to powerful people, either. When the Pope wanted to give English parishes to his Italian cronies, Grosseteste stopped him, even though the Pope suspended Grosseteste and threatened him with excommunication. Grosseteste also led a group of bishops who refused to obey the Pope's orders to pay money over to the king – and doing that meant making enemies in two high places. Almost his last act before he died was to tell the Pope to get lost when the Pope tried to wangle a post in England for his nephew. Grosseteste didn't go in for drama in quite the way that Becket did, and he died in his bed.

# Nicholas Owen

If you're Catholic you'll know this man as St Nicholas Owen. In 1970 Pope Paul VI canonised 40 English and Welsh martyrs, and Nicholas Owen (?–1606) was one of them. We know next to nothing about Owen's background, but we do know that he became a Jesuit lay brother in Elizabeth's reign just when it was very dangerous to do so (see Chapter 12 for information about the persecution of Catholics – and just about any other religious sect). But his great claim to fame is that he built the most amazing priest holes – hiding places for Catholic priests. These holes were no sliding panel jobs (far too easy to detect); Owen was the Thomas Chippendale of priest holes. His masterpiece is at Sawston Hall near Cambridge. You can stand on a stone spiral staircase, with nothing but empty space underneath the step you are standing on, with the solid stone of the staircase clearly visible between the wooden slats, and yet you are standing on the entrance to a priest hole. This chamber doesn't seem humanly possible, but it is – I've been in it.

# John Lilburne

Getting yourself imprisoned by Charles I *and* by Oliver Cromwell takes class, but John Lilburne (c. 1614–57) managed it. Lilburne would stand up to anyone and take any punishment, all in the name of religious liberty. When

Lilburne met a Puritan preacher called John Bastwick, who had had his ears cut off for criticising the Archbishop of Canterbury, he was appalled and spoke out on Bastwick's behalf. William Laud, the archbishop in question, had Lilburne arrested and whipped through the streets. Not surprisingly, Lilburne fought for Parliament in the English Civil War (1642–49), and very well he did, too.

But then Lilburne got into trouble with Parliament. His old pal Bastwick had him arrested for criticising the Speaker of the House of Commons (there's gratitude for you). Parliament put Lilburne in prison and fined him, and then decided he wasn't guilty after all and let him out. Next Lilburne took up the cause of the ordinary parliamentary soldiers, who'd won the Civil War for Parliament but didn't have the vote. He helped found a radical group called the *Levellers*, who criticised the corruption and power-seeking in Parliament. Now it was Cromwell's turn to have Lilburne arrested and charged with treason. For information on these tumultuous years and events, head to Chapter 13.

Lilburne was one of those people who stand up for what they know is right and aren't silenced or intimidated, whatever the government does to them – and whoever is in the government, too. We could do with more people like him. Oh, and like Grosseteste (see the earlier section), he died in his bed, though you wouldn't have put money on his doing so.

# Olaudah Equiano

Olaudah Equiano (c. 1745–c. 97) was a successful writer and explorer in eighteenth-century England. He took part in a number of naval battles in the Seven Years' War and joined an expedition to find the elusive Northwest Passage round the top of Canada. Later he bought a plantation in Central America and retired a wealthy man. Okay, what's so special? What is special about him is that for much of this time he was an African slave. He came from Guinea, and he learned seafaring through being bought by a naval officer. He learned to read and write in the intervals between sea voyages. He managed to raise enough cash to buy his freedom, but he was forever being tricked out of his money. At one point, Olaudah Equiano even seemed about to be re-enslaved. He must be one of the very few former slaves who have become slave-owners, even though he took care to treat the slaves on his Caribbean plantation well. Not surprisingly, he took a keen interest in the movement to abolish the slave trade, which he knew at first hand. The slave trade produced many remarkable life stories, but not many as varied and surprising as Olaudah Equiano's. Check him out.

# John Snow

John Snow (1813–54) was a humble London doctor, but he made his name by solving one of the most urgent medical puzzles of the nineteenth century: What on earth caused cholera? You don't want to catch cholera, believe me. The disease starts with acute diarrhoea, and then all your body fluids drain away through any orifice going: Cholera's a really horrible way to die. Cholera hit London for the first time in 1832 from India, but how it spread was anyone's guess. Most doctors assumed the conductor was something in the air, a *miasma*, as they called it, but Snow thought cholera was more likely to be carried in something people ate or drank. When a very sharp outbreak occurred in one particular part of London's Soho in 1854, Snow looked at the statistics and logged the fatal cases on a map. The answer was staring him in the face: All the people who'd died got their water from one particular pump at the corner of Broad Street; the people who used the pump at the other end of the street were fine. Snow got the pump handle removed and guess what? The deaths slowed down immediately. You won't be surprised to hear that the miasma lobby refused to accept Snow's findings, but Snow had shown how you could use statistics to help isolate the source of cholera. And, of course, he was right.

# Sophia Jex-Blake

In 1865 Elizabeth Garrett Anderson became Britain's first woman doctor, but anyone who thought that women in the medical profession was all plain sailing from now on was in for a rude shock. Sophia Jex-Blake (1840–1912) was a well-educated middle-class lady who, in 1868, decided to train as a doctor. She enrolled at Edinburgh University, or at least she tried to. But Edinburgh put every obstacle it could think of in her way. When they couldn't stop her and her companions enrolling, the university tried to stop them from taking their examinations or from getting their degrees. The students heckled her and tried to force her out of the lecture theatres. Jex-Blake had to spend almost as much time fighting legal battles with the university as she did studying medicine. But she didn't give in. Gradually people began to read about what was happening in Edinburgh. Parliament passed a law allowing women to enrol on medical courses on the same terms as men. Jex-Blake became a successful doctor, and helped found the London Medical School for Women. Not surprisingly, she was an active supporter of Votes for Women, too. Her case ought to be better known, if only because the opposition she faced was so incredibly fierce and just plain nasty. Not one of Edinburgh's finest hours.

# Emily Hobhouse

At the end of the Boer War, British General Sir Horatio Herbert Kitchener had the job of mopping up the Boer guerrilla fighters in the South African veldt. So he burned all crops for miles around, rounded the people up and forced them into a series of concentration camps. Yes, you did read that right. Soon thousands of men, women, and especially children were dying from malnutrition and disease. Which was not surprising, since the camps had almost no food, hardly any medical facilities, and no proper shelter.

Emily Hobhouse (1860–1926) travelled out to South Africa specifically to see these camps for herself. One tough lady, she visited the camps and told the camp commandants exactly what she thought of them. By sheer determination and persistence, she got them to make at least some small improvements – you know, like recognising soap as an essential. Then she went back to Britain to take the issue up with the prime minister. Emily Hobhouse is one of those people who won't just sit and shake their heads at suffering but get up and do something about it. When Bob Geldof saw the news about famine in Ethiopia he got on the phone to create Band Aid; when Emily Hobhouse heard the news from South Africa, she got on a boat to create merry hell.

# Dr Cecil Paine

For every famous figure like Alexander Fleming, the scientist who discovered penicillin, hundreds of Cecil Paines are in the background, and the Flemings wouldn't exist without them. Cecil Paine (1905–94) was a consultant pathologist in Sheffield in the 1930s. He was working on infections, particularly a terrible infection called puerperal fever, which was still killing thousands of mothers in childbirth. No one knew what caused puerperal fever, and the number of mothers dying from it was going up instead of down. Paine worked out that wearing a mask during the delivery helped reduce the risk, and he came *so* close to working out how to use penicillin to eradicate it altogether.

At that time, doctors were still making penicillin by leaving bottles and pans out to develop mould, which was a bit hit-and-miss. Nevertheless, Paine tried using the penicillin mould for eye infections. Now comes the sad bit. Paine found his penicillin so cumbersome that he gave up on it, but his assistant, Howard Florey, went on to crack the problem of how to make penicillin more efficiently for mass production. Thanks to that discovery, puerperal fever virtually disappeared. Florey said that Paine's work was crucial; Paine himself said he was a poor fool who didn't see the obvious when it was stuck in front of him. Well, maybe. But it's poor fools like that who do the work that helps the famous names make their discoveries, and that fact needs pointing it out.

# Chad Varah

Chad Varah (1911–2007) was a young Church of England vicar when, in 1936, he had to conduct the funeral of a young girl who had killed herself. What horrible thing had happened to make this young girl end her life? Her periods had started. Without anyone to tell her what was happening, this fourteen-year-old thought she must have contracted VD. Varah was so appalled that he decided to do something about this ignorance. The first thing, obviously, was to get some sex education going in Britain, and in the 1930s and 1940s, doing so took some courage. If school children today are well informed about their bodies and about sex, thank Chad Varah.

But Varah learned another lesson in that girl's death. She didn't die because her periods had started; she died because, when she most needed help, she felt totally alone, with no one to turn to. Varah decided that no one should ever feel that alone again, and in 1953 he started the telephone helpline that became the Samaritans. In 1953 many families didn't have a telephone, and no one had ever thought of using telephones in that way: Varah's idea – that whoever you were, whatever the problem, if you needed help someone would always be at the end of a phone ready to listen and support, 24/7 – was genuinely visionary thinking. Not many people bring off miracles, but creating the Samaritans seems to me to make Chad Varah one of them. A truly Great Briton.

# Index

## • A •

Act of Settlement (1701), 238
Act of Six Articles (1539), 190
Acts of Union, 12
Adrian IV (pope), 119–120, 380–381
Afghanistan, 304
Africa, 307–311, 352–353
Agincourt, battle at, 140
Agricola, 56–57
Albany, Duke of, 173
Albert (Prince Consort of Queen
    Victoria), 286
Alfred the Great (king of Anglo-Saxons),
    86–88
alliance building, 320–323
Al-Qaida, 372–373
American Revolutionary War, 268–273
Amritsar, massacre at, 331–334
Anarchy, 110–111
André, John (major), 272
Angevin Empire, 117–121
Angles, 71. *See also* Anglo-Saxons
Anglican Church (Church of England), 168,
    189–191
Anglo-Boer War, 313–314
Anglo-Irish, 237
*Anglo-Saxon Chronicle,* 67, 79
Anglo-Saxons
    arrival of, 66–69
    British Christians, 73
    Celtic Church, 74, 76
    church traditions, 73–78
    invasion of Britain by, 69–72
    overview, 65
    rise of Mercia, 78–79
    Roman Church, 76–78
    saints, 75
Anjou, 117
Anne Boleyn (queen of England), 169
Anne of Cleves (queen of England),
    169–170
anti-Catholic protests, 233–234
Anti-Corn Law League, 287

Apartheid, 352–353
aqueducts, 57–58, 257
archaeologist findings, 24–25
Archbishop of Canterbury, 108, 122–124,
    191, 193
Arkwright, Richard (water frame
    inventor), 258
Armagh, 393
Arnold, Benedict (commander), 272
Arthur (king of England), 68
asylum seekers, 19–20
Athelstan the Glorious (king of the
    English), 88
Attlee, Clement (prime minister of U.K.),
    346, 347
Augustine (monk), 76–77
Augustinians, 151
Auld Alliance, 16, 172
Australia, 305–306, 311
Austria, 251

## • B •

Babington Plot (1586), 177
Bacon, Francis (philosopher), 223
Bacon, Roger (Franciscan friar), 153
Balliol, John de (king of Scotland), 133–135
Bane, Donald (self-declared king), 107
Bannister, Roger (athlete), 349
Bannockburn, battle of, 134, 381
Barebones Parliament, 213
battles, 339–340. *See also specific battles
    and wars*
Bayeux Tapestry, 102
BBC, 389
Beaker people, 33, 34
The Beatles, 389
Beaton, David (Cardinal), 195–197
Beauclerc, Henry (son of William, Duke of
    Normandy), 109, 110
Beaumaris, 393
Becket, Thomas à (archbishop of
    Canterbury), 122–124
Bede (monk), 67, 383

Bedoyere, Guy de la (author), 52
Behn, Aphra (author), 264
Belfast, 366–369
Belgium, 40, 45, 275
Benedictines, 150
Berwick upon Tweed, 14
Bessemer, Henry (inventor), 263
Bevan, Aneurin 'Nye' (minister),
    346, 347
Beveridge Report, 346
Bevin, Ernest (trade unionist), 346
*Bible,* 190, 384–385
Bill of Rights, 236
Bishops' War, 206
Black Death (Plague), 155–156, 215
Black Hole of Calcutta, 302–303
Black Prince (son of Edward III), 139
Blair, Tony (prime minister of U.K.),
    368–373
Blitz, 340–341
'Bloody Assizes', 234
'Bloody Sunday', 330–331, 367
boats and bombers, in World War II,
    342–343
Boers (Dutch), 309
bog bodies, 38
Boleyn, Anne (queen of England), 169
Bolingbroke, Henry. *See* Henry IV (king of
    England)
bombings on London underground,
    373–374
Bonaparte, Napoleon (Emperor of France),
    277–278
*Book of Common Prayer* (Cranmer), 191
*The Book of Kells (800),* 383–384
border regions, 14
Bosnia, 322
Boston Tea Party, 270
Bosworth, battle of, 146
Boudica (queen of Icenit tribe), 55–56
Boulton, Matthew (engineer), 262
Boyle, Robert (Irish aristocrat), 227
Brady, Ian (psychopath), 356
"Breeches Bible", 190
Brehan Law, 70
Brigantes tribe, 41, 62
Brindley, James (engineer), 257

Britain. *See also* England; Ireland; Scotland;
    Wales; *specific topics*
countries of, 13–15
    cultural contributions of, 387–390
documents of major historical
    importance, 383–386
formation of, 240–247
France declares war on, 275–276
historical turning points, 379–382
joins Common Market and EEC, 354–355
origin of name, 12
visiting, 391–394
as world power, 353–354
British Christians, 73
British Civil War in America, 208–211
British colonies, 301, 311
British Empire
    Africa, 307–311
    Anglo-Boer War, 313–314
    Australia and New Zealand, 305–306, 311
    Canada, 311
    China, 306–307
    colonies, 301, 311
    end of, 349–353
    India, 302–305
    Irish, 312–313
    Jamaica, 312
    New World Order, 300–302
    overview, 299–300
    role of Britain after losing, 353–358
    Twentieth century, 335–337
*British Military History For Dummies*
    (Perrett), 328
"British Revolution", 279–284
British Union of Fascists (BUF), 335
Britons, 12, 18–19, 69, 71
bronze, making, 36
Bronze Age, 32–33
Brown, Gordon (prime minister of U.K.),
    375–376
Brunel, Isambard Kingdom (technology
    genius), 297–298
Bubonic Plague, 155–156, 215
BUF (British Union of Fascists), 335
Burgess, Guy (British diplomat), 348
Burma, 304
Bush, George W. (president of U.S.),
    372–373

## • C •

Caboto, Giovanni (sailor), 300
Caesar, Gaius Julius (general and consul of Rome), 37, 44, 52, 53–54
Calais, siege of, 138–139
Callaghan, James (prime minister of U.K.), 358
Calvin, John (French lawyer), 186
Campaign for Nuclear Disarmament (CND), 365
Campbell, Robert (captain), 241–242
Canada, 311
Canmore, Malcolm, III (king of Scotland), 104
Caratacus (chieftain), 54–55
Carausius (emperor of Rome), 63
Carthusians, 150
Cartwright, Edmund (clergyman), 259
castles, 105
Catherine Howard (queen of England), 170
Catherine Parr (queen of England), 170
Catholic Irish, 237
Catholics
    anti-Catholic protests, 233–234
    plots against Elizabeth I, 177
    role of church, 183–185
    theology, 182
    view of Elizabeth I's church, 194
    views on Mary I, 192–193
Cato Street conspiracy (1820), 281
Celts
    Celtic Church, 74, 76
    Fianna/Fenians, 18, 43–44
    kingdoms of, 69–72
    overview, 39–40, 66
Channel Islands, 15
Charles I (king of England)
    Civil War, 208–212
    dissolution of Parliament, 204–205
    George Villiers, 203–204
    Ireland, 205–206
    MPs, 381–382
    Puritans, 206
    reformation of Parliament, 207–208
Charles II (king of England), 214, 215
Chatsworth House, 393
children, misconceptions about Victorian cruelty to, 294–295

China, 306–307
Christians and Christianity, 61–62, 73, 126. *See also* church/church traditions
Chronicle (Anglo-Saxon), 67, 79
Church of England, 168, 189–191
church/church traditions. *See also* Catholics; Christians and Christianity; religion
    British Christians, 73
    Celtic Church, 74, 76
    Church of England, 168, 189–191
    courts, 122–123
    Interdict, 127
    Roman Church, 76–78
    Saxon saints, 75
    services, 149–150
Churchill, John (Duke of Marlborough), 239
Churchill, Winston (prime minister of U.K.), 326, 339–340, 356
Cistercians, 150
Cives (Roman-Britons), 66
Civil War (British), 208–211
class structure, during Iron Age, 43
Claudius (emperor of Rome), 54–56
Clifford's Tower, 154
Clinton, William Jefferson (president of U.S.), 368
cloth trade, 257–259
CND (Campaign for Nuclear Disarmament), 365
Cnut (king of Denmark), 93–94
Collins, Michael (Irish leader), 331
colonies (British), 301, 311
Columba (peasant), 74
commodities tax, 269
Common Law (English), 202–203, 388
Common Market, 354
*Common Sense* (Paine), 271
Commonwealth, 349–353
communion, 191–192
Community Charge, 365
Conservatives, 249. *See also* Thatcher, Margaret
Constantius (emperor of Rome), 63
Constitutions of Clarendon, 122–123
Cook (captain), 305–306
Corn Laws, 279–281, 287
Council of Europe (1949), 354
Coventry Cathedral, 394

Cranmer, Thomas (archbishop of Canterbury), 191, 193
Crecy, battle of, 138
Crick, Francis (scientist), 349, 389
cricket, 337
crime and public punishment, 222
Crimean War, 292–294
Croke Park massacre, 330–331
Cro-Magnon, 29
Cromptom, Samuel (fiddler), 259
Cromwell, Oliver (landowner), 212–214
Cromwell, Thomas (chief minister), 188
Cronin, Mike (author), 91, 205, 288, 331
crusades, 126, 185
Crystal Palace's Great Exhibition, 297
cultural contributions of Britain, 387–390
Curthose, Robert (son of William, Duke of Normandy), 109

## • D •

Darby, Abraham (inventor), 263
Dardanelles, 326
Dark Ages, 67
Darwin, Charles (author and scientist), 26, 297–298, 386
*Dauphin,* 141
David I (king of Scotland), 120–121
Davis, Craig (author), 352, 360
D-Day, 343
Declaration of Arbroath (1320), 16, 136, 384
Declaration of Independence, 270–271
Declaration of Indulgence, 215
Defence of the Realm Act (DORA), 324
Depression years, 335
Dermot (king of Leinster), 120
Descartes, René (French thinker), 223–224
design (fashion), 356
devolution, 370–371
Dickson, Keith (author), 344
Disraeli, Benjamin (Conservative leader), 290
Divine Right of Kings, 200
DNA, 389
documents of major historical importance, 383–386
*Domesday Book,* 105–106
Dominicans, 151

DORA (Defence of the Realm Act), 324
*Downing Street Declaration,* 368
Doyle, John (author), 221
Drake, Francis (explorer), 178–179
Druids, 46, 47
Dudley, Robert (Earl of Leicester), 176
Durham, 392
Durotriges tribe, 41
Dutch Boers, 309

## • E •

East Anglia kingdom, 72
Eden, Anthony (prime minister of U.K.), 353–354, 356
Edgar the Ætheling, 96, 98, 103–104
Edict of Fraternity, 275
education, in Middle Ages, 151
Edward I (king of England), 132–135
Edward II (king of England), 136–137
Edward III (king of England), 95, 97–98, 137–141
Edward IV (king of England), 144–145
Edward V (king of England), 144–145
Edward VI (king of England), 170–171, 191–192
Edward VIII (king of England), 336
Edwin of Mercia (English thegn), 104
EEC (European Economic Community), 354–355
EFTA (European Free Trade Association), 354
Egbert (king of Wessex), 86
Egerton, Francis (Duke of Bridgewater), 257
Eighteenth century. *See specific topics*
Eleanor of Aquitane, 115, 117–118, 124–125
Elizabeth I (queen of England)
  Catholic plots against, 177
  colonies in America, 301
  conflict with Mary, Queen of Scots, 176–178
  religion, 193–195
Elizabeth II (queen of England), 349, 374
emperors (Roman), 63
Empire. *See* British Empire
enclosures, 255–256

England. *See also* Britain; *specific monarchs; specific topics*
becomes a republic, 212–213
castles, 105
Common Law, 202–203, 388
conflict with Scotland, 120–121
French connection with, 130
holocaust, 154
invades Ireland (1170), 380–381
leading role of, 15–16
Marcher Lords, 118–119
Norman invasion of, 380
overview, 13
relationship with Scotland during union, 240
second attempt at union with Scotland, 242–243
War of Captain Jenkin's Ear (1739), 251
English Common Law, 202–203, 388
English language, 106
English Renaissance, 217–221
Equiano, Olaudah (writer and explorer), 397
Essex kingdom, 72
Ethelred II (king of the English), 89–91, 94
ethnicity, 18–20
European Economic Community (EEC), 354–355
European Free Trade Association (EFTA), 354
*European History For Dummies* (Lang), 33, 62, 66, 126, 202, 223, 274, 320
excommunication, 176
Eyre, Edward (governor), 312

### • *F* •

factory life, 259–261
Falkland Islands, 363–364
family trees, 143, 164
famine in Ireland, 18, 288
Fashoda, 310–311
Fenians, 18, 43–44
feof, 116
Ferdinand, Franz (Archduke of Habsburg), 322
Festival of Britain, 349
feudal system, 105–106
Fianna, 18, 43–44

'15 rebellion, 243
fighting, 43–44, 271–272. *See also specific battles and wars*
First World War, 323–328
Flamsteed, John (astronomer), 227
food, 60, 254–256
Forkbeard, Svein (king of Denmark), 90
'45 rebellion, 244–245
1455–60 War, 145
1461 War, 145
1462–70 War, 145
1471 War, 146
1485 War, 146
Fox, Charles James (author), 274–275
France. *See also specific monarchs*
Britain signs agreement with, 320–321
declares war on Britain, 275–276
Hundred Years War, 137–141
Franciscans, 151
Franklin, John (naval commander), 306
Frankum, Ronald, Jr. (author), 351
French Revolution, 273–279
fyrd, 99

### • *G* •

Galileo (astronomer), 223
Gallic Wars, 52–53
*Gallic Wars* (Caesar), 44
Gandhi, Mahatma (Indian leader), 336–337, 349–350
Gaveston, Piers (Earl of Cornwall), 136–137
genealogy, 22
*General Belgrano* (British submarine), 364
General Election (145), 345–346
General Strike, 333–334
*Geneva Bible,* 190
George I (king of England), 247
George II (king of England), 247–248
George III (king of England), 248, 280
George IV (king of England), 248
Germany
Hitler attacks Poland, 339
Munich Conference, 338–339
overview, 337–338
Seven Years' War (1756–63), 251
United States declares war on, 328
*Ghandi* (film), 332
Gilbert and Sullivan operettas, 390

Gildas (monk), 67

Gladstone, William Ewart (prime minister of U.K.), 290

'Glorious Revolution', 236

gods, during Iron Age, 46–47

Godwinsson, Harold (king of England), 96, 97–102, 101

Godwinsson, Tostig (brother of Harold), 98, 99–100

*Good Friday Agreement,* 368

Gorbachev, Mikhail (Soviet Union leader), 365

Gordon, George (general), 309–310

Gothic revival, 63–64

Grand Remonstrance, 208

Great Britain, 12. *See also* Britain

Great Exhibition (Crystal Palace), 297

'Great Game', 303–304

Great Reform Act (1832), 283, 382

Great War, 323–328

Grey, Edward (British foreign secretary), 322

Grosseteste, Robert (Bishop of Lincoln), 153, 396

Gruffudd Llewellyn, ap (king of Wales), 95

Gunpowder plot, 201–202

**• H •**

Habeus Corpus (1679), 385

Hadrian's Wall, 58, 392

Haig, Douglas (field marshall), 327–328

Halley, Edmund (astronomer), 226

Hallstatt style, 38–39

Hampden, John (landowner), 207–209

Hampden Clubs, 280

Harald Hardrada (king of Norway), 96, 98, 99–100

Hardie, Keir (Labour MP), 292

Hargreaves, James (spinning wheel inventor), 258

Harold Harefoot (king of England), 94–95

Harvey, William (scientist), 225

Hastings, Battle of, 97, 101–102, 380

Hastings, Warren (governor-general of India), 303

Hawkins, John (explorer), 178–179

Heath, Edward (prime minister of U.K.), 354, 358, 360

Hengist (German chieftain), 68

Henry I (king of England), 116–117

Henry II (king of England), 117–125

Henry III (king of England), 124–125

Henry IV (king of England), 142, 144

Henry V (king of England), 140–141

Henry VII (king of England), 166–167. *See also* Tudors

Henry VIII (king of England), 167–170, 187–191, 381

Hereward the Wake (Saxon thegn), 104

Herodotus (historian), 36–37

High Middle Ages. *See also* Middle Ages

  Black Prince, 139

  Declaration of Arbroath, 16, 136, 384

  Edward I, 132–135

  Edward II, 136–137

  England, 130

  Hundred Years War, 137–141

  Ireland, 130

  Joan of Arc, 141

  overview, 129

  Provisions of Oxford, 131

  Scotland, 130, 133–135

  Wales, 130, 132–133

  Wars of the Roses, 142–146, 165

Highland settlements (Scotland), 255

hill forts (Iron Age), 44

Hillary, Edmund (climber), 349

Hindley, Myra (psychopath), 356

*History* (Bede), 383

*History of the Kings of Britain* (Geoffrey of Monmouth), 46–47

Hitler, Adolf (Nazi Party leader), 339

Hobbes, Thomas (philosopher), 224

Hobhouse, Emily (welfare campaigner), 399

Holbein, Hans (artist), 219

holocaust (English), 154

homage, paying, 116

Home Rule bill (Ireland), 318

honor, 116

Hooke, Robert (philosopher), 227

House of Lancaster, 144

House of Lords, 371–372

House of York, 144–145

Howard, Catherine (queen of England), 170

Howe, Geoffrey (politician), 366

human sacrifices, 47

humours, 152

Hundred Years War, 137–141
Huskisson, William (MP), 262
Hussein, Saddam (dictator of Iraq),
    372–373
Hywel (king of Wales), 86

### • *I* •

Ice Age, 29, 379
ideas, ground-breaking
  politics, 224–225
  religion, 223–224
  science, 225–229
immigrants, 19–20, 355
India, 302–305, 331–334, 349–350
Industrial Revolution
  aqueduct, 57–58, 257
  cloth trade, 257–259
  factories, 259–261
  food, 253–256
  iron, 262–263
  locomotion, 262
  road work, 256–257
  slave trade, 263–264
  steam engine, 261–262
Interdict, 127
Invasion Hypothesis, 39–40
Iona, 391
Iraq, 372–373
IRB (Irish Republican Brotherhood),
    330–331
Ireland (Republic of Ireland). *See also*
    Nothern Ireland
  becomes an island, 30
  Belfast, 366–369
  Catholic Irish, 237
  Charles I, 205–206
  conquest of, 17–18
  Curse of Cromwell, 214
  under Earl of Strafford, 205–206
  Gaelic kingdoms of, 69–71
  during High Middle Ages, 130
  Home Rule bill, 318
  invasion of, 119–120, 380–381
  joins Civil War, 209–210
  joins England and Scotland, 246–247
  Norman influence on, 108
  overview, 14
  penal times, 245–246
  religious conflict, 17

  role in Empire, 312–314
  The Troubles, 330–331
  types of Irish in seventeenth century, 237
  Ulster, 179
  Vikings in, 90
Irish Dalriadans, 71
Irish Famine, 288
*Irish History For Dummies* (Cronin), 91, 205,
    288, 331
Irish Republican Brotherhood (IRB),
    330–331
iron, 262–263
Iron Age
  Belgian invasion, 45
  Celts, 39–40
  Invasion Hypothesis, 39–40
  life during, 40–45
  overview, 35–36
  religion during, 45–47
  styles of, 38–39
  written accounts of Britain during, 36–38
Ironbridge, 394
Isabella (wife of Edward II), 137
Isle of Ely, 104
Isle of Man, 15, 83

### • *J* •

Jacobites, 243
Jamaica, 312
James, Duke of Monmouth, 234
James I (king of England), 200–203. *See also*
    James IV (king of Scotland)
James I (king of Scotland), 135
James II (king of England), 234–236
James II (king of Scotland), 135
James III (king of Scotland), 135
James IV (king of Scotland), 172, 392. *See*
    *also* James I (king of England)
James V (king of Scotland), 172–173
James VI (king of Scotland), 197, 200
Jane Seymour (queen of England), 169
Jeffreys, George (Lord Chief Justice), 234
Jesuits (1580), 177
Jex-Blake, Sophia (doctor), 398
Joan of Arc, 141
John (king of England), 127–128
John of Gaunt, 142, 157–158
Julian of Norwich (Benedictine nun), 153

## • K •

Katharine of Aragon (queen of England), 168
Kay, John (flying shuttle inventor), 258
Keeler, Christine (nude model), 357
Kent kingdom, 72
Kenya, 352
Khartoum, 309–310
"King of the English", 86–88
kings. *See also specific monarchs*
  early Stewart, 135
  of England, 86–88
  overview, 21
  relationship with Vikings, 85
  of Wales, 85–86
Kinnock, Neil (Labour leader), 369
Knight's Fee, 116
Knox, John (Catholic priest), 186–187

## • L •

La Tène style, 125–127
Labour Party, 345–348, 357–358, 369
Lancaster, House of, 144
Lanfranc (archbishop of Canterbury), 108
Lang, Sean (author), 33, 62, 66, 126, 202, 223, 274, 320
language (English), 106
'Lapse' rule, 305
Latin, church services in, 150
Laws of Motion (Newton), 228
legal system, revamped by Henry II, 121
Levellers, 212
Lilburne, John (political agitator), 396–397
Lindisfarne, 74, 76
"Lionheart". *See* Richard I (king of England)
Lischner, Ray (author)
  *Shakespeare For Dummies,* 221
Livingstone, David (missionary explorer), 308
Llewellyn, Prince of Wales, 132–133
Lloyd George, David (prime minister of U.K.), 331, 332–333
locomotion, 262
Lollards, 153–154
Long Parliament. *See* Parliament
longbow, 138–139
*Look Back in Anger* (play), 354

Lord Mansfield's Judgment (1772), 385–386
lordships, 116
Louis XVI (king of France), 275
Luther, Martin (Catholic monk), 185–186

## • M •

Macadam, John Loudon (engineer), 256–257
MacAlpin, Kenneth (Scottish king of Dalraida), 85
Macbeth, 93
MacDonald, Ramsay (prime minister of U.K.), 334–335
MacDonald clan, 241–242
MacGregor, Rob Roy (Jacobite), 244
Maclean, Donald (British diplomat), 348
Macmillan, Harold (prime minister of U.K.), 352–353, 356–357
Magna Carta (1215), 128, 384
Major, John (prime minister of U.K.), 368, 369, 370, 372–373
*Making of the English Working Class* (Thompson), 21
Malayan Emergency, 350–351
Malcolm IV (king of Scotland), 121
Maldon, battle of, 90
manor, 116
March of the Blanketeers (1817), 281
Margaret (patron saint of Scotland), 107
Margaret (queen), 173
Mary (queen of France and Scotland), 173–178, 196
Mary I (queen of England, "Bloody Mary"), 171, 192–193
Mary II (queen of England), 236, 237, 238
Mary of Guise, 196
Matilda (Empress), 110–111
Mau Mau tribe, 352
Maxner, Stephen (author), 351
*Mayflower,* 201
medical care, in Middle Ages, 152–153
members of parliament. *See* prime ministers and MPs
Mercia, 72, 78–79
*Michael Collins* (film), 331
Middle Ages. *See also* High Middle Ages
  Black Death (Plague), 155–156
  education, 151
  English holocaust, 154

John Wyclif, 153–154
medical care, 152–153
Peasants' Revolt, 157–160
Religion, 147–151, 181–187
thinkers, 153
middle class, 43
*The Middle East For Dummies* (Davis), 360
miners' strike, 362–363
Mitterrand, François (president of
France), 364
monasteries and monastic orders,
150–151, 188
monetarism, 362
Monmouth, Geoffrey of (writer and
chronicler), 46–47
Montfort, Simon de (Earl of Leicester), 131
Morcar of Northumbria (English
thegn), 104
Mortimer, Roger (English noble), 137
Mosley, Oswald (Labour MP), 335
Mountbatten, Lord, 351
MPs. *See* prime ministers and MPs
Munich Conference, 338–339
music, during Renaissance, 218–219
Muslim crusades, 126

**• N •**

Nasser, Gamal Abdel (Egyptian ruler),
353–354
National Health Service (NHS), 347
National Service, 348
National Union of Mineworkers (NUM),
362–363
Nationalisation, 347
Natural Philosophy, 226–229
naval supremacy, 321
Neanderthals, 27–28
Nelson, Horatio (admiral), 277–278
neolithic revolution, 30–31
New Model Army, 209
New World Order, 300–302
New Zealand, 305–306, 311
Newcomen, Thomas (steam engine
inventor), 261–262
Newton, Isaac (scientist), 227–229
Newton, John (clergyman), 264
NHS (National Health Service), 347
Nightingale, Florence (nurse), 293

Nineteenth century. *See specific topics*
nobles, 43
Norman invasion of England (1066), 97,
101–102, 380
Normans. *See* William, Duke of Normandy
Norsemen, 82–85
North American settlement, 179
Northern Ireland. *See also* Great Britian
conquest and short history of, 17–18
in twenthieth century, 366–369
in United Kingdom (UK), 11, 12
visiting, 393
Northumbria kingdom, 72
novels, 388
NUM (National Union of Mineworkers),
362–363

**• O •**

Oates, Titus (clergyman), 215
Offa (king of Mercia), 78–79, 85
Olympic Games (1948), 349
opium, 306–307
Orange Order, 238
*Ordinance of Labourers,* 157
organised sport, 388
*The Origin of Species* (Darwin), 26, 386
*Oroonoko* (Behn), 264
Osborne, John (playwright), 354
Oswald (king of Northumbria), 395
Oswy (king of Bernicia), 77–78, 380
Owain Glyn Dwr, 144
Owen, Nicholas (saint), 396
Owen, Robert (factory owner), 260

**• P •**

Paine, Cecil (pathologist), 399
Paine, Tom (author), 271, 276
palaces, during Renaissance, 218–219
Palestine, 336, 351–352
Palmerston, Lord, 289
Parliament
dissolution of, 204–205
People's Budget, 318–319
petition by People's Charter, 292
Provisions of Oxford, 131
Race Relations Act (1965), 355
reformation of, 207–208

Parliamentary government, 387
Parliamentary monarchy, 249–250
Parr, Catherine (queen of England), 170
Passchendaele, 327–328
*Pax Britannica,* 289
Peasants' Revolt, 157–160
Peel, Robert (prime minister of U.K.), 286,
    287–289
penicillin, 390
Peninsula War, 278
Pentrich Rising (1817), 281
People's Budget, 318–319
People's Charter (1838), 291–292, 386
Percy, Henry (Earl of
    Northumberland), 144
Perrett, Bryan (author), 328
Pertinax (emperor of Rome), 63
'Peterloo' and the Six Acts (1819), 281
Petition of Right (1628), 385
Philip II (king of France), 125–127
Philip II (king of Spain), 171, 176
Philip VI (king of France), 137–139
physic garden, 152
Picti tribe, 41, 71–72
Pilgrimage of Grace, 189
Pilgrims, 201
Pinochet (Chilean dictator), 371
Pitt, William (the elder), 252
Pitt, William (the younger), 275
Plague (Black Death), 155–156, 215
Plantagenets, 116
Poitiers, battle of, 139
Poland, 251, 339
political ground-breaking ideas, 224–225
political parties in eighteenth century
    Britain, 249
Poll Tax, 157–158, 365
Pontiac (Chief of the Ottawa), 268
pop music, 356
Postumus (emperor of Rome), 63
poverty, 221–222
Powell, Enoch (Conservative MP), 355
prehistoric man and tools, 24–26
prime ministers and MPs, 381–382. *See also
    specific prime ministers and MPs*
Protestants
    Church of England, 168, 189–191
    in Scotland, 195–196
    settlers in Ulster, 179

theology, 182
view of Elizabeth I's church, 195
views on Edward VI, 191–192
Provisions of Oxford, 131
Punjab, 304
Purgatory, 149
Puritans, 195, 200–201, 206, 213
Pym, John (politician), 207–209

## • Q •

queens, 21. *See also specific monarchs*

## • R •

race, 18–20, 355
Race Relations Act (1965), 355
radar, 340
Rahere (court jester), 152
Raleigh, Walter (writer), 180, 301
rationing, 342, 348
Reagan, Ronald (president of U.S.), 364
rebellions, 243–245
*Reflections on the Revolution in France*
    (Fox), 274–275
reformation. *See* religion
Reivers, 14
religion. *See also* Christians and
    Christianity; church/church traditions
    beliefs, 148–149
    Catholic and Protestant theology, 182
    church services, 149–150
    conflict in Ireland, 17
    Edward VI, 191–192
    Elizabeth I, 175, 193–195
    ground-breaking ideas on, 223–224
    Henry VIII, 187–191
    during Iron Age, 45–47
    Mary I, 192–193
    Middle Ages, 147–151, 181–187
    misconceptions about Victorian ideas,
        295–296
    monastic orders, 150–151
    overview, 147–148
    reformers, 185–187
    role in Catholic Church, 183–185
    Scotland, 195–197

remembrance ceremonies, 330
Renaissance. *See* English Renaissance
Revolt of the Northern Earls (1569), 177
Revolutionary War (American), 268–273
revolutions
  American Revolutionary War, 268–273
  "British Revolution", 279–284
  French Revolution, 273–279
  Industrial Revolution, 253–264
  overview, 268
Reynolds, Albert (Irish taosaich), 368
Rhodes, Cecil (prime minister of U.K.), 310
Rhodesia, 353
Rhodri the Great (king of Gwynedd), 86
Richard I (king of England), 125–127
Richard II (king of England), 142, 159–160
Richard III (king of England), 144–145,
    165–166
Ridolfi Plot (1571), 177
*The Rights of Man* (Paine), 276
road work, 60, 256–257
Roaring Twenties, 334–335
Robert III (king of Scotland), 135
Robert the Bruce, 133–135
Robin Hood, 128
Roe, Thomas (diplomat), 302
Roman Church, 76–78
Roman invasion
  Agricola, 56–57
  arrival of Caesar and Claudius, 53–56
  Brigantes, 62
  Gallic Wars, 52–53
  Gothic revival, 63–64
  Roman emperors, 63
  Roman view of Britain, 51–54
  Roman way of life, 57–62
  withdrawal of troops, 64
Romano-Britons (Cives), 66
*The Romans For Dummies* (Bedoyere), 52
rood screen, 149
'rotten boroughs', 282, 283
rough wooing, 173–174
Royal Family, 20. *See also specific monarchs*
Rufus, William (son of William Duke of
    Normandy), 109
Rump Parliament, 213
Russia, 320–321

**• S •**

sacrifices (human), 47
saints (Saxon), 75
Sands, Bobby (IRA prisoner), 367–368
Saville Enquiry, 367
Saxons, 71, 72. *See also* Anglo-Saxons
Scargill, Arthur (NUM leader), 362–363
Schlieffen, Alfred von (Chief of the German
    General Staff), 323
science and technology, 225–229, 297–298
Scotland. *See also* Britain; *specific
    monarchs*
  conflict with England, 120–121
  conquest of, 16–17
  devolution attempt, 370–371
  during High Middle Ages, 130, 133–135
  Highland settlements, 255
  John de Balliol, 133–135
  joins Civil War, 209–210
  Kenneth MacAlpin (Scottish king of
    Dalraida), 85
  Malcolm Canmore IIIs influence on, 107
  overview, 13
  relationship with England during
    union, 240
  religion, 195–197
  Scots merge with Picti, 72
  second attempt at union with England,
    242–243
  Vikings in, 92–93
Scots-Irish, 237
Scoutus, Duns (Scottish theologian), 153
sea battles, during Great War, 326–327
Seahenge, 32
security, Elizabeth I on, 176
Sedgemoor, battle of, 234
Septimius Severus (emperor of Rome), 63
Seven Years' War (1756-63), 251
sex, misconceptions about Victorian ideas
    on, 295
Seymour, Jane (queen of England), 169
Shakespeare, William (poet and
    playwright), 219–221
*Shakespeare For Dummies* (Doyle and
    Lischner), 221
sheep, 255
Shetland Islands, 15
Simnel, Lambert (baker's son), 166–167

Simpson, Wallis (Duchess of Windsor), 336
Sind (1843), 304
Singapore, fall of (1942), 382
Sinn Fein, 331, 368
*Sixteen Revelations of Divine Love* (Julian of Norwich), 153
Skara Brae, 391
slave class, 43
slave trade, 263–265
Sluys, battle of, 138
Smithfield, 158–160
Snow, John (doctor), 398
Somerset, Duke of, 170–171
Somme, 327
South Sea Bubble, 250
Spa Fields meeting (1816), 280
Spain, 250–251
Spanish Armada, 178–179
spinning jenny, 258
Spitfire, 340
sport (organised), 388
St Albans, battle of, 145
St Boniface (Saxon saint), 75
St Cedd (Saxon saint), 75
St Chad (Saxon saint), 75
St Cuthbert (Saxon Saint), 75
St David (Saxon saint), 75
St Hild (Saxon saint), 75
St Patrick, 61
St Wilfrid (Saxon saint), 75
Stamford Bridge, battle of, 100
Stamp Act, 269, 270
*Statute of Labourers,* 157, 158
steam engine, 261–262
Stephen of Blois (king of England), 118
Stephenson, George (railway locomotive designer), 262
Stephenson, Robert (railway locomotive designer), 262
Stewarts. *See also* Stuarts
  arrive in England, 199–203
  early Stewart kings, 135
  marrying Mary, Queen of Scots, 173–175
  overview, 172–173
Stirling Castle, 392
Stone Age
  archaeologist findings, 24–25
  Cro-Magnon, 29
  Neanderthals, 27–28
  neolithic revolution, 30–31
  overview, 23, 26–27
  Stonehenge, 31–32
  Swanscombe woman, 28
Stonehenge, 31–32
Strafford, Earl of, 205–206
Strongbow (king of Leinster), 120
Stuart, Charles Edward (Bonnie Prince Charlie), 246
Stuart, James Edward (Prince of Wales), 243–245
Stuarts, 210–212. *See also* Stewarts
Suetonius Paulinus (historian), 37, 55–56
Suffragettes, 319
sugar, 269, 301–302
Sussex kingdom, 72
Svein (king of Denmark), 104
Swanscombe woman, 28
Synod of Whitby (664), 380

### • T •

Tacitus (historian), 37
taxation, 269
tea, 390
technology. *See* science and technology
television, invention of, 349, 358
Telford, Thomas (engineer), 257
Tensing, Norgay (sherpa), 349
terrorist attacks, 372–373
Thatcher, Margaret (prime minister of U.K.), 358–366
Theodosius (emperor of Rome), 64
Thompson, E. P. (historian), 21
Throckmorton plot (1584), 177
*Titanic,* 318
tools (prehistoric), 24
Tories, 249
Toulouse, 118
Tower of London, 103
towns (in Roman England), 58–59
trade, during Iron Age, 41–42
trade unions in 1970s, 360–363
transubstantiation, 190, 191
Treaty of Limerick, 245
trenches, 324–325
triangular trade, 263–265
Tribal Hideage, 78–79
tribal structure, during Iron Age, 25, 41

The Troubles, 330–331
Tudor, Henry (Henry VII, king of England), 166–167
Tudors, 163, 164
Twentieth century. *See specific topics*
Tyler, Wat (Kentish rebel), 158–160
Tynwald, 132

# • U •

UDI (Unilateral Declaration of Independence), 353
UK (United Kingdom of Great Britian and Northern Ireland), 5, 11, 12, 15–18. *See also* Britain
Ulaid tribe, 41
Ulster, Protestant settlers in, 179
Unilateral Declaration of Independence (UDI), 353
union
 first attempt, 240–241
 Ireland, 246–247
 joins with England and Scotland, 246–247
 rebellions, 243–245
 Scotland, 242–243
United Kingdom of Great Britian and Northern Ireland (UK), 5, 11, 12, 15–18. *See also* Britain
United States, 328. *See also specific leaders*

# • V •

Varah, Chad (vicar), 400
viaducts, 257
Victoria (queen of England), 285–287
Victorians
 Crimean War, 292–294
 misconceptions about, 294–296
 overview, 285
 People's Charter, 291–292
 Prime Ministers and MPs, 287–291
 and Queen Victoria, 285–287
 science and technology, 297–298
*The Vietnam War For Dummies* (Frankum, Jr. and Maxner), 351
Vikings
 Cnut, 94–96
 image of, 84
 in Ireland, 90

kings, 84–88
Norsemen, 82–83
overview, 81
retreat and return of, 89–93
in Scotland, 92–93
Villiers, George (Duke of Buckingham), 203–204
visiting Britain, 391–394
Vitalinus the Vortigern, 66–69
Votes for Women, 319

# • W •

Wales. *See also* Britain
 conquest of, 17
 devolution attempt, 370–371
 during High Middle Ages, 130, 132–133
 kings of, 85–86
 Marcher Lords, 118–119
 Norman influence on, 108
 overview, 13
Wall Street crash, 334–335
Wallace, William (Scottish nobleman), 134
Walpole, Robert (politician), 249–250
War of American Independence. *See* American Revolutionary War
War of Captain Jenkin's Ear (1739), 251
War of Austrian Succession (1740), 251
War of Spanish Succession (1701), 250–251
Warbeck, Perkin (pretender to English throne), 167
Wars of the Roses, 142–146
Washington, George (president of U.S.), 271–272
Waterloo, battle of, 278–279
Watson, James (scientist), 349, 389
Watt, James (inventor), 261–262
Wedgwood, Josiah (potter), 263
Welfare State, 347
Wessex kingdom, 72
Westminster Abbey, 103
wheel, invention of, 33
Whigs, 249
Whitby Abbey, 77–78
Widgery Report, 367
Wilberforce, William (MP), 264
William, Duke of Normandy, 100, 96, 98, 102–109

William, Prince of Orange (Dutch ruler), 235–236. *See also* William III (king of England)

William III (king of England), 236, 237, 238. *See also* William, Prince of Orange

William the Conqueror, 100, 96, 98, 102–109

Wilson, Harold (prime minister of U.K.), 357–358, 360

'Wind of change' speech (Macmillan), 352–353

*The Wind that Swept the Barley* (film), 331

'winter of our discontent', 361

Wishart, George (preacher), 195–196

Witan, 97–98

witches, 203, 225

woad, 44–45

Wolsey (cardinal), 168, 169

women, oppression of by Victorians, 296

Woodhenge, 32

World Cup (1966), 357

world power, Britain as, 353–354

World War I, 323–328

World War II, 339–344

*World War II For Dummies* (Dickson), 344

Wyclif, John (theologian), 153–154

York, House of, 144–145

### • Z •

Zulu, 307–309

# FOR DUMMIES®

## A world of resources to help you grow

## UK editions

### SELF-HELP

978-0-470-66541-1

978-0-470-66543-5

978-0-470-66086-7

### STUDENTS

978-0-470-68820-5

978-0-470-74711-7

978-0-470-74290-7

### HISTORY

978-0-470-68792-5

978-0-470-74783-4

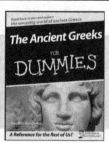
978-0-470-98787-2

Origami Kit For Dummies
978-0-470-75857-1

Overcoming Depression For Dummies
978-0-470-69430-5

Positive Psychology For Dummies
978-0-470-72136-0

PRINCE2 For Dummies, 2009 Edition
978-0-470-71025-8

Psychometric Tests For Dummies
978-0-470-75366-8

Raising Happy Children
For Dummies
978-0-470-05978-4

Reading the Financial Pages
For Dummies
978-0-470-71432-4

Sage 50 Accounts For Dummies
978-0-470-71558-1

Self-Hypnosis For Dummies
978-0-470-66073-7

Starting a Business For Dummies,
2nd Edition
978-0-470-51806-9

Study Skills For Dummies
978-0-470-74047-7

Teaching English as a Foreign
Language For Dummies
978-0-470-74576-2

Teaching Skills For Dummies
978-0-470-74084-2

Time Management For Dummies
978-0-470-77765-7

Work-Life Balance For Dummies
978-0-470-71380-8